ALBA

CELTIC SCOTLAND IN THE MIDDLE AGES

ALBA

Celtic Scotland in the Middle Ages

edited by

EDWARD J. COWAN and R. ANDREW McDONALD

TUCKWELL PRESS

This short run edition published in 2012 by
John Donald, an imprint of Birlinn Ltd
West Newington House
10 Newington Road
Edinburgh
EH9 1QS
www.birlinn.co.uk

First published in 2000 by Tuckwell Press

ISBN: 978 1 906566 57 9

British Library Cataloguing-in-Publication Data
A catalogue record for this book is available from the
British Library

Printed and bound by CPI Group (UK) Ltd, Croydon, CR0 4YY

Contents

Maps

Tables

Illustration

Contributors

STEVE BOARDMAN is a Lecturer in Scottish History at the University of Edinburgh.

DAUVIT BROUN is a Lecturer in Scottish History at the University of Glasgow.

ALAN BRUFORD was a Reader in Scottish Ethnology in the School of Scottish Studies at the University of Edinburgh

EDWARD J. COWAN is Professor of Scottish History at the University of Glasgow.

GRAEME CRUICKSHANK is an independent historian and researcher, and the operator of Edinburgh Historical Enterprises.

ALEXANDER GRANT is a Reader in Medieval British History at the University of Lancaster.

NORMAN MACDOUGALL is a Senior Lecturer in Scottish History at the University of St Andrews.

R. ANDREW MCDONALD is an Assistant Professor of History at the University College of Cape Breton in Nova Scotia, Canada.

DAVID SELLAR, formerly a Senior Lecturer in Scots Law at the University of Edinburgh, is a Research Fellow in Scottish History at the University of Glasgow

KEITH STRINGER is a Reader in Medieval British History at the University of Lancaster.

Abbreviations

Adomnán, *Columba*	*Adomnán's Life of Columba*, ed. A. O. and M. O. Anderson (Edinburgh 1961; repr. Oxford 1991)
ALI	*Acts of the Lords of the Isles, 1336–1493*, ed. J. and R. W. Munro (SHS 1986)
Ann. Clonmacnoise	*The Annals of Clonmacnoise*, ed. D. Murphy (Dublin 1896)
Ann. Connacht	*The Annals of Connacht*, ed. A. M. Freeman (Dublin 1944)
Ann. Four Masters	*Annala Rioghachta Eireann: Annals of the Kingdom of Ireland by the Four Masters*, ed. J. O'Donovan (Dublin 1856)
Ann. Tigernach	'The Annals of Tigernach', ed. W. Stokes (repr., Felinfach, Lampeter, 1993); also in *Revue Celtique*, xvi– xviii (1895–7)
Ann. Ulster	*The Annals of Ulster (to A.D. 1131)*, ed. S. Mac Airt and G. Mac Niocaill (Dublin 1983); also *Annala Uladh: Annals of Ulster ... A Chronicle of Irish Affairs from A.D. 431 to A.D. 1541*, ed. W. M. Hennesy and B. MacCarthy (Dublin 1887–1901)
APS	*The Acts of the Parliaments of Scotland*, ed. T. Thomson and C. Innes (Edinburgh 1814–75)
Argyll Records	*The Records of Argyll*, ed. Lord Archibald Campbell (Edinburgh 1885)
Argyll Trans.	Argyll Transcripts, made by 10th duke of Argyll (photstat copies of extracts in the Department of Scottish History, University of Glasgow)
Beauly Chrs.	*The Charters of the Priory of Beauly*, ed. E. C. Batten (Grampian Club, 1877)
Bede, *HE*	*Bede's Ecclesiastical History of the English People*, ed. B. Colgrave and R. A. B. Mynors (Oxford 1969)
Cal Fearn	*The Calendar of Fearn: Text and Additions, 1471–1667*, ed. R. J. Adam (SHS 1991)
CDS	*Calendar of Documents relating to Scotland*, ed. J. Bain and others (Edinburgh 1881–1986)
Chron. Bower	*Scotichronicon by Walter Bower, in Latin and English*, ed. D. E. R. Watt and others (Aberdeen and Edinburgh, 1987–98)
Chron. Earls of Ross	*Ane Breve Cronicle of the Erlis of Ross*, ed. W. R. Baillie (Edinburgh 1850)
Chron. Fordun	*Johannis de Fordun, Chronica Gentis Scotorum*, ed. W. F. Skene (Edinburgh 1871–2)
Chron. Holyrood	*A Scottish Chronicle known as the Chronicle of Holyrood*, ed. M. O. Anderson (SHS 1938)

Chron. Man	*Cronica Regum Mannie & Insularum*, transcribed and translated by G. Broderick (Douglas 1979)
Chron. Man (Munch and Goss)	*The Chronicle of Man and the Sudreys*, ed. P. A. Munch and Rev. Dr Goss (Manx Soc., 1874)
Chron. Melrose	*Chronicle of Melrose*, facsimile edn, ed. A. O. Anderson and M. O. Anderson (London 1936)
Chron. Picts-Scots	*Chronicles of the Picts: Chronicles of the Scots*, ed. W. F. Skene (Edinburgh 1867)
Chron. Wyntoun (Laing)	Androw of Wyntoun, *The Orygynale Cronykil of Scotland*, ed. D. Laing (Edinburgh, 1872–9)
Chrons. Stephen, etc.	*Chronicles of the Reigns of Stephen, Henry II, and Richard I*, ed. R. Howlett (Rolls Ser., 1884–90)
CPL	*Calendar of Entries in the Papal Registers relating to Great Britain and Ireland: Papal Letters*, ed. W. H. Bliss and others (London 1893–)
CSSR	*Calendar of Scottish Supplications to Rome*, ed. A. I. Dunlop and others (SHS 1934–)
Dryburgh Lib.	*Liber S. Marie de Dryburgh*, ed. W. Fraser (Bannatyne Club, 1847)
ER	*The Exchequer Rolls of Scotland*, ed. J. Stuart and others (Edinburgh 1878–1908)
ES	*Early Sources of Scottish History, A.D. 500 to 1286*, ed. A. O. Anderson (Edinburgh 1922; repr. Stamford 1990)
ESC	*Early Scottish Charters prior to 1153*, ed. A. C. Lawrie (Glasgow 1905)
Highland Papers	*Highland Papers*, ed. J. R. N. Macphail (SHS 1914–34)
HMC	Historical Manuscripts Commission
Holyrood Lib.	*Liber Cartarum Sancte Crucis*, ed. C. Innes (Bannatyne Club, 1840)
Life of Ailred	*The Life of Ailred of Rievaulx by Walter Daniel*, ed. F. M. Powicke (London 1950)
Melrose Lib.	*Liber Sancte Marie de Melros*, ed. C. Innes (Bannatyne Club, 1837)
Moray Reg.	*Registrum Episcopatus Moraviensis*, ed. C. Innes (Bannatyne Club, 1839)
Munro Writs	*Calendar of the Writs of Munro of Foulis*, ed. C. T. McInnes (Scottish Record Soc., 1940)
NAS	National Archives of Scotland, Edinburgh (formerly Scottish Record Office)
OPS	*Origines Parochiales Scotiae*, ed. C. Innes and others (Bannatyne Club, 1850–5)
Orkneyinga Saga	*Orkneyinga Saga: The History of the Earls of Orkney*, trans. H. Pálsson and P. Edwards (Harmondsworth 1978)
Paisley Reg.	*Registrum Monasterii de Passelet*, ed. C. Innes (Maitland Club, 1832)

PSAS	*Proceedings of the Society of Antiquaries of Scotland*
RCAHMS	Royal Commission on the Ancient and Historical Monuments and Constructions of Scotland
Reliquae Celticae	A. Cameron, *Reliquiae Celticae: Texts Papers and Studies in Gaelic Literature and Philology*, ed. A. MacBain and J. Kennedy (Inverness 1892–4)
RMS	*Registrum Magni Sigilli Regum Scotorum*, ed. J. M. Thomson and others (Edinburgh 1882–1914)
Rot. Scot.	*Rotuli Scotiae in Turri Londinensi et in Domo Capitulari Westmonasteriensi asservati*, ed. D. Macpherson and others (Record Commission, 1814–19)
RRS	*Regesta Regum Scottorum*, ed. G. W. S. Barrow and others (Edinburgh 1960
RSS	*Registrum Secreti Sigilli Regum Scotorum*, ed. M. Livingstone and others (Edinburgh 1908–)
SAEC	*Scottish Annals from English Chroniclers, 500 to 1286*, ed. A. O. Anderson (London 1908)
Scots Peerage	*The Scots Peerage*, ed. J. B. Paul (Edinburgh 1904–14)
SHR	*Scottish Historical Review*
SHS	Scottish History Society
Stevenson, *Documents*	*Documents Illustrative of the History of Scotland, 1286–1306*, ed. J. Stevenson (Edinburgh 1870)
TA	*Accounts of the Lord High Treasurer of Scotland*, ed. T. Dickson and J. B. Paul (Edinburgh 1877–1916)
Taymouth Book	*The Black Book of Taymouth*, ed. C. Innes (Bannatyne Club, 1855)
TDGNHAS	*Transactions of the Dumfriesshire and Galloway Natural History and Antiquarian Society*
TGSI	*Transactions of the Gaelic Society of Inverness*
Theiner, *Vetera Monumenta*	*Vetera Monumenta Hibernorum et Scotorum Historiam Illustrantia*, ed. A. Theiner (Rome 1864)
Wigtownshire Chrs.	*Wigtownshire Charters*, ed. R. C. Reid (SHS 1960)

Preface

This book had its genesis in an international conference on 'Alba: Celtic Scotland in the Middle Ages,' that was held at the University of Guelph in Canada to commemorate the one hundredth anniversary of the death of William Forbes Skene, the pioneering historian of Celtic Scotland. A further concern was to remedy what was perceived as a substantial void in the historiography of medieval Scotland where the *Gàidhealtachd* was concerned. This volume is the result.

The ten essays collected here have all been substantially revised since they were first presented, to take account of the most recent scholarship. The editors are particularly grateful to the contributors for their patience and good-humoured co-operation as both travelled far from Guelph. It is with sadness that we note the passing of one of the contributors, Dr. Alan Bruford, whose essay is presented here as it was originally submitted, without the opportunity for revision.

Taken as a whole, the volume spans virtually the entire medieval period, from the Caledonians of Late Antiquity to the rebellions of Donald *Dubh* MacDonald, a claimant to the MacDonald Lordship of the Isles, in the early sixteenth century; it is, therefore, chronologically, if not thematically, comprehensive. Each chapter stands on its own, and addresses a specific problem or issue within the broader framework of 'Celtic Scotland.' The stage is set by Ted Cowan in 'The Invention of Celtic Scotland,' which discusses both perceptions of Celts and Highlanders and the historiography of the *Gàidhealtachd* from the late middle ages to the time of W. F. Skene and beyond. Cowan notes how the apparent dearth of contemporary source materials has often been perceived as a hindrance to the study of Celtic Scotland. It is fitting, then, that the next essay is concerned with a re-evaluation of one particular document. In 'The Seven Kingdoms in *De situ Albanie*: A Record of Pictish Political Geography or imaginary Map of ancient *Alba*?' Dauvit Broun examines the way that this important text has been used by historians since the time of Skene, and asks whether most commentators have read too much into it. Broun argues, in contrast to generations of earlier scholars, that this text cannot be read as a realistic map of Pictish political geography, although he goes on to suggest that this does not necessarily diminish its value for the historian. The Picts also figure prominently in the contributions of both Alan Bruford, 'What happened to the Caledonians?' and Graeme Cruickshank, 'The Battle of Dunnichen and the Aberlemno Battle-Scene,' with each author concentrating on a particular type of evidence. Bruford, relying heavily on linguistic evidence, primarily in the form of place-names, delves into the political geography of North Britain in the post-Roman centuries to offer a speculative reconstruction of the fate of the Caledonians, the early inhabitants of what would become Alba. Cruickshank, taking as his main 'text' the magnificent battle-scene on the Pictish cross-slab in the Aberlemno churchyard, explores what he calls one of 'the biggest clashes of arms in the history of 'Dark Age' Britain' – the battle of Dunnichen in 685, in which the Picts defeated the Northumbrians and threw off their overlordship.

The Picts were, of course, only one of several ethnic groups that went into making up the kingdom of Alba and, later, the medieval kingdom of *Scotia*. Seen from another perspective, *Alba/Scotia* was also put together out of regional building blocks. In his wide-ranging essay on 'The Province of Ross and the Kingdom of Alba,' Alexander Grant explores the mechanisms by which one of those regional building blocks, the northern province of Ross, was incorporated into the kingdom of Alba, reflecting on important problems in the history of that province from Roman times up to the early thirteenth century, and assessing its interactions with a dynamic and emerging kingdom. From Ross, the focus shifts to Galloway, and from largely secular subjects to an ecclesiastical one. Keith Stringer's article on 'Reform Monasticism and Celtic Scotland: Galloway, *c*.1140–*c*.1240,' explores the contribution of one dynasty of 'Celtic' magnates to religious life in medieval Scotland, and adds a new dimension to our understanding of the interplay between native 'Celtic' society and mainstream European life.

The theme of the interactions and relations between Scottish kings and powerful regional lords serves to link the remaining four essays. In 'Rebels without a Cause: The Relations of Fergus of Galloway and Somerled of Argyll with the Scottish Kings, 1153–1164,' R. Andrew McDonald compares and contrasts the relative positions of Fergus and Somerled as powerful, largely autonomous rulers on the margins of the Scottish kingdom, and considers in detail their turbulent and ultimately disastrous relations with the Canmore kings. David Sellar, in 'Hebridean Sea-Kings: The Successors of Somerled, 1164–1316,' takes up with the death of Somerled in 1164 and explores the careers of his descendants, with a special emphasis on the MacDougall Lords of Argyll, highlighting their roles as both Scottish magnates and Hebridean sea-kings. Moving into the later medieval period,

Steve Boardman tackles the question of not only a regional power-base but also the dynamic expansion of one kin-group – the Campbells – at the expense of another – the Stewarts – in 'The Tale of Leper John and the Campbell Acquisition of Argyll.' The volume fittingly concludes with Norman MacDougall's thoughts on the 'decline and fall' of one of the most important institutions of medieval Gaeldom: the MacDonald Lordship of the Isles. In 'Achilles Heel? The Earldom of Ross, the Lordship of the Isles, and the Stewart Kings, 1449–1507,' MacDougall offers compelling insights into the inner dynamics and the mechanisms which ultimately weakened and destroyed this characteristic Gaelic institution.

At the editorial level, it has been thought desirable to maintain a high degree of individuality among the various articles. No effort has been made to standardise personal or place-names, in order to reflect the idiosyncratic nature of current scholarship as well as the present polarisation between those scholars who prefer Gaelicised forms and those who favour Anglicised ones. Similarly, no effort has been made to harmonise points of view between articles, thereby more accurately reflecting the current state of knowledge on various issues and the differing interpretations of historians on contentious matters. Indeed, scholarly disagreement is fundamental to historical dialogue, and the reader will, occasionally, find potentially contradictory opinions voiced, most notably between the contributions of Dauvit Broun and Alan Bruford but also in the footnotes of various other essays. The differing viewpoints on a wide variety of related topics mean that there is bound to be some overlap in these articles, but it is hoped that there is little repetition.

A volume of essays such as this one is almost bound, by definition, to contain chronological and thematic gaps and omissions. Most noticeable in these pages, perhaps, is a lack of material on women in the *Gàidhealtachd* – an omission which it is hoped the imminently forthcoming volume on *Women in Scotland*, edited by E. Ewan and M. Meikle (Tuckwell Press), will go some way to remedying. Similarly, considering the importance of the Church and religion in the Middle Ages, ecclesiastical facets are surely under-represented here, although Keith Stringer's masterly study sheds important light on hitherto undeveloped themes. No doubt more could have been written on any number of themes; at the end of the day, however, it is important to acknowledge that the study of Celtic Scotland is an ongoing, not to mention a dynamic, process. It is hoped that this volume will make some modest contribution to the field, while at the same time stimulating further investigation, discussion, and debate.

Inevitably, a volume like this is a collaborative effort. The editors would like to thank the authors warmly for their contributions – all of which have received multiple peer evaluation – as well as for their patience and co-operation, particularly during the final stages of production. Also deserving of special thanks are Sandy and Alison Grant, Dauvit Broun and Jacqueline Buchanan. We are indebted to Ms Christine Boyle of the University of Guelph for her organisational skills, and to Mrs Dorothy Mallon, Department of Scottish History, Glasgow University, for her assistance with the typescripts. Finally, we thank John and Val Tuckwell, who have once again proved a pleasure to work with, and who have supported this project from the beginning.

E.J.C.
R.A.McD.

1

The Invention of Celtic Scotland

EDWARD J. COWAN

In 1837 William Forbes Skene began his first book on Gaelic-speaking Scotland with a quotation best rendered 'happy are the people without a history'; adopting that criterion, he observed that the Highlanders should have been 'one of the happiest people in Europe'.[1] Some forty-five years later J. G. Mackay, bemoaning 'The Misrepresentation of Highlanders and their History', cited Sir Walter Ralegh's opinion that 'all history is a romance and no further deserving attention than as a record of speculative and hypothetical conjecture'. Though not prepared 'to acquiesce entirely in the opinion of this great man', he thought that so far as books relating to the Highlands were concerned 'there seems to be some ground for this broad and sweeping scepticism'. Mackay, who was addressing the Glasgow Highland Association in 1882, asserted that 'to many Highlanders the extraordinary antipathy and determined antagonism with which they have been treated by pragmatical historians has long been a most unaccountable mystery'. In his view the writers who commented upon the Highlands without knowing anything about them were as much to be dreaded as the activities of Butcher Cumberland. While an Englishman or a Lowlander might be distinguished as a Whig or a Jacobite, 'the Highlander could have no such sentiments, he could only be activated by his love for plunder and bloodshed'.[2]

Two years earlier Skene had completed what may be regarded as the most lasting legacy of his life's work, the great three volume *Celtic Scotland: A History of Ancient Alban*.[3] His impressive scholarly output

---

1 W. F. Skene, *The Highlanders of Scotland: Their origin, History, and Antiquities; with a Sketch of their Manners and Customs, and an account of the clans into which they were divided, and of the state of society which existed among them* (London 1837), i, p. vii.

2 J. G. Mackay, 'The Misrepresentations of the Highlanders and their History. A paper read before the Glasgow Highland Association' (Glasgow 1882), Edinburgh University Library Mackinnon Collection, P. 35/8, pp. 1–7.

3 W. F. Skene, *Celtic Scotland: A History of Ancient Alban* (Edinburgh 1876–80; 2nd edn 1886–90). His editions included: *Book of the Dean of Lismore: English and Gaelic Selections* (Edinburgh 1862); *Chronicles of the Picts, Chronicles of the Scots and other early memorials of Scottish History* (Edinburgh 1867); *The four ancient books of Wales, containing the Cymric poems attributed to the bards of the sixth century*

included several volumes of editions and translations of documents at that time virtually unknown to the world of scholarship, which until comparatively recently persisted in reiterating the fiction that there were no worthwhile sources available to historians of Celtic Scotland in the medieval era. Such wilful neglect, he suggested in his *Highlanders* (a Highland Society of London prize-winning essay), was more deep-rooted than mere ignorance, and should be attributed to

> the influence of that extraordinary prejudice against the Celtic race in general, and against the Scottish and Irish branches of that race in particular, which certainly biased the better judgement of our best historians, who appear to have regarded the Highlands with some-what of the spirit of those who said of old 'Can any good thing come out of Nazareth?' But it is mainly to be attributed to the neglect, by the indiscreet supporters of Highland fables, of that strictly critical accuracy, in point of evidence and reasoning, so indispensable to the value of historical research; the want of which infallibly leads to the loose style of argument and vague assumption so remarkably characteristic of that class of writers, and tends unfortunately to draw down upon the subject itself no small share of the ridicule to which the authors were more justly liable.

He claimed that the production of his essay involved an 'entirely new system of history', namely the exposure of the 'fundamental error' tracing descent of the Gaels from the Dalriadic Scots, demonstrating instead, to his own satisfaction, their Caledonian origins.[4] Forty years later his aim, less ambitiously, was to

> show what the most reliable authorities do really tell us of the early annals of the country, divested of the spurious matter of suppositious authors, the fictitious narratives of our early historians, and the rash assumptions of later writers which have been imported into it.[5]

In this endeavour he was following a well-worn path extending all the way back to the avowals and disclaimers of the medieval chroniclers.

The success of *Celtic Scotland* owed much, as Skene acknowledged, to

(Edinburgh 1868); and John of Fordun, *Chronica Gentis Scotorum* (Historians of Scotland, Edinburgh 1871), vol i. He also edited *Tracts by Dr Gilbert Skeyne, medicinar to His Majesty* (Bannatyne Club, 1860); and *Memorials of the family of Skene of Skene; from the family papers, with other illustrative documents* (New Spalding Club, 1887), as well as publishing numerous articles and pamphlets. All of his work now requires total revision but his more severe modern critics should remember that Skene was not a full-time historian.

4 Skene, *Highlanders*, i, pp. ix–x.
5 Skene, *Celtic Scotland*, i, p. vi.

the publisher David Douglas, who, having enjoyed a personal and professional breakthrough with G. W. Dasent's *Popular Tales from the Norse* (1859), had become something of a specialist in Scottish, notably Gaelic, material. Douglas overcame a number of the technical problems associated with the printing of the language to produce J. F. Campbell's *Popular Tales of the West Highlands* (1860), and he also published such writers as Cosmo Innes, E. W. Robertson and Joseph Anderson, as well as Skene, to become one of the great unsung heroes of nineteenth-century Scottish historical and cultural publishing.[6]

Although Skene became Historiographer Royal for Scotland in 1881, he was a career lawyer, a Writer to the Signet and clerk of the bills in the Court of Session. Born at Inverie, in Knoydart, his love of the history and culture of the Highlands was reinforced through his acquaintance with another famous lawyer, Sir Walter Scott, who arranged for him to be boarded with the Gaelic scholar and minister, Mackintosh Mackay, at Laggan, Inverness-shire, from whom he learned Gaelic. As Aeneas Mackay wrote, 'while never neglecting official and professional duties, his discharge of which was highly appreciated by his clients and the court, he had his eye from earliest manhood on highland history and Celtic scholarship'; in his view William Forbes Skene 'accomplished more for the annals of his native country than any other writer' of the nineteenth century.[7] He did not become a household name, however. None other than Robert Louis Stevenson failed to recognise Skene when, as a young man, he was apprenticed to the law firm of Skene and Edwards, and he later told a correspondent that his former employer was 'a Great Historian – and I was his blessed clerk and did not know it; and you will not be in a state of grace about the Picts till you have studied him'.[8]

Many of Skene's ideas and assertions are no longer tenable but his accomplishment should not be under-rated; it was not his fault that the prejudice towards his subject long survived his lifetime. While the historiography of the *Gàidhealtachd* has greatly improved during the last twenty years or so,[9] there is no room for complacency and there is still some considerable way to go, particularly with reference to the medieval period, which has tended to receive less attention[10] than such familiar

6 G. Thomsen, 'On the character of the Old Northern Poetry', ed. E. J. Cowan and H. Pálsson, *Studia Islandica*, xxxi (Reykjavik 1972), 13–16.

7 *Dictionary of National Biography* (London 1909), lii, 338.

8 *The Letters of Robert Louis Stevenson*, ed. B. A. Booth and E. Mehew (New Haven and London, 1994–5), no. 2782.

9 Cf. E. J. Cowan, *The Historical Highlands: A Guide to Reading* (Edinburgh 1977).

10 Two recent publications are R. A. McDonald, *The Kingdom of the Isles: Scotland's Western Seaboard, c.1100–c.1336* (East Linton 1997); and J. L. Roberts, *Lost Kingdoms: Celtic Scotland and the Middle Ages* (Edinburgh 1997).

subjects as the Jacobites or the Clearances. Among the contributors to this volume are some of the foremost historians of medieval Celtic Scotland – although none of them would ever contemplate a project on the scale that Skene set himself since such massive syntheses, so confidently and eagerly embraced by the Victorians, are no longer fashionable, nor are they attainable, given the pressures of modern academic life. But – quite simply – *Celtic Scotland* cannot be ignored by anyone investigating the first millennium and a half of Scottish history. Skene died in 1892. This volume of essays was conceived as a modest token of respect for his outstanding scholarly achievement; he it was, for good or ill, who placed Celtic Scotland on the historical map once and for all. No one since has seriously doubted its existence though many have quibbled about the label 'Celtic'.

However, as Tom Devine has indicated, there was another side to Skene. In 1847 he was appointed Secretary to the Central Board of Management for Highland Relief, a body charged with alleviating the worst effects of the potato famine. In that capacity he was forced to confront what he considered to be the inadequacies of the contemporary population of the *Gàidhealtachd*. So sensitive were the contents of his letters to Sir Charles Trevelyan, Assistant Secretary to the Treasury and a man centrally involved in both Irish and Scottish relief, that he wrote, 'Pray do not let these find their way into print.' While Skene was by no means totally impervious to the plight of starving and impoverished Gaels, there is no doubt that he was personally implicated in a number of controversial and unpalatable decisions which amounted to subsidising certain landlords while recommending the migration of their socially and economically unreconstructed tenants.[11] One could therefore be forgiven the suspicion that William Forbes Skene sought refuge in the Celtic past as some solace for his failure to truly confront his Gaelic present. But he was neither the first nor the last so to do, and indeed his views can be seen as representative of one of the great streams of Scottish historical consciousness which, swirling with contradiction and ambivalence, ebbed and flowed throughout the centuries.

The word 'Celtic', or for that matter 'Celt', is fraught with difficulty and controversy. The 'Keltoi' first appear in the works of early Greek writers of the fifth century BC, such as Hecataeus of Miletus and Herodotus. Though subsequent historians have found their use of the term infuriatingly imprecise it seems to have conveyed the sense of non-Greek, and hence 'foreigner' or 'barbarian' which in Greek eyes were

11 T. M. Devine, *The Great Highland Famine: Hunger, Emigration and the Scottish Highlands in the Nineteenth Century* (Edinburgh 1988), 128, 132, 171, 247.

one and the same. In modern parlance it defined 'the other'.[12] Like many historical appellatives, 'Celtic' has generated much confusion and, in certain quarters, hostility. It is always a cause of some unease when historians cannot decide upon definitive nomenclature for the period or topic they are investigating – hence the disputes over such descriptors as 'Dark Age', 'medieval', 'Renaissance', feudalism, revolution or nationalism. The problem is compounded when the adjective is also claimed for archaeology, language, culture, religion, music, mysticism, magic, literature and lunatic fringery. For good or ill the Celtic label is now well established and no amount of futile flytings between archaeologists, linguists and historians will change that fact.[13] Skene applied the word to the Celtic-speaking inhabitants of Scotland – Britons, Picts and Gaels, yet during most of the period with which he was primarily concerned the words 'Celt' or 'Celtic' do not appear in any indigenous source. The evolving awareness of these terms in Scotland, as well as of the *Gàidhealtachd* in the context of Scottish historiography, is the theme of what follows.

* * *

The first Scottish chronicler to explicitly discuss the inhabitants of Gaelic Scotland was John of Fordun, who probably composed his *Chronica Gentis Scotorum* in the 1370s; his material was later incorporated into Walter Bower's *Scotichronicon*, written in the 1440s. It is with some diffidence that I quote the relevant and overly familiar passage yet again; but what should be noted is that medieval commentators depended heavily upon the authority of classical writers in formulating their remarks, the voice of antiquity providing verification of empirical observation. Thus Fordun famously noted that the Gaels spoke a different language from that of their civil neighbours, *domestica gens*:

> The people who speak Scots occupy the coastal and lowland regions, while those who speak Gaelic live in the mountainous regions and the outer isles. The coastal people are docile and civilised, trustworthy, long-suffering and courteous, decent in their dress, polite and peaceable, devout in worship, but always ready to resist injuries threatened by their enemies. The island or highland people however are fierce and untameable, uncouth and unpleasant, much given to theft, fond of doing nothing, but their minds are quick to learn, and cunning. They are strikingly handsome in appearance, but their clothing is unsightly. They are always hostile and savage

---

12 M. Chapman, *The Celts: The Construction of a Myth* (London 1992), 24–52.
13 For some illuminating discussion of this topic, see D. E. Evans 'Celticity, identity, and the study of language – fact, speculation and legend', *Archaeologia Cambrensis*, cxl (1992), 1–16.

not only towards the people and language of England, but also towards their fellow Scots because of the difference in language.[14]

For good measure the testimonies of the Roman historian Solinus and the seventh-century encyclopaedist Isidore of Seville were recruited to emphasise Gaelic barbarism, bloodlust, battle-rage and bravery.

John Mair embroidered this account in his *History of Greater Britain*, published in Latin at Paris in 1521.

> Just as among the Scots we find two distinct tongues, so we likewise find two different ways of life and conduct. For some are born in the forests and mountains of the north, and these we call men of the Highland, but the others men of the Lowland. By foreigners the former are called Wild Scots, *Scoti sylvestres*, the latter householding Scots, *Scoti domestici*. The Irish tongue is in use among the former, the English tongue among the latter. One-half of Scotland speaks Irish,[15] and all these as well as the Islanders we reckon to belong to the Wild Scots. In dress, in the manner of their outward life, and in good morals, for example, these come behind the householding Scots – yet they are not less, but rather much more, prompt to fight; and this both because, born as they are in the mountains and dwellers in forests, their very nature is more combative ... These people delight in the chase and a life of indolence; and their chiefs eagerly follow bad men if only they may not have the need to labour; taking no pains to earn their own livelihood, they live upon others, and follow their own savage and worthless chief in all evil courses sooner than they will pursue an honest industry. They are full of mutual dissensions, and war rather than peace is their normal condition.

Yet each of these writers – and the point has not been sufficiently stressed – could, despite their apparently hostile attitudes, detect much of value in the Gaelic population. Fordun and Bower emphasised their loyalty and obedience if properly ruled, while Mair applauded their military abilities and selfless courage. Such ambivalence would prove a recurrent theme.

The views of Hector Boece in his hugely influential *Scotorum Historiae* (1527) were much less qualified; he made no secret of his admiration for the 'auld Scottis' or Gaels, who preserved sturdy and worthy values which

14 *Chron. Fordun*, i, 24; translation from *Chron. Bower*, i, 185.

15 *A History of Greater Britain As Well England as Scotland Compiled from the Ancient Authorities by John Major, by name indeed a Scot, but by profession a theologian 1521*, ed. and trans. A. Constable (SHS 1892), 48; 'at the present day almost half of Scotland speaks the Irish tongue, and not so long ago it was spoken by the majority of us' (p. 50).

eluded his effete contemporaries. He praised the moderation, sobriety and self-sufficiency of former generations as well as their athleticism, inurement to cold weather and a harsh environment, their courage, and capacity for war. Things in his own day were not as they had once been; ancestral frugality had given way to gluttony and luxury.

> For quhare our eldaris had sobriete, we have ebriete and dronkinnes; quhare thay had plente with sufficence, we have immoderat coursis with superfluite; as he war maist noble and honest, that culd devore and swelly [swallow] maist; and be extreme diligence, serchis sa mony deligat [luxurious] coursis, that thay provoke the stomok to ressave mair than it may sufficiently degest.[16]

He wrote at some considerable length about the attributes and manners of his hardy forebears; but what was to trouble posterity, and would bring much ridicule upon Boece's head, was the spurious line of forty kings that he included in his account. These kings had been inherited from Fordun and Bower and originated in the earlier king-lists which Dauvit Broun has recently illuminated so helpfully,[17] but they were to haunt Scottish historiography for two hundred years.

John Leslie bishop of Ross was a great admirer of Boece and shared many of his opinions; his *History* was published at Rome in 1578, a Scots translation appearing in 1596. He too was convinced that the values and manners of the old Scots were preserved by contemporary Gaelic speakers, who for over two thousand years had maintained uncorrupted their language, clothing and way of life. Such writers, interested as they were in manners and the speculative reconstruction of past societies, could be said to have anticipated the much-lauded 'conjectural historians' of the Scottish Enlightenment.[18]

The supreme historian to emerge from Renaissance Scotland was George Buchanan, and he it was who, in his magisterial discussion of the antecedents of the populations of the British Isles, first truly introduced the terms 'Celt' and 'Celtic' to Scottish historiography, drawing upon his profound knowledge of the classical sources. He showed, in the introductory sections of his *Rerum Scoticarum Historia* (1582), that Britons,

---

16 *The Chronicles of Scotland Compiled by Hector Boece Translated into Scots by John Bellenden 1531*, ed. R. W. Chambers, E. C. Batho and H. W. Husbands (Scottish Text Soc., 1938–41), i, p. lv.

17 D. Broun, *The Irish Identity of the Kingdom of the Scots in the Twelfth and Thirteenth Centuries* (Woodbridge 1999). For a wide-ranging exploration of a similar theme, see W. Ferguson, *The Identity of the Scottish Nation: An Historic Quest* (Edinburgh 1998).

18 On this and for further discussion of historiography, see E. J. Cowan 'The discovery of the Gàidhealtachd in sixteenth-century Scotland', *TGSI* (1999), forthcoming.

Picts and Scots shared a common kinship in their descent from the Gauls
or Celts. A native of Killearn, close to Loch Lomond in the earldom of
Lennox, Buchanan was a Gaelic speaker who, as a committed classicist,
could cheerfully anticipate 'the gradual extinction of the ancient Scottish
language', the dying away of its 'harsh sounds', and its replacement with
'the softer and more harmonious tones of the Latin'; thus Gaelic-speakers
would pass from 'rusticity and barbarism to culture and civilization'.

Throughout his discussion Buchanan reserved much of his venom for
the Welsh antiquarian, Humphrey Lloyd, whom he accused of constantly
preferring barbarism to refinement. In Buchanan's view over-population
in the homelands of Gaul – in earlier times a term of much wider
geographic application than it was in Caesar's day – forced the Celts to
migrate to neighbouring lands. He used 'Celt' in the same sense that the
Greeks had understood. Thus from the *Celti*, or *Celtiberi* (Celtiberians),
the people known as the *Celtici* were descended. In another passage he
noted that 'the Irish, and the colonies sent from them, having sprung from
the Celtic inhabitants of Spain, very probably used the Celtic (language)' –
*Hiberni et coloniae ab eis missae a Celtis Hispaniae habitatoribis oriundi, uti
credibile est, Celtica utebantur.*[19] As his translator sensibly observed, 'the
aborigines of Europe were known by the general name of Celts, as the
aborigines of America are known by the general name of Indians'.
Following Pliny's notion that the common origins of nations could be
traced by comparing religion, language and onomastics, Buchanan pointed
to the shared religious practices of the Gauls and the Britons in their
mutual respect for druids and bards; the name and function of the latter
were still preserved, he noted, 'among all nations who use the ancient
language of the Britons'. He was fascinated by the transitory nature of
language, by how it was continually evolving and changing, and he quoted
Horace with approval:

> As from the trees old leaves drop off, and die,
> While others sprout, and a fresh shade supply,
> So fare our words – time withers them, but dead,
> A fresher language rises in their stead.

Thus it was that the languages of the Celts gradually diversified though,
through a learned disquisition on place-names, utilising the unimpeachable
testimony of the classics, Buchanan was able to demonstrate their
common roots:

> I think it rather wonderful that the fundamental principles of a
> language, and the manner of declining it, should be preserved

[19] George Buchanan, *Rerum Scoticarum Historia* (Edinburgh 1582), fols. 17, 21.

among a people so widely scattered, so rarely agreeing in the other rules of life, and so often opposing each other, with such deadly hatred.[20]

He thus initiated a debate which consumed much historical talent in subsequent centuries, which was partially resolved by Kenneth Jackson in 1955,[21] but which still rumbles on in certain quarters.

It is important to realise that Buchanan rooted his entire discussion of Scottish history in his review of what classical writers had to say about the early peoples of Scotland, quoting extensively from Caesar, Tacitus, Cicero, Solinus, and Ammianus Marcellinus, among others, and, incidentally, rehearsing practically every cliché and stereotype about the Celts – and hence by implication the Gaels – repeated by these writers. But Buchanan also sought inspiration for, and corroboration of, his constitutional theories in the Gaelic past; he sought to justify the deposition of Mary Queen of Scots by invoking the antiquity and sanctity of custom as it still survived in the Gàidhealtachd in his own day. Clan chiefs were elected, and were liable to lose office if they did not obey their councils. 'Is it likely', asked Buchanan, 'that those who are so careful in sections of the community would ignore what affects the welfare of the whole nation?' Like Boece and Leslie he was greatly impressed that a culture over two thousand years old survived in his native country; but to him, in the main, belongs the distinction of having revived the Ancient World's identification of the kinship of the Celtic peoples.[22]

Although Buchanan's constitutional views remained familiar throughout the seventeenth century, the distractions of religious controversy and civil war rendered his ideas about the Celts largely irrelevant. The Montrose wars of 1644–5 both widened the gulf and deepened the antipathy between Highlander and Lowlander. Sympathy and admiration for the warrior-like abilities of the Gaels were manifested in several royalist histories,[23] but the

20 George Buchanan, *The History of Scotland translated from the Latin of George Buchanan with Notes and a continuation to the Union in the reign of Queen Anne*, trans. J. Aikman (Glasgow 1827), i, 9, 80, 93, 116.

21 K. H. Jackson, 'The Pictish language', in F. T. Wainwright (ed.), *The Problem of the Picts* (Edinburgh 1955), 129–66.

22 E. J. Cowan 'The political ideas of a covenanting leader: Archibald Campbell, marquis of Argyll 1607–1661', in R. A. Mason (ed.), *Scots and Britons: Scottish political thought and the union of 1603* (Cambridge 1994), 257–8.

23 E.g., George Wishart, *Memoirs of the Most Renowned James Graham, Marquis of Montrose, translated from the Latin of the Rev Doctor George Wishart* (Edinburgh 1819); John Spalding, *Memorialls of the Trubles in Scotland and in England, 1624–1645*, ed. J. Stuart (Spalding Club, 1850); Robert Mentet (Menteith) of Salmonet, *The History of the Trubles of Great Britain*, trans. James Ogilvie (London 1735); Patrick Gordon of Ruthven, *A Short Abridgement of Britane's Distemper, from the yeare of God MDCXXXIX to MDCXLIX*, ed. J. Dunn (Spalding Club, 1844).

climate was apparently overwhelmingly hostile to the reception of an emerging Gaelic voice. As John MacQueen has pointed out, Gaelic-speaking Scotland also experienced a renaissance in the sixteenth century,[24] but there was little awareness of or interest in it in the rest of Scotland. Although histories were composed in the *Gàidhealtachd* they were not to be published for some considerable time.[25]

It is somewhat harsh, however, to claim that Buchanan's notions about the Celts 'had no effect whatever on the learned world, and ... were a cul-de-sac in the history of ideas'.[26] It is a safe bet that everyone with an interest in Scottish history in the seventeenth century read Buchanan more or less critically. Robert Gordon of Straloch expressed some reservations about his theories, while there was a flurry of interest in matters antiquarian towards the end of the century. Sir Robert Sibbald, who was interested in a wide variety of subjects, produced a history of Fife in which he argued that the Picts were Goths, traces of whom survived in the Lowland population, so anticipating by a century the ideas of John Pinkerton. The Irish chronologist and genealogist, Roderic O'Flaherty, well and truly set the cat among the Scottish pigeons with his publication of *Ogygia* (1685) in which he attacked 'the imaginary antiquity of Buchanan's ancestors', describing him as 'a man happier in his poetical genius than in the probability of his accounts'. He was, of course, attacking Buchanan's bogus kings whom he had uncritically borrowed from Boece: 'in comparison with Irish history, the antiquity of all other countries is modern, and in some degree in a state of infancy'.[27] Sir George Mackenzie, with the assistance of Sibbald and Sir James Dalrymple, responded with a 'defence', 'founded on a strange idea that the honour of Scotland depended on the antiquity of the royal line'.[28] None of these

24 J. MacQueen, 'The Renaissance in Scotland', in G. Williams and R. O. Jones (eds.), *The Celts and the Renaissance: Tradition and Innovation. Proceedings of the Eighth International Congress of Celtic Studies 1987* (Cardiff 1990), 41.

25 E.g., Sir Robert Gordon, *A Genealogical History of the Earldom of Sutherland from its origin to the year 1630* (Edinburgh, 1813 edn); *The Book of Clanranald*, in A. Cameron, *Reliquiae Celticae: Texts Papers and Studies in Gaelic Literature and Philology*, ed. A. MacBain and J. Kennedy (Inverness 1892–4); James Fraser, *Chronicles of the Frasers: The Wardlaw Manuscript*, ed. W. Mackay (SHS 1905).

26 P. T. J. Morgan, 'The Abbé Pezron and the Celts', *Transactions of the Honourable Society of Cymmrodorion*, 1965, pt 2, 289.

27 Roderic O'Flaherty, *Ogygia, or a Chronological Account of Irish Events*, trans. James Hely (Dublin 1793), i, pp. lvii–lviii, lxix.

28 John Pinkerton, *An Enquiry into the History of Scotland preceding the reign of Malcolm III, or the year 1056, including the authentic history of that period* (new edn, Edinburgh 1814), i, p. lviii. This edition also contains Pinkerton's *A Dissertation on the Origin and Progress of the Scythians or Goths; being an Introduction to the Ancient and Modern History of Europe* (Edinburgh 1787), which was reprinted in 1789 and 1794.

writers used the word 'Celtic' but they did send readers back to their copies of Buchanan, whose works were to be superbly edited by Thomas Ruddiman in 1715. Meanwhile, in England, John Aubrey had been investigating megalithic sites such as Stonehenge and Avebury and had associated them with druids, thus spawning 'the germ of an idea which was to run like lunatic wildfire through all popular and much learned thought, and particularly emotive feeling, until modern times'.[29]

* * *

The dubious distinction of having first employed the word 'Celt' in English[30] appears to belong to Edward Topsell, curate of St Botolph, Aldersgate, and lifelong zoologist. In 1607 he wrote in his *History of Foure-footed Beastes* that 'Indians were wont to use no bridles like the Grecians and the Celts'.[31] John Milton used 'Celtick' in his 'Mask' (1634) and in 'Paradise Lost'.[32] Professor John Garden of Aberdeen wrote to Aubrey in 1693, noting that 'Druid is a word of Celtick extract, and that the origin thereof is to be sought for in the Celtick tongue such as both the old Gallic and the British tongues were'.[33] Another of Aubrey's informants was the Irish deist and controversialist, John Toland, who commenced working on aspects of Celtic philology shortly after he graduated from Edinburgh University in 1690; he had previously spent two years studying at Glasgow. His publishing history is complex; his book, or rather pamphlet, *The History of the Celtic Religion and Learning: containing an account of the Druids*, first appeared in 1726, though parts of it had clearly existed in draft in the 1690s. Toland's essays represent the first sustained discussion of Scottish megalithic monuments – in a comparative context for he considered those of Ireland, England and Wales as well – though he distinguished them as druidic. He was an admirer of Sibbald and also of Martin Martin, whose *A Description of the Western Islands of Scotland* (1695) he used extensively. In a Scottish context his work deserves to be much better known since he wrote much of interest on a broad range of topics, but for present purposes what is impressive is his confident handling of the word 'Celtic'. Glossaries, appended to his *History*, of Irish, Breton and Latin words are dated 1693 from Oxford. He well understood the relationship between Welsh,

29 S. Piggott, *The Druids* (Harmondsworth 1974), 121.
30 For a parallel discussion to what follows, see C. Kidd, *British Identities before Nationalism: Ethnicity and Nationhood in the Atlantic World, 1600–1800* (Cambridge 1999), ch. 8, 'Constructing the pre-romantic Celt'.
31 *Dictionary of National Biography*, lvii, 59–60; *Oxford English Dictionary*, s.v. 'Celt'.
32 *The Works of John Milton*, ed. F. A. Patterson (New York 1931–8), i, 87; ii, 27.
33 Quoted in S. Piggott, *Ruins in a Landscape: Essays in Antiquarianism* (Edinburgh 1976), 61.

Cornish 'almost extinct', Breton, Irish 'the least corrupted', Manx and Gaelic, and he was emphatic that Celtic and Gothic were 'as different as Latin and Arabic'. He expressed concern that writers such as William Camden, *Britannia* (1586), and his own contemporary, Edward Lhuyd, concentrated too much on Wales in pursuing their 'Celtic' researches, without paying sufficient attention to Irish and Gaelic. Indeed it may have been a communication from Toland which partly inspired Lhuyd's visit to the Highlands and Islands at the turn of the century.[34] Toland was undoubtedly an eccentric of some notoriety but he was perfectly comfortable with expressions such as 'Celtic Antiquary' and 'Celtic original'; nor was he lacking a sense of humour – 'they are apt all over Scotland to make every thing Pictish, whose origin they do not know'.[35]

It is thus not exactly clear what is meant when one commentator asserts that 'Paul Pezron (1639–1706) was in all probability the inventor of the modern Celts, and thus of Celticism', unless it is symptomatic of a type of Welsh celto-centricity, noted by Toland and still to be detected in some of the journal literature.[36] There is no denying the influence of Abbé Pezron's *L'antiquité de la nation et la langue des Celtes* (Paris 1703), which appeared in translation as *The Antiquities of Nations: more Particularly of the Celtae or Gauls, taken to be originally of the same people as our Ancient Britains* (London 1706); but it was very much part of a debate which was well and truly underway. Pezron was mentioned, briefly, in Father Thomas Innes's ground-breaking *Critical Essay on the Ancient Inhabitants of the Northern Parts of Britain or Scotland* (1729), though his greatest debt was clearly to George Buchanan despite his criticism of the latter's work. The *Essay* and his *The Civil and Ecclesiatical History of Scotland* (first published in 1853) lucidly and systematically laid out the early history of Scotland utilising an analytical and critical methodology which was, quite simply, unprecedented; and, in the process, he finally demolished Boece's wretched forty kings. He also, though sparingly, employed the word 'Celtic', but only with reference to language; thus British (or Welsh), Pictish and Irish were 'all originally only different dialects of the same mother tongue, the Celtic'.[37] He argued that the Picts, whom he like Sibbald believed to have originated in Scandinavia, were simply 'the

---

34 John Toland, *The History of the Celtic Religion and Learning: containing an account of the Druids ... With a History of Abaris, the Hyperborian, Priest of the Sun* (repr. Folcroft, Pennsylvania, 1974), 46–7, 69. See also J. L. Campbell and D. Thomson, *Edward Lhuyd in the Scottish Highlands, 1699–1700* (Oxford 1963), *passim*.

35 Toland, *History of Celtic Religion*, 115, 145, 151.

36 Morgan, 'Abbé Pezron', 286.

37 Thomas Innes, *A Critical Essay on the Ancient Inhabitants of the Northern Parts of Britain or Scotland* (Edinburgh 1879), 61; Thomas Innes, *The Civil and Ecclesiastical History of Scotland*, ed. G. Grub (Spalding Club, 1853).

ancient Britons of the north', the Britons themselves deriving from 'the Celtes or Gauls', as Buchanan had suggested.[38]

John Pinkerton provided a review of eighteenth-century historical literature, much of it irrelevant in the present context. David Malcolm published his *Dissertations on the Celtic Language* (1738), 'the first work which had appeared in Scotland upon that subject, which afterwards sleeped, till Ossian had the happy effect to awaken public curiosity'.[39] Malcolm, minister of Duddingston, is noteworthy for his conviction that the Amerindians spoke a form of Gaelic, a conclusion to which he came after interviewing survivors of the failed Darien colony.[40] William Maitland's *History* of 1757[41] was mentioned only to be trashed. The two Macphersons, John and James, were noted as 'the very first authors whom the Highlands of Scotland have ever produced', and hence the 'novelty and oddity of their prejudices', particularly their perceived antipathy towards their Lowland neighbours, were not surprising.[42]

* * *

The problem was (apart from Pinkerton's sour-faced contempt for competitors, real or imagined) that Scottish medieval history was re-invented during the Enlightenment. The two greatest historians of the age (though there were, of course, others) were William Robertson and David Hume; the former published *A History of Scotland* (1759), while the philosopher produced *A History of England to the Revolution of 1688* (1763), adopting the unusual convention of commencing with the sixteenth and seventeenth centuries and then working backwards to complete his account from the time of Julius Caesar; despite the book's title it did contain incidental material on Scotland and a fairly detailed section on Mary Queen of Scots. Both writers were firmly rooted in their

---

38 Innes, *Critical Essay*, 54, 56–7.

39 Pinkerton, *Enquiry*, i, p. lxiv.

40 David Malcolm, *An Essay on the Antiquities of Great Britain and Ireland an attempt to show an affinity between the languages etc of the ancient Britains and the Americans of the Isthmus of Darien* (Edinburgh 1738). Pinkerton may have confused this publication with David Malcolm, *Collection of Letters in which the usefulness of the Celtic is instanced in illustrating the antiquities of the British Isles* (Edinburgh 1764).

41 William Maitland, *The History and Antiquities of Scotland* (London 1757). 'He is a bitter enemy of Innes, of Ireland, of the Piks, and of himself': Pinkerton, *Enquiry*, i, p. lxvi.

42 Pinkerton, *Enquiry*, i, pp. lxvii–lxxi; John Macpherson, *Critical Dissertations on the Origin, Antiquities, Language, Government, Manners, and Religion of the Ancient Caledonians, Their Posterity the Picts, and the British and Irish Scots* (London 1768); James Macpherson, *Introduction to the History of Great Britain and Ireland* (London 1771). For an excellent discussion of historiography in this period, see D. Allan, *Virtue, Learning and the Scottish Enlightenment: Ideas of Scholarship in Early Modern History* (Edinburgh 1993), esp. chs. 3, 4.

own present, a world of progress, improvement and enlightened ideas; both regarded early history as being akin to childhood and medieval and early modern times to youth and early middle age, while their own era was regarded as full adult maturity. By their criteria people on the verge of the third millennium would exist in some historical hereafter or in a twilight zone of geriatric debility. Both men were spared the realisation that progress is an illusion. Both, it might be added, wrote with a certain aloofness which gives the impression that they were not truly engaged with their subject, a condition normally known to historians, fallaciously, as 'objectivity' which is still pursued as a futile quarry in certain modern historiographical circles. Occasionally, however, both betray a glimmer of passion.

Robertson believed that 'no period in the history of one's own country can be considered as altogether uninteresting. Such transactions as tend to illustrate the progress of its constitution, laws or manners, merit the utmost attention.'[43] Upon publication his *History* was given a rapturous reception and extravagant praise for its judiciousness, its balanced and moderate tone and its clarity of style. It treats of the period 1542–1603 with a preface on medieval Scotland. Modern critics have concurred with contemporaries on the merits of Robertson's work. He complained that existing histories were marred by polemic and bias, an observation of some truth. Ever since John Knox some Scottish historians had behaved like advocates entering the court with a distinct point of view or opinion, ready to demolish the opposition with proofs which often took the form of full transcripts of documents entered into their texts. Sometimes dismissed as antiquarians, they were nothing of the kind – though admittedly the authors' analytical abilities were often submerged in a mass of undigested texts, Robert Wodrow's massively documented *The History of the Sufferings of the Church of Scotland* (1721–2) providing one such example. Robertson transcribed his documents in appendix form; it was said of David Hume that he never dirtied his hands in an archive and he kept quotation to a minimum in order to concentrate upon narrative and causation.

Robertson wrote off the first nine hundred years of Scottish History as 'pure fable and conjecture and ought to be totally neglected or abandoned to the industry and credulity of antiquaries';[44] it was not just the Celtic past but all medieval history which was barbaric. The situation, however, gradually improved. The problem throughout Scottish history was the overweening power and ambition of the nobility; over and over again he

[43] William Robertson, *A History of Scotland* (London 1759), i, 201.
[44] Ibid., i, 203.

reiterated the point that 'under the aristocratical form of government established among the Scots, the power of the sovereign was extremely limited', while the Reformation simply strengthened the grip of the nobility[45]. Even under James VI, 'all the defects in the feudal aristocracy were felt more sensibly, perhaps, than at any other period ... and universal licence and anarchy prevailed to a degree scarce consistent with the preservation of society'.[46] In the conclusion to the entire work it is revealed that the process of taming the magnates began in 1603 once James had access to English resources; as elsewhere in Europe their position was 'undermined by the progress of commerce'. Stewart absolutism did the rest. Seventeenth-century Scotland was a miserable place: 'its kings were despotic; its nobles were slaves and tyrants; and the people groaned under the rigorous domination of both'. The nobility fought back at the crown in the covenanting revolution but they were bankrupt by 1660, their power finally shattered by the Union of 1707.

> As commerce advanced in its progress, and government attained nearer to perfection, [feudal privileges] were insensibly circumscribed and at last, by laws no less salutary to the public than fatal to the nobles, they have been almost totally abolished. As the nobles were deprived of power, the people acquired liberty.[47]

Robertson's rather astonishing condemnation of the aristocracy is deserving of notice particularly since his noble contemporaries supported the moderate party in the Kirk of which he was leader. There may have been an element of flattery in all of this to the effect that the nobility, having enjoyed a heroic, if anarchic, past in which they could perhaps take pride, were now members of a polite and enlightened society.

There was, however, an ambivalence in Robertson's attitude towards his country's past. He observed that Scottish geography, 'mountains and fens and rivers, set bounds to despotic power and amidst these (despite the chaos) is the natural seat of freedom and independence'; the nobility too 'owed their personal independence to those very mountains and marshes which saved their country from being conquered'. He seems to have realised that the nobility, for all their faults, checked the excesses of the monarch and preserved the constitution and liberties of Scotland. He admitted to some surprise that so many documents from the sixteenth century were 'remarkable for a precision and vigour of expression, which we are surprised to meet with in an age so unpolished'. He may even have temporarily questioned his own commitment to progress when he

---

45 Ibid., i, 405–6, 111, 77.
46 Ibid., iii, 93–4.
47 Ibid., iii, 181–6.

articulated the realisation that 'the vices of another age astonish and shock us; the vices of our own become familiar and excite little horror'.[48]

David Hume, who attempted in his lengthy history to prove the constancy of human nature, was equally dismissive of the medieval period.

> The curiosity, entertained by all civilized nations, of enquiring into the exploits and adventures of their ancestors, commonly excites a regret that the history of remote ages should always be so much involved in obscurity, uncertainty, and contradiction. Ingenious men, possessed of leisure, are apt to push their researches beyond the period in which literary monuments are framed or preserved; without reflecting, that the history of past events is immediately lost or disfigured when entrusted to memory and oral tradition, and that the adventures of barbarous nations, even if they were recorded, could afford little or no entertainment to men born in a more cultivated age. The convulsions of a civilized state usually compose the most instructive and most interesting part of its history; but the sudden, violent, and unprepared revolutions incident to barbarians, are so much guided by caprice and terminate so often in cruelty, that they disgust us by the uniformity of their appearance; and it is rather fortunate for letters that they are buried in silence and oblivion. The only certain means by which nations can indulge their curiosity in researches concerning their remote origin, is to consider the language, manners, and customs of their ancestors, and to compare them with those of their neighbouring nations. The fables which are commonly employed to supply the place of true history, ought entirely to be disregarded.

For the reasons stated he was resolved to begin his account with the Romans, 'neglecting all traditions, or rather tales' concerning early history, and to 'hasten through the obscure and uninteresting period of Saxon annals'.[49] In fact he devoted some four volumes to medieval England, but he implied that Scotland had no 'real history' before the reign of Edward I, and 'so few events of moment, that to avoid tediousness' he omitted them. Very quickly the reader is introduced to a barbarous, rude people, 'more accustomed to arms than inured to laws'. In 1296 'even the turbulent highlanders, ever refractory to their own princes, and averse to the restraint of laws' submitted to Edward who, for good measure carried off the Stone of Scone, venerated by 'popular superstition'. Hume dismissed the Scots' claim that the English king destroyed their records,

[48] Ibid., i, 222–3, 405–7, ii, 156.
[49] David Hume, *The History of England from the Invasion of Julius Caesar to the Revolution in 1688* (London 1823), i, 1–2.

doubting that they had any history the loss of which might be regretted. His patriotism gained strength in contemplating the careers of Wallace and Bruce, as 'the genius of the nation' was aroused to throw off the English yoke; but he could not help regretting that Edward's plans for union had not been realised. He took a dim view of the avarice, fanaticism and 'absurd severity' of the Reformers, particularly in their harsh treatment of Mary. He had no regrets that the regnal union in 1603 foreshadowed the loss of Scottish independence and he proceeded to paint a dismal picture of Scots and Scotland on the eve of the covenanting revolution, a people thrawn, cantankerous, uncultivated and thirled to Calvin.[50] It was of course the religious dimension which so disgusted Hume and which inspired the utter contempt in which he held his predecessors. Sir David Dalrymple, Lord Hailes, who has some claim to be regarded as Scotland's first true medievalist, who was equally judicious in historical dissection and the selection of the *mot juste*, and who proved himself a superb manipulator of the trope of irony, dismissed the period before Malcolm Canmore as 'involved in obscurity and fable', and denounced the superstition of a bygone age.[51]

* * *

It is something of a relief to turn from this depiction of near-relentless gloom to the pages of Gilbert Stuart, who chose to seek his inspiration in a more distant Scottish past, in 'the democratical genius of the Scottish constitution' by which the subjects could resist the tyranny of the monarch and, 'making him a sacrifice to justice, and an instruction to posterity, conduct him from the throne to the scaffold'. He participated in the lively contemporary debate on the militia, opposed as he was to the standing army as a potential instrument of tyrannical whim, and oppression through taxation. Stuart rejoiced that he lived 'in this enlightened age of philosophy and reflection',[52] and he serves as a reminder that Robertson and Hume did not have everything their own way. Between them, however, these two luminaries of the historian's craft mustered little credibility for the value of studying the history of medieval Scotland. They were aided and abetted by Adam Smith and Dugald Stewart whose pursuit of 'conjectural history' was predicated on the absence of a worthwhile or instructive medieval Scottish experience. The

---

50 Ibid., ii, 245, 282–3, 317–18, v, 39–54.
51 Sir David Dalrymple, Lord Hailes, *Remarks Concerning the History of Scotland* (Edinburgh 1773); Sir David Dalrymple, Lord Hailes, *Annals of Scotland from the Accession of Malcolm III Surnamed Canmore to the Accession of Robert I* (Edinburgh 1776).
52 Gilbert Stuart, *The History of Scotland from the Establishment of the Reformation till the Death of Queen Mary* (London 1782).

situation was to be retrieved by two men who conspired in the greatest
literary phenomenon of the century, namely James Macpherson and
Hugh Blair.

Macpherson, a native of Badenoch, published his *Fragments of Ancient
Poetry* (1760), which purported to be the compositions of the legendary bard
Ossian, at the prompting of his friend, Blair, who was shortly to become
the first professor of Rhetoric and Belles Lettres at Edinburgh University.
The Gael was troubled by the prejudice directed against the ancient inhabitants of his country who were 'thought to be incapable of the generous
sentiments to be met with in the poems of Ossian'. Such was the popularity
of the *Fragments* that the public demanded more, so generating the
notorious controversy involving accusations of forgery and worse. What
is significant for present purposes is that Macpherson confidently used the
word 'Celtic'. He was also convinced that the old Highland way of life was
passing due to commerce and migration.[53] Aware of the scepticism which
greeted his publications, he was careful to construct, in his prefaces, a
bogus historical context for his – at the very least – questionable effusions.
In this endeavour he was ably supported by Blair's hugely influential *A
Critical Dissertation on the Poems of Ossian the son of Fingal* (the first version
of which appeared in 1763), which commenced with a double assertion:
'Among the monuments of the ancient state of nations, few are more
valuable than their poems or songs. History, when it treats of remote and
dark ages, is seldom very instructive.' In short order he demonstrated that
he had no hesitation about terminology.

> That the ancient Scots were of Celtic original, is past all doubt.
> Their conformity with the Celtic nations in language, manners and
> religion, proves it to a full demonstration. The Celtae, a great and
> mighty people, altogether distinct from the Goths and Teutones,
> once extended their dominion over all of the west of Europe; but
> seem to have had their most full and compleat establishment in
> Gaul. Wherever the Celtae or Gauls are mentioned by ancient
> writers, we seldom fail to hear of their Druids and their Bards; the
> institution of which two orders, was the capital distinction of their
> manners and policy.[54]

Blair, however, was not only endorsing Scotland's Celtic heritage; he
also provided much Celtic accretion such as druids and bards. It may be
suspected that both Blair and Macpherson as critic and translator sought
to usurp the function of the poet which Aristotle had distinguished as 'not

---

53 James Macpherson, *The Poems of Ossian and related Works*, ed. H. Gaskill
   (Edinburgh 1996), 37–8, 43–4, 51.
54 Ibid., 345, 349–50, 362.

to be a mere annalist of facts, but to embellish truth with beautiful, probable, and useful fictions'. So similar are the sentiments expressed by the pair in their various writings that collusion can be fairly and certainly assumed. To bards and druids were added clans, chiefs and consanguinity as well as wild and romantic scenery.

> The extended heath by the sea shore; the mountain shaded with mist; the torrent rushing through a solitary valley; the scattered oaks, and the tombs of the warriors overgrown with moss; all produce a solemn attention in the mind, and prepare it for great and extraordinary events.

Ossianic simile abounded in images of landscape and nature, weather and mist, so providing information on the relationship between the Celts and their environment. When superstition and mythology,[55] together with a love of warfare and the lamentation for times and peoples past, were added to this heady brew, the contents of the Celtic cauldron appear pretty much as we would recognise them today.

Anne Grant wrote in 1785: 'I am determined my children shall drink "from the pure wells of Celtic undefiled".'[56] Such was the vogue for Ossian and things Ossianic that it is hardly surprising that John Pinkerton could remark, unhappily, that 'this may be called the Celtic century, for all Europe has been inundated with nonsense about the Celts'. He was much wider of the mark when he predicted that 'when we come to the truth about them, and time always draws truth out of the well, the Celtic mist will vanish, or become a mere cloud'.[57] Pinkerton initially embraced Ossian but later changed his mind, scornfully noting, in his inimitable irascible fashion, that 'even little misses lisp about the authenticity of Ossian, and the antique purity of the Celtic language', while bitterly dismissing the 'phantasmagoria in which a dark mirror sends forth unreal images to captivate the vulgar'.[58]

If Blair had proved something of a celto-maniac, Pinkerton was an

55 Ibid., 356, 366–9. For a useful discussion, see S. Rizza, 'A Bulky and Foolish Treatise? Hugh Blair's *Critical Dissertation* reconsidered', in H. Gaskill (ed.), *Ossian Revisited* (Edinburgh 1991), 129–46.

56 Anne Grant, *Letters from the Mountains; being the real Correspondence of a lady, between the years 1773 and 1807* (Edinburgh 1809), ii, 94; quoted in P. Womak, *Improvement and Romance: Constructing the Myth of the Highlands* (London 1989), 133.

57 Pinkerton, *Dissertation*, 124.

58 Pinkerton, *Enquiry*, pp. iv–v. Johnson and Boswell encountered the theory that the Scythians were the ancestors of the Celts in conversation with the Rev. M'Queen in Skye, prompting Johnson's reflection that 'languages are the pedigrees of nations': *Johnson's Journey to the Western Islands of Scotland and Boswell's Journal of A Tour to the Hebrides with Samuel Johnson, LL.D.*, ed. R. W. Chapman (Oxford 1979), 310.

unrepentant celto-phobe who elevated the supposed Scandinavian origin of the Picts into a full-blown theory of Teutonism; he was convinced that the ancestry of all the northern European nations was to be sought among the Scythians or Goths. In the 1787 version of his *Dissertation* he argued that Scottish backwardness had prevailed during several centuries of potentially beneficent Gothic influence (including, of course, that of the Vikings) due to the country's Celtic population which, even in the late eighteenth century, had

> not yet advanced even to the state of barbarism; and if any foreigner doubts this, he has only to step into the Celtic part of Wales, Ireland or Scotland, and look at them, for they are just as they were, incapable of industry or civilisation even after half their blood is Gothic and remain as marked by the ancients, fond of lies and enemies of truth ... For the Celts were so inferior a people, being to the Scythians as a negro to a European, that, as all history shows, to see them was to conquer them.[59]

Although these repugnant statements survived the edition of the *Dissertation* published in 1789 they were dropped from that of 1814, which suggests that Pinkerton's Teutonic hide was insufficiently thick to resist the hail of critical arrows which rained down upon it. Horace Walpole, for example, greeted the first edition with the observation, 'I think you make yourself too much a party against the Celts: I do not think they were or are worthy of hatred'.[60] George Dempster of Dunnichen, the prominent and well-respected antiquary, gently mocked his friend by noting the paradox that in the Lowlands 'all the ancient names are Celtic, and the inhabitants radically and fundamentally Goths', whereas in the *Gàidhealtachd* the order of things was 'quite reversed, the names of all the islands Gothic, and the inhabitants Celts'. He also mischievously enquired whether the Celts might be so-called from wearing the 'kelt' or philabeg.[61] Despite his offensive views, Pinkerton pursued his thesis with much energy and massive erudition, in the process drowning his opponents, past and present, in vitriolic ink. He opined that 'fiction was the natural product of the Celtic mind';[62] while Lowlanders were perceived to be 'acute, industrious, sensible, erect, free', Highlanders were 'indolent, slavish, strangers to industry'.[63] Some years ago, I argued that the developing interest in the saga literature of medieval Iceland fed the Teutonist

---

[59] Pinkerton, *Dissertation*, 69, 123.
[60] *The Literary Correspondence of John Pinkerton* (London 1830) i, 224.
[61] Ibid., i, 221, 230.
[62] Pinkerton, *Dissertation*, 73 n.
[63] Pinkerton, *Enquiry*, 339.

appetites of the late eighteenth and early nineteenth centuries; while Colin Kidd has indicated how such primitive ethnology fed into whiggish ideology and British identity,[64] but supporters of the Goths did not have everything their own way. The immensely influential visit to Scotland by the Icelandic scholar, Grimur Thorkelin, in the 1780s was inspired by a desire to explore the links between the Vikings and the Celts, and despite Pinkerton's best efforts the celticists were far from vanquished. Indeed it may be suggested that his extreme views actually reinforced the case he wished to destroy.

Skene made good use of the sagas in his *Highlanders*. One of two people whose assistance he acknowledged was T.G. Repp, who was for some time curator of the Scandinavian books in the Advocates Library, an unhappy individual who did not find a conducive environment in Edinburgh.[65] The other was Donald Gregory, secretary of the Society of Antiquaries of Scotland and author of the indispensable *History of the Western Highlands and Isles of Scotland from AD 1493 to AD 1625* (first published 1836, second edition 1881), a volume which neatly complemented Skene's own work. Both men also collaborated on the *Collectanea* volume for the Iona Club.[66]

John Gibson Lockhart once referred to Sir Walter Scott's 'celtified pageantry', but Scott, despite the themes of some of his poems and novels, as well as his later well-known fascination with highlandism and tartanry, was by no means Celt-obsessed. Sir Walter was a true child of Enlightenment historiography in that he rejected the medieval barbarism symbolised by the Highlands, which he stressed almost *ad nauseam* in *Tales of a Grandfather*, but he also fancied himself the heir of Ossian, the last minstrel singing the last lay about what had made Scotland, Scotland. In modern popular criticism he remains more written about than read, but the full complexity of his relationship with the *Gàidhealtachd* still awaits proper investigation. He noted that the Highlanders were, 'like the Welsh, the unmixed aboriginal natives of the island, speaking a dialect of the ancient Celtic, once the language of all of Britain'.[67] He never greatly stressed the Celtic antecedents of his beloved Borderland but in his *Minstrelsy* he quoted an

---

64 E. J. Cowan, 'Icelandic studies in eighteenth- and nineteenth-century Scotland', *Studia Islandica*, xxxi (1972), 109–51; C. Kidd, 'Teutonist ethnology and Scottish nationalist inhibition, 1780–1880', *SHR* lxxiv (1995), 45–68.

65 Cowan 'Icelandic studies', 124.

66 *Collectanea de Rebus Albanicis: consisting of original papers and documents relating to the history of the Highlands and Islands of Scotland* (Iona Club, 1847). This was the first and last publication of the Iona Club. Gregory also wrote *Inquiry into the earlier history of Clan Gregor, with a view to ascertaining the causes which led to their proscription in 1603* (Edinburgh 1831).

67 Sir Walter Scott, *Manners, Customs, and History of the Highlanders of Scotland* (repr. New York 1993), 29. The articles in this little book were originally published in the *Quarterly Review*, of which, at the time, Lockhart was editor.

epigram of 1613 which humorously alluded to the Welsh heritage of the Southern Uplands:

> From Rice ap Richard, sprung from Dick a Cow,
> Be cod, was right gud gentleman, look ye now.[68]

In chapter six of *The Antiquary* he made much fun of the Celtic–Teutonic debate which had so distracted Pinkerton and his predecessors, but Scott had no interest in the cult of Celticism as such. While it is true that in his Highland novels such as *Rob Roy* and *A Legend of Montrose* he often displayed impatience at the attitudes and antics of unregenerate Gaels, he was not guilty of the frequently levelled charge of completely ignoring the contemporary plight of the Highlanders:

> in but too many instances, the glens of the Highlands have been drained, not of their superfluity of population, but of the whole mass of the inhabitants, dispossessed by an unrelenting avarice, which will be one day found to have been as shortsighted as it is unjust and selfish.[69]

According to Lockhart, Scott in 1820 became a member of the Celtic Society of Edinburgh, which existed to promote kilt-wearing and cultural activities as well as providing some financial relief for destitute Gaels; it was to provide the inspiration for George IV's 'Highland Jaunt' in 1822, an episode which, in the minds of many commentators, sealed Scott's reputation as the prime mover in the creation of plastic Scotland. The nineteenth-century proliferation of such societies – equally well-intentioned but just as manipulative – particularly in Glasgow, secured his dubious legacy.

*   *   *

It is noteworthy that although the Celtic label was secure by the time Skene's *Highlanders* appeared there was little or no awareness of the pan-Celticism implied in Geoffrey of Monmouth's twelfth-century recitation of the 'Prophecies of Merlin', later exploited by the propaganda department of Robert Bruce,[70] nor of the politically inspired revival version of the same phenomenon which emerged in the later nineteenth century.[71] During Skene's lifetime men like Ernest Renan and Matthew

---

[68] Sir Walter Scott, *Minstrelsy of the Scottish Border: consisting of Historical and Romantic Ballads* (London 1839), 92.

[69] Scott, *Manners, Customs*, 111.

[70] E. J. Cowan, 'Myth and identity in early medieval Scotland', *SHR* lxiii (1984), 133–4; E. J. Cowan, 'Identity, freedom and the Declaration of Arbroath', in D. Broun, R. J. Finlay and M. Lynch (eds.), *Image and Identity: The Making and Re-making of Scotland through the Ages* (Edinburgh 1998), 56–8.

[71] J. Hunter, 'The Gaelic connection: the Highlands, Ireland and nationalism, 1873–1922', *SHR* liv (1975), 178–204.

Arnold were busily constructing a Celtic myth which would ultimately be swallowed by the Celts themselves.[72] However much they tried to conceal their agendas under the bogus screen of objective scholarship, establishment males at the height of the British Empire, saturated in the language and rhetoric of a previous imperial age, applied the same terminology to their Welsh, Irish and Scottish neighbours as the Greeks and Romans had used to describe the barbarians. Thus it was that Skene, the epitome of the Edinburgh North British establishment could combine his scholarly interests in Celtic Scotland with a rational rejection of contemporary Gaeldom. Fortunately, he did not survive to witness the worst excesses of the Celtic movement which involved such figures as Patrick Geddes, Charles Rennie Mackintosh and his wife, Margaret Macdonald, as well as Lady Gregory and W. B. Yeats in Ireland. William Sharp, writing under his female Celtic pseudonym of 'Fiona Macleod', contributed much to the notion of a 'Celtic Twilight' in such books as *Pharais* (1894), *The Washer of the Ford* (1895) and *The Winged Destiny* (1904), drawing upon a weird amalgam of Pre-Raphaelite mysticism, Gaelic folklore and a seriously warped imagination. By 1963, J. R. R. Tolkien, who was briefly a lecturer at Edinburgh University, could write:

> To many, perhaps to most people ... 'Celtic' of any sort is ... a magic bag into which anything may be put, and out of which almost anything may come ... Anything is possible in the fabulous Celtic twilight, which is not so much a twilight of the Gods as of the reason.[73]

Yet through his *Rings* cycle Tolkien himself, notable scholar though he was, contributed greatly to the Celtic craze of the later twentieth century, the eighties and nineties of which have generated a veritable deluge of Celtic book titles not to mention the clamjamfry of nonsense that is now popularly deemed to constitute part of Celtic heritage. John Pinkerton must be birling in his grave. He was not to know that the twentieth would truly be the 'Celtic century'; it remains to be seen what the twenty-first will make of this remarkable phenomenon, now worldwide, which craves the attention of scholarly investigation rather than the arrogance of academic dismissal. One thing is certain: the invention of Celtic Scotland is not yet complete; it is an ongoing process.

72 P. Sims-Williams, 'The visionary Celt: the construction of an ethnic preconception', *Cambridge Medieval Studies*, xi (1986), 71–96.
73 J. R. R. Tolkien, 'English and Welsh', in *Angles and Britons* (O'Donnell Lectures, Cardiff 1963), 29–30; quoted in Chapman, *The Celts*, 1.

2

The Seven Kingdoms in *De situ Albanie*: A Record of Pictish political Geography or imaginary Map of ancient *Alba*?[1]

DAUVIT BROUN

It is well known and much lamented that there are few documentary sources surviving for the history of the Picts before Pictland disappeared from contemporary record in 900 and *Alba* took its place.[2] Such material as does remain for Pictish political history relates chiefly to the kings who are also found in extant Pictish king-lists. Lesser kings are mentioned only rarely, such as the sub-king of the Orkneys whom St Columba met at the court of King Bridei *filius Meilochon*,[3] and the king of Atholl drowned in 739 by one of the most formidable Pictish kings on record, Onuist son of Uurguist.[4] It is not surprising, therefore, that scholars seeking a more complete picture of Pictland's political geography have turned to sources which have a less obvious claim to be contemporary. In particular, the legendary division of *Alba* into seven kingdoms described in *De situ Albanie* (datable to 1202 × 14)[5] has been regarded as a record of Pictish kingdoms, and has been used to construct a detailed map of Pictland's political landscape. Not all historians, however, have been prepared to accept everything in this part of *De situ Albanie* as historically accurate.

---

[1] This is a substantially revised version of an earlier unpublished paper, 'The seven Pictish provinces and the origins of *Alba*'. I am very grateful to Thomas Clancy, Stephen Driscoll, Katherine Forsyth, Simon Taylor and Alex Woolf, and particularly to David Dumville, for their comments on the earlier version. I am, needless to say, entirely responsible for any errors that remain.

[2] See, e.g., D. Broun, 'The origin of Scottish identity', in C. Bjørn, A. Grant and K. J. Stringer (eds.), *Nations, Nationalism and Patriotism in the European Past* (Copenhagen 1994), 40–5.

[3] In Adomnán, *Columba*, 166–7 (II. 42); the most recent translation is Adomnán of Iona, *Life of St Columba*, trans. R. Sharpe (Harmondsworth 1995), 196. The name of King Bridei's father is given in Bede, *HE*, 222 (III. 4), and in *Ann. Ulster*, 559; it is commonly rendered as Maelchu or Maelchon, but these are Gaelic forms rather than Pictish, and since it is unclear what the Pictish form would actually have been, it is best to let Bede's wording stand.

[4] *Ann. Ulster*, 739. 7; *Ann. Tigernach*, i, 243 (739. 6).

[5] See below, page 27.

Isabel Henderson has commented that *De situ Albanie* 'is a much more careless piece of work than writers have admitted and its evidence should not be given too much weight'.[6] In the thirty years since this remark was made, however, historians have not shown much inclination to abandon *De situ Albanie* as a major source for Pictish political geography, although they have tended to use its evidence selectively. This essay aims to review the different ways this key text has been regarded by historians from Skene to the present day, and to ask whether most have not read too much historical reality into what may have been written not as a passive (and, to some unagreed extent, inaccurate) record of the past, but as a learned attempt by one or more medieval scholars, long after the Picts had disappeared, to interpret a legend of the division of *Alba* into seven kingdoms.

To set the scene, we should return not to Pictish times but to the early thirteenth century, and recall a historian somewhere in the east midlands north of the Forth and south of the Mounth who assembled a number of pieces relating to the history of the Scottish kingdom into what may have been a small volume consisting of a single gathering. The collection survives only in a fourteenth-century manuscript produced in York for a Roger of Poppleton.[7] Four texts (none with titles) lie at the heart of the collection: a Pictish king-list (designated *Series Longior* 1 by Molly Miller);[8] the 'Chronicle of the Kings of *Alba*' (otherwise the 'Old Scottish Chronicle') which runs from Cinaed mac Alpín (died 858) to Cinaed mac Maíle Choluim (971–95);[9] a list of kings of *Dál Riata* and Cinaed mac Alpín's successors to William I (1165–1214) (known as king-list 'E');[10] and a copy of the royal genealogy headed by William I which consistently features

---

6 I. Henderson, *The Picts* (London 1967), 36.

7 M. O. Anderson, *Kings and Kingship in Early Scotland* (2nd edn, Edinburgh 1980), 240–60. For discussion, see ibid., 235–40; E. J. Cowan, 'The Scottish chronicle in the Poppleton manuscript', *Innes Review*, xxxii (1981), 3–21; M. Miller, 'Matriliny by treaty: the Pictish foundation-legend', in D. Whitelock and others (eds.), *Ireland in Early Mediaeval Europe* (Cambridge 1982), 138–42; J. C. Crick, *The Historia Regum Britannie of Geoffrey of Monmouth*, vol. III: *Summary Catalogue of the Manuscripts* (Woodbridge 1989), 256–61.

8 Or *SL*1 for short (Miller, 'Pictish foundation-legend', 159–60); referred to in earlier works as 'list A'.

9 The name 'Chronicle of the Kings of Alba' is used by D. N. Dumville, *The Churches of North Britain in the First Viking-Age*, Fifth Whithorn Lecture, 14 September 1996 (Whithorn 1997), 36 n.107. Molly Miller referred to it as the 'Old Scottish Chronicle': e.g., M. Miller, 'The last century of Pictish succession', *Scottish Studies*, xxiii (1979), 39–67. Before M. O. Anderson, 'Scottish materials in a Paris manuscript', *SHR* xxviii (1949), 31–42, it used to be regarded as an organic part of Pictish king-list *SL*1 (known to earlier scholars as list 'A'). Note the title given by B. T. Hudson, 'The Scottish Chronicle', *SHR* lxxvii (1998), 130–61.

10 It also includes passages praising David I and his sisters: see Anderson, *Kings and Kingship*, 68–70.

Gaelic spelling-conventions.[11] These texts appear to have been copied faithfully into the collection: the only change which the collection's compiler may have made was to add William I and his father to the genealogy. It is a measure of the importance of this collection that any critical edition of these texts would have to be based on the copies preserved in Poppleton's manuscript: indeed, in the case of the 'Chronicle of the Kings of *Alba*' there is no other witness.[12]

These texts are preceded by two items: the compiler himself was the author of one, and he interpolated the second. The first is *De situ Albanie*, 'Concerning the topography of *Alba*'.[13] Marjorie Anderson has drawn attention to references in this tract to other pieces in the collection – the 'Chronicle of the Kings of *Alba*', king-list E and the genealogy – which suggests that *De situ Albanie* was written by the compiler himself.[14] The second item is a collection of passages drawn almost entirely from Isidore of Seville's *Etymologiae*.[15] It has not, however, been put together by the compiler himself. It is concerned with rather more than just Pictish or Scottish origins; moreover, it finishes abruptly with the words *de hiis ista sufficiunt* (in effect 'that is enough of that'), which could suggest that the compiler has broken off from copying a longer work. The compiler has done more than simply copy this text, however: he has also introduced a passage on Scota daughter of Pharaoh which David Dumville and Molly Miller have shown to derive probably from a Sawley manuscript of *Historia Brittonum* at a stage in the manuscript's history dating from sometime after 1202.[16] There can be little doubt that the compiler's work

---

11 Discussed in D. Broun, 'Gaelic literacy in eastern Scotland, 1124–1249', in H. Pryce (ed.), *Literacy in Medieval Celtic Societies* (Cambridge 1998), 189.

12 List E is the only complete witness of the archetype of Marjorie Anderson's Y group of king-lists; the Pictish king-list (*SL1*) is the only copy of *SL* before the text was partially Gaelicised; and, although there are other texts of the royal genealogy with a Scottish provenance datable to the 12th and 13th centuries, there are no other copies of the version found in the collection.

13 Its full title is *De situ Albanie que in se figuram hominis habet quomodo fuit primitus in septem regionibus diuisa quibusque nominibus antiquitus sit uocata et a quibus inhabitata*, 'Concerning the topography of Alba which takes the shape of a man; in what way it was originally divided into seven kingdoms, and by what names it may have been called of old and by whom inhabited'. It is edited in Anderson, *Kings and Kingship*, 240–3, and translated in *ES* i, cxv–cxviii.

14 Anderson, *Kings and Kingship*, 235–6.

15 It is entitled *Cronica de origine antiquorum Pictorum*, 'Chronicle concerning Pictish origins': it is edited in ibid., 243–5. The title is problematic, not least because the text is concerned as much with the origins of *Scoti* as *Picti*. See ibid., 243 n.233.

16 Miller, 'Matriliny by treaty', 138. It may be noted that Marjorie Anderson (*Kings and Kingship*, 140) argued for a date of composition between 1165 and 1184 on the grounds that Andrew, Bishop of Caithness (d.1184) is not referred to as deceased. The textual link with Cambridge University Library MS Ff.1.27 is more compelling, however.

belongs to the reign of William I, which leaves little or no scope for the passage on Scota to have been introduced into the Isidorian text *before* the compiler saw it. The passage on Scota, therefore, enables the compiler's work itself to be dated to 1202 × 14. It also shows that the compiler was prepared to interpolate the material he copied from the text of Isidorian extracts: there are two other instances where additions have been made concerning Scottish or Pictish origins which may, therefore, be attributed to him.[17] The final item in the collection is a copy of the shorter version of the St Andrews' foundation-legend.[18]

Be this as it may, the collection can be recognised as a scholarly attempt to compile a record of the history of the Scottish kingdom. It has been suggested that the collection represents 'materials made by someone ... who contemplated writing a history of ancient Scotland', and that '*De situ*, though ill composed and imperfectly digested, could be a draft for what would have been an opening geographical chapter'.[19] There is no compelling reason, however, to regard the collection as in any way unfinished: as for *De situ Albanie*, its flaws arise from its author's determination to bring together conflicting information, which is consistent with his overall intention to record a range of material about the kingdom's past. There is no indication that the collection as a whole was meant to be anything other than a kind of scholar's reference-booklet for the kingdom's history.

De situ Albanie, the only item in the collection which the compiler himself composed, consists of a very brief summary of *Scotia*'s earlier names and inhabitants; an account of its topography comparing it with the head, body, arms and legs of a man; a detailed breakdown of its ancient division by seven brothers into seven kingdoms; and finally brief notes on the advent of Fergus Mór mac Eirc, the kingdom of *Dál Riata* and the reign of Cinaed mac Alpín. The most extensive part of the tract is its account of *Scotia*'s ancient division into seven kingdoms, and it is this section which has attracted the most attention. For reasons which will be explained below, it has generally been regarded as containing detailed information about the extent of Pictish kingdoms. There are problems with this view, however, which have not been fully confronted, not least the fact that *De situ Albanie* was composed three centuries after the Picts disappeared from contemporary record.

17 He adds 'or *Scotia*' to the statement that *Hibernia* was the destination of the *Scotti* in the fourth age; and he states after *Albani* that *Scoti* and *Picti* take their origin from them.

18 Known as version 'A'. I am currently preparing a new edition after identifying two previously unnoticed manuscripts of the complete text (London, British Library MS Cotton Tiberius D iii, fos. 93r–94r, and London, British Library MS Arundel 36, fos. 15v–16v).

19 Anderson, *Kings and Kingship*, 236.

De situ Albanie, in fact, has not one but two accounts of an ancient sevenfold division (which will be referred to hereafter as DSa and DSb). They read as follows:

DSa:

> And this land was anciently divided by seven brothers into seven parts, of which the principal part is Angus with the Mearns (*Enegus cum Moerne*), so named after Angus the first-born of the brothers.
>
> And the second part is Atholl and the Gowrie (*Adtheodle et Gouerin*).
>
> The third part, then, is Strathearn with Menteith (*Sradeern cum Meneted*).
>
> The fourth part of the parts (*pars partium*) is Fife with Fothriff (*Fif cum Fothreue*).
>
> And the fifth part is Mar with Buchan (*Marr cum Buchen*).
>
> And the sixth part is Moray and Ross (*Muref et Ros*).
>
> The seventh part, then, is Caithness (*Cathanesia*) this side of the mountain and beyond the mountain,[20] because the mountain of *Mound* divides Caithness through the middle.
>
> Each of these parts, therefore, was then called a *regio* [kingdom] and because each of them had in it a *subregio* [sub-kingdom] it follows from this – having seven under-kings beneath them – that these aforesaid seven brothers were regarded as seven kings.

DSb:

> These seven brothers divided the kingdom of *Albania* into seven kingdoms (*regna*), and each of them in his time reigned in his kingdom (*regnum*).
>
> The first kingdom – as a trustworthy informant has told me, namely Andrew, a venerable man, bishop of Caithness,[21] by nation a Gael (*nacione Scoctus*), and a monk of Dunfermline – <stretched> from that excellent water which is called in Gaelic (*Scottice*) *Froch*,[22] in Britonnic (*Britannice*) *Werid*, and in French (*Romane*) *Scottewatre*,[23]

---

20 The Ord of Caithness is meant: 'this side' is evidently the south, and apparently encompassed south-east Sutherland, while 'beyond' is the north.

21 Bishop Andrew died in 1184, and was a regular witness of royal charters from c.1147: see G. W. S. Barrow, *Scotland and its Neighbours in the Middle Ages* (London 1992), 60. The haziness of DSb's treatment of northern Scotland suggests that Bishop Andrew may not have seen his diocese before he wrote this account; for evidence that DSb is a copy of a written source, see Anderson, *Kings and Kingship*, 242 n.20.

22 Read *Forth*?

23 *Romane* means 'in French', but *Scottewatre* is English. This kind of confusion is found in England in the late 12th and 13th centuries, and has been interpreted as 'an example either of diglossia or code-shifting – the largely unconscious bilingual

that is the water of the Scots (*aqua Scottorum*), because it divides the kingdoms of the Scots and the English, and runs near the town of Stirling, as far as another noble river, which is called the Tay (*Tae*).

The second kingdom to the Isla, encircling < the first > like the sea as far as the mountain that is called *Athran* [Airthrey?]²⁴, in the northern region (*aquilonali plaga*) of Stirling.

The third kingdom from the Isla (*Hilef*) to the Dee (*De*).

The fourth kingdom from the Dee (*De*) up to the great and wonderful river called the Spey (*Spe*), the greatest and best in all *Scocia*.

The fifth kingdom from the Spey (*Spe*) to the mountain Drumalban (*Brumalban*).

The sixth kingdom was Moray and Ross (*Mure <f> ²⁵ et Ros*).

The seventh kingdom was Argyll (*Arregaithil*).

While DSa is easy enough to follow, this cannot be said of DSb. A particular problem is its description of the fifth kingdom. 'From the Spey to Drumalban' could be taken as a rather contorted way of describing Atholl.²⁶ A less forced interpretation, however, is that it referred to Moray and Ross. Earlier in *De situ Albanie*, where the topography of *Scotia* is likened to the shape of a man, the man's arms are equated with 'the mountains which divide *Scotia* from Argyll', which evidently meant Drumalban. Because the man's body is identified with the mountain-range 'called the Mounth' running from the Irish Sea to the North Sea, there would seem to be little doubt that Drumalban was understood to extend further north than Atholl: 'from the Spey to Drumalban', therefore, would have naturally embraced Moray and Ross. The problem, of course, is that this would mean that the sixth kingdom, described as 'Moray and Ross', repeats the fifth. The fifth kingdom in DSb, therefore, is either unconvincing or confused. It is impossible, however, to tell whether the flaw originated with Bishop Andrew (who conceivably never saw his diocese)²⁷ or with the author of *De situ Albanie*.²⁸

practice of moving between two equally familiar languages': I. Short, '*Tam Angli quam Franci*: self-definition in Anglo-Norman England', in C. Harper-Bill (ed.), *Anglo-Norman Studies, 18 (1995)* (Woodbridge 1996), 158 (see also references cited at p. 158, nn. 21–2). In a Scottish context it is conceivable that an English form of a place-name like this could have been used when speaking French.

24 W. F. Skene, *Celtic Scotland* (Edinburgh 1876–80), iii, 45.

25 *Mures*, MS.

26 So Skene, *Celtic Scotland*, iii, 46.

27 See note 23, above, for his regular attendance at the royal court.

28 There is a confused passage in the section describing the topography of *Alba* in the shape of a man: it reads *latus dextere partis ex Muref et Ros et Mar <r> et Buchen*, which seems to mean that Moray, Ross, Mar and Buchan extended along the right flank. If, however, the man was facing up (as might be expected), these areas should be on his left flank. The text as it survives says nothing about the left flank. The left flank

Another problem is that the two accounts do not always tally: for instance, DSb does not have a division corresponding to 'Atholl and the Gowrie', instead joining the Gowrie (and perhaps Atholl as well) with what is apparently meant to be Strathearn and Menteith. It is also notable that DSa includes Caithness but not Argyll, while DSb includes Argyll but omits Caithness. If DSa and DSb are taken together, therefore, it would be hard to disagree with Isabel Henderson's remark about the carelessness and unreliability of *De situ Albanie*.[29]

Before Isabel Henderson raised doubts about the value of *De situ Albanie*, the prevailing view of the previous century had been to accept DSa and DSb as authentic records of earlier territorial divisions. W. F. Skene's discussions in *Chronicles of the Picts, Chronicles of the Scots* (1867)[30] and the third volume of *Celtic Scotland* (1880)[31] were particularly influential. He argued that because DSa confined itself to Pictland, it represented a situation which pertained prior to the ninth century, before the north was lost to Vikings and Pictland was (allegedly) united with Argyll by Cinaed mac Alpín.[32] On the other hand DSb, he argued, described the situation following the (alleged) union of Argyll and Pictland and loss of the north to Vikings. Not only did this involve the inclusion of Argyll and absence of Caithness and Sutherland, but he maintained that 'changes thus produced upon the provincial distribution of the population by the formation of the kingdom of Alban or Scotia in the ninth century'[33] resulted in the other differences between DSa and DSb.

A. O. Anderson noted that an even earlier account of Pictland's seven-fold division was recounted in a Gaelic tract on Pictish origins embedded in *Lebor Bretnach* and *Lebor Gabála Érenn*.[34] This described a division of

should run from the leg (described as the Spey) and the arm (Drumalban, to the west): Mar and Buchan, however, are east, not west of the Spey. If the passage from *Muref* to *Buchen* originally described the left flank, then the author's knowledge of geography north of the Mounth would seem to have been rather confused.

29 Henderson, *Picts*, 36.
30 *Chron. Picts-Scots*, pp. lxxxiv–lxxxvi.
31 Skene, *Celtic Scotland*, iii, 42–7.
32 For recent criticism of the idea of a Picto-Scottish union see, e.g., D. Broun, 'The origin of Scottish identity in its European context', in B. E. Crawford (ed.), *Scotland in Dark Age Europe* (St Andrews 1994), 21–31; and Dumville, *Churches of North Britain in the first Viking-Age*. The idea of Cinaed mac Alpín as conqueror of the Picts has recently been defended by P. Wormald, 'The emergence of the *regnum Scottorum*: a Carolingian hegemony?', in B. E. Crawford (ed.), *Scotland in Dark Age Britain* (St Andrews 1996), 131–60.
33 Skene, *Celtic Scotland*, iii, 46.
34 *ES* i, p. cxvii n.2. The tract is designated *SL3* by Molly Miller, and its witnesses are listed in her 'Pictish foundation-legend', 160–1. See also Anderson, *Kings and Kingship*, 82–3; W. J. Watson, *The History of the Celtic Place-Names of Scotland* (1926; repr. Edinburgh 1993), 107; and *Chron. Picts-Scots*, 24–7, 323–5, for text and translation.

Alba among seven sons of Cruithne (*Cruithne* being 'Pict' in medieval Gaelic). In the course of the tract this was summarised in a stanza which Anderson translated:

> Cruithne's seven children divided
> Scotland[35] into seven parts:
> Cait, Ce, Cirig, a warlike[36] family;
> Fib, Fidach, Fotla, Fortrend.

He also noted that Cruithne and his seven sons appear as the first kings in the longer Pictish regnal list: following *Series Longior* 1,[37] they are:

> *Circin* < *n* > .*lx.* < *annis* > *regnauit.*
> *Fidaich .xl.*
> *Fort* < *r* > *enn .lxx.*
> *Floclaid .xxx.*
> *Got .xii.*
> *Ce .xv.*
> *Fib(aid) .xxiiij.*[38]

Anderson recognised that Cruithne and his sons 'were invented as eponymous rulers of the kingdom and its districts'.

The association of these names with known regions was explored more fully by W. J. Watson.[39] He readily recognised *Fib* and *Cait* in the modern Gaelic area-names *Fiobh* (medieval *Fíb*), 'Fife', and *Cataibh*, 'Sutherland' (from earlier *i Cattaib*, 'among the Cats'). Because 'Caithness' means 'headland of Cait' he also saw *Cait* as incorporating both south-east Sutherland and Caithness. He also recognised *Fotla* as the second element in the medieval Gaelic *Athfhotla*, 'Atholl' (modern Gaelic *Athall*), which he analysed as *Ath Fhotla*, 'New Ireland'.[40]

Of the four remaining names, two are found in Irish chronicles derived from the 'Chronicle of Ireland' (to 911) and, ultimately, the 'Iona Chronicle' (to *c*.740).[41] Watson noted references in Irish texts to *Círcinn* as the genitive

35 *Alba.*
36 *cethach*, amended by Anderson to *cathach.*
37 Anderson, *Kings and Kingship*, 245–9 (the extant witness of the copy which the author of *De situ Albanie* made as part of his collection).
38 Earlier in *SL*1 Cruithne's sons are listed without reign-lengths, where 'Circin' appears more correctly as 'Circinn', 'Fidaich' as 'Fidach', 'Fortenn' as 'Fortrenn' and 'Fibaid' as 'Fib'. 'Floclaid' may be amended to 'Foltlaid' (i.e. *Fótlaig*).
39 Watson, *Celtic Place-Names*, 107–17, and 30 (for *Cataibh*).
40 Ibid., 228–9.
41 On these, see K. Grabowski and D. N. Dumville, *Chronicles and Annals of Mediaeval Ireland and Wales: The Clonmacnoise-group Texts* (Woodbridge 1984), 55–6, and references cited there; and M. Herbert, *Iona, Kells and Derry: The History and Hagiography of the Monastic Familia of Columba* (Oxford 1988), 22–3, and works cited there.

form of a place-name in north Britain which he understood to represent *Círcenn* in the nominative, 'Crest-headed'. He also argued that in Irish texts this name appeared in *Mag Gergind* (or similar forms), 'Plain of Gerrchenn' (with *Gergind* as the genitive of a personal name *Gerrchenn*). He observed that 'it is difficult, if not impossible, to correlate it [*Círcinn*] with *Gerginn*'.[42] Conceivably, therefore, references to *Mag Círcinn*, 'Plain of Círcenn' and *Mag Gergind* were not, in fact, to the same plain at all. This ambiguity is unfortunate, because the only evidence for localising *Círcenn* is actually a reference to *Mag Gergind*: a Life of St Patrick (*Vita II*) informs us that Palladius died at Fordun *in Campo Girgin*, 'in Mag Gergind'.[43] In *Lebor na hUidre* this statement is found with 'the Mearns' instead of 'Mag Gergind', which lends support to the association of Mag Gergind with the Mearns (and also helps to rule out the Fordun in Strathearn).[44]

The other region found in Irish chronicles represented by a son of Cruithne is 'Fortriu'. It appears frequently, and is often found in the genitive form *Fortrenn* (as in *rex Fortrenn*, the royal title given to a number of kings who appear in the Pictish regnal list): from this and other attested forms of the name Watson deduced a hypothetical nominative singular **Fortriu*.[45] Skene had earlier drawn attention to a battle won against Vikings in 904 which the 'Chronicle of the Kings of *Alba*' reported as 'in Strathearn': the *Annals of Ulster* referred to the victors as *fir Fortrenn*, 'the men of **Fortriu*', which showed that Strathearn was at least part of **Fortriu* if it was not, in fact, equivalent to it.[46]

Two names therefore remained: *Cé* and *Fidach*. Watson remarked that 'the position of these two ancient provinces ... is uncertain'.[47] He assumed that, by a process of elimination, *Cé* and *Fidach* must refer to DSa's 'Mar and Buchan' and 'Moray and Ross'. He was inclined (by analogy with *Circinn* and *Fortrenn* in the legend) to take *Fidach* as a genitive of an unattested **Fidaid*. He noted a possible connection between *Fidach* and *Gleann Fithich*, Glen Fiddich (in the highlands of Banffshire), and an Irish literary reference to *Mag Cé*, 'Plain of Cé'.[48] He rejected a link between *Cé*

42　Watson, *Celtic Place-Names*, 109.

43　*Four Latin Lives of St Patrick*, ed. L. Bieler, in *Scriptores Latini Hiberniae*, vol. VIII (Dublin 1971), 77; at p. 12, Bieler dated *Vita II* to sometime in or after the first half of the 8th century and not later than the 11th.

44　Noted in Watson, *Celtic Place-Names*, 110.

45　Ibid., 68–9. See, most recently, D. Broun, '*Fortriu/Fortrenn*': an editorial confession', *Innes Review*, xlix (1998), 93–4.

46　*Ann. Ulster*, 904. 4; Skene, *Celtic Scotland*, iii, 43 n.4.

47　Watson, *Celtic Place-Names*, 114.

48　Ibid., 115; see further M. E. Dobbs, 'Cé: the Pictish name of a district in eastern Scotland', *Scottish Gaelic Studies*, vi (1947–9), 137–8.

and *Baile Ché* (Keith, Banffshire), which appears to have been *Céith* in the Middle Ages.

Putting all this together, Watson charted how in his view the divisions denoted by Cruithne's seven sons corresponded with the kingdoms held by seven brothers in DSa:[49]

> *Círcenn* (or *Círig*): Angus and the Mearns;
> *Fotla*: Atholl and the Gowrie;
> *Fortriu: Strathearn and Menteith;
> *Fíb*: Fife and Fothriff;
> *Cé*: Mar and Buchan;
> **Fidaid?* (gen. *Fidach*): Moray and (Easter) Ross;
> *Cat*: Caithness and (S.E.) Sutherland.

This scheme was adopted (with minor adjustments) by H. M. Chadwick[50] and F. T. Wainwright;[51] a rare sign of dissent was T. F. O'Rahilly's suggestion that *Fortriu was 'much more extensive than Skene's definitions would imply, and probably included Fife and Forfar [that is, Angus]', although he did not expand on this.[52] Chadwick also suggested that DSa may have been composed by someone who had the legend of Cruithne's sons in front of him, and that 'his intention was merely to reproduce it in a modernised form, omitting all obsolete names'.[53] He observed how the identification of Angus and the Mearns in DSa as the 'principal part' named after Angus the eldest of the brothers could show knowledge of the longer Pictish king-list (*SL*), where 'Circinn' is the first of Cruithne's sons to succeed him in the kingship.[54]

Before Isabel Henderson's warning against placing too much weight on the evidence of *De situ Albanie*, therefore, DSa was central to modern reconstructions of Pictish political geography, and DSb was regarded as important evidence for *Alba*'s internal divisions in the period c.850–950.[55] Attitudes to DSa and DSb have changed in the last thirty years: Isabel Henderson's warning, however, seems to have had a greater impact on archaeologists than historians. Charles Thomas, for instance, has remarked that 'great uncertainty must surround the whole matter';[56] more

---

49 Watson, *Celtic Place-Names*, 108.
50 H. M. Chadwick, *Early Scotland: The Picts, the Scots and the Welsh of Southern Scotland* (Cambridge 1949), 38–9.
51 F. T. Wainwright (ed.), *The Problem of the Picts* (Edinburgh 1955; repr. Perth 1980), 1–53, at 46–7; see also map 1b.
52 T. F. O'Rahilly, *Early Irish History and Mythology* (Dublin 1946), 371 n.3.
53 Chadwick, *Early Scotland*, 40.
54 Ibid., 39, 42.
55 See esp. ibid., 38.
56 C. Thomas, *Celtic Britain* (London 1986), 86.

recently Sally Foster has abandoned DSa and DSb altogether in a brief discussion of the regions represented by Cruithne's sons, and confined herself to identifying only the three which survive in some form in modern Gaelic: *Cat, Fíb* and *(Ath)Fhotla*.[57] Among historians there has been a general inclination to continue to use DSa and DSb as evidence for ancient political divisions, but not to accept either account in its entirety as a snapshot of political geography at a given stage between the eighth and tenth centuries.[58] As a result there has been notable variation in how these accounts have been used to interpret the areas named in the legend of Cruithne's sons.

The most thorough recent discussion of Pictish regions, by Marjorie Anderson, generally followed Watson's scheme.[59] She suggested, however, that DSb's second kingdom, which she interpreted as encompassing Strathearn, Menteith and 'at least the southern part of Gowrie, including Scone', is preferable to DSa's 'Strathearn and Menteith' as a description of **Fortriu*.[60] She also suggested that by the ninth century 'it is just possible that the term [**Fortriu*] was acquiring a wider meaning and could legitimately be understood as the equivalent of *rex Pictorum*'.[61] She pointed, for instance, to a place-name *Wertermorum* which is found associated with Dunnottar in a record of Æthelstan's invasion of 934:[62] *Werter* has been identified as a P-Celtic form of **Fortriu*.[63] She suggested, therefore, that this 'implies that Fortriu was thought of [latterly] as extending northwards as far as the Mounth that divides the valley of the Dee from Strathmore'.[64]

Since Anderson there have been a number of brief treatments of these Pictish regional divisions. The most radical departure from Watson's scheme has been advanced by A. A. M. Duncan, who regarded the list of seven as suspiciously alliterative and suggested that 'behind the myth lies a

57 S. M. Foster, *Picts, Gaels and Scots* (London 1996), 35.

58 As well as the scholars cited in what follows, note D. P. Kirby, '... per universas Pictorum provincias', in G. Bonner (ed.), *Famulus Christi: Essays in Commemoration of the Thirteenth Century of the Birth of the Venerable Bede* (London 1976), 316–17 n.40, who commented that Henderson's strictures are 'appropriate', but that *De situ Albanie* 'is, however, a most valuable document'. At 292–3 he expressed reservations about its veracity, but nevertheless identified Bridei *filius Meilochon* with Fidach because of his association with Inverness (see, e.g., p. 307), thus apparently following Watson.

59 Anderson, *Kings and Kingship*, 139–44.

60 Ibid., 140–1; also 198–9.

61 Ibid., 174; see also Wainwright, *Problem of the Picts*, 51.

62 *SAEC*, 68 and n.5 (quoting a north English chronicle associated with Symeon of Durham's *Historia Regum*: see *Symeonis Monachi Opera Omnia*, ed. T. Arnold [Rolls Ser., 1882–5], ii, 93, 124).

63 Watson, *Celtic Place-Names*, 68–9.

64 Anderson, *Kings and Kingship*, 174.

larger number of people and provinces each at some stage with its own king'.[65] On this basis he made no attempt to cover all Pictish territory in his identification of the seven kingdoms. He restricted *Fíb* to Fife and *Fotla* to Atholl, in line with attested Gaelic usage, and also confined **Fortriu* to Strathearn, *Cait* to Caithness, and suggested tentatively that *Fidach* equated only with Moray: he otherwise adopted both DSa and DSb's divisions for *Cé* (Mar and Buchan) and *Círcenn* (Angus and the Mearns).[66] A more conservative approach was taken by Alfred Smyth, who departed from Watson's scheme only in confining *Fíb* to Fife and *Fotla* to Atholl.[67] This, in turn, has been followed most recently by Benjamin Hudson, with the exception of extending *Fidach* to include Banffshire (presumably following Watson's suggestion of a possible link with Glen Fiddich).[68]

Although DSa has continued to influence modern reconstructions of Pictish kingdoms, its evidence is no longer entirely accepted. There are, indeed, a number of difficulties with DSa's evidence which serve to reinforce Isabel Henderson's scepticism about the text's historical value. One possible cause for disquiet is its comment that 'Angus and the Mearns' is so called after Angus, the first-born of the seven brothers, which suggests ignorance of Cruithne's sons as transmitted to us, none of whom is called Angus. Angus may have been the only brother named in DSa because, of all the area-names cited, Angus was the only one that obviously corresponded to a personal name.[69] As noted earlier, however, Chadwick argued that the notion that Angus was the eldest of Cruithne's sons was an updated reference to *Círcenn*. This cannot be entirely discounted, though there is no way of telling, of course, how much freedom may have been taken in reinterpreting the legend – in particular with regard to the bounds of obsolete regions such as *Círcenn*, supposing that these were known. If the reinterpretation was the work of the author of *De situ Albanie* himself, however, it is noteworthy that he has made no reference to the names of Cruithne's seven sons in his copy of *SL* (despite including information in *De situ Albanie* from other texts in his collection, as appropriate). This could suggest that he did not recognise them in *SL*, so that any knowledge he had of the regions represented by Cruithne's

---

65 A. A. M. Duncan, *Scotland: The Making of the Kingdom* (Edinburgh 1975), 48.
66 Ibid., 47.
67 A. P. Smyth, *Warlords and Holy Men: Scotland AD 80–1000* (London 1984), 69.
68 B. T. Hudson, *Kings of Celtic Scotland* (Westport, Connecticut, 1994), 9. A selective approach to DSa is also in evidence in maps of early Scotland published recently in more general books: see M. Lynch, *Scotland: A New History* (London 1991), 20; and L. and J. Laing, *The Picts and the Scots* (Stroud 1993), 14.
69 See Anderson, *Kings and Kingship*, 142 n.106, for a suggestion as to why Angus may have been regarded as the kingdom's core in the reign of William I.

sons may not, therefore, have extended to their names. DSa shares stylistic shortcomings which Marjorie Anderson has identified generally in *De situ Albanie*, so it would appear unlikely that the author of *De situ Albanie* has simply copied it (in contrast to DSb, where these stylistic shortcomings are absent, suggesting that DSb was copied from a written account by Bishop Andrew).[70] Chadwick's proposal, therefore, would only seem to remain a serious possibility if the author of *De situ Albanie* simply reproduced DSa from an oral source – a possibility which cannot be decisively proved or disproved.

A more straightforward difficulty with DSa is the equation of *Fotla* with 'Atholl and the Gowrie'. If *Fotla* stood for *Athfhotla*, 'Atholl', then how (it must be asked) could it also mean Atholl *and* the Gowrie?[71] A recognition of this contradiction presumably lies behind the recent tendency to interpret *Fotla* as Atholl alone. A plausible explanation of DSa's 'Atholl and the Gowrie', however, would be that, again, its author did not know that *Fotla* was one of the seven kingdoms. If so, this would indicate ignorance not only of the regions represented by Cruithne's sons, but also an attested Pictish kingdom.[72]

'Atholl and the Gowrie' is not the only equation of an earlier kingdom with a pairing of twelfth-century regions which can be questioned. 'Mar and Buchan' are not known ever to have been contiguous: there is no positive indication that the territory between them, which included the Garioch, Formartin and Strathbogie, was anciently regarded as part of either region. Neither is there any indication that Mar ever exercised authority over Buchan (or Angus over the Mearns, for that matter).[73] In the case of 'Fife and Fothriff', however, these areas were frequently paired

---

[70] Anderson, *Kings and Kingship*, 242 n.20.

[71] Given DSa's scheme that in each pair of regions corresponding to a kingdom one region was subordinate to the other, it might be asked whether Atholl ('new Fótla') formed only part of a wider region known as *Fótla*, and that the Gowrie may have earlier been (old) *Fótla*. In DSa, however, the Gowrie is subordinate to Atholl, a relationship which should surely be reversed if the Gowrie was indeed ever '(old) *Fótla*'.

[72] See note 2, above. If DSa was meant to preserve a Pictish view of Pictland's territorial divisions, might it not also be expected to refer to Orkney's sub-king mentioned by Adomnán (see note 2), even if Orkney was (for the sake of argument) regarded as a sub-kingdom of *Cait*?

[73] For the limits of Mar, see W. D. Simpson, *The Province of Mar* (Aberdeen 1943), 3–5. Aberdeen in Mar only became the royal and ecclesiastical capital of Mar and Buchan (and the lands in between) in the reign of David I (1124–53). As for the Mearns as a subordinate region of Angus, Watson interpreted Mearns as the 'Stewartry' (*Celtic Place-Names*, 110–11). The name is attested in the 'Chronicle of the Kings of Alba', and is presumably therefore as old as the 10th century. There is no evidence, however, that it was subordinate to Angus (as opposed, e.g., to the king).

together in the twelfth century:[74] moreover, there is place-name evidence which suggests that Fothriff was once regarded as part of Fife.[75] 'Strathearn and Menteith' for their part could tally with the diocese of Dunblane: Strathearn's status as senior partner could therefore be reflected in the earl of Strathearn's role as patron of the see, as well as the occasional designation of the bishop as 'of Strathearn'.[76] Although 'Fife and Fothriff' and 'Strathearn and Menteith' may boost confidence in DSa's pairings and its idea of one in each pair as subordinate to the other, it is also possible that the author of DSa developed his scheme from his knowledge of Fothriff's dependence on Fife and Strathearn's rights in a diocese which included Menteith. More evidence would be needed to allay the suspicion that the pattern described in DSa of two regions per kingdom, with one subordinate to the other, has been contrived in the cases of Mar and Buchan, Angus and the Mearns, Atholl and the Gowrie, and probably also Moray and Ross:[77] indeed, the attempt to make Caithness into a pair seems to show that the pattern was consciously maintained even where the author could not name two regions to form a pair.

As for DSb, no-one appears now to regard it as a record of *Alba*'s territorial divisions. As noted already, Marjorie Anderson has used it to supply a more credible description of the bounds of **Fortriu*. Because it includes Argyll at the same time as omitting to mention anywhere north of Ross, however, it is difficult to argue that it derives ultimately from a Pictish account. There is also the problem of its fifth kingdom, which has been garbled (if, indeed, it ever made sense). This unfortunately means that the fifth kingdom cannot be cited with any confidence as evidence that, unlike DSa, DSb correctly identified Atholl on its own as one of the kingdoms. Atholl may have been intended to fall within DSb's second kingdom stretching from north of Stirling to the Isla, which would reduce the second kingdom's credibility as an accurate record of **Fortriu*.

As noted already, **Fortriu* in any case appears to be attested in the name *Wertermorum*, apparently 'upland of **Fortriu*', which is mentioned with Dunnottar in a north-English source as the furthest that Æthelstan reached into Scotland in his invasion of 934. As Marjorie Anderson pointed out, 'uplands of **Fortriu*' appears to refer to the Mounth, which according to Watson's scheme should have been the northern limit of

---

[74] See, e.g., *RRS* i, no.118, and *RRS* ii, nos. 30, 38.

[75] Simon Taylor informs me that Rosyth in Fothriff represents *Ros Fhíbe*, 'the promontory of Fife'.

[76] Duncan, *Making of the Kingdom*, 179; I. B. Cowan and D. E. Easson, *Medieval Religious Houses: Scotland* (2nd edn, London 1976), 204.

[77] Note, however, the suggestion in Duncan, *Making of the Kingdom*, 191, that Ross may have originally been part of Moray.

Círcenn. (The Mounth was apparently a Pictish name,[78] however: *Wertermorum*, therefore, probably represented only part of the Mounth – such as the Braes of Angus.) Her suggestion that this refers to a later usage of **Fortriu* in a wider sense cannot be unequivocally rejected: there may, indeed, have been a 'greater **Fortriu*' as well as a more restricted 'lesser **Fortriu*' or '**Fortriu* proper' at least since the reign of Bridei son of Bile, victor at Dunnichen in 685, the first king in the Pictish regnal list to be called *rex Fortrenn* in Irish chronicles. This may signify that *rex Fortrenn* held a predominant position at least among the southern Picts. If DSa and DSb are recognised as potentially flawed, however, then it is difficult to accept the existence of a 'lesser **Fortriu*' on their evidence alone. The most economical explanation would be that **Fortriu* did, in fact, extend from (at least) Strathearn in the south to (part of) the Mounth in the north, and that the regnal list which has been taken to represent a list of kings of Picts and Pictland as a whole may in origin have been simply a **Fortriu* regnal list.

If information in DSa and DSb is inaccurate, this begs the question why *any* of its detail can be taken as evidence for territorial divisions which applied three or four hundred years before *De situ Albanie* was composed. This is especially pressing in the case of **Fortriu, Círcenn, Cé* and *Fidach* which, by the early thirteenth century, had probably been obsolete for centuries. The cornerstone for accepting these accounts (and DSa in particular) as at least generally authentic has been their partial coverage of Scotland north of the Firths of Forth and Clyde. Since Skene it has commonly been inferred from the correspondence of DSa with (mainland) Pictland that DSa is based on a Pictish account; DSb's correspondence with what was, until recently, generally regarded as the bounds of the 'united' kingdom of Picts and Scots before the incorporation of territory south of the Forth in the reign of Illulb mac Custantín (954–62) has also been taken to show that it belonged to the period *c.*850–950.[79] None of this is necessarily true, however. The country designated as *Alba* in Gaelic, and *Albania* or *Scotia* in Latin, was not normally understood in the eleventh and twelfth centuries to correspond with the territory ruled by *rí Alban/rex Scottorum*. It is only from 1216, for example, that chroniclers in Melrose began to use *Scotia* to include the kingdom's territory south of the Forth. There was, in fact, some flexibility in how *Albania/Scotia* was applied: we need look no further than *De situ Albanie* to appreciate this. In the topographical description comparing *Scotia* to the shape of a man we are told that Argyll 'in the western part of *Scotia*' represents the head; we

---

[78] Witnessed in the phrase *citra Monoth*: *Ann. Ulster*, 782. 1
[79] E.g. Chadwick, *Early Scotland*, 35, 38.

are also told, however, that 'the range of mountains which divide *Scotia* from Argyll' represent the arms.[80] Before the thirteenth century the only landward border of *Scotia* which appears to have been generally agreed was its southern limit defined by the Forth. An example of this is the explanation in DSb of the Forth's Latin name *Aqua Scottorum*, 'Water of the Scots', 'because it divides the kingdoms of the Scots and the English'.[81] If it was possible for the author of *De situ Albanie* himself to think that Argyll was not necessarily part of *Scotia*, or for his contemporaries to regard the Forth as marking *Scotia*'s southern boundary, then the mere fact that DSa excluded Argyll and territory south of the Forth from its account of *Scotia* cannot be taken as evidence for the account's origin in Pictish times. The only unusual feature of DSb, for its part, is its failure to mention the area north of Ross, which is especially curious given that the bishop of Caithness is cited as its source.[82]

In summary, then, there is reason to doubt that either DSa or DSb was written with the knowledge of the names of the regions represented by Cruithne's sons. Moreover, neither can be dated positively to before the twelfth century. Also, when measured against the very little that is known independently about Pictish kingdoms, they do not conform convincingly with evidence for a kingdom of Atholl or for the northern limit of *Fortriu. It would be wrong, however, to conclude that there was no link between *De situ Albanie* and the legend of Cruithne's sons. Both share the idea of seven brothers dividing *Alba* into seven kingdoms, and both DSa and the legend of Cruithne's sons define *Alba* as Pictland. It would appear, however, that before the twelfth century the names of Cruithne's sons were probably forgotten, presumably because many had become obsolete. I would suggest, therefore, that the most convincing interpretation of DSa is as an intelligent attempt by someone to describe, in terms of the political geography of his time, how the area between Caithness, the

---

80 Other evidence of the variable territorial extent of *Alba* or *Scotia* is discussed in D. Broun, 'Defining Scotland and the Scots before the wars of independence', in D. Broun, R. Finlay and M. Lynch (eds.), *Image and Identity: The Making and Remaking of Scotland through the Ages* (Edinburgh 1998), 4–17.

81 The use of the phrase 'kingdom of Scotland' or 'kingdom of the Scots' to describe the whole territory of the kingdom first came into use in charters in the 1160s and became common only towards the end of the century: G. W. S. Barrow, *The Anglo-Norman Era in Scottish History* (Oxford 1980), 153–4. It is quite possible, therefore, that Bishop Andrew, and even the author of *De situ Albanie* himself, could still have envisaged the Forth as defining the kingdom's southern limit.

82 It is possible, given that DSb appears to be a copy of something written by Bishop Andrew (see Anderson, *Kings and Kingship*, 242 n.20), that Andrew wrote it before he became bishop of Caithness, which would make his omission of his diocese less puzzling. It should also be noted that the description of *Scotia* in the shape of a man in *De situ Albanie* does not specify anywhere north of Ross either.

Forth and Drumalban could have been divided (more or less equally)
among seven brothers. The suspiciously artificial pattern of two regions
per kingdom with one subordinate to the other may therefore be
explained as an ingenious attempt to interpret the sevenfold division in
relation principally to mormaerdoms – the main regional power-blocks in
the central Middle Ages. The author of DSb, on the other hand, took
geography as his guide when he attempted to explain the seven kingdoms.
Insofar as DSa and DSb tally (often only imprecisely), it is only where
geographical features provide natural boundaries for political units. DSb's
author, moreover, was not only ignorant of the regions represented by
Cruithne's sons, but he had also lost the idea that the legend defined *Alba*
as Pictland.

In the end, I would argue that it would be safest to disregard DSa and
DSb as evidence for Pictish political geography. This does not make it
impossible, however, to suggest a plausible map of Pictish regions south of
the Mounth in the eighth century. It would feature *Fortriu* stretching
from Strathearn (if not the Forth) to the Mounth and including the
Gowrie and Angus (perhaps *Wertermorum* represented the Braes of
Angus), with the kingdom of Atholl to the north, Fife (including Fothriff)
to the east, and perhaps *Círcenn* confined to the Mearns. It is possible,
however, that the Mearns, as *Mag Gergenn*, was quite distinct from *Mag
Círcinn*, the 'Plain of Círcenn'.[83] If so, we would be free to place *Círcenn*
elsewhere. An intriguing reference to *Círcenn* is found in material in the
Annals of Tigernach added to an event noted in the *Annals of Ulster*.[84] In
the latter, the entry for 596.3 reads *Iugulatio filiorum Aedán, .i. Brain 7
Domangairt*, 'the slaying of the sons of Aedán (king of *Dál Riata*), namely
Bran and Domangart'. Adomnán in his *Life of St Columba* has the saint
foretell Domangart's death *in Saxonia*, 'in England': presumably it was
this event which is recorded here in the *Annals of Ulster*.[85] The notice of
this event in the *Annals of Tigernach*, however, has been expanded
(probably by a Clonmacnoise redactor in the tenth century),[86] so that it
reads: *Iugulacio filiorum Aedán, .i. Bran 7 Domungort 7 Eochaid Find 7
Artúr i cath Chírchind in quo uictus est Aedhán*, 'the slaying of the sons of
Aedán, namely Bran and Domangart and Eochaid Find and Artúr in the
battle of Círcenn in which Aedán was defeated'. Now, according to

83 See above, page 41.
84 The texts are quoted and discussed in Grabowski and Dumville, *Chronicles and
   Annals of Mediaeval Ireland*, 126, and J. Bannerman, *Studies in the History of Dalriada*
   (Edinburgh 1974), 84–5.
85 Adomnán, *Columba*, 32–3 (I. 9). There is no reason to link this with Aedán's
   defeat against Anglians at Degsastan in 603, as suggested in *ES* i, 118 n.5: see
   Adomnán, *Columba*, xxi.
86 Grabowski and Dumville, *Chronicles and Annals of Mediaeval Ireland*, 126.

Adomnán, Eochaid Find and Artúr fell in battle against *Miathi*, a people who have been identified with the *Maeatae* mentioned by Dio Cassius and have been located in an area running north and south of Stirling.[87] The tenth-century Clonmacnoise redactor seems, therefore, to have conflated two separate events.[88] For as long as *Círcenn* was regarded by modern scholars as equivalent to Angus and the Mearns, however, it appeared that the 'battle of *Círcenn*' could not refer to the battle against a people located around Stirling, so that *three* events would seem to have been conflated: the slaughter of Bran and Domangart, the deaths of Eochaid Find and Artuir (against *Miathi*), and a battle in *Círcenn* somewhere in Angus or the Mearns. Moreover, the battle against *Miathi* was a victory for Aedán (although costly), while the battle of *Círcenn* was a defeat.[89] If DSa's privileged position as a source for Pictish political geography is rejected, however, then it no longer becomes necessary to separate the battle of *Círcenn* from the battle against *Miathi* because *Círcenn* has to be Angus and the Mearns. Could *Círcenn*, therefore, have been a Gaelic name for an area where *Dál Riata* and *Miathi* might have fought a battle? It is conceivable that a battle in which (according to Adomnán) Aedán suffered significant losses could have been reported as a defeat in a contemporary annal but as a victory by Adomnán a century or more later. Unfortunately too little is known about the Clonmacnoise redaction to be able to say whether its record of the battle of *Círcenn* ultimately represents a contemporary annal, or to explain confidently how it came to be attached to a different event altogether. As things stand, there is at least a possibility that the battle of *Círcenn* and the battle against *Miathi* are one and the same, and that *Círcenn* denoted an area equivalent to, or encompassing, *Miathi* territory around Stirling.[90]

If we abandon DSa and DSb as evidence for the extent of the seven kingdoms, we must acknowledge that the political landscape north of the

---

[87] Adomnán, *Columba*, 32–3 (I. 9); for discussion, see pp. xix–xx.

[88] Pointed out by O'Rahilly, *Early Irish History*, 505.

[89] Bannerman, *Studies in Dalriada*, 85; Adomnán, *Columba*, p. xx, which suggests that a 6th-century battle of Círchenn may have been 'remembered in tradition', in which Bridei *filius Meilochon* was killed (see also Anderson, *Kings and Kingship*, 36–7). Anderson notes that in *Ann. Tigernach*, *cath Chírchind* is Gaelic, while the rest of the entry is Latin. Given the tendency of scribes writing annals to flit between Latin and Gaelic (even more so by the 10th century), I doubt whether this shows that *cath Chírchind* was a 'further addition'.

[90] There may be some etymological resemblance between *Círcenn*, 'Crest-headed', and Old Welsh *Bannauc* (literally 'horned': see *Geiriadur Prifysgol Cymru: A Dictionary of the Welsh Language* (Caerdydd 1950–67), i, 255, s.v. bannog[2]), the range of hills which separated the Picts from Gododdin: this name appears in the medieval settlement 'Bannock' and the nearby 'Bannockburn': see K. Jackson, *The Gododdin: The Oldest Scottish Poem* (Edinburgh 1969), 5–6, 78–9.

Mounth is impenetrably obscure, with the exception of *Cait* in the north. While we may lose evidence for the eighth or ninth centuries, we should also gain, however, for the twelfth and early thirteenth. In DSa and DSb we can see how scholars in the central middle ages imagined ancient *Alba*. We can appreciate the powerful attraction for them of the idea of a distant sevenfold division – a notion which apparently informed the 'Appeal of the Seven Earls' in the winter of 1290–1.[91] And we can recognise how Pictland continued to influence the way *Alba* could be defined three centuries after Pictland itself disappeared from contemporary record. Finally, in the author of *De situ Albanie* we see one of the last generation of scholars who regarded *Alba* or *Scotia* as a country of varying extent. In the thirteenth century a new approach took root, which allowed only a single definition of the country – namely as equivalent to the territory ruled by the king of Scots. With this new more concrete idea of kingdom and country, ancient *Alba* may be said to have become modern Scotland.

91 See G. W. S. Barrow, *Robert Bruce and the Community of the Realm of Scotland* (3rd edn, Edinburgh 1988), 44–5; Barrow perceptively comments (p. 44) that the idea of the Seven Earls was 'a mixture of fact and myth, and the myth surely outweighed the fact'.

3

What happened to the Caledonians?

ALAN BRUFORD†

This is a paper about the Picts, and anything about the Picts must be highly speculative. The rarity of recorded accounts of that mysterious people, and the fact that their few remaining inscriptions are almost entirely indecipherable, means that anything about their political history – as against what can be deduced about their way of life from excavation, artefacts and stone-carvings – depends on deductions from an exiguous collection of references by foreigners, which are inevitably garbled by misunderstanding and distorted by prejudice. The deductions in this paper are based largely on names, which are about all that survive of the reasonably comprehensible P-Celtic language that seems to have been spoken by the rulers, at least, of Pictland: this avenue of speculation has not been much explored before, but it does provide what I hope are convincing answers to several outstanding questions, and even if some parts of the argument can be overturned, this need not bring down the rest.

The term 'Caledonian' is well known as a mock-learned synonym for 'Scottish' or 'a Scot', used both jocularly (by Englishmen) and romantically (by Scots) since the second half of the seventeenth century. Many people take it for granted that *Caledonia* was the Roman name for Scotland as *Hibernia* was that for Ireland, though of course it took another thousand years to establish something like the present frontiers of Scotland, and the *Oxford English Dictionary* rightly reminds us that Caledonia was just a name for 'some part of northern Britain'.[1] What matters more is that the

---

[1] Kenneth Jackson, with characteristic caution, said that 'the name Caledonia ... cannot be proved to be Celtic, and may therefore very possibly be pre-Celtic': K. H. Jackson, 'The Pictish language', in F. T. Wainwright (ed.), *The Problem of the Picts* (Edinburgh 1955), 129–66. It can however plausibly be derived from the Celtic root which appears in early Irish as *calad* and Welsh as *caled*, though apparently *calet-* in Gaulish, meaning 'hard' – a hardy race: H. Pedersen, *Vergleichende Grammatik der keltischen Sprachen* (Göttingen 1913), ii, 37. Jackson's caution might have been better applied to the beginning of his sentence: my quotation above omits 'Caledonia, which was synonymous with Scotland to the Romans', which needs a lot of qualification.

place-name is first used by Tacitus in his *Agricola* for the area north of the
Forth. Very few other classical authors use it as a place-name, but there
are more instances of the adjective which gave us 'Caledonian' in place-
names (the Caledonian Forest, the Caledonian Ocean and so on) and
particularly in what seems to be the basic form, the name of a tribe or
group of tribes called *Caledonii* or less often *Caledones*.

Ptolemy's map locates the *Kaledonioi* somewhere in the Central
Highlands:[2] his co-ordinates have been interpreted as meaning that they
lived just south of Inverness or that they lived in central Perthshire, and
there is some reason to believe that their tribal territory may have
extended from one area to the other across Drumochter. The fact that the
name of this tribe was used for northern peoples in general, whereas the
other ten or eleven tribes that inhabited the area according to Ptolemy are
seldom or never mentioned by other authors, strongly suggests that the
Caledonii were the leading tribe of a confederacy. It may be significant
that the four tribes Ptolemy locates apparently along the coast of the
North-West Highlands all have names that alliterate with theirs: *Creones,
Carnonacae, Caereni, Cornavii*.[3] It was this alliteration that first suggested
to me the significance of the way the names of later Pictish regions
alliterate, which we shall come to shortly.

There is no doubt that the Caledonians were leaders of some of the
tribes that later became known as Picts. The name *Picti* is probably just
what it seems, a Latin word meaning 'painted people' – whether that
means literally painted with woad or warpaint, or as is more often
suggested, tattooed with patterns like the symbols that later Picts carved
on stones, or something else again. It does not need to be a pejorative
description; it could even be what the Picts called themselves. *Picti* may be
a rough translation of the name **Priteni*, the earlier form of Welsh
Prydyn, 'Picts'; the Q-Celtic equivalent **Quriteni* became *Cruithni*, the
early Irish name for them, and the name is fairly obviously connected
with the root of Welsh *pryd* and Irish *cruth*, 'form, shape'. It could mean

2 For the 'northern Scottish' names in Ptolemy's map, see A. L. F. Rivet and
   C. Smith, *The Place-Names of Roman Britain* (Cambridge 1979), 140–1.

3 I am still not convinced that these are real tribal names: they look very like a
   series of epithets extracted from an alliterative poem about the Caledonians which
   Ptolemy happened to have picked up. I have to admit that the meanings for these
   epithets which I cheerfully suggested in earlier oral versions of this paper – given
   in Edinburgh to a late session of the Third International Conference on the
   Languages of Scotland (July 1991), to the Pictish Arts Society (October 1991) and
   the Cosmos Project Conference on Cosmology and History (February 1992) – are
   mainly based on modern Gaelic and unlikely to be the real meanings, though they
   fit in very well with the false picture of the Picts as a stereotyped 'lost race'
   accepted by most Scots until recently: 'little people, living in little mounds, eating
   berries on headlands'.

'shapely people', but more likely as Kenneth Jackson said 'may mean the people of the designs, i.e. tattoos'.[4] Jackson went on to suggest that a Southern British variant of the same name, *Pritani*, later Welsh *Prydain*, was slightly corrupted into Latin *Britanni* from which *Britannia* and 'Britain', and by some less clear process *Brittones* and 'Britons', were deduced. Middle Welsh documents keep confusing the words for Britain and Pictland, and Tacitus, who writes of *Caledonia* but calls the inhabitants Britons, may be doing the same sort of thing.

In any case classical authors actually say that the Caledonians were Picts: the name *Picti* first appears in a Latin panegyric dated AD 297, and about a dozen years later another panegyric mentions '*Caledones* and other Picts'. Ammianus Marcellinus in 368 writes that the Picts were divided into two peoples, the *Dicalydones* and the *Verturiones*.[5] 'Dicalydones' seems to mean 'double Caledonians', suggesting that the Caledonians themselves were divided into two parts, perhaps on either side of the Grampians: it reflects Ptolemy's much earlier name for the sea to the west of Scotland, *Okeanos Douekaledonios*, which may include an early Celtic prefix for 'two', *dve*.[6] About AD 200 Dio Cassius had written that there were two main tribes in the independent part of Britain, whose names were taken to incorporate other vassal tribes, the *Caledonii* and the *Maeatae*, and that the latter were further south, towards the 'wall that divides the island' – perhaps the Antonine Wall rather than Hadrian's. Their name is thought to be carried on by Dumyat and Myot Hill, two hills in the Stirling area, and may be in a sixth-century *bellum Miathorum*, 'battle with the *Miathi*', mentioned in Adomnán's *Life of St Columba*.

4 Jackson, 'Pictish Language', 158 ff.; fuller discussion in K. H. Jackson, 'Two early Scottish names', *SHR* xxxiii (1954), 14–18. See also T. F. O'Rahilly, *Early Irish History and Mythology* (Dublin 1946), 341–6, 444–52. W. F. H. Nicolaisen, *Scottish Place-Names* (London 1976), 150–1, refuses to accept that *Picti* is a Latin nickname, but does not consider the possibility that it may be a rough translation of *Priteni*. As far as I know nobody has discussed the significance of the nominative/accusative form *Pictores*, 'painters', used by *Ann. Ulster* around 700 (M. O. Anderson, *Kings and Kingship in Early Scotland* [2nd edn, Edinburgh 1980], 39 and n.160), which suggests that by then Pictish artists were admired, but not for their face or body-painting.

5 See F. T. Wainwright, 'The Picts and the Problem', in Wainwright, *Problem of the Picts*, 1–53. This chapter gives a comprehensive collection of early references. In this case, however, see also Anderson, *Kings and Kingship*, 126, who quotes the whole passage and points out that the *Picti in duas gentes diuisi, Dicalydonas* [sic] *et Verturiones* are only those reported as ravaging Roman Britain along with the unidentified *Attacotti* and the *Scotti* (ever since identified as the Irish, though no convincing Gaelic derivation for the Latin name has yet been suggested). But for Ptolemy's reference (below), it would be tempting to dismiss the first syllable of *Dicalydones* as a scribal dittography from the word before, *diuisi*.

6 Wainwright, 'Picts', 53; Jackson, 'Pictish Language', 136 n.3; cf. Pedersen, *Grammatik*, ii, 127.

Otherwise the *Maeatae* vanish from the record as soon as they appear, and are apparently replaced by the *Verturiones*, who again may be mentioned only once in Roman times but can probably be identified with a later Pictish people called *fir Fortrenn* ('the men of **Fortriu*') in Irish sources,[7] who certainly were based further south than the Caledonians seem to have been.[8]

The Caledonians, too, vanish from the record and are not mentioned at all in post-Roman sources after the Romans left Britain, but they are well attested from the first to fourth centuries and have left post-Roman traces in place-names. The name survived in *Coit Celidon*, the Caledonian Wood (or Forest perhaps), which is mentioned in the ninth-century Welsh annals attributed to Nennius as the site of one of Arthur's battles, and turns up occasionally as a location for distant adventures in medieval Welsh tales.[9] More significantly, it is an element in the modern place-names of Dunkeld, 'the hill-fort (*dún*) of the Caledonians' – the English form has lost the final syllable, but the Gaelic *Dún Chailleann*, early Irish *Dún Cailden*, has not, and derives regularly from *Caledonii* – and Rohallion, 'the ring-fort (*ráth*) of the Caledonians' a farm just across the Tay from it; as well as Schiehallion, 'the fairy hill (*síd*) of the Caledonians', the striking pointed mountain that dominates Loch Rannoch.[10] All of these are in central or northern Perthshire, and reinforce the argument for at least the southern half of the Caledonians having a base there, which was remembered when Gaelic-speakers first settled in the area. But the tribe is not mentioned in the list of Pictish kingdoms given by Irish writers in sources which may well date from the ninth century or earlier, or in any Irish annals, Bede or any later source until 'Caledonia' was rediscovered by Renaissance scholars like George Buchanan. So what happened to the Caledonians?

The Irish list of Pictish kingdoms is actually best known from the so-called 'Pictish Chronicle' as preserved in a Latin manuscript copied in Northern England in the fourteenth century, the Poppleton MS, and is ostensibly a list of the seven sons of the eponymous ancestor of the

7   W. J. Watson, *The History of the Celtic Place-Names of Scotland* (1926; repr. Edinburgh 1993), 68–9.

8   Wainwright, 'Picts', 50–3. It might be significant that the place-names thought to be derived from the name of the *Maeatae* are on both sides of the upper Forth estuary, just like the names which locate the area called in early Welsh sources *Manau* (see below, note 47), and *Manau* and *Maeatae* alliterate.

9   See J. R. F. Piette, 'Calidon and the Caledonian Forest', *Bulletin of the Board of Celtic Studies*, xxiii (1969), 191–201, for an overview of literary references to this 'vague location' in the north.

10   Wainwright, 'Picts', 52; Jackson, 'Pictish Language', 135; O'Rahilly, *Early Irish History*, 355, makes a pertinent comparison between Dunkeld and Dumbarton as names bestowed by Gaels on foreign capitals.

Cruithni or Picts, *Cruithne*. The form of that name is enough to show that the original source was Gaelic, and old enough to have been inserted in Irish manuscripts of the *Lebor Gabála Érenn* (*Book of the Conquest of Ireland*) of similar date: inventing characters after whom places were called was one of the typical techniques of the pseudo-historians who had been compiling that imaginary history of prehistoric Ireland since at least the ninth century. The seven names have been identified with seven provinces listed as having been ruled by seven brothers in a twelfth-century tract, *De situ Albanie*, also preserved in the Poppleton MS.[11] The grounds for identification vary. Obviously *Fib* must be Fife (with its western dependencies, *Fothreve*). *Fidach* is identified as Moray and Ross because all the other provinces of the *De situ* have been at least tentatively identified. *Fotla* (the basic form deduced from corruptions such as *Floclaid* in the 'Chronicle') would seem to be Atholl (with Gowrie), whose name appears in the *Annals of Ulster* as *Athfoithle* (genitive),[12] which seems to be *Fotla* with the Gaelic prefix *ath-*, 'new' or 'second': more of this later. *Fortrenn* has already been mentioned as the genitive of the Irish *Fortriu, apparently derived from the *Verturiones*: its kings appear in Irish annals as those high kings of the Picts who are associated with Strathearn by later writers, so it is thought to correspond to Strathearn and Menteith in *De situ*. *Cait* or *Got* is obviously Caithness and Sutherland, *Cathanesia citra montem et ultra montem*, either side of the Ord, perhaps: the element survives both in Norse *Catanes* whence Caithness, and in the Gaelic name for Sutherland, *Cataibh*.[13] *Cé* may be Aberdeenshire (Mar and Buchan) if the name of Bennachie means the Peaks of Cé (*benna Ché*).[14] *Circinn* is probably

---

11 Wainwright, 'Picts', 46–7; Anderson, *Kings and Kingship*, 80–1, 235 ff; and see Dauvit Broun's essay, above.

12 *Ann. Ulster*, 739.

13 *Cataibh* is a fossilised dative plural, used in a locative sense, 'among the Cats' (Clan Chattan is of course conjectured to be of Sutherland origin). Caithness itself is *Gallaibh*, 'among the Norsemen': compare earlier *Innse Gall* for the Hebrides.

14 *Beinn* being literally a peak, and Bennachie a ridge with several small peaks – and a probable Pictish fort on the highest, the Mither Tap (R. W. Feachem, 'Fortifications', in Wainwright, *Problem of the Picts*, 76) – the plural is more appropriate. A derivation, as has sometimes been assumed, from a name on the regular pattern of *Beinn na Caiche*, 'The Peak of the Breast', would be inappropriate, and a form such as *Beinnnan Caioch*, 'The Peak [sic] of the Breasts', would be likely to have 'g' rather than '*ch*' in the middle. See M. E. Dobbs, 'Cé: the Pictish name of a district in eastern Scotland', *Scottish Gaelic Studies*, vi (1947–9), 137–8, who first pointed out that the name appears in two titles among the *oircne*, 'ravagings' or 'massacres', in the Middle Irish tale-lists: *Orgain Maighi Ce la Galo mac Fephail*, 'The Ravaging of the Plain of Ce by Galo son of Febail', which heads this section of the list, and also *Orgain Beinne Ce*, 'The Massacre of Bennachie (?)' For the background to these titles, see P. Mac Cana, *The Learned Tales of Medieval Ireland* (Dublin 1980), 46–7, 61, 63, 77, 85, and *passim*; the same author's note 'On a title in the MI Tale-Lists', *Celtica*, xi (1979), 128–32, accepts that though there seems to have been a

another genitive which turns up in forms like *Mag Gerginn*, 'the Plain of Gergiu (?)', in Irish sources, and seems to mean Angus and Mearns.[15]

It will be noticed that these seven kingdoms divide into two alliterative groups, three beginning with *C*, *Cat*, *Cé* and *Cirig*, and four (in their Gaelicised forms) with *F*, *Fib*, *Fidach*, *Fotla* and *Fortriu*. The two groups do not divide north and south of the Grampians, as Bede says the Picts were divided (though he evidently considered Argyll, the West Highlands and Hebrides, where Columba preached, to be in the northern half).[16] It should also be noted that *De situ Albanie* almost immediately repeats the list of provinces (first described as *partes*, now as *regna*) with their boundaries, but whereas number seven was *Cathanesia* in the first list, it is *Arregaithil*, Argyll, in the second. Should there really be eight provinces, despite the seven sons? And if there was an eighth province beginning with *C*, could it not have been Caledonia, as we might as well call it for want of the Pictish form of the word?

Anthony Jackson openly sets out to provoke new speculation about the Picts.[17] His reconstruction of their patterns of intermarriage and the workings of succession by male kings through the female line is based on a people he has studied in southern China, but it may nevertheless approximate to Pictish patterns of thought. There is certainly some reason to think that they divided things in halves, and may have married in moieties. Yet though his system works best with a set of eight lineages, he accepts the 'well-known fact that the Picts had a predilection for the number seven',[18] and later has to discard three of the seven names as southern tribes who did not much use Pictish symbols and divide the others into halves to get his set of eight. The 'well-known fact' is used to support his contention that just twenty-eight symbols are of importance, and his later theory (which has convinced nobody) that the Pictish ogham inscriptions are not a written language at all but a calendar system for calculating dates of festivals, in which multiples of seven strokes, corresponding no doubt to weeks, appear to recur. The only other evidence he gives for it is that, 'In old Irish legends and even contemporary Celtic folklore we know that seventh sons of seventh sons were especially gifted

Mag Ce in Ireland, this tale may be about Scotland, but suggests that *Orgain Beinne Ce* is a misreading of *Orgain Becce*, a story mentioned elsewhere of the massacre of an Irish poet Becc and his retinue. This would still suggest that the scribe knew the place-name *Benna Che*.

15 *ES* i, 118, 241. See Anderson, *Kings and Kingship*, 36–7, on the unreliability of these two annals of battles, which are only in the late *Ann. Tigernach*; 594 and 752, see also below, note 65.

16 Bede, *HE*, 222–3 (III. 4). The mountains which divide the Picts are, of course, not named.

17 A. Jackson, *The Symbol Stones of Scotland* (Stromness 1984).

18 Ibid., 61.

in magic arts.'[19] Since I know of no early Irish 'legend' that says this, and since the belief that seventh sons of seventh sons have healing or divinatory (rather than strictly magic) powers is shared by the Highlands with England and probably most of Europe, this seems weak evidence for Pictish beliefs.

What has been established recently is that early Irish clerics of the sort who wrote the *Book of the Conquest* had a strong predilection for the number seven. Liam Breatnach has recently published an edition of *Uraicecht na Riar*,[20] *The Handbook of Ranks*, a legal text dealing with the early Irish poetic grades, which also tended to be arranged in lists of seven – but there are several different texts which divide poets (*filid*) and the lower grades of bards sometimes into one hierarchy of seven ranks, sometimes into two, and with different selections of names for the various grades. The whole thing is clearly a playground for inventive pedants, probably canon lawyers rather than secular lawyers. Breatnach quotes an article by a medieval historian, R. E. Reynolds,[21] who notes that in the organisation of the Church throughout Europe from the seventh century onwards a system of seven grades, rather than five or nine as earlier, became the norm, apparently under the influence of Irish scholars, and was associated with other groups of seven such as the seven gifts of the Holy Spirit. Breatnach suggests that the system which started with the Church came to be applied also to secular systems of rank throughout the early Irish laws, sometimes with demonstrably artificial results. This is certainly the argument of a leading member of the so-called 'anti-nativist' school, which tends to find the origins of everything in early Ireland in Judeo-Christian tradition rather than the Celtic paganism favoured by the 'nativists', but in this case I find it convincing. It could well be that most sets of seven in insular Celtic law go back to the prominence of sevens in Judeo-Christian belief rather than having any basis in pagan Celtic belief. Even the seven-day week, despite its days named after Roman gods, only reached Rome with Constantine: the pagan Roman week, from market-day to market-day, lasted eight days.[22] There may be some exceptions: for instance, noblemen's sons in early Ireland were sent for fosterage from the ages of seven (or earlier) to fourteen, but even there some sources suggest it went

---

19 Ibid., 63. See I. Opie and M. Tatem, *A Dictionary of Superstitions* (Oxford 1989), 346–7, for a useful set of references to belief in the healing powers of the seventh child since the 16th century (the earlier Welsh one is spurious), mostly from England.

20 *Uraicecht na Riar*, ed. L. Breathnach (Dublin Institute for Advanced Studies, 1987); see esp. 81–9.

21 Ibid., 85–6, citing R. E. Reynolds, 'At sixes and sevens – and eights and nines: the sacred mathematics of sacred orders in the early Middle Ages', *Speculum*, liv (1979), 669–84.

22 R. M. Ogilvie, *The Romans and their Gods in the Age of Augustus* (London 1969), 71–2.

on until seventeen – implying perhaps different ideas of the normal age of puberty – and it is probably more significant that they reached full manhood, when they could marry and hold land, according to the law tracts, at twenty, not twenty-one.[23]

So the seven sons of Cruithne and their seven kingdoms of the Picts may not be part of genuine pagan Pictish tradition: the whole idea may have been invented by Gaelic historians writing after the collapse of the Pictish kingdoms. There may actually have been just seven provinces in the last stages of independent Pictland, but this does not mean that there always had been, or had to be because of the significance of the number: that is all that I am arguing.[24]

Given that the *Caledones* and *Verturiones* were the leading tribes of the Picts in the fourth century AD, it seems very possible that the affiliations of their client tribes could have been signalled by alliteration, and with the seven province names we have two alliterating groups of four: Caledonians, *Cait, Cé, Circinn*; *Fortriu* (earlier *Verturiones*), *Fib, Fotla, Fidach*. There may indeed have been more than this, if the presence of Pictish symbol stones can be taken as proving a Pictish presence in Skye and the Outer Hebrides as well as in Orkney and Shetland: it hardly seems likely that these outlying areas all came under the lineage of *Cait*, as Jackson suggests, though they may not originally have been part of the mainland Pictish kingdom. The well-established Celtic name of the *Orcades*, apparently implying a pig totem, does not fit the alliterative pattern, and it is not at all clear whether the *Orcadum regulus* whom Adomnán mentions as being at King Bridei's court in Inverness was one of his established followers or had only recently submitted to him.[25] On the other hand there is a suggestion from an unidentified Irish source that Shetland may have been known as *Innse Cat*, the Islands of the Cats,[26] which would imply at least a totem shared with Caithness. But leaving the Northern and Western Isles

---

23 F. Kelly, *A Guide to Early Irish Law* (Dublin Institute for Advanced Studies, 1988), 82–4, 88; the most significant ages seem to be seven, 14 and 20, but 10, 12 and 17 are also dividing lines for certain purposes. Note that early Irish lawyers deliberately collected sets of seven – 'heptads' – rather than the triads used by other scholars: ibid., 266, no. 3.

24 And see Dauvit Broun's essay, above.

25 Adomnán, *Columba*, 166–7 (II. 42). See note 60 below for the under-king's probable status. It seems possible that the Western and Northern Isles, and perhaps parts of the west coast of the mainland, had a separate group of tribal names alliterating on vowels (all vowels alliterate together in Celtic and Anglo-Saxon verse): the *tuatha Orc ocus Iboth*, 'tribes of Orkney and the (southern?) Hebrides' of Irish legend would represent the best-remembered of these names (see O'Rahilly, *Early Irish History*, 538, esp. n.6). Their leaders might once have been the mysterious *Attacotti* (see note 5 above).

26 See O'Rahilly, *Early Irish History*, 344 n1.

aside, there are still three questions to be resolved. Where did the eighth tribe live? If *Fotla* simply means Atholl, why are the forts and fairy hills of the Caledonians commemorated in that area? And what happened to the Caledonians?

The answer I want to suggest to all three of these questions is that *Fotla* originally meant Argyll, and that people from there occupied Atholl – 'new *Fotla*' – and drove out the Caledonians. There is a sequel, but first the arguments for this much. As I have said already, even if not all the details are convincing, the general argument may still be plausible enough to consider.

Bede, in the description of St Columba already mentioned,[27] is quite definite that his mission was to 'the provinces of the northern Picts': Argyll seems to be considered part of the northern half because it is beyond the mountains. What he says next – with some doubt himself, apparently – is that the southern Picts, this side of the mountains, were said already to have been converted by St Ninian. This is now thought very doubtful, and could derive from a piece of Christian Pictish propaganda: so could the claim that it was the 'most powerful Pictish king Bridei *filius Meilochon*'[28] who granted Iona to Columba. On the other hand, though Adomnán mentions Columba staying with Conall son of Comgell, king of Dál Riata, before coming to Iona,[29] he never says that Conall gave him the island, though this is claimed in Conall's obituary in the *Annals of Ulster* for 574, probably not a contemporary source or any earlier than Adomnán. It seems more likely that someone leaving Ireland in self-imposed exile looking for a hermitage would choose a site among people of another race and language than his own: Iona is not such a small or barren island that it is likely to have been totally uninhabited before Columba came, and certainly Mull, a short boat journey away, was not. The evidence for Gaelic-speaking inhabitants in Mull and the islands north of Islay is tenuous, depending on questionable deductions from passages in Adomnán. If, as Bannerman suggests, Bridei may have 'considered himself overlord of the islands inhabited by the Dál Riata',[30] including Mull and Iona, I think this must mean that they were still at the very least debatable land.

The linguistic argument which follows accounts for my identification of Argyll as the original *Fotla*. The traditional view is that *áth Fhotla* means 'new Ireland', using the name *Fódla*, one of the three names of Ireland said in the *Book of the Conquest* to have been taken from three early queens (or

---

[27] See note 16 above.

[28] See Dauvit Broun's essay, above, note 3, for this form of the name.

[29] Adomnán, *Columba*, 30–1 (I.7).

[30] J. Bannerman, *Studies in the History of Dalriada* (Edinburgh 1974), 79.

goddesses), *Eire*, *Fódla* and *Banba*.[31] All that it necessarily means is 'another *Fotla*'. (The form in early Irish is most often *Fotla* for the name of Ireland as well as the Pictish place-name: in Old Irish orthography this means that it was pronounced '*Fodla*' with a *d* sound, rather than the corresponding fricative, the sound of *th* in 'that', which was written in the middle of a word with a *d*, later *dh*, and in modern Irish and Scottish Gaelic is silent. *Fodla* seems to be an unexplained rarer variant of *Fotla* which later became the normal form.)[32] What W. J. Watson claimed as appearances of the other two names, *Éire* and *Banba*, in the north-east of Scotland, as evidence of early penetration by the Scots there, has recently been dismissed by the foremost authority on Scottish place-names.[33] In any case, a very plausible meaning for Irish *Fotla* was suggested over sixty years ago by the late M. A. O'Brien.[34] The suggestion is one of a set on the names of Ireland which, as the speculations of a relatively young scholar, not yet the authoritative linguist he became, may have received less attention than they deserve: O'Brien himself was notoriously indifferent to the reception of his ideas. Whatever the other suggestions in this article are worth, this one seemed to me so convincing when I first read it thirty years ago that I have never forgotten it, and am prepared to defend it on the grounds that it makes good sense, even if there are linguistic difficulties which made O'Brien himself call it a 'very tentative explanation'. He suggests a derivation of the name *Fotla* from a genitive form, **vo-dolo*, 'of going down', used perhaps in a combination like the modern *Inis Fódhla*, which would mean 'The Isle of the Going Down (namely, of the Sun)', equivalent to Latin *Insula Occidentalis*, the Western Island. With familiarity *Inis* might be dropped, leaving a nominative *Fotla*.

The weaknesses in this argument are the derivation from a genitive form and doubts about the history of the irregular verbal noun *dul*, 'going'. The strength of the argument lies in the Welsh word which O'Brien went on to derive from the same hypothetical common Celtic root. Again he had to use a form other than the nominative singular to

31 See M.-L. Sjoestedt, *Gods and Heroes of the Celts* (London 1949), 10–11.

32 The MS form of the goddess's name, e.g. in the version of the *Book of the Conquest* in the *Book of Leinster*, ed. R. I. Best, O. Bergin and M. A. O'Brien (Dublin 1954), 35 ff., is regularly *Fotla* with a '*t*'. The long '*o*' in later Irish forms may be no more than compensatory lengthening for the now silent '*dh*'.

33 W. F. H. Nicolaisen, 'Names in the landscape of the Moray Firth', in W. D. H. Sellar (ed.), *Moray, Province and People* (Edinburgh 1993), 260–1, questioning Watson, *Celtic Place-Names*, 228–32, with the more authority since the names in question seem to be originally river-names; Nicolaisen has 'been studying river names for almost forty years', and sees these forms as nothing exceptional or necessarily imported.

34 M. A. O'Brien, 'Hibernica: 6. On the names of Ireland', *Zeitschrift für celtische Philologie*, xiv (1923), 326–33.

reach the one he wanted to account for, but again it was a plausible one: a plural adjective *vodoli*, 'Sundowners' or 'Westerners', which the Britons might have used to describe the inhabitants of the island to their west, could with the sound changes characteristic of Welsh develop into the modern Welsh word for 'Irishmen', *Gwyddyl*, from which the singular *Gwyddel* would be a back-formation. No derivation half so convincing for this word has been suggested: the current front-runner is something to do with *gŵydd*, 'wild', or possibly *gwŷdd*, 'wood';[35] 'wild men' might be an uncomplimentary description of people who were apt to invade Wales about the time the Romans left, 'woodsmen' sounds a lot less likely, and in neither case do the quantities of the vowels match those in *Gwyddyl*. The importance of this Welsh word is that it is the generally accepted origin of the Irish word *Goídil*, 'Gaels', from which all forms of that name derive; while *Goídelc*, whence descend modern words for the Gaelic language, carries over the typically Welsh adjectival ending shown by modern *Gwyddeleg*.[36]

If the Irish adopted a Welsh name for themselves as 'Westerners' (and whoever first borrowed the word surely knew enough Welsh to have thought twice about a word for his own people that he knew meant 'wild men'), it seems quite likely that they had a corresponding word for 'Easterners', and I suggest that it lies behind modern *Albannaigh*, 'Scotsmen'. This derives of course from Old Irish *Albu*, modern Scottish Gaelic *Alba*, Scotland. The name *Albu* originally meant all Britain to Irishmen, and later, perhaps after Kenneth mac Alpín's time, was narrowed down to mean the part of Britain successfully colonised by their own people. It is generally agreed to be the same as Albion, which appears in ancient Greek as a name for Britain. T. F. O'Rahilly, with typical assurance, declares it to be related to a Welsh word *elfydd*, 'earth',[37] which presumably would be the natives' own name for their country. Most other scholars accept that it derives from the same root as Latin *albus*, 'white', and probably refers to the white cliffs of Dover and other parts of the Channel coast which might be seen by those entering the country from ancient Gaul.[38] But such a reference would mean nothing to an Irishman. 'Low Latin' *alba*, whence French *aube*, *aubade* etc., means dawn, the white light in the east; though the poets preferred to use the name of

---

35 See *Geiriadur Prifysgol Cymru*, ed. R. J. Thomas (Cardiff 1950), 1754, s.v. *Gwyddel*.

36 The Royal Irish Academy, *Contributions to a Dictionary of the Irish Language* (Dublin 1913–76), s.v. *Goidel*, *Goidelc*.

37 O'Rahilly, *Early Irish History*, 385 ff. See also *Contributions to Dictionary of Irish Language*, s.v. *Albu*.

38 See Watson, *Celtic Place-Names*, 11–12; and E. Partridge, *Origins* (London 1958), 11, s.v. *alb*. 4.

the goddess Aurora, writers like Caesar at least used the related verbs *albeo* and *albesco* of the breaking of day, and it seems very likely that *alba* was a normal term for daybreak in the spoken language long before it was recognised in literary usage. Might not the Celtic languages, closely related to Latin, have used a form from the same stem to mean the dawn, therefore the east, and Irishmen have used a derivative for the country behind the dawn, to their east?[39] Certainly I would rather believe I came from the Land of the Rising Sun than from the hinterland of the white cliffs of Dover!

To return to the original argument, we know too little of the phonology of Pictish to doubt that *Fotla* (representing the Irish adaptation of what the Picts, who seem to have kept the original Celtic initial *W* sound that became *F* in Irish and *Gw* in Welsh,[40] probably pronounced as **Wodla*) is the Pictish form of Irish *Fodla*, and the Gaels seem to have accepted it as such. If the Irish form may mean a western region, so may the Pictish. There is in fact a further argument for identifying it with Argyll. The original form of that name, *Airer Goídel*, seems to mean 'Shore' or 'Borderland of the Gaels'.[41] I know of no evidence for the use of this name before the ninth century, and it was only about that time that *Goídil* itself seems to have become a common term used by Gaels to identify themselves, particularly to distinguish themselves from the Norse invaders. But by that time Gaelic language and culture had apparently spread well beyond their original foothold in Argyll and were about to become the dominant language and culture of Scotland north of Forth and Clyde: they could claim other coasts than this one where their hold was already being undermined by Norse raiding. About Columba's time, when Scottish Dál Riata was at most roughly equivalent to the former counties of Argyll and Bute, the Irish seldom if ever thought of themselves as a race covering the whole island. The term used in the law tracts, probably closer to this period, is *Féni*, which seems to mean the ruling aristocracy, possibly only in the kingdoms of Tara (which only later laid claim to the high-kingship of Ireland) and Cashel[42] – and it seems unlikely that such a term would be used, or needed, for a colony which still belonged to one independent petty dynasty, which later fought against the king of Tara. However, it seems perfectly possible that the Picts referred to Argyll, perhaps in the broadest sense of the later name, including the west coast north of

---

[39] Ibid., 3; cf. any Latin dictionary, s.v. *aurora* and *albesco*.
[40] Jackson, 'Pictish Language', 163.
[41] Watson, *Celtic Place-Names*, 120–1.
[42] F. J. Byrne, *Irish Kings and High-Kings* (London 1973), 8–9, 36, and *passim* on the high kingship.

Ardnamurchan up to Loch Broom,[43] as 'the west coast' or 'the coast of *Fotla*', and that this was later translated by Scots then occupying it into Gaelic (or Welsh-Gaelic) words which were still recognised at that time to be cognate in form and meaning – though by this time *Goídel* had come to imply 'Gaelic-speakers' and the name therefore constituted a recognition of current ownership. In other words Argyll, like most of the other province-names of Northern Scotland, could derive from a Pictish name.

Before embarking on my totally hypothetical suggestion of what may have happened to the Caledonians – which will account for some anomalies mentioned above – I need to define a couple of terms. It may be convenient to describe the Pictish divisions which I have so far called kingdoms as 'tribes'. This does not necessarily imply anything as unified as modern African or Amerindian tribes: it very probably means much the same as the early Irish *tuath*, which is often translated as 'tribe' but is better defined as the smallest unit ruled by a king. (Incidentally, there is no evidence at all that I know to show that the *tuath* system which in theory at least covered all Ireland was ever transferred to Scotland, which was colonised by a single otherwise not very important *tuath*, but probably like later colonies attracted adventurers from quite different backgrounds.[44] The nearest approach to a *tuath* system that can be traced is actually the clan system of the sixteenth century, where few of the significant clans seem to have been founded much more than a century

43 Watson, *Celtic Place-Names*, 121. A region called *Iardoman*, 'Western World', is mentioned in *Ann. Ulster*, 567, 568, as the scene of a raid led by Colman Bec of the Southern Uí Neill and Conall son of Comgall king of Dál Riata. A later gloss to a version of this annal in a list of kings of Tara in the *Book of Leinster*, 95, followed by the 17th-century *Ann. Four Masters*, explains these as Seil(?) and Islay; on the strength of this and a mention in the *Book of Invasions* (*Book of Leinster*, 20) of 'Domon and Erdomon in North Britain(?)' (*co Domon & co Herdomon i tuascirt Alban*), Watson (*Celtic Place-Names*, 41), followed by Bannerman (*Dalriada*, 79), takes it 'to be the old designation of the Inner Hebrides', with the first element being *ar*, 'near', or even 'east', rather than *iar*, 'west'. I suggest that it is an early translation of Pictish *Uotla and may well refer to a part of the province still under Pictish rule, possibly no further north or east than Mull or Morvern.

44 Bannerman, *Dalriada*, 134–7, suggests that in the 7th century there may have been half a dozen heads of houses among the Scottish Dál Riata as powerful as a typical Irish *tuath*, but there is no evidence. Anderson, *Kings and Kingship*, 163, says that other 'evidence is hardly to be expected', and goes on to assume that the kings of Dál Riata were over-kings of seven (sic!) *tuatha*. However, it is very doubtful whether conventions that applied (according to later accounts) in the relative stability of Ireland would have much force in the conditions of the expanding colony in Scotland: it seems more likely that individual successful warlords might claim the title of king if they could assert a degree of independence from the king of Dál Riata recognised by others. In any case, there is no evidence for the use of *tuath* in this sense in Scotland, and in modern Scottish Gaelic it means 'landowners', 'farmers', 'tenants' or even according to the dictionaries 'peasantry'.

earlier; the same may well be true of the significant *tuatha* of sixth-century Ireland – and feudal ideas tend to distort the older pattern.) A *tuath*, like a Highland clan, can be described as basically an aristocratic lineage, including those eligible to succeed to the kingship or chiefship and more distant relatives, along with their followers, warriors, poets, craftsmen and so on, and tenants who were clearly not related at all to the ruling lineage and are often referred to with contempt in the early literature – not to mention slaves, who seem to have remained an important part of the economy of very early Christian Ireland. A Pictish 'tribe' would probably have been something similar, with a peasantry who may not even have spoken the same language as their masters,[45] but with a ruling lineage reckoned not in the male line but – unless you are convinced by the arguments of Alfred Smyth – according to some system in which inheritance passed through the mother.[46] The corollary is that 'conquest' does not mean the extermination of a whole population, or fighting by peasant levies, though peasants would no doubt be killed trying to prevent the pillaging of their livestock or granaries. Once the members of the warrior aristocracy have been killed, enslaved, or driven into hiding or exile, the 'tribe' and its name will disappear, and this must be what happened to the Caledonians.

The reconstruction I suggest starts with the Dál Riata settling in the Picts' western province, *Votla* (for consistency the names of Pictish provinces will normally be spelt with a *V*, unless the Gaelic forms with *F* are used, but it denotes the same *W* pronunciation as in personal names like Uurguist written with *U*). Its area may have been roughly equivalent to the recent county of Argyll. The peasantry very likely remained the same, but became tenants of an aristocracy speaking a different sort of Celtic language. Their Pictish overlords must have been defeated in battle by the Scots, and driven back from the coast towards what is now west Perthshire and the head-waters of the Tay: this area of Breadalbane may already have been in their territory. A. O. Anderson's 'possible migration-route from the sea ... by Loch Awe and Glen Lyon, into Fortriu ... marked by the remains of a series of ring-forts, similar to the cashels of Ireland',[47] could be a sign of Pictish retreat rather than Scottish expansion.

---

45 Jackson, 'Pictish Language', 152–8.
46 See A. P. Smyth, *Warlords and Holy Men: Scotland AD 80–1000* (London 1984), 58–76, esp. 67–72. Matrilinear succession of course need not imply matriarchy, or require the use of metronymics instead of patronymics. [And see now A. Woolf, 'Pictish matriliny reconsidered', *Innes Review*, xlix (1998), 147–67: Ed.]
47 Anderson, 'Ninian and the Southern Picts', in *SHR* xxvii (1948), 25–47, 32. In this rather unreliable paper Anderson, who is here as on the following page probably following the arguments of W. J. Watson, seems to suggest that these forts may have been built by the Scots of Dalriada, but also possibly by Irish *Cruithni* who,

The alliteration suggests that *Votla* and *Verturiones* were two elements of a confederation which also included the men of Fife: at this stage I suspect that the fourth of the later *F*-names, *Fidach*, had not yet been created, and if there was a fourth alliterating tribe it was actually the *Votadini* of Lothian, whose territory of *Manau Guotodin* extended north of the Forth.[48] The *Votadini* are generally considered to be Britons, speaking the form of P-Celtic that later became Welsh, because Cunedda of Manau Guotodin, according to Nennius's *Historia Brittonum*, came to North Wales about the end of the fourth century with eight sons who gave their names to territories and noble lineages there,[49] and because Aneirin's great elegy for the last champions of the *Votadini*, the *Gododdin*, was preserved in Wales in Welsh. But the borderline between what became Welsh and Pictish need not have been on the Forth; there have been finds of Pictish symbols, though mostly on movable objects, south of the Forth; and a number of early Welsh heroes along with the cleric Gildas, our only contemporary source for the history of sixth-century Britain, are claimed in later legend to have been born in Pictland.[50] It may in fact have been Cunedda's migration, which has been interpreted as the enlistment of a substantial band of mercenaries to resist Irish invaders in Wales, followed in the sixth century by the first Anglian attacks on their Lothian homeland, that weakened the *Votadini* before the desperate last foray recounted in the *Gododdin*, which is dated to the beginning of the seventh century.[51] In any case they may already have tended to side with the Romanised Britons, since the *Verturiones* are apparently named as

he claims, may have founded the kingdom of Fortriu, or even by descendants of the broch-builders from Edinshall in Berwickshire who rebelled against the Romans, since the forts 'are said to have had door-checks like the brochs'! Feachem, 'Fortifications', 71–6, has no difficulty in accepting more easterly examples as Pictish, though some 'might have been built by peoples moving eastwards from the western seaboard' and their 'builders might have been Scots' – but might just as well have been retreating Picts: the resemblance of these simple structures to Irish cashels need not mean that they are derived from them.

48 Clackmannan north of the Forth and Slamannan to the south both contain the name Manau: see Watson, *Celtic Place-Names*, 103–4.

49 *Nennius, British History and the Welsh Annals*, ed. J. Morris, (London 1980), 79: *atavus illius* [of Maelgwn of Gwynedd], *id est Cunedag, cum filiis suis, quorum numerus octo erat, veberat prius de parte sinistrali, id est de regione quae vocatur Manau Guotodin.*

50 Gildas is traditionally described as son of a Northern king, in Welsh called Caw of *Prydyn*, Pictland (though this tends to be confused with *Prydein*, Britain). For a recent discussion of Caw, father of saints and warriors, see *Culhwch and Olwen*, ed. R. Bromwich and D. S. Evans (Cardiff, 1992), 128–9, and 77–8; cf. ibid., 74 for a mention of the original Tristan, Drystan mab Talluch, whose name seems to be a Welsh form of the Pictish royal names Drosten son of Talorc.

51 See K. H. Jackson, *Language and History in Early Britain* (Edinburgh 1953), 213–14.

undisputed leaders of this section of the Picts as early as 368. At that time
the division between the southern Picts whose tribal names began with *V*
and the northern ones whose tribal names began with *C* may have been
primarily a ritual one between two halves of a dualistically organised
nation or confederacy, and any rivalry may have been on the level of that
between Glasgow and Edinburgh today rather than that between
Orangemen and Catholics. The *Verturiones*, however, seem to have come
to perceive the Caledonians as rivals, perhaps as weak rivals with less
recent experience of warfare than they themselves had gained from raiding
the Romanised regions just to their south. I suggest that they encouraged
their confederates from *Votla* to expand down the Tay valley and win
themselves a new homeland in central Perthshire, soon to be called 'new
Votla', which in Gaelic translation became Atholl. Probably the *Verturiones*
and their other confederates from Fife attacked from the south, up the
Tay, at the same time as the *Votla* attacked down the river from the west,
and drove what was left of the southern Caledonian aristocracy out of the
Dunkeld area and over Drumochter into the arms of their northern
kinsfolk. Perhaps they still thought of their southern and western fellow-
Picts as merely ritual rivals and were taken by surprise by this treacherous
onslaught.

This would explain why the name of Atholl came to be applied to the
area where place-names record Caledonian fortresses and spiritual centres
(I translated Schiehallion in modern terms as 'fairy hill of the Caledonians',
but *síd* in Old Irish really meant the Otherworld, the abode of the pagan
gods, and it should be thought of as the Caledonians' Olympus, if not
their Delphi.) It would also help to explain why in 761 the *Annals of Ulster*
(and other Irish annals which probably borrowed details of Scottish affairs
from them) stop describing the over-kings of the Picts listed in the 'Pictish
Chronicle' in their obituaries and other entries as *rex Pictorum* and call
them *rex Fortrenn*, 'king of Fortriu', from 763 to 834. Then *rex Pictorum*
returns for a while for the obits of Kenneth mac Alpín and three of his
successors, before the appearance in 900 of the new geographical rather
than racial term (now completely in Irish, and probably reflecting the
king's actual Gaelic title), *rí Alban*, 'king of Alba', for Kenneth's grandson
Donald son of Constantine and all his successors.[52] We will consider the
meaning of the later changes shortly, but meanwhile it seems clear that the
Verturiones or *Fortrinn* had become the leading lineage of all the Picts. The

---

52 See *Ann. Ulster*, 580, 584, 629, 631, 653, 657, 729, 736, 761 (*rex Pictorum*); 693, 763,
775, 820, 834 (*rex Fortrenn*); 858, 862, 876, 878 (*rex Pictorum* again); 900, 952, 954,
967, 971 etc. (*rex Alban*). See also references to Fortriu or *fir Fortrenn*, probably
meaning the Picts in general, ibid., 736, 839 and as late as 904: *fir Alban* replaces
the term in 918.

title *rex Fortrenn* first actually appears for Bridei son of Bile's obit in 693, and if we accept Marjorie Anderson's argument that instances of *rex Pictorum* before this date were probably retrospective interpolations,[53] it may be concluded that the two terms were by then regarded as equivalent in much the same way as the lesser term 'king of Tara' and the greater 'king of Ireland' were claimed to be much later – though the kings of Fortriu were probably acknowledged by all Pictland much more often than any king of Tara was recognised as over-king by even four of the five provinces of Ireland. The *Annals of Ulster* refer to Fortriu and the men of Fortriu from 736 until as late as 904, generally in terms which can be as well interpreted as meaning all Pictland as merely a province, for instance in 866 when Norse invaders 'go to Fortriu and plunder all *Cruithentuath*' – a rare use in this source of a term for 'the nation of the Picts' designed to avoid confusion with their very distant relatives the Irish Cruthin, meaning primarily the Ulster kingdom of Dál nAraide whose kings appear regularly in the annals as *rex Cruithne*.[54] It may also be significant that the only clear reference to a king of the southern Picts, *Dubtolarg rex Pictorum citra Monoth*, 'Black-haired Talorc king of the Picts this side of the Mounth' who died in 781, does not call him king of Fortriu, though this is the title regularly given at the same period to more important kings of the Picts, including Constantine and Oengus sons of Fergus who were also kings of the Scots of Dál Riata.[55] In other words *rex Fortrinn* implied the over-kingship of all the Picts.

Whatever the date of this conquest – presumably between the arrival of the Scots and 693 – it is only a first phase, and I think it may have been quite quickly followed by a second phase for which it is possible to suggest a date. The lineage of the Caledonians disappeared entirely, not just from Perthshire, and if they still held the territory they seem to have had in Roman times they could have retreated as suggested above to the northern part around Inverness. In the reconstructed list of Pictish kingdoms this is identified with Fidach, the furthest north of the group that alliterates on *F*. It seems to me that this can best be explained as the result of this second phase. The *F*-Picts could not leave the Caledonians in Moray plotting a come-back with the help of the other *C*-tribes: as soon as they had consolidated their position in Atholl and the border area of

53 Anderson, *Kings and Kingship*, 173: at p. 174 the wider meaning of Fortriu in the 9th century is admitted, and p. 151 discusses why Eochaid Buide of Dál Riata (d.629) should be called *rex Pictorum*.

54 *Ann. Ulster*, 629, 645, 646, 708, 727, 749, 774, has obits of *rex Cruithne*. From 790 *rí Dal nAraide* becomes the regular form: see O'Rahilly, *Early Irish History*, 344, and more generally 341–52.

55 *Ann. Ulster*, 781. The Gaelic forms Oengus and Fergus correspond to Pictish Onuist and Uurguist, and do not necessarily imply Scottish descent.

Gowrie, they must have pressed on themselves over Drumochter by land, probably combining this with a pincer movement into the Moray Firth by sea. Very likely one of the Caledonians' mistakes was not to keep up the sea power they surely had when Ptolemy called an ocean after them: if their main centre of power was well up the Tay, they may have kept a few river boats there – if they used skin boats like Irish curachs, as Gildas's account of both Picts and Scots says,[56] river boats may have been no smaller than their sea-going craft, but the *Fortrinn* would have controlled the estuary below them, and the main Caledonian fleet must have been based in the Moray Firth. Their confederates in *Cé* and *Circinn* had a coastline of steep cliffs and few safe havens, whereas the *Fortrinn*, whose territory seems to have stretched from the upper Firth of Forth to the upper Firth of Tay, with their confederates controlling the ports of East Fife, had every chance to build up a navy which could have got its training raiding late Roman Britain, though with less success in the long run than the Angles, who certainly had wooden ships.

In any case, the northern Caledonians disappear, and *Fidach* apparently takes their place. The most likely explanation seems to be that one ruling lineage was wiped out or at least driven into exile and replaced by one related to the conquerors, the only *F*-Pictish 'tribe' north of the Grampians. Whether this involved elevating a cadet branch of an existing royal lineage to under-king status or there was already a fourth royal lineage in the group (perhaps replacing the *Votadini?*) in some outlying district which could be given the conquered province we cannot tell: the Gaelicised form of the name looks like the adjective from *fid*, 'wood', and if it translates a Pictish cognate[57] it could be an epithet either for 'woodsmen' settled in the forests of Inverness-shire or ones who came from somewhere like the Trossachs.

As I said, it is possible to suggest a very plausible date for this final defeat of the Caledonians. The only over-king of the Picts in historical times who is clearly described in an early source as not ruling from the Fortriu heartland between Scone and Forteviot is Bede's 'powerful king' Bridei *filius Meilochon*, who according to Adomnán was visited by St Columba in a fortress which was evidently near the river Ness and which Reeves identified as the hill fort of Craig Phádraig just west of Inverness.[58] This is generally taken to mean that he was a king of the northern Picts

---

56 Quoted by Bannerman, *Dalriada*, 153.
57 The Welsh cognate *gwydd* is sometimes cited in explanations of Gwyddel (see note 34 above); the royal name Uuid might conceivably be a Pictish cognate, but the Gaelic equivalent Foith suggests not.
58 Anderson, *Kings and Kingship*, 49–51; Wainwright, 'Picts', 21; both following indications in Adomnán, *Columba*, 62–5 (II. 33–4).

who became over-king, and from Bede's mention of the supposed conversion of the southern Picts by Ninian before the arrival of Columba in the ninth year of Bridei to convert 'this island' (apparently meaning Britain!), Wainwright deduces that 'Bede describes his [Bridei's] people as the "northern Picts"'.[59] But the fact that he was in a fort near Inverness when Columba visited him could also mean that this 'powerful Pictish king' had recently conquered the area and had set up his headquarters where he could supervise the pacification and resettlement of the province. The presence before Bridei,[60] during one visit of Columba's to him 'staying beyond Drumalban', of an under-king (*regulus*) of Orkney may suggest that he used Inverness as a base for the subjugation of more than one province, and certainly by sea rather than land.[61]

The annals actually mention a 'flight before the son of Maelchu' a few years before this.[62] Tigernach's 'flight of the Scots' (*teichedh do Albanchaib*) (559) is obviously a late scribe's misinterpretation of the double entry (558 and 560) in the *Annals of Ulster* – nobody before the ninth century would have called the Dál Riata *Albanaig* – and I suggest that this was the expulsion of the Caledonians, possibly even that the two entries in the *Annals* are not duplicates but record the driving of the Caledonians first out of Atholl and just two years later out of their northern province by Bridei and the men of Fortriu.[63] The puzzling entry for the (non-violent) death of another *rex Pictorum*, Cennalath, apparently the *Galam Cennaleph* who precedes Bridei in the king-lists, just four years before Bridei himself, could then mean the

59 Wainwright, 'Picts', following Bede, as note 16 above.
60 The apparent diphthong in the final syllable of the Pictish form *Bridei* or *Bredei* is one of several features which suggest that Pictish like British had had a penultimate stress accent before the Celtic final syllables were lost (cf. Jackson, *Language and History*, 265 ff.) and retained the resultant stress on the final syllable perhaps for longer than early Welsh did. This would help to explain the variation in the first vowel between *Bredei*, *Bridei*, Bede's *Bridius* and Adomnán's *Brudeus* (cf. Jackson, 'Pictish Language', 161, and Anderson, *Kings and Kingship*, 246 n.77). The usual Gaelic form *Bruide* may be influenced by the form of the native Irish name Bruidge (e.g. *Ann. Ulster*, 579).
61 See note 25 above. Brude had taken the Orkney king's hostages (*cujus obsides in manu tua sunt*), which was the normal way, at least in Ireland at that time, of asserting overlordship.
62 Discussed in Anderson, *Kings and Kingship*, 138–9; see *ES* i, 21, for Tigernach's version.
63 *Ann. Ulster*, 558, record a rout (*fuga*), which could be the immediate result of a battle, while the entry for 560 uses the Irish word *immirge*, used for the flitting of a family or the emigration of a complete tuath. This could either mean the families of defeated Caledonians being encouraged to take refuge across Drumochter, leaving their lands and most of their possessions open to the victors; or more likely, after two whole years, the final defeat leaving the survivors of the kindred to wander in exile. There is no need to see the two entries as duplicates, though the death of Gabrán of Dál Riata is duplicated beside each.

death of the last Caledonian king in exile: the existence of Pictish exiles in
Dál Riata in Columba's time is attested by Adomnán.[64]

How the remaining Picts of the C-tribes and the neighbouring peoples
were affected by this conquest we can only guess. Indeed we do not know
what the previous system of high-kingship, if any, may have been: it could
have alternated between Caledonians and *Verturiones*, or rotated among all
seven or eight 'tribes'; it could have been the prerogative of Caledonians
alone; or the *F*- and *C*-groups could each have had their own equal over-
king, like the Irish provincial kings. On the whole the last seems the most
likely, and the transition from it to a single high-king from the Fortriu
lineage would have been a comparatively easy one. The other C-tribes no
doubt resisted, but with a wedge between them on land and an enemy
with enough command of the sea to make Orkney submit, *Cait* and *Cé* are
unlikely to have held out for long. The richer lands of *Circinn* may have
been another matter. The record of a battle there in the 590s in which
Aedán son of Gabrán of Dál Riata was defeated and some of his sons
killed suggests that Aedán, who also had enough naval power to attack
Orkney in 580, could have sailed round to assist the native tribe against
their overlords, who may have lost command of the sea to him: this seems
more likely than an attack overland which would have to come through
the Fortriu heartland.[65] Moreover an anomalous annal preserved by
Tigernach records the death of 'Bruidhi mac Maelchon' in the battle of
Asreth *in terra Circin* between Picts on both sides. This is dated to 752,
whereas Bridei died according to the *Annals of Ulster* in 584: but if we
accept O'Rahilly's suggestion that this period of 168 years represents
exactly two of the 84-year cycles used for calculating the date of Easter on
which the annals were based, so that the entry is at the right position in
the wrong cycle, we may have a record of the C-tribes' ultimate vengeance,
though it does not seem to have destroyed the hegemony of Fortriu.[66] The

---

[64] *ES*, i, 61; Adomnán, *Columba*, 126–7 (II. 23). The death of Cennalath (*Ann. Ulster*,
580) is discussed by Wainwright, 'Picts', 21, and his reign four years before Bridei
and one year 'with' him in footnotes in Anderson, *Kings and Kingship*, 116, 130. It
is possible that a scribe assimilated the epithet (if as the earlier king-lists suggest it
was such to the name *Galam*) to Irish *cennalad*, 'particoloured head' (ibid., 91
n.55), but dare one suggest that the original Irish form translating a Pictish epithet
might have been *cennchalad*, 'hard-headed' – or 'king of the Caledonians'? This
would go some way towards explaining why the corresponding name in the other
set of lists is *Tagalad* (F and I), or a related form.

[65] *ES*, i, 118.

[66] O'Rahilly, *Early Irish History*, 508; cf. Anderson, *Kings and Kingship*, 36–7. The
entry in *Ann. Ulster*, 584, records *Mors Bruide mc. Maelcon*, which would not
normally suggest death in battle; Tigernach says he fell (*cecidit*) in the battle, using
the term one would expect, but possibly he literally fell, wounded, and died later
of his wounds.

battle of Dunnichen against the Northumbrians 101 years later was fought on what must surely have been the territory of *Circinn*, west of Forfar, but *Tigernach* calls the victor Bridei son of Bile 'king of Fortriu', as the *Annals of Ulster* do at his death.[67] Very possibly it was the external threat of Northumbrian conquest that ensured a final armistice in the feud between the two groups of Picts.

There is also a tradition preserved in the Irish genealogies that there was a branch of the Eoganacht, the royal line of Munster, the Eoganacht of *Mag Gergind* in Alba, to which Oengus king of Alba (presumably one or other of the kings of Picts and Scots known to Gaels as Oengus son of Fergus) belonged.[68] It is difficult to identify *Mag Gergind* as anywhere but a plain in *Circinn*, probably the Howe of the Mearns, and it has been suggested that Angus, the major part of ancient *Circinn*, is called after king Oengus.[69] However their ancestor belongs to the mythical stratum and his great-nephews are described as contemporaries of St Patrick, so he may represent an alliance rather than actual immigration after the time of St Columba. The genealogies also mention an even earlier connection between the Eoganacht and the men of the Lennox,[70] and I think all we can deduce is that individual Munster noblemen may have settled, perhaps as mercenaries like the later galloglasses, in Strathclyde and Pictland, and their provincial kings therefore took an interest in the affairs of this distant region.

It is likely enough that dissension among the Picts made both sides encourage Gaelic settlers who could help in war, and though we may dismiss several of Watson's suggested Gaelic names in Pictland,[71] there is no need to doubt that there was both clerical and lay penetration. 'What happened to the Picts?' is not the question I set out to answer, but I would like to finish by trying to clarify what did *not* happen under Kenneth mac Alpín. The first point that needs to be made is that neither Kenneth's name nor that of his father is Gaelic. The Old Irish form which gives English Kenneth, *Cinaed*, is accepted by Brian Ó Cuív in the only authoritative recent study of early Gaelic personal names as being of

---

67 *ES*, i, 192–3; *Ann. Ulster*, 693.
68 *Corpus Genealogiarum Hiberniae*, ed. M. A. O'Brien, vol. I (Dublin 1962), 196. See details in O'Rahilly, *Early Irish History*, 370–2.
69 Ibid., 371 n.3. Anderson, *Kings and Kingship*, 188, seems to reject this because it would not be of the same date as names like Cowal or Lorn, a strange piece of reasoning.
70 O'Brien, *Corpus Genealogiarum Hiberniae*, 358; the lines 'meet at' the fictional *Éber*, one of the first Gaels to land in Ireland according to the pseudo-historians!
71 See note 32 above. Gowrie similarly need not be connected to Gabrán father of Aedán (Watson, *Celtic Place-Names*, 112–13): the Gaelic name, and possibly a Pictish cognate, simply suggests a good area for horses.

Pictish origin.[72] It is an anomalous name, apparently meant to be stressed
on the last syllable, which did not survive much beyond the eleventh
century in either Scottish or Irish Gaelic. The name translated as Kenneth
since written records began in Scottish Gaelic is a superficially similar
form better adapted to the sound-system of Gaelic, *Coinneach*, derived
from Old Irish *Cainnech* (meaning 'nice person'), the name of a contemporary of St Columba usually called in Ireland St Canice. The original
form of the royal name Kenneth simply could not survive in Gaelic: but it
was quite fashionable, perhaps romantically exotic, among the Irish
aristocracy about Kenneth mac Alpín's own time, and on its own would
not prove that he was not a Gael. His father's name Alpín or Elpín,
however, contains a *p* and is clearly not of Q-Celtic origin: it is almost
certainly the Pictish cognate of the Welsh name Elffin.[73] The fact that
three kings of Dál Riata, all called Alpín son of Eochaid, appear at
different places in the king-list and nowhere in the annals, suggests that
royal genealogists a century or more after Kenneth's own time made two
botched attempts to attach his father to the Dalriadic royal line before
coming up with a more plausible third: the name consistently given for his
grandfather, Eochaid, is certainly Gaelic in form but may translate a
Pictish cognate, like Oengus for Onuist.[74]

No text which hails Kenneth as first Gaelic king of Alba can be shown
to be earlier than the tenth century, and as we have noticed already the
annals continue to describe him and his successors as *rex Pictorum* until his
grandson Donald son of Constantine is called *rí Alban* on his death in 900.
(Constantine is a name used by Welsh and Pictish, not Irish kings, and
Domnall, 'Donald', certainly has a Welsh cognate, Dyfnwal, and probably
had a Pictish one.) Molly Miller has drawn attention to the nature of the
succession in these years, which follows a Pictish pattern, brothers
succeeding brothers, rather than the typical Gaelic pattern of cousins
succeeding cousins, often by killing them (so that a brother may eventually

---

[72] At least he doubts the suggestion that it could go back to Latin *cinaedus*,
'sodomite, catamite', and offers no other alternative but Pictish origin: B. Ó Cuív,
'Aspects of Irish Personal Names', *Celtica*, xviii (1986) 162. Cinaed is treated as a
compound of the common Gaelic name Aed, 'fire', borne by Kenneth mac
Alpín's younger son and later by the ancestor of the Mackays: see O'Rahilly,
Early Irish History, 362–3. This suggests that even in Irish it might have been
stressed on the final syllable, though forms apparently closer to the Pictish such as
Ciniod have a quite different version of this.

[73] See O'Rahilly, *Early Irish History*, 362–3, who suggests that the Welsh name is a
borrowing from the Pictish and may be ultimately from the name of Clodius
Albinus, the second-century Roman governor of Britain.

[74] See Anderson, *Kings and Kingship*, 46, 182–3, 195–6, and index, for the three
Alpíns, one of whom she suggests was also a king of the Picts.

succeed his brother after avenging his death).[75] This became the pattern among Kenneth's descendants in the tenth century, after a final recurrence of the original Pictish style of inheritance through the mother which brought Eochaid son of Rhun of Strathclyde to the throne under the tutelage of the mysterious 'Giric son of Dúngal', who I suspect was actually his Strathclyde Welsh great-uncle.[76] It seems to have been in reaction to this Welsh take-over that the Gaelic nature of the succession and indeed the kingship of 'Alba' was definitively established.

What happened in or around the years 842 to 848 is difficult to reconstruct, but it is unlikely to have been an invasion of dominant Pictland by the king of a Dál Riata which had virtually become a Pictish province over the previous hundred years,[77] followed by a genocide which wiped out the Picts and their language at one stroke. It must have involved some change great enough to be seen in retrospect as a turning-point in what was surely a process of gradual infiltration, at first by Gaelic clerics with new beliefs and Gaelic warriors with new fighting skills, not by peasants, followed by a gradual spread down the social scale of the new language that need not have been complete even by the eleventh century, since it left no record. The inheritance of the Pictish throne by a Scot with an improbably Pictish name and patronymic through his mother, even if the Picts had not apparently by that date given up much of their matrilineal

---

75 M. Miller, 'The last century of Pictish succession', *Scottish Studies*, xxiii (1979), 39–67.

76 The patronymic is Dúngal in most lists, Domnall in a sub-group: Anderson, *Kings and Kingship*, 71. Smyth, *Warlords and Holy Men*, 215–21, simply ignores the usual form and identifies Domnall as Kenneth mac Alpín's brother. However, early Welsh Dumnagual, later Dyfnwal, resembles Irish Dúngal on paper but is actually cognate with Domnall and might be translated as such by a bilingual scholar: this could explain the confusion. Dumnagual was the name of the father of Artgal of Strathclyde, killed in 872 'on the advice of Constantine son of Kenneth' (Smyth *Warlords and Holy Men*, 64, 215), and Giric who killed Constantine's brother Aed in 878 could well have been Artgal's avenging brother, who added old-style legitimacy to his reign in Pictland by nominally sharing it with his great-nephew, the small son of Aed's sister. His name, Ciricius in the Poppleton MS (Anderson, *Kings and Kingship*, 251), is no doubt the Welsh version of the name of St Cyriacus seen in the place-name Capel Curig in Gwynedd.

77 This is the fairly obvious reading of the evidence by W. F. Skene, *Celtic Scotland* (Edinburgh 1876–80), i, 292–308. Anderson, *Kings and Kingship*, 188–95, claims that it has been discredited; but this depends entirely on the author's determination to find some truth in the obviously confused and faked genealogies of the Dalriadan kings after 741. Why, for example, does she allow 'the eighth-century Oengus son of Forgus' to be a Pict, but insist on making his 9th-century namesake son of a Dalriadan Fergus? (For the nature of the confusion between Forggus, the exact equivalent of Pictish Uurguist, and the more usual Gaelic Fergus, see O'Rahilly, *Early Irish History*, 368 n.3.) Anderson also chooses to overlook the difference between the names *Eochu* and *Eochaid*.

system, would not mark such a turning-point; indeed Alfred Smyth's suggestion that Kenneth's brother Donald (if not himself) may have had a Norse mother is intriguing, though the evidence for this, the epithet which seems to describe Kenneth's brother in the prophecy of Berchan,[78] is from a source at least two centuries later, and 820 or so seems very early for the Norse raiders to have brought women with them. The legend accepted by Irish writers a century or two later, *Braflang Scóine*, 'the Pitfall of Scone', where the Pictish nobles were invited to a feast and dropped into a pit below the tables when drunk, has been shown to be an old fable used to account for a swift reversal of fortune, first recorded by Herodotus of the Medes' defeat of their Scythian conquerors and later attached mainly to rapid conquests, notably Hengist's murder of the British nobles at a peace conference in Nennius and Geoffrey of Monmouth.[79] It does however suggest that Kenneth won his throne by force of arms against the opposition of most of the Picts; so do the king-lists which name other Pictish kings between 842 and 848.[80]

It is beginning to seem that what we may be looking at is the success of a rebel or exiled Pict, not necessarily a member of any recognised line of under-kings, very possibly with support from the Scots among whom his line was exiled, and perhaps, as fairly early sources say, taking advantage of a recent defeat of the Pictish royal forces by Norse invaders.[81] Once he came to power, Kenneth mac Alpín could not claim to be the legitimate heir to the kingdom of Fortriu, but there was no strongly supported claimant to the throne of Dál Riata either, where the last king recorded in the annals had died in 792 and the credible genealogical record arguably ran out as long ago as 696.[82] Kenneth may have been related, perhaps in the female line (which would give him no claim at all by Irish law), to

---

78 Smyth, *Warlords and Holy Men*, 190–1.
79 Herodotus, *The Histories*, trans. A. de Selincourt (Harmondsworth 1954), 57; Geoffrey of Monmouth, *The History of the Kings of Britain*, trans. L. Thorpe (Harmondsworth 1966), 164–5. See full discussion in Mac Cana, *Learned Tales of Medieval Ireland*, 142–5 (Appendix B), and further parallels listed by Miller, 'Last century of Pictish succession', 50 and n. 27.
80 Anderson, *Kings and Kingship*, 197, 233.
81 *Ann. Ulster*, 839: see Smyth, *Warlords and Holy Men*, 180, and Anderson, *Kings and Kingship*, 195, for two rather different estimates of the part played by this defeat in Kenneth's (or his father's) success.
82 Anderson, *Kings and Kingship*, 179–95. 'The pedigree of Aed Find is not above all possible doubt' (ibid., 189), and most of his predecessors were of Cenél Loairn, whose relationship in the genealogies to earlier Dalriadan kings of Cenél nGabráin is probably an invention (Bannerman, *Dalriada*, 121–32). Indeed, since the modern Gaelic form of the place-name Lorn is *Latharna*, the same as the early Irish tuath to the south of Dál Riata, around Larne, it is tempting to wonder whether they were Dál Riata at all or settlers from a neighbouring 'tribe', and the form Loarn is itself an invention to muddy the record.

some branch of a Dalriadic royal line, or he may simply have had Scottish military helpers to reward and the need for the prestige and administrative skills of the Scottish clergy. One of the things Irish clerics and the (by this date) allied bardic class undoubtedly knew how to do was to forge a genealogy, especially when it was to their advantage. It suited everyone to proclaim Kenneth as first Scottish king of a united kingdom, and he sealed the deal, according to the 'Chronicle of the Kings of Alba', by bringing some of the relics of St Columba from Iona, threatened by regular Norse raids, to 'a church which he had built'.[83]

What church this was is not clear, but if it had been at the established religious centres of St Andrews or Abernethy it is surprising that the name was not mentioned. In fact the only place mentioned in connection with Kenneth by the Chronicle is Forteviot (*Fothíurtabaicht*), depicted in some later traditions as an important residence of the kings of the Picts, specifically perhaps the main centre of Fortriu, where he is said to have died. The legend mentioned above connects the beginning of his reign with Scone, whose importance as an inaugural site for all Pictland could be conjectured to date back to the time of the Caledonians,[84] though it is not mentioned in any source demonstrably older than the tenth century. Kenneth's new church, however, may have been further north again, at Dunkeld as Skene conjectured: indeed it seems quite possible that the name of Dunkeld, which appears a line or two below in the MS as one of two limits of 'Danish' devastation, has been misplaced by scribal error.[85] A few years later its abbot was already 'principal bishop of Fortriu' according to the *Annals of Ulster*, and the attribution of its foundation to an earlier king of the Picts, Constantin son of Uurguist, rests on fairly flimsy evidence.[86]

If Dunkeld was the site Kenneth mac Alpín chose to found his church,

---

[83] Anderson, *Kings and Kingship*, 250. This chronicle is also known as the 'Scottish Chronicle', the 'Old Scottish Chronicle' and the 'Pictish Chronicle'; cf. Dauvit Broun's essay, above, at note 9.

[84] The choice of Scone as an inaugural site could well date back to a time when the over-kingship of the Picts was shared in some way by Fortriu and Caledonians, since it must have been close to the boundary of their territories: cf. Anderson, *Kings and Kingship*, 141, noting a conflict between the two versions of *De situ Albanie* on which kingdom included Gowrie and Scone with it.

[85] See Skene, *Celtic Scotland*, i, 305, 310. Smyth, *Warlords and Holy Men*, 186–8, brings together the main references to Dunkeld in the 9th century.

[86] Anderson, *Kings and Kingship*, 174, 194. *Ann. Ulster*, 865, records not only the death of this *Tuathal m. Artgusso* (the names could be Gaelicised Pictish ones) *prim-epscop Fortrenn & abbas Duin Caillenn*, but also that of Cellach son of Ailill, abbot of Kildare and Iona, *in regione Pictorum*, which suggests that the connection between Iona and Pictland remained a strong one after Kenneth's death.

rather than bringing the relics to an established church in Fortriu[87] or Fife, is it coincidence that he chose the place that still bore the name of the Caledonians? It may seem a romantic fantasy to suggest that he may still have been proud after nearly three centuries to trace his descent, whether in the female or the male line, from a Caledonian survivor who perhaps took refuge among the Scots, or perhaps in *Circinn* or some part of the Highlands where neither the king of Fortriu nor the king of Dál Riata had much authority. But is it more fantastic than accepting that this nobleman – who need not have been too poor to keep a family bard and genealogist – with his Pictish name and patronymic, could trace descent in the male line from Aedán son of Gabrán of Dál Riata at the same period?

[87] Abernethy, near the mouth of the Earn, is now in Perthshire rather than Fife and presumably belonged to Fortriu, the kingdom whose centre was Strathearn.

4

The Battle of Dunnichen and the Aberlemno Battle-Scene[1]

GRAEME D. R. CRUICKSHANK

Historians of the medieval period have available to them documentary sources other than writings on parchment and vellum. One such document is a slab of sandstone, standing over seven feet high (see page 77 below), located in the churchyard of the hamlet of Aberlemno, which lies halfway between Forfar and Brechin in the county of Angus, in east-central Scotland. It is a product of Pictish craftmanship, and belongs to the middle phase of their stone-cut art which was prevalent in the seventh and eighth centuries AD. Uniquely, this stone illustrates a battle, and the purpose of the present enquiry is two-fold: to examine and analyse the various incidents which comprise the scene of conflict depicted, and to make a case for regarding this scene as the portrayal of an actual historical event – the battle of 685 which was known to the Scots as *Duin Neachtain*, to the Britons as *Lin Garan*, to the Angles as *Nechtanesmere*, and to present-day historians as Dunnichen. To that end, it is also necessary to study the battle itself.

Of course, comprehending the battle of Dunnichen being played out across a sheet of sandstone in Aberlemno churchyard requires a sympathetic appreciation of the content, the meaning, the execution, and the dating of this piece of sculpture. Those who seek proof that this is indeed the battle in question are liable to be forever disappointed, for there are too many imponderables and uncertainties for this view to be put forward dogmatically. However, by pointing out all the factors in favour of this interpretation, an argument can be presented which may be regarded as compellingly persuasive.

---

[1] Both of the principal topics examined in this article have been written up in considerably more detail by the author: *The Battle of Dunnichen*, in summary form, was published in 1991, a new edition of which is currently in press, and a comprehensive study is in the course of preparation; while an exhaustive study of *The Aberlemno Battle-Scene* is due for imminent publication. In both instances, the publisher is the Pinkfoot Press, the leading publisher of Pictish material, which is happily situated two miles from Dunnichen and three miles from Aberlemno: The Pinkfoot Press, Balgavies Farm Cottage, by Forfar, Angus, DD8 2TH.

The key to the conflict between the Picts and the Northumbrians, which reached its climax at the battle of Dunnichen, lay in the disappearance of *Gododdin*; this was the name of the territory, and also of the people who occupied it, which lay in the area of what was to become the Lothians, though probably extending west and south of the boundaries of the modern counties. The *Gododdin* suffered a major catastrophe around the year 600 when its heroic warband marched out of *Din Eidyn* (Edinburgh) and into Northumbrian territory, only to be almost totally annihilated at *Catraeth* (Catterick). The story is told in the epic heroic poem *Y Gododdin* by Aneirin, who was said to be the sole survivor of the campaign.[2] With *Gododdin* on the wane, the question was which of its neighbours would move in and annex the territory. The cousins of the *Gododdin*, the Britons of Strathclyde, were pinned back by the remorseless Northumbrian advance in the west. Alarmed by this, the Scots of Dál Riata marched to repel them, but were decisively defeated at the battle of Degastan in 603. This left the Northumbrians as the obvious power to take over the *Gododdin* territory, and during the next few decades they pursued their objective of capturing its key strongholds, which climaxed in the siege and fall of *Din Eidyn* in 638. Its north-western extension of *Manau* may have held out a little longer, but was under Northumbrian control by the middle of the century.

This meant that the Picts and the Northumbrians now had some form of common border: they would have faced each other across the Firth of Forth, and they would have been even closer up-river in the Stirling area. Warfare was inevitable – but not immediate. The reason, at least in part, was the blood relationship which existed between one royal lineage of the Picts and that of the Northumbrians. Eanfrith, who had ruled in Northumbria in 632, had earlier married a Pictish princess. This important dynastic marriage had a very important result: if the succession of the Pictish kingship was open to female descent,[3] a son of this Northumbrian prince could become a Pictish king, and so indeed it transpired. Talorcan, who became king of the Picts in 658, had for an uncle Oswiu, the powerful and aggressive king of the Northumbrians, whose influence must have been considerable. He may well have assisted Talorcan to gain the throne during an unsettled period in Pictland, and supported him in

---

[2] For further details, see K. Jackson, *The Gododdin: The oldest Scottish Poem* (Edinburgh 1969); A. Jarman, *Aneurin, Y Gododdin: Britain's oldest heroic Poem* (Llandysul 1988); and *The Triumph Tree: Scotland's Earliest Poetry, AD 550–1350*, ed. T. O. Clancy (Edinburgh 1998), 46–78.

[3] The Pictish succession system has generally been taken to have been matrilinear; but see, now, A. Woolf, 'Pictish matriliny reconsidered', *Innes Review*, xlix (1998), 147–67.

his victory over the Scots about that time. Northumbria thus gained a measure of control over Pictland, but Talorcan died in 662, and during the remaining eight years of Oswiu's reign, such understandings may well have turned into resented obligations. There is a strong suspicion that Talorcan's successors, the brothers Gartnait and Drest, sons of Donuel, were also placed on the throne at Oswiu's instigation, and made to rule successively for at least a decade as Northumbrian puppet-kings.[4]

There can be no doubt that a sizeable part of Pictland lay under Northumbrian control. Just what form this took is uncertain; it may have been military occupation, or alternatively the exaction of tribute perhaps backed up by the holding of hostages. Whatever it was, the southern Picts had become an oppressed people; nor were they alone, for the Britons of Strathclyde had been in a similar position for some time, and the Scots of Dál Riata were also in like circumstances. The power of Northumbria appeared to grow unchallenged throughout northern Britain.

This situation was to change dramatically following the death of Oswiu in 670. He was succeeded by his son, Ecgfrith, though it seems that there was an initial period of readjustment before the new king assumed full control. Although we have no details, it would appear that the Picts took advantage of the brief unsettling effect of the change in Northumbrian leadership to make an attempt to 'throw off the yoke of slavery', as it was expressed a few years later by Eddius Stephanus.[5] Whatever the precise nature of the Pictish initiative, it infuriated Ecgfrith, who decided to forestall any planned or incipient rebellion by attacking the Picts with ruthless ferocity. The battle took place in *c.*672, on the Plain of *Manau* (in the vicinity of the modern Grangemouth), and resulted in a horrendous defeat for the Picts; the gruesome account of Eddius says that two rivers were filled with the corpses of the Pictish dead, so that the Northumbrians were able to cross over dry-shod to pursue and kill great numbers of the fugitives. Thus the Picts in the area of Northumbrian control were again reduced to a state of slavery.

The new Pictish king, Bridei son of Bile, faced an immense task. For a start, recovering from such appalling losses would have been a slow process. We do not know which king was on the throne at the time of the horrendous defeat of *c.*672: had it still been Drest, that would surely have led to his expulsion, which occurred about then, and Bridei's first task would have been to restore some measure of confidence among his shattered people. On the other hand, if Drest had already been expelled

---

[4] For a perceptive insight into this fluid period of Pictish history, see M. Miller, 'Eanfrith's Pictish son', *Northern History*, xiv (1978), 47–66.

[5] *The Life of Bishop Wilfrid by Eddius Stephanus*, ed. B. Colgrave (Cambridge 1927), ch. 19.

and Bridei had led the Picts to such a disastrous defeat, he would have had the additional problem of re-establishing his own credibility as a military leader. It is therefore not surprising that a dozen years elapsed before he felt sufficiently confident in both his own situation, and that of his people, to launch a bid to regain his nation's freedom. It seems likely, however, that by 685 Bridei had forged Pictland into a single kingdom, and established his own position as king of all the Picts, ready and able to challenge the power of Ecgfrith. Nothing has been recorded to indicate the reasons which impelled Ecgfrith to invade Pictland at this time, but it may well have been the same type of circumstances which had prevailed a dozen years earlier. The scene was set for one of the biggest clashes of arms in the history of 'Dark Age' Britain.

In the late spring of 685, Ecgfrith, the king of the Northumbrians, led his army north to do battle with the Picts under their king, Bridei. The precise location where the conflict occurred is not known with absolute certainty, but it is reasonable to assume that Ecgfrith marched through and beyond the area of southern Pictland under Northumbrian control, which doubtless meant proceeding north of both the Forth and the Tay. His most likely route would then have taken him up Strathmore, but it appears that he deviated eastwards somewhere in the region of Forfar, and headed for Dunnichen.[6] The reason for this may be contained in Bede's account of the conflict, in which he relates how the Picts feigned flight, and lured the Northumbrians into mountainous country.

The employment of such a judicious strategy by Bridei would have demonstrated his determination to avoid the mistakes of the previous encounter which had ended in catastrophe. It is therefore reasonable to suppose that the Picts had a plan to bring them victory. The battle of c.672 had been fought on flat land, where large armies could be marshalled and deployed; this time the Northumbrians would be forced to fight on Bridei's choice of territory, which was distinctly different. The words of Bede suggest how this was achieved: a small part of the Pictish army showed itself to the invaders, and then pretended to run from them, drawing them after in pursuit, in the hope of an easy victory. The idea would have been to lure the enemy into an ambush, making full use of the local topography to entrap them and help secure their defeat. If events transpired as suggested here, the Northumbrians, in hot pursuit, burst through the defile where the modern hamlet of Dunnichen now stands, only to find the Picts, whom they had imagined to be in full flight,

---

6 A slightly different location has recently been suggested in L. Alcock, 'The site of the "battle of Dunnichen"', *SHR* lxxv (1996), 130–42. The topographical arguments used are quite persuasive, but in the view of this writer, the place-name connection is a more compelling factor.

standing firm before them. Too late, they saw with dread the ramparts of Dun Nechtan looming above them. A detachment of Picts from the fort swiftly barred the path of their retreat, while the main Pictish host gathered on the brow of the hill, preparing for the onslaught. On their only open side lay the pool and marshland of Nechtan's Mire, which for many of them would soon become a watery grave. The trap could now be sprung.

Of course, such a description of the battle is totally speculative, but it does take account of the local topography, and it represents both the hill-fort and the mire as important factors in the successful outcome of the Pictish victory, which accords with the names given to the engagement in the Irish annals, and an English chronicle, respectively. What we do know with certainty – every source of information about the battle states it – is that the Northumbrians were routed, the majority of their forces, including King Ecgfrith himself, being slain. In one of his lesser works, Bede adds the detail that the royal bodyguard died to a man, vainly fighting to protect their beleaguered monarch. Of the survivors, of which there were not many, most were enslaved by the Picts; only a few struggled back home to break the awesome news to their people.

The battle of Dunnichen represents a mighty clash of arms which can have had few equals in early British history. No indication whatsoever has come down to us regarding the size of the respective armies, but there is little doubt that they would have consisted of the maximum potency which each side could muster. Despite so many uncertainties about the battle, we know one important fact about it with an astonishing degree of accuracy, and that is *when* it was fought. By drawing together a number of references, not all of them relating directly to the battle, it can be stated with confidence that it took place at around three o'clock in the afternoon of Saturday 20 May, 685.

The outcome of the battle of Dunnichen had far-reaching consequences, not only for the Picts and the Northumbrians, but also for their neighbours, and for the future of northern Britain in terms of the development into nationhood of Scotland and England. For the Picts, the greatest of all their victories brought freedom from Northumbrian domination, both actual and threatened. The enemy was driven entirely from Pictland, and whether there had been a physical occupation, a tribute system, or a combination of the two, it was now at an end. The see of Abercorn, established only four years earlier, was abandoned. Thus all the incursions of the Northumbrians, effected during the previous thirty years by dynastic, political, religious, and military means, were brought to nought. Furthermore, it was not only the Picts who benefitted, but also the Scots of Dál Riata and the Britons of Strathclyde; they too had been under some form of Northumbrian domination, and now they also recovered their independence.[7]

The power of Northumbria, and the policy of aggressive expansion which it nurtured, had been checked – permanently, as it turned out – but it had not been broken, and it is something of an irony that, as kingdoms go, Northumbria was to outlast Pictland by several decades. Nor was war ended between the two, for there were to be several more major battles between them, with mixed results. A clash in 698 seems to have given the Picts another victory, though in 711 it was the Northumbrians who triumphed on the Plain of *Manau*, somewhere in the region of their devastating success of half a century earlier. Perhaps when the Pictish king, Nechtan, sent a letter to Abbot Ceolfrith of Jarrow in *c.*715 asking advice on certain matters of Christian doctrine, he was actually making an overture for the establishment of a state of peaceful co-existence.

If Bridei indeed had a plan to bring victory in battle against the Northumbrians, then it is reasonable to suppose that he also had a series of objectives in mind should he gain the victory. It can be no more than unverifiable speculation, but in practical terms, he may have formulated these five aims: to avenge the horrendous defeat of *c.*672; to prevent any more of Pictland falling under Northumbrian control; to liberate that part of Pictland which had already come under Northumbrian domination; to place a permanent check upon the Northumbrian policy of territorial expansion at the expense of Pictland; and to establish a southern boundary which would not be subject to the threat of continued Northumbrian aggression. It may be reckoned that Bridei scored four and a half out of five, and considering the scale of the battle, a success rating in the region of 90% must represent a major achievement. The consequences of this success were vital for the future nationhood of Scotland.

Any attempt to construct the story of the battle of Dunnichen must of necessity rest on flimsy foundations. The main problem is a dearth of primary historical sources. Only four sources[8] can claim to be anything like contemporary, and the sum total of information they contain is meagre. We must lean heavily on the account of the battle given by Bede in his *Historia Ecclesiastica Gentis Anglorum*, which he completed in 731. Annoyingly incomplete and brief it may be, but it is by far the most detailed and valuable historical source that exists. Using only phrases where sentences would have been so much more informative, Bede nonetheless contrives to describe Ecgfrith's attitude, the terrain he

---

[7] Bede, *HE*, 429 (IV. 26).

[8] Adomnán, *Columba*, 178–9 (II.46); *Vita Sancti Cuthberti Auctore Anonymo*, ch. 8, and *Vita Sancti Cuthberti Auctore Beda*, ch. 24, both in *Two Lives of Saint Cuthbert*, ed. B. Colgrave (Cambridge 1940); *Life of Bishop Wilfrid by Eddius Stephanus*, ch. 44.

encountered, the Pictish tactics, the outcome of the conflict, the exact date, and the consequences of the Northumbrian defeat. Even though he may have had mixed feelings about the fate of Ecgfrith, Bede can only have grieved over the catastrophe which befell the Northumbrian forces. He was, after all, a Northumbrian, and alive at the time of the battle – he would have been a boy of about twelve years of age. This may account for his failure to give details, even important ones such as the name of the victorious Pictish king and the place where this momentous event occurred.

It is left to the next layer of historical record to provide a name for the battle, and while such sources are not contemporary with the event, they give the impression of drawing upon material which was. As the battle was fought in Pictish territory, and the Picts were the victors, their name should be the one we use, but they have left no written record of the battle, and so we must turn to English chronicles and Irish annals. The *Historia Brittonum* of *Nennius* calls it *Gueith Lin Garan*, 'the Battle of the Pool of the Heron'.[9] This seems to have come by way of the Britons of Strathclyde and may be close to, or even the same as, the name used by the Picts themselves. Three Irish annals – the *Annals of Ulster*, the *Annals of Tigernach*, and the *Fragmentary Irish Annals* – favour *Cath Duin Neachtain* (with variations), 'the Battle of Dun Nechtan'.[10] Their entries relating to Scotland seem to be based on a single compilation probably originating on Iona,[11] which suggests that this is how it was known to the Scots. Finally, Simeon of Durham, writing his *History of the Church of Durham*,[12] uses the name *Nechtanesmer*, which presumably was how the battle was known to the Northumbrians. It is the linking of Dun Nechtan with the modern place-name of Dunnichen, as propounded by George Chalmers in his *Caledonia* of 1807,[13] which points to the probable location of the battle.

There is another document which provides a tantalising insight into the background of the battle. It is a fragment of verse which may be contemporary, and which, although not written by a Pict, could have been written in Pictland. It appears to be part of a song of victory in commemoration of the battle and of the victorious king. The twelve lines of verse have been preserved in a document known as the *Fragmentary*

9   *Nennius, British History and The Welsh Annals*, ed. J. Morris (London 1980), 77.
10 *Ann. Ulster*, 685; *Ann. Tigernach*, 686; *Fragmentary Annals of Ireland*, ed. J. N. Radner (Dublin 1978), 685.
11 J. Bannerman, *Studies in the History of Dalriada* (Edinburgh 1974), 9–26.
12 Simeon of Durham, *Historia Dunhelmensis Ecclesiae*, in *Symeonis Monachi Opera Omnia*, ed. T. Arnold (Rolls Ser., 1882–5), i, 32.
13 G. Chalmers, *Caledonia* (London, 1807–24), i, 210, 255.

Irish Annals, copied from ancient sources by Duald MacFibris. It is a curious compilation, apparently based as much on legend as on historical fact, and the date of the sources from which these fragments were copied is unknown. The Dunnichen verse is credited to Riaguil of Bennchor, an Irish cleric who was seemingly in Pictland at the time of the battle. However, it has proved awkward to translate, and the several enigmas which it contains provoke further questions, rather than supply answers.[14]

It is a matter of lasting sorrow that no records written by the Picts themselves have survived which tell of their feelings about the battle of Dunnichen: how they planned to overcome the might of the Northumbrians, how they achieved their victory, how they viewed its significance, and how they celebrated the devastating manner of its achievement. No parchment or vellum text has survived, but this deficiency of history may be compensated for in the form of a dramatic narrative scene carved in stone.

The Pictish monolith which currently stands in Aberlemno Churchyard is a masterpiece of stone-cut art. On one side of the great slab there appears what is arguably the finest example of a Pictish cross, while on the other side, the stone bears witness to a battle – the only rendition of such a subject in the whole field of Pictish art. It is important to recognise the unique status of this battle-scene. It is not a hunting scene, nor a parade scene, both of which feature quite frequently on Pictish stones; nor does it show warriors either on their way to battle, or in the aftermath of battle – two interpretations which have appeared in print. What is depicted here is a battle in progress, and this is the only Pictish stone to illustrate such an occurrence. (One other stone is comparable – Sueno's Stone, near Forres – but it can be argued that it is not truly Pictish, nor does its martial content constitute a battle.)

14 The Dunnichen victory song has proved notoriously difficult to translate. The version offered below is taken from *The Battle of Dunnichen* (see note 1, above), 22–3. A detailed consideration of the options and their historical implications is in the course of preparation.

> This day Bridei fights a battle
> for the heritage of his grandfather,
>
> Unless the son of God wills it otherwise,
> he will die in it;
>
> This day the son of Oswiu has been struck down
> in a battle against blue swords,
>
> Although he has spoken penitence,
> it is penitence too late;
>
> This day the son of Oswiu has been struck down,
> who had the black draughts,
>
> Christ heard our supplications,
> they spared Bridei the brave.

The Aberlemno Stone

What we witness at Aberlemno is a scene showing warriors engaged in warfare. At least two-thirds of these men are in the act of using their weapons against other men, or have adopted aggressive postures towards them, and there are at least two instances of armed engagement between adversaries. These men are warriors in action; this scene indubitably shows a battle. Moreover, the portrayal is so realistic that it is not difficult to regard what is shown here as a real battle – no imagined happening, but a rendition of an actual historical event. It then becomes tempting to regard this as a lithic record of the battle of Dunnichen.

The tableau consists of nine fighting men – five on horseback, three on foot, and one other. It is readily apparent that what is shown is not the general mêlée of a free-for-all fight, but an engagement between two defined sides, at least one of which has assumed a pre-planned formation. The most obvious way of telling the sides apart is that one grouping of men is bare-headed, while the other grouping wears helmets. The helmeted and unhelmeted men are separated by a clear, though unmarked, roughly vertical division, with the latter on the left and the former on the right. As this is a Pictish stone (and should there be any doubt, the two great symbols which surmount the battle-scene demonstrate this to be so), then it is reasonable to assume that at least one of these groupings is Pictish. The archaeological record, admittedly very weak for Pictish times, has not revealed any trace of Pictish helmets, nor do helmeted men appear on any other Pictish stone.[15] Indeed, Picts are characteristically portrayed on a great many stones as having long, flowing hair and pointed beards, appearing just as the left-side group does at Aberlemno, and therefore we may safely assume that these five helmetless soldiers are Picts.

It follows that the four helmeted soliders on the right are not Pictish, and therefore this scene cannot represent any internal power struggle within Pictland. This raises the crucial question: who are these foreign warriors, seen doing battle with the Picts? The Scots of Dál Riata might be considered as contenders, but there is no evidence that their soldiers wore helmets either. The Picts' other major adversaries were the Northumbrians, and here the physical remains of antiquity can be of vital assistance. The four helmets carved on the Aberlemno stone, all depicted in profile, are shown sufficiently clearly to indicate certain points of detail. The most obvious feature is that each one is fitted with a prominent nasal – a metal nose-guard which affords some protection for the face without obscuring vision to any great extent – which here has a pronounced outward slant. The line of each helmet shows a

---

15 For a full discussion of this topic, see G. D. R. Cruickshank, 'Did the Picts wear helmets?', *Pictish Arts Society Journal*, v (1994), 8–11; C. Cessford, 'Pictish helmets', *Pictish Arts Society Journal*, vi (1994), 33–4; G. D. R. Cruickshank, 'Of Pictish helmets and other objects', *Pictish Arts Society Journal*, vii (1995), 23–8.

broadening in both directions as it reaches the lower back of the head, suggesting the attachment of cheek-guards and a neck guard. The helmets also appear to be quite high, possibly indicating a crest or ridge on top.

An essential clue as to their origin is provided by the Franks Casket.[16] This is an oblong box made of cetacian bone, and the stylistic treatment of its intricate carving has led scholars to believe that it was made in Northumbria, and to ascribe to it a date of around 700. The casket (which was presented to the British Museum by Sir Augustus Franks in 1867) provides an intriguing link with the Aberlemno battle-scene, for three of the scenes depict soldiers wearing helmets which possess, to a certain extent, the characteristics described above. Each has a very prominent nasal, and neck and cheek protection; in addition, two have pronounced crests. The appearance of these three soldiers on the Franks Casket provides a good case for claiming that the helmets depicted on the Aberlemno stone came from Northumbria, and, by extension, such a deduction would also apply to those who are seen wearing them.

What would strengthen the case greatly would be the discovery of an actual example of this type of helmet, and by a stroke of good fortune we have just that. In 1982, during excavations for a new building at the Coppergate in York – the old capital of Northumbria – a digging machine chanced to uncover a plank-lined pit containing, among other objects, what appeared to be a helmet. After long and meticulous conservation, the details of this fine helmet could be studied.[17] Three features link it decisively with the helmets on the Aberlemno stone: a prominent nasal, hinged cheek-guards, and a mail neck-guard. Also, a band of decorated metal runs over the top, giving it a crest of sorts. When the helmet was buried in c.890, it was already quite old, as evidenced by clear signs of both heavy wear and repair.

The nasal is of particular interest, supporting an outstandingly beautiful example of decorative brasswork. This cast brass mount bears a pair of confronted intertwined biped creatures. Each animal is characterised by a set of long jaws with bulbous ends, a high rounded forehead, and a tapering body the hindquarters of which develop into interlace. On art-historical grounds, this can be used to date the helmet, and taking into account its archaeological context and comparisons with somewhat similar European examples as well, it may be regarded as dating from the period 750–75. It is quite possible that very similar helmets with nasals, though lacking such elaborate nasal-mounts, were in use at a slightly earlier period, making them roughly contemporary with the battle. The Coppergate

---

16 J. Beckwith, *Ivory Carvings in Early Medieval England* (London, 1972), 117 for description, 13–15 for illustrations.
17 D. Tweddle, *The Coppergate Helmet* (York 1984), *passim*.

Helmet may fall short of providing us with definite proof, but it does offer the strong likelihood that the helmets carved in stone at Aberlemno are Northumbrian, and that the warriors who wear them are Northumbrians.

It is therefore reasonable to suppose that here on the Aberlemno stone we are witness to a military clash between the forces of Pictland and Northumbria. To be commemorated in this way, it must have been a major event – not just in terms of the scale of the conflict, but also regarding the nature of the consequences which stemmed from it. It seems very probable that what we are looking at at Aberlemno is the artistic rendering of an actual battle against the Northumbrians, and one which meant a great deal to the Picts. No conflict better fits the picture than the near-by battle of Dunnichen.

The nine figures of soldiers which appear in the battle-scene are arranged in three registers, though only the second register definitely depicts a single incident; the first one probably does, while the third most likely records two incidents. There is no way of telling how the Pictish sculptor wished this scene to be viewed – as a single scene, as four separate incidents, or as the four-episode development of a single event – for there is not the slightest suggestion of a division anywhere on that area of the stone which bears the figures. It may be valid, then, to regard it as a single scene composed of four incidents.

Incident 1, which occupies the top register, shows a Pictish horseman apparently chasing a Northumbrian horseman from the field of battle. The Pict has his sword raised, holding it vertically in his right hand. The Northumbrian appears to have dropped his weapons in his haste to flee, for behind him, between the two riders, lie what would seem to be his shield and beside it his sword, while in the top-left corner is an object which may be his scabbard. The apparent flight of the Northumbrian is emphasised by the fact that his horse has adopted a sort of leaping motion, doubtless intended to represent a gallop (though we now know, thanks to high-speed photography, that real horses do not gallop in this way or anything like it). While it is not unique – though it is sometimes claimed to be – this leaping horse looks very different from the other horses in the scene with their typical prancing style of trot, and may be regarded as conveying a sense of swiftness and urgency.

However, there are serious inconsistencies with this seemingly straight-forward interpretation. There is another criterion to be considered when dividing the combatants into two sides, and that is the length of the horses' tails. The Pictish horses on the left (whose riders are bare-headed) have full tails, while the Northumbrian horses on the right (whose riders wear distinctive helmets) have trimmed tails – except for the horse in the top-right corner. The rider may be clearly identified as a Northumbrian, yet the horse would appear to be Pictish, both in its overall proportions and by virtue of its full tail. There are problems, too, with the identification of the weapons. A comparison of the dropped shield with the other shields in the scene indicates that it is Pictish, probably belonging to a Pictish horseman, while an analysis of the sword type suggests that this weapon too is Pictish rather than Northumbrian.

These unexpected revelations must cause us to reassess what is happening in this incident. The basic premise already established holds good: a Pictish horseman chases a mounted Northumbrian from the battlefield; but now it is apparent that the latter is not riding his own horse but that of a Pict who has been dismounted and whose sword and shield lie on the ground nearby. The horse's unconventional leg position, possibly suggestive of a rearing motion, may indicate the animal's displeasure at being mounted by an unfamiliar rider, unschooled in the arts of Pictish horsemanship. The use of the rein is relevant here; if the Northumbrian is fleeing on his own horse, he would surely give the animal its head, but by holding the rein taut he is indicating that his priority is to control the horse in an attempt to prevent it from rearing and/or bolting. Because this incident contains a seemingly contradictory helmet/horse connection, it is clear that it does not represent a straightforward contest, as depicted in the two registers below. We are unlikely ever to know precisely what this incident represents, but we are left with the distinct feeling that however enigmatic it may be to the modern observer, it was, by dint of either immediate recognition or tutored instruction, profoundly meaningful to those who viewed it when the design was freshly cut and the stone recently erected, and for a long time thereafter.

Incident 2, which occupies the middle register, shows three Pictish infantrymen being engaged by one Northumbrian horseman. The most intriguing feature of this section of the scene is that it illustrates the Pictish battle tactics. The three Pictish infantrymen stand one behind the other, each seemingly wearing a form of battledress, the garment being more extensive than the normal Pictish tunic. The leading man has his sword in his right hand, raised over his shoulder in an attacking attitude. In his left hand he holds his shield, grasping it by some form of handle located in the centre. He holds his shield out in front of him, with his arm half-extended, and as its boss carries a large spike, it is itself a weapon of some potency.

The second Pictish infantryman may be described (slightly anachronistically) as a pikeman. He wields a large two-handed weapon, designed for thrusting rather than throwing. The manner in which he holds it, with his left (leading) hand gripping from below and his right (trailing) hand gripping from above, suggests that he is preparing for an upward thrust, the action required to unseat an approaching horseman. It must have been a heavy weapon to handle, for its length is greater than his height, and it consists of a robust pole with a large metal head. It requires both hands to hold it horizontally, and yet the pikeman still has the protection of his spiked shield. Presumably some form of strapping, possibly fixed to his shoulder and forearm, holds it in position; indeed, two incised arced lines may be observed, which could represent just such equipment. The reason why the shield of the second infantryman is markedly larger than those of his colleagues, either mounted or on foot, may be because, not being hand-held and consequently more static than the others, it was required to give protective cover to a greater area of his body.

The most illuminating aspect of this incident is the relative positions of the first and second infantrymen. The point of the second man's pike actually extends in front of the shield of his brother in arms, and it would appear that these two foot soldiers – and presumably the whole of the two front ranks – are working in concert. Any attacker would thus have to face three lethal weapons simultaneously: the jabbing spike on the shield of the first infantryman, the slashing sword of the same man, and the thrusting pike of his colleague behind him. Was this the Pictish tactic which wrongfooted the Northumbrians and won the day at Dunnichen?

Behind these two is a third infantryman holding a spear. This appears to be a much lighter weapon than the pike and would be used for either jabbing or throwing at an opponent. Unlike all the other weapons featured in the scene, we cannot be sure how this one was used, as the infantryman holds it vertically in an inert position. However, he is hard up against the frame of the scene, allowing the sculptor no opportunity to show him in action. Perhaps, indeed, he was not active at the time. Being in the third rank, he might have been held in reserve, waiting until the Northumbrian attacker had either committed himself to the engagement or had been repulsed and turned away, at which time he would have thrown his spear. Thus the attacking Northumbrian cavalry might have had to face four weapons wielded by the massed ranks of Pictish infantry: spiked shield, sword, pike, and spear. It might also be significant, in the context of the actual engagement, that the front foot of each infantryman is slightly raised compared with the back one. This may be indicative of a walking motion, doubtless in closed-rank formation, in a very controlled and disciplined fashion, as the Pictish infantry advance to meet the charging Northumbrian cavalry.

All these aspects of the formation and deployment of the Pictish infantry point to the use of carefully devised and well rehearsed tactics. Whether Pictish armies of the period adopted such tactics habitually, or whether they were devised especially for the occasion, we cannot say. It could be that such tactics, if not used before against the Northumbrians, caught them unprepared and unable to offer adequate countermeasures, and thus were an important factor in the defeat of the invaders. Perhaps Bridei was not just a skilled strategist but also an inventive tactician, in which case there would be a double reason to hail him as the architect of the Dunnichen victory.

Incident 3, which occupies most of the bottom register, shows a Pictish horseman and a Northumbrian horseman confronting each other. In his left hand, the Pict holds his round shield; it is seen in profile, as with those of the infantrymen, the spiked boss being especially prominent. In this instance, however, it is not used as a weapon, as the shield is held high and tilted back to protect its bearer from the thrusting spear of his opponent. In his right hand, the Pict holds a javelin. His arm is nearly fully extended backwards, as if just prior to launching his weapon, which is pointed but does not appear to have a flanged head. The Northumbrian who confronts him is virtually an exact copy of the Northumbrian in the previous incident, though his horse is somewhat larger than that of his compatriot above. He approaches in an aggressive attitude: in his right hand, he holds aloft a spear, his positioning suggesting that he is about to hurl it, or at least thrust with it, at his opponent. On his left arm, he carries a small round shield, which lacks any indication of having a spiked boss, while by his left flank hangs his sword.

Having these two horsemen in direct opposition to each other allows two interesting and perhaps highly significant comparisons to be made. One concerns the standard of horsemanship exhibited by the respective riders, in particular the use of reins to control their horses. That the Pict commands a superior technique is readily apparent. This may be shown for propaganda reasons, though if it is an accurate rendition of the relative skills of the two sets of horsemen, then it has profound implications for the conduct and outcome of the battle. The Pict rides with a loose rein, which he does not even hold, yet his horse is collected and controlled. The Pictish rider achieves this by the use of his legs, a technique which must have required much practice to perfect. The important consequence of this equine mastery is that it leaves both hands free to deploy his javelin and shield; he is thus able to attack and defend simultaneously.

The Northumbrian, by contrast, rides with a taut rein, this being emphasised by the posture of his horse's head, which is held much more vertically than that of his opponent's horse. He presumably holds the rein in his left hand. He wields a spear in his right hand, but his shield lies inert on his left arm. Although he can attack, he cannot also defend very effectively. Thus the Pict is well equipped to ward off the Northumbrian's spear and to hurl his own javelin with a higher degree of expectation that it will reach its mark. It would therefore seem that the Pictish cavalry, as well as the Pictish infantry, were employing cleverly devised and well rehearsed tactics to confound and defeat their enemy. Indeed, there is more than a suggestion of a symbiotic relationship between the Pictish rider and his horse; this could have been the trump card played by the Picts in the clash at Dunnichen.

The other comparison which this incident readily allows, even invites, is the distinction which may be observed between the Pictish and Northumbrian horses. The contrast between the full tail of the Pictish horse and the trimmed tail of the Northumbrian animal has already been mentioned, but there are other differences of much greater significance. The Pictish horse is of light weight, well balanced, and has a sprightly air. The disparity between this and the Northumbrian horse is very evident, and it may clearly be seen that the latter is a much heavier animal, this being particularly noticeable in the size of its neck and of its rump, and it also has a longer body. The obvious deduction is that the Picts had succeeded in refining their breed into a dextrous and adroit animal, well adapted to close-quarter fighting, whereas the Northumbrian animal, while being considerably more powerful, appears to be much less agile, and if the battle was indeed fought on the margins of a mire, then lightness of foot and ease of manoeuvrability would have been critical factors.

Incident 4 occupies the bottom-right corner of the lower register, and shows an unnaturally large unmounted Northumbrian in close proximity to a large bird. The man is wearing the typical Northumbrian helmet with nasal, and his round shield lies close to him, but there is no sign of any weapons. He is dressed in a long, knee-length tunic, which is divided from just below the hip and has the appearance of being a birny (a long coat of chain mail). The pronounced division at the bottom of this garment could indicate that he is a horseman who has been unmounted, for this device would make riding much more comfortable, and it is worth remembering that all the other Northumbrians are depicted on horseback.

The large bird seems to be acting aggressively towards the Northumbrian, pecking at his throat. From the man's attitude, he may be staggering backwards from an attack by a bird of prey, though it is curious that he does not use his shield to protect himself. A more likely explanation is that he is one of the casualties of battle; his corpse lies where he was struck down, and is being pecked at by a carrion bird. His shield, no protection now, lies beside his prostrate form where he has dropped it. The bird is probably a raven or an eagle – most likely a raven because its beak is small and straight, not large and hooked, and because it has walking feet, not talons.

This incident may be interpreted on two levels. First, there is the factual meaning. Considering that it occurs at the conclusion of a battle-scene, it may well illustrate the reality of the situation: the bodies of the vanquished being left on the field to be disposed of by carrion birds. Additionally, it may have been employed as a metaphor for 'death in battle', carrying the implication of total defeat, the fallen warrior's army being so badly routed that his comrades were unable to claim and bury their dead. Sadly, no Pictish literature has survived, but the Welsh poem *Y Goddodin*,[18] which is not too far removed – geographically, temporally and culturally – from the Picts of Dunnichen, includes fourteen references to dead warriors becoming food for scavenging wildlife: specifically, the wolf (2), birds in general (4), the eagle (2), and the raven (6). Thus the metaphor employed in the rendition of this incident may well represent a powerful visual equivalent of an established literary device. There can be little doubt as to the general meaning which it is intended to convey: this battle ended with Northumbrian carnage.

Moreover, the size of the Northumbrian figure may be perceived as broadcasting a more specific message. He is big; or, to be more precise, he is disproportionately bigger than the other figures in the scene. While the lower half of his body is consistent with that of the other warriors on both sides, his upper body is markedly larger. It is more than possible that allegory is operating here also, and in showing this dead Northumbrian as a big man, the sculptor's intention is to indicate that he is of particular importance. We know that Ecgfrith, the Northumbrian king and leader, was killed at the battle of Dunnichen, and so the climax of the battle-scene at Aberlemno, and the climax of the actual battle of Dunnichen, might well come together in this single incident.

If a case is to be made for the Aberlemno battle-scene being a representation of the battle of Dunnichen, then it must be shown to be reasonably close in both time and place to that event. However, dating Pictish stones is notoriously difficult, even to a century in many cases, let alone a decade. It is therefore necessary to study other dateable objects, which possess similar characteristics to a greater or lesser degree. The Franks Casket (dated very approximately to 700) and the Coppergate Helmet (dated to 750×775 on the basis of its nasal mount) have already proved helpful in this respect. Another vital clue may be found much closer to home – on

18 See note 2, above.

the other side of this very stone. Elements in the decoration of the slab around the cross are clearly derivative, and close parallels may be found elsewhere. This applies especially to the S-creatures which appear to the left of the cross shaft, which closely resemble intertwined creatures in the Lindisfarne Gospels. That illuminated manuscript may be dated 698 × 721, probably being close to 700.

However, the late seventh and early eighth centuries were not a good time for cultural transference between Northumbria and Pictland because of continued hostilities between the two after the battle of Dunnichen. The letter of Nechtan, king of the Picts, to Abbot Ceolfrith of Jarrow in *c.*715 provided a more amenable climate, and so it is reasonable to ascribe a date of *c.*720 or a little later to the cross side of the stone. This raises the vital question: must the battle-scene side be dated similarly? The answer is no; the reason is that the two sides are almost certainly not contemporary.

Two factors point to a substantial difference in date between the two sides of the Kirkton of Aberlemno stone (neither factor being unique to this particular Pictish stone). First, there is the disparate nature of the sculptural technique. The cross is executed in full relief, albeit delicate, and the surrounding decoration stands out in sharp relief. By contrast, the battle-scene is executed in low relief, sometimes so shallow that it is little more than an incised line separating the subject matter from the background, and indeed some elements are rendered purely by linear incision, a characteristically earlier technique. This marked difference indicates that several decades may have elapsed between the sculpting of the two sides.

Such a notion is supported by the second factor, the disparity in height between the decorated areas on the two sides. If the stone is placed in the ground so that the bottom of the cross is at ground level, the bottom of the battle-scene is over twenty inches above this. The blank portion underneath consists of a wasted area of dressed stone, below which is an area of undressed stone which was surely intended to be buried. The glaring conclusion is that the stone, bearing the battle-scene, was re-erected at a later date to accommodate the later cross. If the cross side dates from the 720s, then the battle side must be earlier – probably by a few decades, placing it in the 680s or thereby. Notwithstanding the inevitable lack of absolute dating, this is quite sufficient to link it closely with the battle of Dunnichen.

So why is this stone not sited at Dunnichen? A number of explanations can be offered, all fanciful, but two factors strongly suggest that it has been moved. One, just referred to, is the blank area below the battle-scene, especially the triangular section of stone which has broken off at the bottom-left corner. The other factor is the hole which has been bored right through the slab in one of the cross-rings, emerging in such a position as to severely disfigure one of the Pictish symbols. Such an act would have been sacrilegious to the Picts, so we must assume that it was done in post-Pictish times, perhaps for no better reason than to accommodate a strong rope by which the slab could be raised and moved. There is no good reason to assume that the stone has always stood in its present location, or very close by; Aberlemno Church is not an ancient foundation, and the earliest date we have for this stone being at Kirkton of Aberlemno in 1569. If it was indeed moved into the churchyard before that date, then it is by no means far-fetched to envisage it trundling the three and a half miles from Dunnichen.

The battle-scene at Aberlemno may be interpreted in a number of ways. One is to regard it as representing a snap-shot in stone of the crucial moment in the conflict: the Pictish infantry, by using cleverly devised and carefully rehearsed tactics, repulses the main body of Northumbrian cavalry, while the Pictish cavalry, deployed on the flanks, defeats the Northumbrian cavalry by more skilful horsemanship, putting the foe to flight or leaving him dead upon the field of battle. The other main option is to see Incidents 2 and 3 as indicative of the principal elements in the Pictish victory, illustrating precisely how their infantry and their cavalry defeated the mounted Northumbrian army. Incidents 1 and 4 may then be seen as linked sequential occurrences; Bridei chases Ecgfrith from the battlefield, and, having caught him, leaves his corpse as food for the carrion bird. Either way, what we see may be regarded as a dramatic and realistic rendition of the Picts' finest hour under arms. They have left us nothing by way of written records relating to their victory at Dunnichen; it may well be that at Aberlemno they have bequeathed to us this wonderful testimony in stone to their greatest triumph.

5

The Province of Ross and the Kingdom of Alba[1]

ALEXANDER GRANT

The kingdom of Alba and subsequently of Scotland was put together between the ninth and the thirteenth centuries out of a number of regional building-blocks, most of which survived into the later Middle Ages in the form of the old 'provincial' earldoms and lordships. This essay looks at one of those building-blocks, the northern province and earldom of Ross, considers some issues about its early history, and reflects on its relationship with the emerging kingdom.

The word 'Ross' could be either Pictish or Gaelic. If Pictish, it is probably the equivalent of the Welsh *rhos*, moor, and so denotes an expanse of moorland; if Gaelic, it probably means promontory, and would therefore denote the great promontory jutting out to Tarbat Ness. In his first discussion of the question, W. J. Watson preferred the former explanation, but subsequently he stated that there was 'nothing decisive in favour of either meaning'[2] – and it is presumably possible that both could apply.[3] In either case, the name will have referred simply to the eastern and central areas of modern Ross, which is where the medieval earldom of Ross was originally located; the western areas, beyond the 'Drumalban' watershed, were not included in the earldom until well into the fourteenth century, though they were held by the earl of Ross in 1293 as part of the separate 'North Argyll'.[4] Moreover, on the east the thirteenth-century

---

[1] This essay has developed from a paper given to a History Department Seminar at Aberdeen University; I am grateful for the opportunity to discuss my thoughts on early Ross, and for the helpful comments that were made. I am also grateful for kind assistance and advice (though not always taken!) from Dauvit Broun, Alison Grant, David Sellar, Keith Stringer, Hector MacQueen, Simon Taylor and John Todd.

[2] W. J. Watson, *Place Names of Ross and Cromarty* (1904; repr., Ross and Cromarty Heritage Soc., 1976), p. xxi; W. J. Watson, *The History of the Celtic Place-Names of Scotland* (1926; repr. Edinburgh 1993), 116.

[3] I.e. that 'Ross' is a Pictish/Gaelic 'false friend', applying equally well to the province in either language, but describing different geographical features.

[4] *APS* i, 447: *terra Comitis de Ros in Nort Argail.* In 1312 the boundary of Moray ran *per mare vsque ad marchias borialis Ergadie que est comitis de Ross et sic per marchias illas vsque ad marchias Rossie: RRS* v, no. 389.

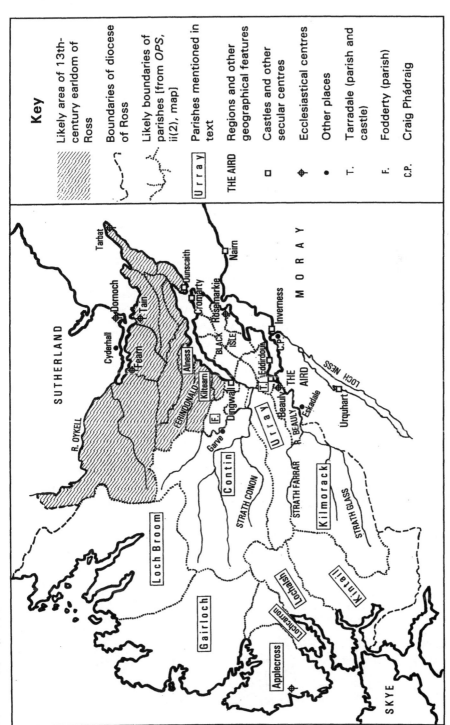

Key

(hatched area)	Likely area of 13th-century earldom of Ross
(dashed line)	Boundaries of diocese of Ross
(dotted line)	Likely boundaries of parishes [from *OPS*, iii(2), map]
Urray	Parishes mentioned in text
THE AIRD	Regions and other geographical features
□	Castles and other secular centres
⊕	Ecclesiastical centres
•	Other places
T.	Tarradale (parish and castle)
F.	Fodderty (parish)
C.P.	Craig Phádraig

Map I. Early Medieval Ross

earldom covered only part of the modern county. It was not until Robert I
granted Dingwall, Cromarty, Tarradale, Urray, Strathconon and Strathglass
to the early fourteenth-century earls that most of the south-eastern and
south-central areas of modern Ross came within the earldom;[5] before
then, it was limited to the territory lying between the River Oykel and
the Dornoch Firth to the north and the shore of the Cromarty Firth
(north of Dingwall) to the south.

That does not imply, however, that the broader concept of the province
of Ross was similarly limited before the fourteenth century; the lands of
the early Scottish earldoms never covered more than part of the provinces
from which they took their names.[6] In fact, the province must have
extended southwards, beyond the modern county line, as far as the River
Beauly or Farrar (as it was originally called); in 1248, for instance, the
davoch of Erchless on the north bank of the Beauly was said to be 'in
Ross'.[7] The Beauly was also the south-eastern boundary of the medieval
diocese based at Rosemarkie, which came to be known as the diocese of
Ross,[8] and so the province of Ross should presumably be equated with
this rather than with the earldom – at least so far as the eastern and central
areas are concerned. But on the west, although by 1255 the parishes from
Kintail to Loch Broom were already subject to the bishop of Ross, they
were described then as 'the churches of Argyll belonging to the foresaid
church [of Rosemarkie]',[9] which indicates that, like the earl's lands of
'North Argyll', they were not yet regarded as being within the province
of Ross.

*   *   *

It is one thing to consider the extent of the province of Ross, quite
another to approach its early history. As Dauvit Broun remarks in his
essay on *De situ Albanie* (above, chapter 2), for the earlier Middle Ages 'we
must acknowledge that the political landscape north of the Mounth is
impenetrably obscure'. Indeed it is not until the later thirteenth century –
beyond the scope of this essay – that the historical mist (or perhaps *haar*,
to use local terminology) which shrouds the dawn of Ross's history clears
sufficiently to make a coherent account of the province and earldom

---

5   Ibid., nos. 77, 196; *RMS* i, app. II, nos. 63–4.
6   A. Grant, 'Thanes and thanages, from the eleventh to the fourteenth centuries', in
    A. Grant and K. J. Stringer (eds.), *Medieval Scotland: Crown, Lordship and
    Community* (Edinburgh 1993), 44–6.
7   *Moray Reg.*, no. 122.
8   *OPS* ii (2), 568 and map. But note that the parish of Ardersier, opposite Rosemarkie
    across the Beauly Firth, was a detached part of the diocese; and also that until
    1226 the bishops of Ross claimed that the parish of Kiltarlity, east and south of
    the River Beauly, belonged to it: ibid., 593–4; *Moray Reg.*, no. 75.
9   Theiner, *Vetera Monumenta*, no. 172.

possible. Before then, all we have are occasional glimpses of what was happening – so that all that can be attempted here is constructive speculation about what might have been going on in Ross, and about how that might be related to the early kingdom of Alba.

Oddly enough, however, it is possible nowadays to suggest that Ross might have featured at the very beginning of recorded Highland history, namely the battle of Mons Graupius in AD 83. Although currently the favoured location for Mons Graupius is near Bennachie in Aberdeenshire, recent archaeology has postulated a chain of Agricolan fortifications along the southern shore of the Moray Firth past Nairn, and even perhaps a Roman site across the Beauly Firth, at Tarradale in southern Ross.[10] Admittedly this is hotly disputed,[11] and in the absence of cast-iron archaeological evidence the question may never be settled absolutely conclusively. Yet it is certainly relevant to consider the possibility that these fortifications do exist, and, in particular, that the Tarradale site is Roman – in which case the final Agricolan campaign, and hence presumably Mons Graupius, would be brought into the province of Ross. But wherever Mons Graupius was fought, it is clear that, broadly speaking, the limit of Roman penetration into Scotland must have been around the Moray–Ross boundary. As will be seen, this raises one of the main themes in the history of Ross: that of the frontier.[12]

That the Romans may have reached as far as Ross is interesting but hardly of long-term importance, because wherever they went in northern Britain they did not stay for any length of time. What is more significant is the information about the Highlands brought back from Agricola's campaigns, which appears to have been used in the second-century treatise on *Geography* by the Alexandrian mathematician Claudius Ptolemaeus.[13] The account of the Highland tribes in 'Ptolemy's Map' starts with five which inhabited the west coast from Kintyre to Cape Wrath, and so must all have been west of the 'Drumalban' watershed. Next, it locates the *Caledonii* across the central Highlands, from Loch Long in the south-west as far as the 'Varar' estuary – the Beauly Firth – in the north-east. Then there are three tribes beyond the Beauly Firth, of which the first, the

---

10 B. Jones, I. Keillar and K. Maude, 'The Moray aerial survey: discovering the prehistoric and proto-historic landscape', in W. D. H. Sellar (ed.), *Moray: Province and People* (Edinburgh 1993), 64–70. I am indebted to my wife for pointing this out to me; since I come from Tarradale, my interest will be obvious.

11 E.g., W. S. Hanson, *Agricola and the Conquest of the North* (London 1987), 97, note.

12 Cf. B. E. Crawford, 'The making of a frontier: the Firthlands from the ninth to twelfth centuries', in J. R. Baldwin (ed.), *Firthlands of Ross and Sutherland* (Edinburgh 1986).

13 A. L. F. Rivet and C. Smith, *The Place-Names of Roman Britain* (Cambridge 1979), 140–1; A. Strang, 'Explaining Ptolemy's Roman Britain', *Britannia*, xxviii (1997), 26–30.

Decantae, should presumably be situated in eastern Ross. In other words, the origins of the province of Ross are surely to be found in the *Decantae* tribal territory. It should be noted, however, that the recent reconstruction of Ptolemy's Map by Alastair Strang, who convincingly corrects its distortions and fits it successfully to the geographical reality, restricts the *Caledonii* to the eastern side of the Great Glen, and places the *Decantae* into a region stretching from the Oykel to the Beauly but continuing southwards to include the territory later known as the Aird, which lies roughly between the Beauly and Loch Ness.[14] Although in more recent times the Aird was part of the province, diocese, and earldom of Moray, if it had originally been within the *Decantae* territory that might explain the close connections between it and Ross that are found later.

During the centuries that followed, most of the northern British tribes listed by Ptolemy are believed to have coalesced into the Picts, who formed two main groupings, northern and southern.[15] Almost all the information we have about Pictish history concerns the southern Picts, while their northern cousins are virtually a complete blank. A well-known exception, however, is the 'most powerful' northern king Bridei *filius Meilochon* (died *c*.586), who was visited several times at his stronghold near Inverness by St Columba.[16] Bridei's power base would thus have been as close (indeed closer) to the *Decantae* territory as it was to that of the *Caledonii* or of the other north-eastern tribe, the *Vacomagi* (who, according to Ptolemy, occupied a region from lower Strathspey to Tayside) – especially if the traditional identification of the stronghold with the hillfort of Craig Phádraig west of the River Ness is valid.[17] It is not impossible that the over-kingship of the Picts exercised by Bridei emanated from the area of the *Decantae*, that is, from Ross and the Aird; that may

14 Ibid., 27.
15 E.g., A. A. M. Duncan, *Scotland: The Making of the Kingdom* (Edinburgh 1975), 25–8, 36, 46–7.
16 Bede, *HE*, 222 (III. 4); Adomnán, *Columba*, pp. xxxiii–xxxv. See Dauvit Broun's essay, above, note 3, for this form of the name.
17 Excavation of Craig Phádraig's ramparts has cast doubt on its identification with Bridei's stronghold; on the other hand, a mould for a piece of ornamental metalwork was found there, which indicates a significant workshop there *c*.600, comparable with that at Dunadd in Argyll, the main contemporary Scottish centre. Also, the largest known Pictish silver chain was discovered west of the Ness, i.e. near Craig Phádraig, when the Caledonian Canal was dug. See: A. Small and M. B. Cottam, *Craig Phadrig: Interim Report on 1971 Excavation* (Dundee University, Geography Dept. occasional paper, no. 1, 1972) (which includes R. B. K. Stevenson, 'Note on mould from Craig Phadraig'); A. Small, 'The hill forts of the Inverness area', in L. Maclean (ed.), *The Hub of the Highlands: The Book of Inverness and District* (Inverness 1975), 79–87; J. A. Smith, 'Silver chains of double rings found in Scotland', *PSAS* xv (1880–1), 64; I. Henderson, 'Inverness, a Pictish capital', in Maclean, *Hub of the Highlands*, 96–7, 103; and Adomnán, *Columba*, p. xxxiv.

be the message of the early Pictish symbol stones in this region.[18] Following Bridei's death, however, the political balance in Pictland seems to have shifted decisively to the south, ultimately to what is known as the kingdom of Fortriu, and nothing further is known about northern politics, except that Bridei's son was hostile to Columba. Yet while, thereafter, the southern Picts appear to have been dominant, at least according to the sources, we should note a reference under the year 782 to the death of Talorgan (son of one of the greatest Pictish kings, Onuist son of Uurguist), who is called king *citra Month*, in other words south of the Mounth or Grampians;[19] the implication is that a separate kingship of northern Pictland may still have survived, though perhaps under southern over-kingship.[20]

One thing, of course, that did happen in northern Pictland was christianisation. In Ross, this is strikingly attested by magnificent stone carvings (especially at Rosemarkie), and also, potentially, by the current excavations of the religious site at Tarbat.[21] But while these indicate that Christianity was well established there by the ninth century, the process of conversion in Ross remains elusive, with the only clues coming from hagiographies, church dedications and place-names. What is clear, however, is that it is not attributable to Columba; despite his famous visits to King Bridei, he appears not to have carried out any significant missionary activity among the northern Picts, and even on the West Coast probably did not reach as far north as Kintail.[22] There are, indeed, no church dedications to Columba anywhere in the mainland of Ross, which is a striking testimony to his lack of impact here. Instead, it is likely that the Irish missionary activity in Wester Ross was headed first by Columba's contemporary St Donnán (killed on Eigg in 617), and then, over half a century later, by St Mael Rubha (died ?722), who came from Bangor and, independently of Iona, founded his monastery at Applecross. It is almost certainly with Mael Rubha, in the later seventh century, that the western mainland of Ross was christianised; beyond Applecross, there are

---

18   Ibid., 104; I. Henderson, 'The origin centre of the Pictish symbol stones', *PSAS* xci (1957–8), 55–7.

19   *Ann. Ulster*, 782; *ES* i, 253.

20   But note Martin Carver's provisional conclusion from the excavations at Tarbat, that 'it is not impossible to imagine' a very localised power structure, 'with no recognised king and no established church, enduring in north-east Scotland at least until the ninth century': M. Carver, 'Conversion and politics on the eastern seaboard of Britain: some archaeological indicators', in B. E. Crawford (ed.), *Conversion and Christianity in the North Sea World* (St Andrews 1998), 35–7.

21   I. Henderson, *The Art and Function of Rosemarkie's Pictish Monuments* (Rosemarkie, Groam House Lecture, 1989); Carver, 'Conversion and politics', 29–37.

22   A. P. Smyth, *Warlords and Holy Men: Scotland AD 80–1000* (London 1984), 107–12; Watson, *Place Names of Ross*, p. lxvii.

dedications to him at Lochcarron, Gairloch and Loch Maree. And he also presumably worked in the east, since he is commemorated at Contin, Strathpeffer, and Keith in Banffshire.[23]

If it was Mael Rubha who led the evangelisation of eastern Ross,[24] however, his work would have been superseded by the activity of St Curadán or Boniface, who appears to have been based at Rosemarkie in the early eighth century. Curadán was probably the 'Bishop Curetán' who was a guarantor of the 'Law of Innocents' promulgated by St Adomnán of Iona at the Synod of Birr in Ireland in 697, and his legend (as Boniface) in the *Aberdeen Breviary* claimed that he founded 150 churches among the Picts![25] The reality would have been very different, but dedications to Curadán are to be found near Inverness, in the Aird, at the lower end of Loch Ness, in Glen Urquhart, in Strathglass, in Novar north of Dingwall, and near Alness[26] – an area which corresponds remarkably closely with what was suggested above may have been the land of the *Decantae* and perhaps the power base of King Bridei *filius Meilochon*. Moreover, this contains (albeit with an extension into south-east Sutherland) what Simon Taylor has identified as one of two significant clusters of place-names beginning with *cill* (church) in eastern Scotland. He argues that the other cluster, in Fife, reflects church foundations in the early eighth century spreading out from a centre at Kinrimonth (later St Andrews) under the

---

23 Watson, *Celtic Place-Names*, 287–9; there are also dedications to him in Argyll, Harris, Lairg in Sutherland, Fife, and Perthshire. For Mael Rubha in general, see A. B. Scott, 'Saint Maolrubha', *SHR* vi (1909), 260–80 (which shows that the common belief that he died at Urquhart in the Black Isle is wrong); A. Boyle, 'Notes on Scottish saints', *Innes Review*, xxxii (1981), 72–3; A. Macquarrie, *The Saints of Scotland: Essays in Scottish Church History, AD 450–1093* (Edinburgh 1997), 166–71; and B. T. Hudson, 'Kings and Church in early Scotland', *SHR* lxxiii (1994), 150.

24 It has been suggested that St Moluóc, an older contemporary of Columba and founder of the monastery at Lismore in Lorn, had been active in eastern Ross well before Mael Rubha, since there is a dedication to him at Rosemarkie: I. Henderson, 'Rosemarkie and the reformation of the Pictish Church in the early eighth century', in E. Meldrum (ed.), *The Dark Ages in the Highlands* (Inverness, 1971), 50–2. But it is more likely that Moluóc's cult was brought to Rosemarkie later, after the takeover of Ross by Cenél Loairn: A. MacDonald, *Curadán, Boniface and the early Church of Rosemarkie* (Rosemarkie, Groam House Lecture, 1992), 28–9.

25 The scanty but complex material concerning Curadán/Boniface is fully presented and unravelled (insofar as that is possible) in Aidan MacDonald's Groam House lecture: ibid., *passim*. In the discussion of Boniface's companions (pp. 17–18, 25), it may be added that: one, 'Madianus', could perhaps be equated with the 'St Madidus' to whom the church of Urray, in southern Ross, was dedicated: I. B. Cowan, *The Parishes of Medieval Scotland* (Scottish Record Soc., 1967), 206. Urray was originally known as Inveraferan (from Gaelic *inbhear* and *aifreann*), meaning 'the confluence of the offering', which implies an early church: Watson, *Celtic Place-Names*, 473.

26 MacDonald, *Curadán*, 25, 38; Watson, *Place Names of Ross*, pp. lxix–xx; Watson, *Celtic Place-Names*, 315.

patronage of the southern Pictish king, Nechtan son of Derile, who in about 715 'modernised' and Romanised the Church in his dominions, expelling Iona-based Columban clergy from them. Hence Taylor finds it 'tempting' to connect the north-eastern *cill*-names with Curadán of Rosemarkie, who may have carried out a similar process in the north.[27] This is plausible, for, like the Romanised stone church which Nechtan founded (probably *Egglespether* near Restenneth in Angus), the church at Rosemarkie is dedicated to St Peter.[28] One possible scenario would be to link Curadán with southern Pictish over-kings,[29] and to see him as being sent to northern Pictland after about 715; there are perhaps parallels with what looks like a similar mission to Orkney at around the same time.[30] Whatever the case, Curadán must presumably be regarded as a bishop for the whole of northern Pictland – the ecclesiastical focus of which, judging by his base at Rosemarkie together with the distribution patterns of his dedications and (perhaps) the north-eastern *cill*-names, must have been in the old *Decantae* territory of eastern Ross and the Aird.

Yet, while the ecclesiastical evidence directs attention eastwards, what was to become Wester Ross should not be ignored: both the absence from it of Columban activity, and Mael Rubha's likely west–east missions, suggest that it might be linked more with the eastern part of the later province than with the west-coast region south of Kintail. And that is a conclusion which seems to emerge from another, secular, body of evidence, namely the Scandinavian place-names which denote the later Norse settlements in Orkney and Shetland, in the eastern mainland north of the Moray Firth, and throughout the entire western seaboard and the Hebrides. These include place-names derived from Norse units of local assessment called 'ouncelands' and 'pennylands', which are unique to Scandinavianised Scotland and appear in every part of it – except for the province of Ross, both east and west.[31] The best explanation for the absence of ouncelands and pennylands from Ross is surely that when it came under Norse rule, there already was an effective system of local assessment through which tribute and taxes could be levied, based no

---

[27] S. Taylor, 'Place-names and the early Church in eastern Scotland', in B. E. Crawford (ed.), *Scotland in Dark Age Britain* (St Andrews 1996), esp. 102.

[28] Bede, *HE*, 532–3 (v. 21); *RRS* i, no. 195; *Moray Reg.*, no. 258; cf. MacDonald, *Curadán*, 18–19.

[29] Note that another guarantor of the 'Law of Innocents' at Birr was Bridei son of Derile, king of the Picts, a brother and predecessor of King Nechtan: ibid., 5.

[30] R. Lamb, 'Pictland, Northumbria and the Carolingian Empire', in Crawford, *Conversion and Christianity*, 41–5, 47–9; cf. Henderson, 'Rosemarkie and the reformation of the Pictish Church'.

[31] B. E. Crawford, *Scandinavian Scotland* (Leicester 1987), 86–8; A. Easson, 'Medieval land assessment', in P. G. B. McNeill and H. L. MacQueen (eds.), *Atlas of Scottish History to 1707* (Edinburgh 1996), 284.

doubt on the ubiquitous davach.[32] But this, or any other, explanation must apply to the west of Ross as well as the east. What the ounceland/pennyland evidence suggests, therefore, is that during the pre-Scandinavian era both eastern and western Ross were already encompassed within an effectively run Pictish kingdom. It may, as argued above, have been based on the old *Decantae* territory, but, in that case, it must have been extended to the western sea-board. In Pictish Ross, east and west seem already to have been brought together – perhaps, indeed, by the time of Bridei *filius Meilochon*, which would give one reason why Columba's missionary activity did not penetrate Wester Ross.

One further point should be made here. In both the lists of Pictish divisions contained in *De situ Albanie*, one of the parts or kingdoms is 'Moray and Ross'. But the second list (DSb in Dauvit Broun's essay, above) describes the 'fifth kingdom' as 'from the Spey to the mountain Drumalban'. Broun points out that that 'would have naturally embraced Moray and Ross', which means that this kingdom 'is either unconvincing or confused'. That is certainly valid, if we were keeping strictly to the later province or earldom boundaries. Since the compiler of this list was so passionate about the River Spey,[33] however, might he have known what he was talking about with respect to that part of Scotland? 'From the Spey to Drumalban' is not an impossible kingdom; it tallies quite well with the later Badenoch and Lochaber, which formed a territorial unit in the thirteenth century.[34] And in that case, it might be that the sixth kingdom, 'Moray and Ross', was intended to represent a region covering Ross (both east and west, not stopping at Drumalban) plus the Aird and the area north-west of Loch Ness, which were subsequently parts of Moray. Coastal Moray might also have been meant to be included, for 'from the Spey' could mean from the upper part of the river; yet although a kingdom lying round the shores of the Moray Firth is possible, it seems more likely (especially in view of the ecclesiastical evidence) that coastal Moray was separate from Ross. We must, of course, remember that the lists in *De Situ Albanie* are not contemporary evidence about Pictland's structures, but ideas dating from *c*.1200, centuries later. Nevertheless, DSb's 'fifth' and 'sixth' kingdoms might just perhaps reflect vague memories of some of the northern Pictish political structures.

*   *   *

[32] Ibid.; M. Bangor-Jones, 'Land assessments and settlement history in Sutherland and Easter Ross', in Baldwin, *Firthlands of Ross and Sutherland*, 153–9; G. W. S. Barrow, *The Kingdom of the Scots* (London 1973), 268–78.

[33] '... the great and wonderful river called the Spey, the greatest and best in all *Scocia*'.

[34] Barrow, *Kingdom of the Scots*, 378.

Be that as it may, none of the Pictish kingdoms, north or south, survived the ninth century. While southern Pictland was conquered by or amalgamated with the Scottish kingdom of the Dalriadic Cenél nGabráin, eventually producing the kingdom of Alba, northern Pictland was taken over from two directions: from the south-west by the other main Dalriadic kindred, Cenél Loairn, which probably moved up the Great Glen to create the tenth- and eleventh-century kingdom based on Moray; and from the north and west by the Norse, following their conquests of the Orkneys and Hebrides.[35] The chronology of the Cenél Loairn invasion is unknown, though if Benjamin Hudson's plausible argument that the southern Scottish king, Giric (*c*.878–*c*.889), was a Cenél Loairn interloper in the line of Cenél nGabráin kings is correct,[36] then, since Giric's main power base was Dundurn near the foot of Loch Earn,[37] it may be assumed that the main Cenél Loairn move into Moray would not have occurred until after his death in *c*.889. In that case, it would have followed the Norse invasion of northern Pictland, about which some narrative detail may be found in the various Scandinavian sagas. According to the *Orkneyinga Saga*, Earl Sigurd the Mighty of Orkney and Thorstein the Red (from the Hebrides) 'conquered the whole of Caithness and a large part of Argyll, Moray and Ross' during the years after about 870.[38] It is they who were presumably responsible for the collapse of the northern Picts. But Sigurd is said to have killed 'Scottish earls' with Gaelic names: a Mael Duin (husband of a daughter of an Irish king), and a Mael Brigte; so it is likely that they had come into conflict with Cenél Loairn, possibly in the Great Glen region. And they were not invincible: Thorstein was killed by Scots, while Sigurd died in *c*.892 after his battle with Mael Brigte.[39] Their deaths seem to have halted the impetus of the Norse conquest, and that probably provided the opportunity for the Cenél Loairn advance into Moray.

35 What follows on the Norse derives mostly from Crawford, *Scandinavian Scotland*, esp. chs. 2–4.
36 B. T. Hudson, *Kings of Celtic Scotland* (Westport, Connecticut, 1994), 56–7, 128–32. But note Dauvit Broun's reservations in his review: *SHR* lxxv (1996), 248.
37 Hudson, *Kings of Celtic Scotland*, 132–3. But the remark (p. 131) that 'Fordun preserves the interesting information that it was Giric who subdued the northern and western coasts of Scotland' is mistaken, for Fordun is clearly referring to the north and west of *England*: *Chron. Fordun*, i, 159–60.
38 *Orkneyinga Saga*, ch. 5; *ES* i, 371.
39 *The Book of Settlements (Landnámabók)*, trans. H. Pálsson and P. Edwards (University of Manitoba 1972), chs. 95–6; *Orkneyinga Saga*, ch. 5; *ES* i, 370–1, 378–9, 384. Their probable aim of controlling the east–west route through the Great Glen is stressed in Crawford, *Scandinavian Scotland*, 22–4, 57. G. W. S. Barrow, 'Macbeth and other mormaers of Moray', in Maclean, *Hub of the Highlands*, 111, suggests that Mael Brigte belonged to the kindred of the later rulers of Moray.

Sigurd was buried at what is now called Cyderhall ('Sigurd's howe') on the northern shore of the Dornoch Firth near the mouth of the Oykel estuary: in other words, just north of the Ross–Sutherland boundary.[40] His body would have been brought back to territory securely under Norse control, which, according to Snorri Sturluson's *Heimskringla*, ended at the Oykel.[41] Now if, as it appears, Orkney/Caithness was hit by internal conflicts after Sigurd's death, then the southern part of northern Pictland as far north as the Oykel – in other words, including Ross – might have been taken over by Cenél Loairn. But that may be doubted. After all, the Cenél Loairn acquisition of Moray had to be consolidated, and indeed in the mid-tenth century Moray appears to have been under attack by both Cenél nGabráin kings of Alba from the south and Scandinavians from the north.[42] Thus there is no reason to suppose that Moray was any stronger than Orkney/Caithness. Admittedly, in the later tenth century northern Caithness suffered raids from Moray (presumably sea-borne); but the last of these was repulsed by another powerful Earl Sigurd, 'the Stout', who seems to have been the major figure in northern Scotland from *c.*990 until his death at Clontarf in 1014. Subsequently his son, Earl Thorfinn the Mighty (died *c.*1060),[43] similarly dealt with a Moray attack led almost certainly by Macbeth (the future Scottish king), and went on to defeat him in a battle which was probably off Tarbat Ness, at the eastern tip of Ross.[44] *Njal's Saga* states that Sigurd the Stout 'owned ... Ross and Moray, Sutherland and the Dales [in Caithness]', while Earl Thorfinn was said to have conquered nine earldoms in Scotland.[45] These claims are no doubt exaggerated, but they do indicate that under Sigurd and Thorfinn the dominions of the earls of Orkney/Caithness must have extended beyond the Oykel.

That is confirmed by the place-name evidence. There are no – or next to no – Scandinavian place-names in Moray,[46] whereas eastern Ross contains

---

40 B. E. Crawford, 'Making of a frontier', 38–9.
41 Crawford, *Scandinavian Scotland*, 58–9; Snorri Sturluson, *Heimskringla: History of the Kings of Norway*, trans. L. M. Hollander (Austin, Texas, 1964), 78; *ES* i, 370.
42 Hudson, *Kings of Celtic Scotland*, 87, 91–2.
43 See note 63, below.
44 Crawford, *Scandinavian Scotland*, 64–8, 71–4.
45 *Njal's Saga*, trans. M. Magnusson and H. Pálsson (Harmondsworth 1966), ch. 86; *Orkneyinga Saga*, ch. 32; *ES* i, 499; ii, 3. Note also that before the battle off Tarbat Ness, Thorfinn's main follower joined Thorfinn in Moray with 'all the troops from Caithness, Sutherland and Ross': *Orkneyinga Saga*, ch. 20.
46 W. F. H. Nicolaisen, 'Names in the landscape of the Moray Firth', in Sellar, *Moray: Province and People*, 258: 'there is no place-name evidence to indicate that any Scandinavians ever held sway over our area'. But G. W. S. Barrow, 'Badenoch and Strathspey, 1130–1312, 1: secular and political', *Northern Scotland*, viii (1988), 11, nn. 18, 22, states that Budgate (near Cawdor) and Kerdale (in upper Strathnairn) are

at least thirty-five of them.[47] The density of Scandinavian place-names in eastern Ross, while far from that in the heavily settled Caithness, is not unlike what is found in Sutherland and Wester Ross,[48] which certainly were under Norse rule. As for the distribution, it is fairly even across the region, as far south as Tarradale at the head of the Beauly Firth and Eskadale on the southern bank of the River Beauly.[49] In eastern Ross, however, few of these place-names denote specific farmsteads; the majority are topographic, especially compounds of '-dale' (*dalr*), which are mostly applied to the valleys of minor streams and the tributaries of the larger rivers. The pattern seems to indicate a significant Norse presence, but probably not so much intensive farming settlement as an upper level of lordship or control over the indigenous population;[50] this has recently been convincingly connected with the exploitation of eastern Ross's woodlands, which would have been invaluable for Norse shipbuilding; and it is suggested that the focal point of this exploitation was at Dingwall, at the head of the Cromarty Firth.[51] Moreover, Dingwall (*þing völlr*, 'place of assembly') was presumably an important administrative centre; this therefore demonstrates a significant Norse presence in the south-eastern quarter of Ross.[52]

The place-names, however, surely indicate a Norse control of Ross that lasted for longer than merely the seventy or so years spanning the careers of Sigurd the Stout and Thorfinn the Mighty. The likelihood is, indeed, that it went back to the time of Sigurd the Mighty in the late ninth century, and thus that the *Heimskringla* statement about a boundary at the Oykel is mistaken. Alternatively, tenth-century Ross might for a time have been a no-man's land between Orkney/Caithness and Moray which groups of individual Norse could have penetrated independently, before it eventually came under the control of the earls of Orkney. Whatever the

both apparently Scandinavian. The west-coast part of the later Randolph earldom of Moray, which was in the diocese of Argyll, has not, of course, been counted here.

[47] Thirty-four counted in Watson, *Place Names of Ross*, plus 'Scuddel', the old name of Conon Bridge: Crawford, 'Making of a frontier', 34–5.

[48] Watson, *Place Names of Ross*, xvii–xix; I. A. Fraser, 'Norse and Celtic place-names around the Dornoch Firth', in Baldwin, *Firthlands of Ross and Sutherland*, 29–32.

[49] *Tarfrdalr*, 'bull-dale': Watson, *Place-Names of Ross*, 108; *eskidalr*, 'ash-dale': Watson, *Celtic Place-Names*, 1.

[50] Crawford, *Scandinavian Scotland*, 96.

[51] B. E. Crawford, *Earl and Mormaer: Norse–Pictish Relationships in Northern Scotland* (Rosemarkie, Groam House Lecture, 1994), 11–28.

[52] Watson, *Place Names of Ross*, 93; Crawford, *Earl and Mormaer*, 18–20. The place-name Scatwell, in the middle of lower Strathconon, may also reflect Norse administration, if it derives from *scat völlr*, 'tax-place', as argued in Crawford, 'Making of a frontier', 43–4. But Barbara Crawford now suggests it is the same as a Norwegian place-name, Scatval, which relates to woodland clearance: Crawford, *Earl and Mormaer*, 22–3.

case, it is unlikely that the indigenous Pictish population was swept away, which implies that there may have been a much longer or different kind of Pictish survival in Ross (and indeed in Sutherland and even Caithness) than south of the Moray Firth, where, following the ninth-century Scottish political take-over, the Picts either disappeared or were rapidly Gaelicised. And, irrespective of what happened to the Picts of Ross, what the Norse place-names illustrate most clearly is the emergence of a new political and cultural frontier. Whereas in the pre-Norse era there had probably been a political division or subdivision in northern Pictland along the line of the lower Great Glen, in the tenth century the Ross–Moray frontier was established at the Beauly River and Firth, with the Aird now being part of Moray rather than Ross. This frontier was to last more or less exactly, with respect to provinces, dioceses, earldoms, presbyteries, counties and districts, until the present day. But in the present context the main point is that, from the late ninth to the mid-eleventh centuries, the province of Ross was effectively outside the Gaelic power structures that were being brought together to create the kingdom of Alba.

*   *   *

When did that change? How did Ross come to be incorporated within the kingdom of Alba? The beginnings of the process may perhaps be found in the early eleventh century, when Earl Sigurd the Stout of Orkney/ Caithness married the daughter of a Scottish King Malcolm.[53] It has been argued that she was a daughter of Mael Coluim mac Maíl Brigti, Cenél Loairn king of Moray,[54] but that is most unlikely, because the marriage must have taken place by 1008 at the latest,[55] whereas Mael Coluim did not come to power in Moray until 1020.[56] Thus Sigurd's father-in-law would have been the Cenél nGabráin king of Alba, Malcolm II (1005–34), who is described in one source as 'king of the Mounth'.[57] That probably indicates that he was the first Cenél nGabráin ruler to assert effective kingship across the Grampians in Moray, beyond the original core area of Alba;[58] his daughter's marriage to Sigurd, which would have created an

---

53 *Orkneyinga Saga*, ch. 12; *ES* i, 510 (where A. O. Anderson suggested that the marriage was before 1000, when there was no Scottish king called Malcolm; but the saga accounts compress the chronology of Earl Sigurd's career).

54 Hudson, *Kings of Celtic Scotland*, 135.

55 The son of the marriage, Thorfinn, was five years old when his father was killed in 1014: *Orkneyinga Saga*, ch. 13; *ES* i, 542.

56 *Ann. Ulster*, 1020, 1029; *Ann. Tigernach*, 1020, 1029; Hudson, *Kings of Celtic Scotland*, 134–5.

57 K. Jackson, 'The Duan Albanach', *SHR* xxxvi (1957), 133; cf. E. J. Cowan, 'The historical MacBeth', in Sellar, *Moray: Province and People*, 121.

58 It seems likely that when Mael Coluim mac Maíl Brigti was displaced by his Cenél Loairn cousin and rival Macbethad mac Finnlaích (the future King Macbeth) in 1029, it was with Malcolm II's support; subsequently, Macbeth was probably

alliance that pressurised Moray from both north and south, was no doubt part of the process. But after Sigurd's death, and before his young son Thorfinn grew to manhood, Malcolm II may perhaps have established a temporary foothold in Ross as well. This is suggested because Dingwall, as well as being a Norse centre, was also subsequently a Scottish thanage belonging to the crown. The royal thanages of Scotland were units of crown estates and authority run by royal agents or thanes, and although the terminology is probably later, they were almost certainly established before the end of Malcolm II's reign. Dingwall is the most northerly, lying beyond the chain of Moray thanages running from Fochabers to Kinmylies (just past Inverness). These thanages, mostly located at strategic points on river crossings, are consistent with Malcolm II's assertion of his kingship in Moray, and so the thanage of Dingwall may well represent a push into southern Ross.[59]

On the other hand, when Sigurd's son Thorfinn grew up (and after Malcolm II's death in 1034), he reasserted Norse power in northern Scotland with his victory over Macbeth near Tarbat Ness in north-east Ross.[60] Thus any Scottish gains in Ross were presumably short-lived; while Thorfinn ruled Orkney and Caithness, the frontier would have been back at the Moray Firth. That said, the concept of Scottish lordship over not only Ross, but also Sutherland and Caithness, can be found during Thorfinn's time as earl. The *Orkneyinga Saga* relates that when, early in his career, he was commanded by the king of Norway to accept Norwegian suzerainty, Thorfinn replied that he could not do so because he was already 'the earl of the king of Scots and subject to him'.[61] The implication is that Ross and the provinces to the north all technically belonged to Alba. Yet, while the concept is important, Thorfinn's statement would have had little practical significance; its purpose was doubtless merely to block Norwegian demands, not recognise Scottish ones, and although he might have had a good relationship with the Scottish crown during the reign of his grandfather Malcolm II, that clearly ended with Malcolm's death.[62]

mormaer of Moray under Malcolm and his successor Duncan I (1034–40): Hudson, *Kings of Celtic Scotland*, 138. The Irish chronicler Marianus Scotus called Macbeth the '*dux*' of Duncan I (ibid.); while Anderson translated that as 'earl' (*ES* i, 579), it might have meant 'duke' as in 'duke of Normandy', reflecting the fact that Moray was much larger and more important than the provinces of Alba.

59 Barrow, *Kingdom of the Scots*, 39–68; Grant, 'Thanes and thanages', 40–9.
60 Crawford, *Scandinavian Scotland*, 70–2; Cowan, 'Historical MacBeth', 121.
61 *Orkneyinga Saga*, ch. 18; *ES* i, 562.
62 After Malcolm III's death, Thorfinn apparently regarded Caithness as 'his proper inheritance from his grandfather and refused to pay any tribute for it' to the new king: *Orkneyinga Saga*, ch. 20.

When Earl Thorfinn himself died sometime around 1060,[63] however, the situation changed radically.

> The earl was greatly mourned in the lands he had inherited, though in those regions he had taken by force people thought it very oppressive to live under his rule, so most of the places he had conquered broke away and the people there looked for protection from those who held the lands by birthright. It was soon clear what a great loss his death was.[64]

This passage demonstrates that, outside the core area of Orkney/Caithness, the conquests by Thorfinn (and no doubt by his predecessors) had been achieved by simply imposing his lordship upon the local power structures; but that his two sons, who were apparently joint earls, were unable to do that. Much of the 'loss' was presumably in the west, but it is likely that the local lords within Ross would similarly have refused to acknowledge the new earls' lordship. That would have provided the then king of Alba, Malcolm III, with another opportunity to extend Scottish kingship across the frontier into Ross.

While the politics of Malcolm III's reign are usually discussed in terms of relations with England,[65] it should be remembered that the north must have been equally important to him, though the focus was no doubt on Moray. Malcolm's father Duncan I had been killed by the Cenél Loairn ruler of Moray, Macbeth, who then took over the kingship of Alba; and when Malcolm won the crown in 1057-8, he had to defeat not only Macbeth but also the next head of Cenél Loairn, Lulach, who was briefly king of Alba too. Malcolm's initial policy in the north appears to have been to let Lulach's son Mael Snechta act as mormaer for him in Moray;[66] but, like Malcolm II, he no doubt put his own men into the Moray thanages. And, also like Malcolm II, he looked beyond Moray to Orkney/Caithness. Earl Thorfinn probably died soon after Malcolm established himself as king, and according to the sagas he married Ingibjorg, who had been Thorfinn's wife;[67] that made him stepfather to

---

63 Although Thorfinn's death is usually given as *c.*1065, the dating in the sagas is extremely vague: cf. *ES* i, 542; ii, 2–4. All that is known for certain is that his sons, as joint earls, were with King Harald of Norway before the battle of Stamford Bridge in 1066; but that was 'some time after the brothers ... began ruling in Orkney', so Thorfinn's death was probably several years earlier: *Orkneyinga Saga*, ch. 34.

64 Ibid., ch. 32; cf. *ES* ii, 2.

65 For Malcolm III's reign in general, see Duncan, *Making of the Kingdom*, 117–24, and G. W. S. Barrow, *Kingship and Unity: Scotland 1000–1306* (London 1981), 25–31.

66 That is implied by the fact that Mael Snechta was called 'king of Moray' in *Ann. Ulster*, 1085: cf. *ES* ii, 46.

67 *Orkneyinga Saga*, ch. 33; *ES* ii, 4–5. It has been suggested that she was Thorfinn's daughter rather than his wife (Duncan, *Making of the Kingdom*, 100, 118), but

the new earls of Orkney/Caithness. Although Ingibjorg must have been dead by about 1070,[68] the marriage would have put Malcolm in a good position to exploit the retreat of Norse power from Ross – provided, that is, that Moray was not troublesome. In fact, Mael Snechta must have rebelled, for in 1078 Malcolm 'won the mother of Mael Snechta [that is, King Lulach's widow] ... and all his best men, his treasures and his cattle'.[69] That was the third defeat for Cenél Loairn at Malcolm's hands in twenty-one years, and it looks as if he imprisoned Mael Snechta's main supporters. As for Mael Snechta himself, he was not killed but may have had to enter a monastery; when he died in 1085 the *Annals of Ulster* listed him among various churchmen who all ended their lives 'happily', that is, religiously.[70] By the end of the 1070s, therefore, Moray must have been under Malcolm III's control. There would therefore have been nothing to stop him asserting his power in Ross as well. Although there is no narrative evidence that he did so, it is difficult to believe that he did not; this is certainly consistent with the strong fifteenth-century traditions that he confirmed the privileges of Tain, especially the famous girth or sanctuary.[71]

That does not mean, however, that Malcolm III would have ruled Ross in person. The normal early medieval practice was to entrust newly acquired outlying regions to provincial governors, especially members of the royal kin,[72] and there is no reason to suppose that Malcolm did not do this in the north. Also, although it has been suggested that in this period Moray and Ross went together, that derives from the pairing of provinces made by the author of *De situ Albanie*, which need not be taken seriously.[73] In fact the earldom of Ross, when it can first be delineated, was north of

Orkneyinga Saga is explicit: 'Ingibjorg the Earls'-Mother married Malcolm, King of Scots, known as Long-Neck'. There is, admittedly, a question about her age. If, as Crawford suggests, she married Thorfinn before 1030 (*Scandinavian Scotland*, 77), she would have been born in *c*.1020 at the latest, in which case she would have been in her 40s during the 1060s – when the Ingibjorg who married Malcolm III had at least one son by him. But that is not impossible (and she may have married Thorfinn rather later, after 1035); therefore the saga statement is probably to be believed. The suggestion in W. D. H. Sellar, 'Marriage, divorce and concubinage in Gaelic Scotland', *TGSI* li (1978–80), 476, that Thorfinn might have divorced Ingibjorg, should also be noted.

68 Malcolm III's second marriage, to (St) Margaret, is normally dated 1070×1. There is no reason to believe that (as has sometimes been said) Ingibjorg was set aside by Malcolm.

69 *SAEC*, 100.

70 *Ann. Ulster*, 1085; *ES* ii, 46.

71 *ALI*, no. 28; R. W. and J. Munro, *Tain through the Centuries* (Tain 1966), 14–17; J. Durkan, 'The sanctuary and college of Tain', *Innes Review*, xiii (1962), 147–8.

72 A. Woolf, 'Pictish matriliny reconsidered', *Innes Review*, xlix (1998), 156–8.

73 See Dauvit Broun's chapter, above.

Dingwall; between it and Moray lay the thanage of Dingwall,[74] the Black Isle (which was perhaps another thanage, of Cromarty),[75] other parts of southern Ross such as Tarradale, and the large territory of the Aird, which was in the diocese of Moray but may not have belonged to the mormaer or earl.[76] This makes it highly improbable that what was to become the earldom of Ross was simply combined with Moray. Therefore when, as is most likely, Malcolm III brought it under Scottish rule, he would surely have used a subordinate ruler or mormaer to run it for him.

It follows that the origins of the earldom of Ross are likely to have been in the reign of Malcolm III – but we shall never know who the first mormaer or earl was. One suggestion, however, would be his brother Donald *Bán*; nothing is known of Donald's activities under Malcolm III, but given his antagonism to the English followers of Queen Margaret, he might well have been employed in the north. Another possibility is raised by a pair of entries in the *Annals of Ulster*: in 1085 'Domnall mac Maíl Choluim king of Alba' died unhappily (probably by violence), and in 1116 'Ladhmunn mac Domnaill, grandson of the king of Alba, was killed by the men of Moray.'[77] These were, presumably, father and son, and it seems almost certain that Domnall, or Donald, was a son of Malcolm III. With his Gaelic name, his mother would not have been Margaret; was she Ingibjorg? If so, then Donald would have been Malcolm's second son,

---

74 The thanage of Dingwall was probably much larger than the small modern parish. To the east, across the Conon estuary, there is the territory of Ferintosh, which means 'land of the *toíseach*', and hence (since *toíseach*, lord, is how 'thane' was rendered in Gaelic) equates with the versions of 'thane's toun' found further south (e.g. Thainstone in Kintore thanage: *RRS* vi, no. 397). Watson, *Place Names of Ross*, 114, identified the 'toíseach' in Ferintosh with the thane of Cawdor, who acquired the territory in the 15th century; but Ferintosh is mentioned in the late 13th century, in conjunction with Dingwall (*CDS* ii, no. 1631), and so must surely be the 'thane's toun' attached to Dingwall. Ferintosh is, however, roughly as large as Dingwall parish, which indicates that Dingwall thanage would have been considerably bigger; it probably extended up the Peffrey valley beyond modern Strathpeffer, incorporating the old parishes of Fodderty and Kinnetes (for these, see *OPS* ii (2), 484–504).

75 Cromarty is never recorded as a thanage in surviving documents. But in the early 15th century Wyntoun called Macbeth thane of Cromarty (*Chron. Wyntoun* [Laing], ii, 128), and although his account of Macbeth is full of legends, that could perhaps be true. In the 1260s both Dingwall and Cromarty had become the bases for sheriffs (*ER* i, 26), just as happened with the more southerly thanages of Aberdeen, Kincardine, Forfar, Scone, Auchterarder, and Kinross: Grant, 'Thanes and thanages', 51. Also, the sheriff of Cromarty held six davachs there hereditarily for a feu-farm of 24 merks (*ER* i, 26), which looks like the render for an erstwhile thanage. If Malcolm II had established a thanage at Cromarty, then it could well have been run by Macbeth before he became mormaer of Moray; cf. J. Bannerman, 'MacDuff of Fife', in Grant and Stringer, *Medieval Scotland*, 26–7.

76 See below, page 116.

77 *Ann. Ulster*, 1085, 1116; *ES* ii, 47, 160.

younger than the Duncan who became a hostage in England in 1072, and would be an obvious candidate for authority in Ross. That his son had a Scandinavian name, Lodmund, and was killed in the north, would also fit. Unfortunately, it is not entirely clear that a second son of Malcolm and Ingibjorg could have been old enough to have been employed in Ross by the mid-1080s.[78] On the other hand, he could have been illegitimate, born before Malcolm's marriage to Ingibjorg; that would not affect the basic point. And whatever may have happened, it is worth pointing out that the southern 'quarter' of the original earldom of Ross, consisting of the parishes of Kiltearn and Alness just north of Dingwall, was known as 'Ferindonald', that is, 'the land of Donald'.[79] Traditionally, this Donald is said to have been the progenitor of the Munros, who possessed most of the land later, but there is no evidence of their presence there before the fourteenth century.[80] So it is at least equally possible that the 'Donald' was someone else, and the suggestion may be made that it was one of the Donalds who were Malcolm III's close kin: either his brother, or (perhaps more likely) his son who died in 1085.

The above is, of course, speculation, but the main point is clear: that, very probably, it was Malcolm III who was responsible for bringing all of eastern Ross under the kings of Alba for the first time. This would have taken the effective frontier of the kingdom from the southern to the northern edge of Ross, at the River Oykell and the Dornoch Firth. And that was followed, five years after Malcolm's death, by the treaty made by his son King Edgar with King Magnus of Norway in 1098, which, while ceding the Western Isles to Norway, appears to have agreed Scottish possession of the mainland – including Caithness.[81] Edgar has been criticised for relinquishing Scottish claims on the Isles, including Iona, but it is likely that those were well beyond his control. What is more important in the present context is the apparent Norwegian recognition of Scottish sovereignty all the way to the shore of the Pentland Firth coast. And this seems to have been accepted by the earls of Orkney/Caithness: in the 1120s, for instance, Earl Harald Hakonarson (great-grandson of Thorfinn

---

78 For that, he would have had to have been in his late teens, at least. If he was around 20 when he died, he would have been born in c.1065; he could, therefore, have been Ingibjorg's second son, if her marriage to Malcolm III took place in about 1060; cf. note 57, above.

79 Watson, *Place Names of Ross*, p. xxiv.

80 *The Munro Tree*, ed. R. W. Munro (Edinburgh 1978), 1–3. Cf. W. F. Skene, *The Highlanders of Scotland*, ed. A. Macbain (2nd edn, Stirling 1902), 416–17 (note by Macbain); and note 124, below.

81 This treaty or agreement is known only from the sagas; see, e.g. *Orkneyinga Saga*, ch. 41; *ES* ii, 112–15. No mention is made of Caithness, but Scottish suzerainty over it is subsequently implied. Cf. A. A. M. Duncan and A. L. Brown, 'Argyll and the Isles in the earlier Middle Ages', *PSAS* xc (1956–7), 193–4.

the Mighty) 'held the fief of Caithness from the King of Scots'.[82] Thus the internal frontier in north-eastern Scotland had, technically at least, been removed altogether. The next stage in the construction of Scotland ought therefore to have been to consolidate these gains by asserting full royal authority over the northern provinces of Ross and Caithness.

*   *   *

That, however, took well over a hundred years to achieve.[83] Rather than seeing the consolidation of Scottish rule in the far north, the twelfth and early thirteenth centuries witnessed a long sequence of trouble there, so that at times the effective frontier reverted to the southern edge of Ross. Under Alexander I, as already noted, the men of Moray killed Lodmund, grandson of the king of Alba. Also, Wyntoun's *Orygynale Cronykil* relates that Alexander himself was attacked by northern rebels at Invergowrie; he chased them back across the Mounth and over the 'Stockford' (on the Beauly) into Ross, where they were defeated and killed.[84] Then, when David I was king, there was a major rebellion in which Óengus, earl or 'king' of Moray,[85] was killed by royal forces in 1130, while his co-rebel Malcolm MacHeth (*Mael Coluim mac Aeda*) was eventually captured in 1134, and was imprisoned for the rest of the reign. After David's death, Malcolm MacHeth's sons rebelled against Malcolm IV, in conjunction with their uncle Somerled of Argyll, whose sister was MacHeth's wife. One son, Donald, was captured and used as a hostage for his father – who was released, and was recognised as earl of Ross; he is its first known earl. But when Earl Malcolm MacHeth died in 1168, the new king, William I, did not let his descendants have the earldom; instead, he suppressed it. Another northern rebellion followed in the late 1170s, headed by Earl Harald Maddadson of Orkney/Caithness, who was married to Malcolm MacHeth's sister, and may have threatened to take over Ross as his Norse predecessors had done. William I led an army into Ross in 1179, and built two castles there, at Eddirdour (now Redcastle) on the southern Black Isle and at Dunscaith opposite Cromarty. Then, in 1181, Donald MacWilliam, a great-grandson of Malcolm III through Malcolm's eldest son Duncan (by

---

82 *Orkneyinga Saga*, ch. 54; *ES* ii, 140 n. Cf. B. E. Crawford, 'The earldom of Caithness and the kingdom of Scotland, 1150–1266', in K. J. Stringer (ed.), *Essays on the Nobility of Medieval Scotland* (Edinburgh 1985), 25–8.

83 The narrative outline in this paragraph derives essentially from Duncan, *Making of the Kingdom*, chs. 7–8.

84 *Chron. Wyntoun* (Laing), ii, 174. The 'Stockford' was apparently a ford 'secured by means of wooden stakes or tree trunks' on the Beauly River near the modern Lovat Bridge: G. W. S. Barrow, *Scotland and its Neighbours in the Middle Ages* (London 1992), 213.

85 Earl in *Chron. Melrose*, 33, and in Robert de Torigni's Chronicle (*ES* ii, 174); king in *Ann. Ulster*, 1130.

Ingibjorg), launched a claim to the throne. Again the rebellion focused on Ross, where MacWilliam appears to have been backed by Aed son of Donald, probably a son of Donald MacHeth; he 'wrested from his king the whole of Ross ... and ... for no little time held the whole of Moray'.[86] This, the greatest of the northern rebellions, was eventually put down in 1187, when royal forces caught and defeated Donald MacWilliam at *Mam Garvia*, a moor in southern Ross which was surely near the modern Garve.[87] Next, there was more fighting near the Ross–Moray border in 1196–1201, against sons of Earl Harald of Orkney/Caithness; when William I defeated these, he made Harald repudiate his MacHeth wife and mutilated her son. Thereafter, Ross seemed pacified, but as King William aged, yet another rebellion broke out in 1211. Godfrey ('Guthred', *Gofraid*) MacWilliam invaded from Ireland, apparently encouraged by local thanes in Ross;[88] after initial success, which included capturing the castles, he was betrayed and executed in 1212, and the king 'destroyed' those who had supported him.[89] But trouble continued. In 1215, following Alexander II's accession, another Donald MacWilliam, supported by Kenneth MacHeth and an Irish king, attacked Ross once more. This time they were defeated and killed by a local leader called Farquhar MacTaggart (*mac an tSacairt*: son of the priest), who was subsequently given the earldom of Ross.[90] That, at last, was the end of the MacHeths, though MacWilliam disturbances continued until 1230.

This well-known narrative of events is reasonably straightforward, but how is it to be interpreted? One obvious way is to see the early rebellions against Alexander I and David I as representing continued opposition by the Cenél Loairn of Moray to the Cenél nGabráin kings of Alba: Lodmund was killed by the men of Moray, Óengus was the son of King Lulach's daughter. And, not so obviously but nevertheless plausibly, the later MacWilliam rebellions have been viewed like that as well: William fitz Duncan, son of Duncan II and father of Donald MacWilliam, is described in one source as 'earl of Moray', and it has been argued that he was married to a sister or cousin of Óengus, which would mean that Donald MacWilliam could have headed Cenél Loairn.[91] But Donald MacWilliam also, of course, had a claim to the throne as the grandson of Duncan II,

86 *Chron. Fordun*, i, 268; ii, 263; cf. *RRS* ii, 12–13.
87 As suggested by Barrow, *Scotland and its Neighbours*, 77; cf. Barrow, 'Macbeth and other mormaers', 120.
88 *Chron. Fordun*, i, 278; ii, 274. Here 'thane' may be taken as representing 'native lord'.
89 *Chron. Melrose*, 56; *ES* ii, 389.
90 *RMS* i, App. II, no. 1.
91 *RRS* ii, 12–13; Barrow, 'Macbeth and other mormaers', 119; cf. Duncan, *Making of the Kingdom*, 193.

Malcolm III's eldest son; the fact that his father did not assert it would not
have prevented Donald from doing so, especially if (as seems likely) he
was 'frozen out' by William I. This more recent royal descent must have
been at least an equally important element in the MacWilliam challenge.

Such an interpretation, however, takes little account of the role of Earl
Malcolm MacHeth of Ross, and his descendants. At first sight this appears
to have been purely secondary, as supporters initially of Óengus of
Moray, later of the MacWilliams, and in the 1150s perhaps of Somerled of
Argyll; certainly Malcolm MacHeth is portrayed as subordinate to
Óengus in the *Gesta Annalia* attributed to Fordun.[92] On the other hand,
the only reliable contemporary comment, by Ailred of Rievaulx, implies
that Malcolm was a major rebel leader.[93] Also, Malcolm's marriage
alliances – he married Somerled's sister, and his daughter married Harald
Maddadson, earl of Orkney/Caithness – show that he was of primary
importance. And, as has been pointed out, the fact that Malcolm was
imprisoned not killed, and was eventually released and made an earl,
indicates a relationship with the immediate royal family which Óengus
did not have.[94] This is surely confirmed by the names of the MacHeth
kindred, Malcolm, Donald, Aed and Kenneth; they were all borne by
kings of Alba, but do not appear in the families of other twelfth-century
earls, except that of the royally descended earls of Fife.[95]

Where would Malcolm MacHeth's royal blood have come from? The
name 'MacHeth' disproves the assertion by Ordericus Vitalis that he was
an illegitimate son of Alexander I.[96] The only other specific statement
about his parentage is in the later *Gesta Annalia*: that he claimed to be the
son of Óengus of Moray, but lied, because he was the son of MacHeth.[97]
Taking that literally would make MacHeth a kindred name, like MacDuff
of Fife,[98] and it could perhaps be taken back to the line of King Aed, son
of Kenneth mac Alpín, whose descendants were kings until Constantine III
(died 997). More probably, however, MacHeth is a simple patronymic – in

---

92 *Chron Fordun*, i, 254; ii, 249: 'Upon his death [i.e. Angus's], this Malcolm
    MacHeth rose against King David, as it were a son who would avenge his father's
    death ...'
93 Ailred of Rievaulx, *Relatio de Standardo*, in *Chrons. Stephen, etc.*, iii, 193. Ailred
    portrays Robert de Brus reminding David I that he and other 'Normans' had won
    the kingdom for David's brothers Duncan and Edgar, had put pressure on Alex-
    ander I to let David have the territory bequeathed him by Edgar, and the previous
    year had with great efforts withstood and captured Malcolm (MacHeth).
94 E.g., Duncan, *Making of the Kingdom*, 166; R. A. McDonald, *The Kingdom of the
    Isles: Scotland's Western Seaboard, c.1100–c.1336* (East Linton 1997), 45–6.
95 Cf. Bannerman, 'MacDuff of Fife', 24–5.
96 *SAEC*, 158.
97 *Chron. Fordun*, i, 254; ii, 249.
98 Cf. Bannerman, 'MacDuff of Fife', 20–5, 28–9.

which case his father is likely to have been the Earl Aed who witnessed two of David I's early charters and also, probably, Alexander I's foundation of Scone Priory.[99] The documents do not assign any earldom to Aed, but, since the other earldoms are all accounted for at this time, it is usually reckoned that he must have been earl of either Moray or Ross.[100] Given that Óengus, son of Lulach's daughter, was earl of Moray in 1130, Ross is the better bet – which would indicate that in the 1160s Malcolm MacHeth was restored to his father's earldom. Now it was argued above that when Ross came under the control of the kings of Alba, probably in the reign of Malcolm III, it is likely to have been entrusted to a member of the royal kindred. A royal descent for Earl Aed is therefore entirely reasonable, and the hypothesis suggested here is that he was a son of the Donald son of King Malcolm who died in 1085, and hence perhaps a brother of the Lodmund who was killed in 1116. This is one way of reconciling the MacHeths' probable royal descent with the fact that they backed the MacWilliams: the MacHeths would be descended from a second, or illegitimate, son of Malcolm III, whereas the MacWilliams were descended from his eldest son.

This hypothesis would also account for their antagonism towards the descendants of Malcolm and his second queen, Margaret, which appears to have gone back to Earl Aed, because Ailred described Malcolm MacHeth as 'the heir of paternal hatred and persecution'.[101] That does not necessarily conflict with Aed's appearance as a charter witness early in David I's reign and also probably for Alexander I; after all, Malcolm MacHeth witnessed under Malcolm IV.[102] But an alternative and perhaps more likely suggestion is that Aed supported Alexander I and worked for him in the troublesome north after 1116, and that the 'paternal hatred' was directed more specifically against David I: Alexander I's relations with David may have been tense,[103] and a supporter of his with a power base in northern Scotland could well have resented David I's Anglo-Norman followers. A falling-out between David and Earl Aed is therefore not impossible; and if, as is likely, Aed died in or shortly before 1130, that may have been a catalyst for the subsequent rebellion. The troubles of 1130–4 may reflect MacHeth claims to the throne, as much as those of Óengus of Moray.

---

99 *ESC*, nos. 74, 94; and no. 36 for what purports to be the Scone foundation charter (scholarly opinion on the reliability of the latter's witness list varies).
100 Duncan (*Making of the Kingdom*, 165–6) suggests Moray; Barrow (e.g., *Scotland and its Neighbours*, 61 n.97; 'Macbeth and other mormaers', 118) suggests Ross.
101 *Chrons. Stephen, etc.*, iii, 193.
102 *RRS* i, nos. 209, 292.
103 Especially over David's demand to be given the principality in southern Scotland bequeathed him by Edgar; he had threatened Alexander with armed force based on his Anglo-Norman followers: Duncan, *Making of the Kingdom*, 134.

Admittedly, the above arguments are again only speculative, and various other scenarios could be presented. But no matter what is made of the individuals and their political roles, three fundamental points remain. First, what was going on in Ross during the twelfth and early thirteenth centuries must have been intimately if obscurely bound up with the process of shedding excluded segments of the royal kindred, which is such a major theme in the history of Alba's kingship. Second, during the middle decades of the twelfth century the MacHeths were at the centre of a wider 'opposition' which included Somerled of Argyll and Harald Maddadson of Orkney/Caithness, and which produced what can best be regarded as revolts of the peripheral regions of the north and west, not so much against the centre *per se* as against the essentially south-eastern kingdom of Alba. And third, while the two previous points can be applied to Moray as well, over the twelfth and early thirteenth centuries as a whole Ross was a much more troublesome region, providing as it did a base and springboard for almost all the rebellions, and several times falling entirely outside royal control. Thus the frontier between Ross and Moray was still, in many respects, the effective frontier for the kings of Alba – which is the most important point of all about twelfth- and early thirteenth-century Ross.

*   *   *

The Ross–Moray frontier is neatly highlighted by the different treatment which the two provinces received from the Scottish crown. After the earldom of Moray was suppressed in the 1130s,[104] the province was organised into sheriffdoms, and along its coastal plain royal burghs were established, religious houses were founded, and several incomers, notably Flemings, were granted land by feudal tenure;[105] this is much the same as what happened in the more southerly parts of Scotland. In contrast, after the MacHeth earldom of Ross was suppressed (in 1168), that did not happen there. Twelfth-century Ross had no new sheriffdoms, burghs or religious houses,[106] and although William I built his castles at Eddirdour and Dunscaith, and possibly maintained others at Dingwall and Cromarty,[107]

---

[104] It was probably held for a few years after 1130 by William fitz Duncan: Barrow, 'Macbeth and other mormaers', 119.

[105] *ESC*, nos. 110, 255; *RRS* i, nos. 175, 266, and pp. 43–4; *RRS* ii, nos. 116–17, 132, 139, 153, 213, 281, 359–62, 589, and pp. 39–40; *Moray Reg.*, nos. 30–1, 35, 106–7, 112; Barrow, 'Badenoch and Strathspey, I', 2–4; Duncan, *Making of the Kingdom*, 190–1.

[106] Though there was, of course, the ancient bishopric of Rosemarkie, on the southern shore of the Black Isle; and Dunfermline Abbey must have held land in Ross: *RRS* i, no. 179; ii, no. 500.

[107] The fact that William I built castles at Eddirdour and Dunscaith does not necessarily mean that there were no castles elsewhere. As a thanage, Dingwall was an early

there is no evidence of any 'feudal' grants of land to the crown's southern followers before the end of the reign in 1214 – though, remarkably, to the north of Ross William did grant all or most of Sutherland to Hugh de Moravia.[108] Two caveats are needed, however. Most of the evidence for Moray comes from the episcopal muniments, which have not survived for the diocese of Ross. Also, and more significantly, under Alexander II the Aird, just beyond the southern boundary of Ross, was held by the incomer John Bisset – but his lordship stretched across the River Beauly into Ross, to include what is now the parish of Kilmorack (where he endowed his foundation of Beauly Priory) and in addition the castle and land of Eddirdour; although Bisset cannot be proved to have had this territory before 1214, it is quite likely that he was granted it towards the end of William I's reign, after the defeat of the 1211–12 rebellion.[109] Otherwise, however, it appears clear that before Alexander II came to the throne there were no crown grants of land in Ross.[110] Thus, in contrast to Moray, no 'balance of new and old' is to be found in Ross until well after the death of William I; it was almost entirely 'old'.[111]

But the absence of 'Norman' settlement in twelfth- and early thirteenth-century Ross does not mean that there were no local lords there at all. Frustratingly, there was once a 'roll of twelve membranes of recognitions and old charters of the time of King William and King Alexander his son [concerning?] those to whom the said kings formerly gave their peace, and those who stood with MacWilliam'.[112] This would no doubt have provided a great deal of detail about local lordship in Ross around the end

royal base, and might be expected to have had some kind of fortification; and the same could be argued for Cromarty. The new castle at Dunscaith, on the northern side of the entrance to the Cromarty Firth, surely makes little sense unless there was a complementary fortification opposite, at Cromarty. Thus the later castles at Dingwall and Cromarty, which would have been in existence by the 1260s when both were the seats of sheriffdoms (*ER* i, 19, 26), may well have dated from the 12th century. Note that the reference in *RRS* ii, no. 500, to William I's building-work at 'my castles in Ross' does not specify them, nor say how many there were.

108   *RRS* ii, no. 520.

109   *Beauly Chrs.*, 14–19, 63–4; *OPS* ii (2), 507–18; Duncan, *Making of the Kingdom*, 197.

110   Duncan (ibid.) suggests that 'the Mowat lordship of Cromarty fits logically with the castle of Dunscaith', but the Mowats are not known to have been in Cromarty until 1266 (*ER* i, 19). 'M[ichael?] de Mowat' was sheriff of Inverness in 1234 (*Moray Reg.*, no. 85), and the family probably acquired the sheriffship of Cromarty sometime after that; cf. G. F. Black, *The Surnames of Scotland* (New York 1946), 614. Similarly, while the Murrays of Petty had Avoch in the Black Isle at the end of the 13th century (*CDS* ii, no. 922), there is no evidence that they possessed it significantly earlier.

111   G. W. S. Barrow, *David I of Scotland: The Balance of New and Old* (Reading 1985); repr. in Barrow, *Scotland and its Neighbours*, ch. 3.

112   *APS* i, 114.

of William I's reign, had it not been lost in England after 1296 along with
the rest of the Scottish state muniments. As it is, the only way that the
subject of native Gaelic landholding in Ross can be approached is through
the few scraps of evidence which have survived from later periods.

The starting-point is on the southern edge of Ross, and beyond it in the
Aird. It was argued above that originally the Aird was closely linked to
Ross, but that after the Norse established a frontier on the Beauly, it
became attached to Moray instead. Nevertheless, as has been seen, when
John Bisset was lord of the Aird in the thirteenth century his territory
spilled over into Ross, and that was probably true of his predecessors
there, too. They were almost certainly descendants of the Gilleoin of the
Aird (*Gilleoin na hAird*) who is recorded as the progenitor of three Cenél
Loairn clans in the major fifteenth-century collection of Highland
pedigrees known as 'MS 1467'.[113] These are discussed below; what is
relevant here is the argument by David Sellar[114] that Gilleoin of the Aird
was also the ancestor of John del Ard (of the Aird), who was said in 1297
to be the leading figure in the country near Urquhart Castle on the west
shore of Loch Ness, and of his son Sir Cristin del Ard, captured at Dunbar
in 1296 in the retinue of the earl of Ross.[115] The fact that John del Ard's
son was called Cristin makes it highly likely that he himself should be
identified with the John son of Cristin MacGilleoin who witnessed two
charters to Beauly Priory in the 1270s and one by Elizabeth Bisset to the
earl of Ross in *c*.1300.[116] Now, according to 'MS 1467', Gilleoin of the
Aird had a son called Cristin,[117] and so it might be thought that John del
Ard was Gilleoin's grandson. That is unlikely, however, for a great-great-
grandson of Gilleoin, as recorded in 'MS 1467', was active in 1263–6.[118]
Thus it can be assumed either that there were some more generations
between Gilleoin of the Aird and John del Ard, or that, in the name of
John's father, 'MacGilleoin' was a surname rather than a patronymic;
either is possible. Whatever the case, the frequent occurrence of the name
Cristin in connection with the Aird means there is no reason to doubt
Sellar's identification of this kindred.[119] But in the thirteenth century it

---

113 National Library of Scotland, Adv. MS 72.1.1; used (unsatisfactorily) in
W. F. Skene, *Celtic Scotland* (2nd edn, Edinburgh 1886–90), iii, App. VIII. See
W. D. H. Sellar, 'Highland family origins – pedigree making and pedigree faking',
in L. Maclean (ed.), *The Middle Ages in the Highlands* (Inverness 1981), 104.

114 Ibid., 112.

115 *CDS* ii, no. 923.

116 *Beauly Chrs.*, 61, 64 (as 'Johanne filio Cristini' and 'Johanne filio Christini
MacGillo'); *Munro Writs*, no. 1 (as 'Johanne filio Cristene MacGillone').

117 Sellar, 'Highland family origins', 114.

118 Ibid.; i.e. the 'Kermac Macmaghan' (Kenneth son of Mathghamhain) of *ER* i, 19.

119 Other members of it include Harald son of Dofnald of the Aird (*Beauly Chrs.*, 74,
79, 84), whose first name perhaps reflects enduring Scandinavian connections on

did not possess the lordship of the Aird itself, for that had been given to John Bisset; and, indeed, the lands known subsequently to be held by the del Ards were not acquired until the reign of Robert I. Thus the del Ards were presumably a native kindred over whom 'feudal' lordship was imposed – just as happened with the process of 'Normanisation' elsewhere in Scotland, in Wales, and in Ireland.

As already said, however, 'MS 1467' indicates that three other kindreds stemmed from Gilleoin of the Aird. Two of these are the MacKenzies and the Mathesons. Sellar accepts their descents as 'probably correct', and according to his interpretation of the genealogies the MacKenzies stemmed from Gilleoin's grandson Kenneth, the Mathesons from his great-grandson Mathghamhain.[120] These may be considered west-coast clans; the MacKenzies are associated especially with Kintail, the Mathesons with Lochalsh. But although at first sight those areas seem far removed from the east-coast Aird, in fact they are not. The parish of Kilmorack, running up Strathfarrar and Strathglass, adjoins Kintail; and to the north, the parish of Urray, which starts on the edge of the Black Isle, similarly stretches westwards to Lochalsh. Thus the territory of Gilleoin of the Aird's descendants, the del Ards, MacKenzies and Mathesons, can actually be seen as forming a contiguous block which straddled northern Scotland, from the southern shore of the Beauly Firth across to the west coast. Moreover, since at least part of Strathconon (the parish of Contin) seems to have been occupied by the MacKenzies in the early fourteenth century,[121] their lands may well have included that and perhaps some Highland areas of the parish of Urray (between Contin and Kilmorack) as well. This is a large amount of territory – but not so large as the west-coast lordship or kingdom of Somerled of Argyll in the mid-twelfth century. Gilleoin of the Aird was probably a contemporary of Somerled: his great-great-grandson, Kenneth son of 'Mathan' (*Coinneach mac Mathghamhain*, literally the first of the Mathesons) worked for the crown in Wester Ross at the time of the Norwegian attack in 1263,[122] and counting four thirty-year generations back from that would date Gilleoin to around 1140. It may well be that Gilleoin was like Somerled, in that he too presumably

the edge of Ross. The submission of 'William fiz Stevene de Arde' is recorded in the 1296 Ragman Roll (*CDS* ii, p. 210), where Scottish names are often garbled; Stephen could be a French-speaking clerk's garbling of Cristin, *via* Etienne, so he may have been a brother of John son of Cristin, and the 'William' might perhaps be a similar garbling of Gilleoin.

120 Sellar, 'Highland family origins', 110–12, 114.

121 The wife of a 14th-century MacKenzie chief fell or was thrown over the bridge at Scatwell, in Contin parish: W. Matheson, 'Traditions of the MacKenzies', *TGSI* xxxix/xl (1942–50), 194–5, 208, 211–12.

122 *ER* i, 19–20.

built up a great lordship in the early twelfth century, which would surely have been independent of the mormaers or earls of Moray. The likelihood is that he expanded his power outwards from the Aird to fill what may have been a vacuum in southern Ross left by the retreat of Norse power during the previous half century. And, just as with the kindred of Somerled, after his death his descendants fragmented into three separate clans, who subsequently occupied the Aird, part of south Ross, and the adjoining southern areas of North Argyll.

The other kindred said in 'MS 1467' to descend from Gilleoin of the Aird is that of the Gillanders (*Clann Ghille Ainnriais*).[123] In later centuries this was believed locally to have included the kindred of the Rosses; as Sir Robert Gordon's *History of the Earldom of Sutherland* (1639) put it, 'all the Rosses in that province ar unto this day called in the Irish language Clan-Leamdreis'.[124] But, as both Gordon and the early seventeenth-century chronicler of the earls of Ross stated, this was not the kindred of Farquhar MacTaggart and his successors. Instead, in the early fifteenth century, when the earldom had gone to an heiress and the headship of the kin had gone to the Rosses of Balnagown, the second of these, Walter Ross, married the daughter of a notorious Highland freebooter called Paul Mactire ('wolf's son') – 'after qlk marriage Ross are called Clan Lendris'.[125] Thus the Gillanders were the kindred of Paul Mactire, not the Rosses. That is shown in 'MS 1467', where Paul's great-great-grandfather is given as a Gillanders, who is eight generations on from Gilleoin of the Aird. But those are too many generations, because Paul Mactire can be dated to the 1360s. Thus, as Sellar points out, it is likely that Paul's genealogy has been combined with Gilleoin's descendants, and that it should really start with another Paul, who in 'MS 1467' is Gillanders's grandfather.[126] Now, according to William Matheson, that earlier Paul was possibly Pall Bálkason, '*vice-comes*' of Skye for the kings of Man in the early thirteenth century, from whose father both the MacPhails ('sons of Paul') and the MacLeods ('sons of Ljótr') appear to descend.[127] Paul Mactire's kindred

---

123 Sellar, 'Highland family origins', 107, 110–11, 114.

124 Sir Robert Gordon, *A Genealogical History of the Earldom of Sutherland from its origin to the year 1630* (Edinburgh, 1813 edn), 36.

125 *Chron. Earls of Ross*, 41; see also p. 26. The name Paul Mactire is attested by *RMS* i, no. 423. In MS 1467 his genealogy runs *Paul mac Tyre mac* [or *mhic*] *Eogan* ... (David Sellar informs me that either *mac* or *mhic* could be read); but *Tire* means 'wolf', and so, as Sellar remarks, 'it is not clear whether "Mactire" is patronymic or a byname': 'Highland family origins', 116 n.36. In his table, Sellar takes it as a patronymic (Tire is given as Paul's father), but here I follow William Matheson and guess that it is a byname denoting 'Paul the wolf': W. Matheson, 'The Pape riot and its sequel in Lewis', *TGSI* xlviii (1972–4), 426, 434 n.110.

126 Sellar, 'Highland family origins', 114.

127 Matheson, 'Pape riot', 424–7; *The Blind Harper: The Songs of Roderick Morison and*

would thus be an offshoot of the MacPhails, would have been based in the northern part of Wester Ross (which ties in with a grant of Gairloch to Paul Mactire by the earl of Ross in 1366),[128] and would originally have been Scandinavian.

It may be questioned, however, whether the 'MS 1467' genealogy from the earlier Paul (Bálkason?) *via* Gillanders to Paul Mactire is necessarily reliable. Later Ross tradition had it that 'thair was thrie sones of the King of Denmark, callit Gwine, Loid and Leandres', who conquered parts of northern Scotland: 'Gwine' in Caithness, hence the Gunns; 'Loid' in Lewis, hence the MacLeods; and 'Leandres' with his son 'Tyre' and grandson Paul Mactire in northern Ross, hence Clan Gillanders.[129] Gillanders, however, is not Scandinavian but Gaelic in origin, and means the servant of (St) Andrew. It is fairly common in medieval Scotland,[130] but two instances of the name in the Beauly Priory charters are significant here: a Gillanders MacIsaac witnessed in 1231, and an Isaac MacGillanders witnessed twice in the 1270s.[131] Gillanders MacIsaac was in the company of John Bisset of the Aird, while Isaac MacGillanders was with John son of Cristin MacGilleoin (both times), the earl of Sutherland, and the earl of Ross. That indicates that Gillanders and Isaac, who were no doubt father and son, were prominent figures in eastern Ross during the thirteenth century, on a par with John (del Ard) son of Cristin. And the fact that Gillanders MacIsaac's *floruit* of *c*.1231 makes him a likely contemporary of the Gillanders in Paul Mactire's genealogy raises the question of whether that is simply a coincidence, or whether the two Gillanders may have been the same person. In other words, did Clan Gillanders – which, as has been seen, was later regarded as the senior kindred in Ross – actually derive from the Gillanders MacIsaac of eastern Ross rather than from the Pall Bálkason of the west? That could have happened if one of

---

his Music, ed. W. Matheson (Scottish Gaelic Texts Soc., 1970) 108. The connection with the MacLeods, which is a tradition both in Easter Ross and in Harris, seems to be confirmed by the early 15th-century name Leod mac Ghille Ainnraiis, because Leod or Ljótr is a very rare personal name: Matheson, 'Pape riot', 427. David Sellar tells me, however, that he doubts this descent for the MacLeods: see W. D. H. Sellar, 'The origins of the MacLeods reconsidered', *TGSI*, forthcoming.

128 *RMS* i, no. 423. Earlier, Pall Bálkason and his family may have worked with the earl of Ross: *ES* ii, 458–9, and below, page 123.

129 *Chron. Earls of Ross*, 30–1.

130 Black, *Surnames of Scotland*, 301–2, 498. One that should be noted here is Gillanders son of Alfwin mac Archil, who like his father was *rannaire* or food distributor for Malcolm IV: *RRS* i, 32. He is no doubt the 'Gyllandrys-Ergemawche' who, according to Wyntoun, was involved in the 1157 rebellion against Malcolm IV: *Chron. Wyntoun* (Laing), ii, 197. It is thus wrong to identify this Gillanders with an earl of Ross, either Malcolm MacHeth or a predecessor, as in *Scots Peerage*, vii, 231, and Skene, *Celtic Scotland*, iii, 291–2.

131 *Beauly Chrs.*, 33, 60–1, 63–4.

Paul Mactire's forebears had married a daughter of Gillanders MacIsaac, and had carried on the line after Isaac MacGillanders's death, just as happened later when marriage with Paul Mactire's daughter led to the incorporation of the Rosses within Clan Gillanders; the 'MS 1467' genealogy could easily have been muddled. That is only a hypothesis, but knowledge of the difficulties experienced by 'feudal' landowning families in maintaining father–son succession should encourage scepticism about the neat descents presented in the later Gaelic genealogies.[132] Here, therefore, it is proposed that the real Gillanders kindred was based in eastern Ross, north of the territory occupied by Gilleoin of the Aird's kindred, but probably south of the lands of the earldom of Ross itself.[133] That suggests that its lands – or at least those of Gillanders MacIsaac – may have been in the Black Isle, or lower Strathconon, or around Dingwall; but there is no way to be certain.

Whatever may have been the case, with the descendants of Gilleoin of the Aird and Clan Gillanders it is possible to glimpse major native kindreds who must have been very important within the province of Ross during the twelfth century and perhaps even earlier. Unfortunately, no more native kindreds can be tentatively identified in the same way. One is, perhaps, represented by the Munros, who possessed most of the area of Ferindonald (now Kiltearn and Alness) in the fourteenth century; but there is no evidence to support their family traditions of an early presence there.[134] The few surviving documents from before 1300 do, however, name some Gaels who were presumably prominent in the thirteenth century: Lulach 'MacImantokell' (whose name is an interesting reminder of the Cenél Loairn King Lulach), Colin MacGillecongal, Gilchrist 'MacGilliduffi', Duncan Duff, 'Bochly' or 'Bolan Beg', and Colin Gow.[135] The first two witnessed for Earl Farquhar of Ross, and so were possibly

132 Cf. A. Grant, 'Extinction of direct male lines among Scottish noble families in the fourteenth and fifteenth centuries', in Stringer, *Essays on the Nobility*, 210–31.

133 Although Isaac MacGillanders was once a co-witness with an earl of Ross (*Beauly Chrs.*, 64), neither he nor Gillanders MacIsaac witness the (very few) surviving charters of the 13th-century earls, which suggests that they were not major tenants of the earldom.

134 See above, page 105 and note 80. Local tradition made the Munros come from the area of the River Roe in Co. Derry, Ireland: 'a Munro is always *Rothach*, "a Roman", in Gaelic': Watson, *Celtic Place-Names*, 116. Hence they may well represent a Gaelic kindred; but it cannot be proved.

135 *Moray Reg.*, no. 259; *Beauly Chrs.*, 60–1, 64; *Munro Writs*, no. 1; the forms given here are those found in Black, *Surnames of Scotland*. The early MacGillecongalls mentioned there (p. 499) are from Galloway, so perhaps Colin was recruited from there by Earl Farquhar, just as he brought monks from Whithorn to his new abbey at Fearn (*Chron. Earls of Ross*, 1–3; *Cal. Fearn*, 28–9). Duncan Duff is no doubt simply Duncan *Dubh* (black).

based north of the Cromarty Firth, while the others are associated with grants relating to south-east Ross, and perhaps came from there; Colin Gow was constable of Tarradale Castle in 1278. None of them is anything more than a name, except for Gilchrist MacGilliduffi. Taken literally, that represents *Gille Críosd mac Ghille Dhuibh shídhe*, which may be translated as 'the servant of Christ, son of the servant of the black one of the fairy mound'![136] It comes, however, from the Beauly charters, which survive only in an early seventeenth-century transcription, and so the final '-i' in MacGilliduffi may not be accurate.[137] Thus an alternative, and more likely, original for the surname would be *mac Ghille Duib*, 'son of the servant of *Dub*' – which might perhaps link him with the MacDuff earls of Fife, descendants of King Dub (died 966).[138] As for his forename, *Gille Críosd* is the same as Cristin, the name of several descendants of Gilleoin of the Aird; and it was particularly common among the MacRaes, a kindred which was subordinate to the MacKenzies on the west, but which apparently came from Clunes in the Aird.[139] Gilchrist MacGilliduffi might therefore have been connected with those kindreds. His significance, however, is not so much in his name as in the fact that, unlike the other Gaelic lords discussed above, he is known to have been a 'feudal' landowner, and was, indeed, the superior of an incoming 'Norman'. He appears in the charter of *c.*1270 to Beauly Priory, which is a grant by a David of Inverlunan of the half davach of Ochtertarradale which David held in feu-farm of Gilchrist; this had Gilchrist's consent, and followed Gilchrist's own charter of the same land.[140] Gilchrist must therefore have been the lord of Tarradale, and was probably the builder of the castle there;[141] he may also, perhaps, have held adjoining territory in Urray to the west.[142]

*   *   *

One other native Gaelic lord remains to be considered: the new earl of Ross, Farquhar MacTaggart, himself. He is usually believed to have been a west-coast potentate, who was hereditary lay abbot of the secularised monastery of Applecross, originally founded by St Mael Rubha.[143] But if so, then his surname ought to have been MacNab (*mac an Aba*, son of the

---

136 Following Bannerman, 'MacDuff of Fife', 21.

137 *Beauly Chrs.*, 60. It is in the genitive case, so the '-i' may simply be grammatical.

138 Bannerman, 'MacDuff of Fife', 21–6.

139 Matheson, 'Traditions of the MacKenzies', 216.

140 *Beauly Charters*, 60–1. Gilchrist's own charter has disappeared, but cf. ibid., 17, 61–2.

141 Ibid., 64 (Colin Gow, constable of Tarradale, 1274); *CDS* ii, no. 1633.

142 Later, Urray (called Inveraferan; cf. note 25 above) and Tarradale were granted together to Earl Hugh of Ross by Robert I: *RMS* i, App. II, nos. 64, 381.

143 E.g., Duncan, *Making of the Kingdom*, 197 and note.

abbot) rather than MacTaggart.[144] In fact, the idea of Earl Farquhar's connection with Applecross originated no earlier than the mid-nineteenth-century speculation of W. F. Skene and W. Reeves.[145] Admittedly, speculation is essential when dealing with the early history of Ross (as this essay makes only too clear), but in that case it is distinctly unsound.

Skene and Reeves seem to have combined three sources. First, *The Book of Clanranald* has an account of a Gilpatrick Roy (*Ghillipadraig rúaigh*), killed at Harlaw in 1411, in which his pedigree is given as: 'Gilpatrick Roy, son of Rory, son of the Green Abbot, son of the earl of Ross, whose [that is, Gilpatrick's] surname was of the Rosses'.[146] Next, Hugh Macdonald's *History of the Macdonalds* calls the same person 'Patrick Obeolan, surnamed the Red', and adds that 'This surname Obeolan was the surnames [*sic*] of the Earls of Ross, till Farquhar, born in Ross, was created earl by King Alexander, and so carried the name of Ross ever since, as best answering the English tongue.'[147] Thirdly, Sir Robert Gordon's *History of the Earls of Sutherland* states that 'the laird of Balnagown his surname should not be Rosse, seing ther wes never any Earle of Rosse of that surname; bot the Earle of Rosse wer first of the surname of Builton, then they were Leslies, and last of all that earldom fell by inheritance to the lords of the Yles'.[148] On their own, these statements are not necessarily significant, but Hugh Macdonald also gives the crucial information that 'This Obeolan had its descent of the ancient tribe of the Manapii; of this tribe is also St Rice or Rufus.' Reeves (with Skene) identified St Rice with St Mael Rubha of Applecross, understood Hugh Macdonald to mean that Earl Farquhar of Ross was descended from the same kindred, and went on to claim that Farquhar was either the son of the abbot of Applecross, or

---

144 I am indebted to Geoffrey Barrow for first pointing this out to me. Cf. Barrow, 'Macbeth and other mormaers', 121. It should be added, however, that in Gaelic tradition Mael Rubha was commonly known as '*Sagart Ruadh*', i.e. 'the red priest (which is one way of translating Mael Rubha): Scott, 'Saint Maolrubha', 260–1. Thus Farquhar's second name could possibly have denoted a link with Maelrubhai himself, rather than a later abbot – except, of course, that there were countless other priests in medieval Ross. Note that Scott dismisses all claims, by Rosses, MacKenzies, Reids and MacDonalds, to descent from St Mael Rubha: ibid., 280.

145 W. Reeves, 'Saint Maelrubha: his history and churches', *PSAS* iii (1862), 275–6, which acknowledges Skene's advice; Skene then stated the same point in his notes to *Chron. Fordun*, ii, 434 (citing Reeves's article), and repeated it in *Celtic Scotland*, i, 483–4 (citing Reeves's article and the *Chron. Fordun* note). Reeves's article meant that the suggestion published the same year in E. W. Robertson, *Scotland under her early Kings* (Edinburgh 1862), ii, 4 n., that Farquhar was 'probably the *Cowarb* of the church lands in Ross, representing the head of the old family of the district', was simply ignored.

146 *Reliquiae Celticae*, ii, 212–13.

147 *Highland Papers*, i, 34.

148 Gordon, *Earldom of Sutherland*, 36.

the son of its 'erenach' (*airchinneach*) or lay administrator, since a family called O'Beólan apparently had the office of *airchinneach* in the church of St Columba at Drumcliff near Sligo.[149]

Hugh Macdonald, however, states only that the earls of Ross belonged to the same kindred as 'St Rice', not that they were his descendants; says that Farquhar was born in Ross, probably meaning Easter Ross; and makes no direct connection with Applecross. Also, as already said, Farquhar was 'son of the priest', not son of an abbot or *airchinneach*. Now Reeves remarks that at Applecross 'there exists, indeed, a vivid tradition of an individual styled the "Red Priest of Applecross", who is said to have conveyed to his daughter the rich estates with which this church was endowed, and which, down to his time, had been enjoyed by his predecessors in office'.[150] That led G. F. Black to state in his *Surnames of Scotland* that Earl Farquhar was 'son of the red priest of Applecross'.[151] Reeves, however, identifies the 'red priest' with the Gilpatrick Roy who died in 1411;[152] it is most confusing. The main point, however, is that the 'red priest' had the church lands of Applecross, which means that they would not have gone with Earl Farquhar to the earls of Ross.

Another point is that the existence of an *airchinneach* in County Sligo called O'Beólan does not prove that the same surname was used for the holder of that office at Applecross. Indeed, *Beólan* was a fairly common Gaelic name and, since it means 'little mouth',[153] could well have been a nickname – which might explain how it was applied to the earls of Ross. In a passage on the battle of Halidon Hill (1333), Gordon's *History of Sutherland* states that 'in this field was Hugh Builton, Erle of Rosse, slain; and with him was killed the laird of Foulls, surnamed Monroe'. Gordon goes on to describe the Munros, in a way which indicates that he was using their traditions.[154] It is likely, therefore, that that is where he found the name 'Hugh Builton'; in which case 'Beólan' might have been Earl Hugh's nickname, not his family surname. That could account for the application of 'O'Beólan' to Gilpatrick Roy, the grandson of an abbot who was the son of an earl of Ross, for in the later fourteenth century, two abbots of Fearn

149 Reeves, 'Saint Maelrubha', 275-6, citing *The Life of Columba written by Adamnan*, ed. W. Reeves (Dublin 1857), 279, 400. Although this is not specifically stated, Skene and Reeves were probably thinking of the 'Gyllandrys-Ergemawche' in Wyntoun's account of the 1157 rebellion, whom Skene subsequently identified as an earl of Ross (see note 130, above).

150 Reeves, 'Saint Maelrubha', 275.

151 Black, *Surnames of Scotland*, 565.

152 Reeves, 'Saint Maelrubha', 275-6. The original 'red priest' may well have been Mael Rubha (Scott, 'St Maolruba', 260-1), but the genealogical claims are meaningless.

153 Black, *Surnames of Scotland*, 69.

154 Gordon, *Earldom of Sutherland*, 46.

(which was founded by Earl Farquhar) were kin to the earls: one was said to be the nephew of Earl William, Hugh's successor, while the other's name was Mark Ross.[155] Either might have been descended from Earl Hugh and have been the grandfather of Gilpatrick Roy; and if Earl Hugh was nicknamed Beólan, that could have been garbled by Hugh Macdonald or his source into a general family name for the earls of Ross.

That, however, is equally speculative. What is much more significant is that, although the idea that Earl Farquhar's family belonged to a kindred of O'Beólans was believed by seventeenth-century historians of the MacDonalds and the Sutherlands,[156] it was totally unknown at the same period to the family chroniclers of the Rosses. That the Rosses' own account of themselves is more reliable can be seen by comparing their and Sir Robert Gordon's treatment of the fact that in Gaelic their kindred was called *Clann Ghille Ainnriais*: Gordon uses this to support his manifestly false contention that the earls of Ross never had the surname Ross, while (as seen above) the Ross chronicler – who states categorically that the first earls were 'Ross of surname' – explains it in terms of the marriage to the daughter of Paul Mactire, whose descent from a Gillanders is given independently in 'MS 1467'. On the other hand, when it comes to Earl Farquhar, the chronicler of the earls of Ross descends into utter fantasy, making Farquhar appear from nowhere at the coronation of Edward I in 1272, and defeat a Frenchman called Dougall Duncanson at wrestling, for which he was rewarded by King Alexander with the earldom of Ross![157] That nonsense proves that the Rosses themselves had no idea of what Earl Farquhar's pedigree was; had they had any inkling that he belonged to the same kindred as St Mael Rubha, there can be no question that they would have said so. Against that, it might be argued that Hugh Macdonald's *History of the MacDonalds* drew on west-coast genealogies which were unknown to the Ross chronicler on the east. But if so, they ought to have been included earlier in 'MS 1467', the main compilation of such genealogies. This gives the pedigrees of clans in areas controlled by or claimed by the Lords of the Isles,[158] which in the fifteenth century included Ross; but while there is a pedigree (albeit partly false) for the Gillanders, there is not one for the earls of Ross. Again, it is hard to

---

155 *Munro Writs*, no. 8; *Chron. Earls of Ross*, 5–7; cf. *Cal Fearn*, 29 n., 85.

156 And also, perhaps, by those of the Macraes: David Sellar has pointed out to me that the 17th-century genealogy of the Macraes states that the first Macrae in Kintail married a daughter or grand-daughter of 'MacBeolan who possessed a large part of Kintail' (*Highland Papers*, i, 209) – though that does not necessarily equate 'MacBeolan' with the earl of Ross.

157 *Chron. Earls of Ross*, 1–2, 26, 41; Gordon, *Earldom of Sutherland*, 38.

158 J. W. M. Bannerman, 'The Lordship of the Isles', in J. M. Brown (ed.), *Scottish Society in the Fifteenth Century* (London 1977), 211.

believe that a descent from Mael Rubha or his kindred would not have been included for them, had the compiler of 'MS 1467' known about it. In other words, although in the seventeenth century, historians of the MacDonalds and Sutherlands claimed to know what Earl Farquhar's kindred was, his own descendants did not know it, and neither did the fifteenth-century pedigree writers. The latter are surely to be believed – which means that Farquhar should not be regarded as being descended from the abbot of Applecross.

It follows that the idea of Farquhar MacTaggart coming from the west coast to defeat the MacWilliam/MacHeth rising and take over Easter Ross – which would have been a most remarkable achievement – has to be jettisoned. Instead, there is no reason not to locate him in Easter Ross, which, in fact, tallies with Hugh Macdonald's description of him as 'Farquhar, born in Ross'. Where he was born, however, is impossible to say. The best guess might be Tain – where he appears to have died[159] – which, with St Duthac's shrine and girth, was the main religious centre in north-east Ross. The girth may well be crucial. Such sanctuaries were usually ecclesiastical, attached to a church; that that was so at Tain is proved by the fact that it was marked out by four crosses.[160] But in the later Middle Ages the girth at Tain was supervised by the earls of Ross, along with the 'kirkmen'.[161] This secular oversight of an ecclesiastical girth is most unusual, and it is difficult to see how it could have originated – unless, that is, the earls of Ross exercised it because it had once been the function of their ancestor Farquhar, 'son of the priest'.[162]

In that case, it would be possible to see Farquhar and his father as heirs or successors of St Duthac; Farquhar may have been the coarb (*comharba*) of Duthac, albeit not as a member of Duthac's kin, for otherwise he would surely not have been known simply as '*mac an tSacairt*'.[163] This

159 *Chron. Earls of Ross*, 4.
160 Munro and Munro, *Tain through the Centuries*, 14–17, cf. MacQueen, 'Girth' (forthcoming), and W. Davies, '"Protected Space" in Britain and Ireland in the Middle Ages', in Crawford, *Scotland in Dark Age Britain*, 1–13.
161 Munro and Munro, *Tain through the Centuries*, 14–17, *APS* ii, 248. As Hector MacQueen has pointed out to me, this would explain why in 1306 the earl of Ross denied sanctuary to Robert I's queen and her entourage: they had been associated with Robert's 'bootless' crime of killing John Comyn in a church.
162 Note that the other main sanctuary in northern Scotland was that of Mael Rubha at Applecross (Watson, *Celtic Place-Names*, 124–5). Thus, if Hugh Macdonald did link the earls of Ross with St Mael Rubha, might it be because he or his source confused and conflated the two sanctuaries?
163 Although heredity was very important in the Celtic Church, it must be remembered that (given the accidents of human reproduction) the founders of monasteries would not necessarily have left children or have belonged to thriving kindreds. There is no evidence that Duthac actually established his kindred at Tain.

function or office could explain his obvious influence in early thirteenth-century Ross, especially if other local leaders had been removed by William I in 1212. Nevertheless, it should be stressed that if Farqhuar was, as it seems, a man without a significant pedigree, then he was out of place in the traditional kin-based world. Indeed as the son of a priest he might be thought to have been more generally out of place.[164] On the other hand, after he defeated and killed Donald MacWilliam and Kenneth MacHeth – thereby presumably demonstrating his personal qualities as a military leader – Alexander II knighted him, which established him within the new Anglo-Norman-French social world of the thirteenth century, wherein all knights were equal and knighthood could be earned by some special action. And that, in turn, made him eligible to be made an earl, which would have been unthinkable for a kinless man in traditional Gaelic kin-based society. Thus although, above, Farquhar is called a 'native Gaelic lord', that is not entirely appropriate; he was probably an anomaly in Gaelic Alba, and is best regarded as a 'phenomenon'[165] of the hybrid Scotland created by its twelfth- and thirteenth-century kings – as his subsequent career as earl demonstrates.

                                    *   *   *

The rise of Farquhar MacTaggart, which must be among the most spectacular in the whole of Scottish medieval history, marks a fundamental turning-point for the province of Ross. This is when it at last became an integral part of the kingdom. What is known of Farquhar's career after 1215 illustrates this perfectly.[166] His promotion to the rank of earl – certainly by 1226 and probably by 1223[167] – may have been a consequence of Alexander II's expedition to Inverness in 1221, which prompted an ordinance defining military obligations that highlighted the role of the earls in recruitment and leadership.[168] Be that as it may, he must clearly have acted effectively as the local military commander, for there were no more rebellions in Ross after 1215, despite further MacWilliam risings elsewhere in the Highlands. And Farquhar not only kept eastern Ross

---

164 It is an interesting coincidence (but nothing more) that Farquhar means 'very dear one' (Black, *Surnames of Scotland*, 255), much the same as the meaning of both names of that much more famous bastard of a priest, Desiderius Erasmus.

165 Duncan, *Making of the Kingdom*, 197.

166 For a longer discussion of him, see R. A. McDonald, 'Old and New in the Far North: Farquhar MacTaggart and the early earls of Ross', in S. Boardman (ed.), *Scottish Native Kindreds in the Middle Ages* (East Linton, forthcoming).

167 *Moray Reg.*, no. 258, which was witnessed by 'F comite de Ros', is earlier than no. 75, which is dated 1226; so Farquhar must already have been an earl by then (*Scots Peerage*, vii, 232, seems to have these the wrong way round, and so dates Farquhar's earldom to after 1236). The Manx Chronicle says he was already earl of Ross in 1223: *ES*, ii, 458–9.

168 *APS*, i, 398, c.2.

quiet but also dealt with the west coast, from which the earlier rebellions had probably been launched; by 1223 his daughter was married to Olaf of Man, and he helped Olaf and Pall Bálkason to defeat their rivals in Skye.[169] This action, the beginning of the take-over of North Argyll by the thirteenth-century earls of Ross, probably helped to pave the way for Alexander II's campaigns on the west. In addition, he fought for Alexander in southern Scotland, playing a significant role in crushing the Galloway revolt of 1235.[170] More peaceful contacts with Galloway are reflected in his foundation of a Premonstratensian priory at Fearn, which was staffed by canons from Whithorn.[171] Founding a religious house was the typical act of a new magnate of this period, and its dedication to the Scottish but not Gaelic St Ninian rather than to a local saint such as Duthac or Mael Rubha perhaps signifies a rejection of the traditional Gaelic church in which he presumably grew up. But his most striking rejection of his past – whatever it had been – is to be seen in the names given to his sons, William and Malcolm.[172] They must have been called after Alexander's predecessors as kings of Scots; it is as if Farquhar, who had no established kindred of his own, was looking to enter the royal *familia*. And that, of course, was what his promotion to the closely restricted rank of earl did for him. His new position was maintained by his eldest son, who married the daughter of William Comyn, earl of Buchan, and by his successors;[173] in the later thirteenth and fourteenth centuries indeed, the earls of Ross were among the most prominent magnates of Scotland.

That Ross was incorporated fully into the kingdom, however, was not simply a matter of Earl Farquhar's remarkable career; it also reflects a new royal policy. During the twelfth century the crown had a *laissez faire* attitude to the regions beyond coastal Moray; it suppressed the two troublesome

---

169 *ES* ii, 458–9.
170 *Chron. Melrose*, 84; *ES*, ii, 496.
171 *Chron. Earls of Ross*, 1–3. When that took place is unknown; Fearn's early muni-
     ments, including the papal bull of foundation, were accidentally destroyed in
     1427: *Cal. Fearn*, 28–9; *ALI*, no. 90. Its dating to the 1220s in I. B. Cowan and D. E.
     Easson, *Medieval Religious Houses: Scotland* (2nd edn, London 1976), 101, is only a
     suggestion. The Ross Chronicle makes it follow Farquhar's fictitious wrestling
     match (see above, page 120): he is said to have sworn that if he won his 'battle' he
     would found an abbey staffed by the first religious men he met, and these turned
     out to be 'two quhite channonis in Galloway'. If anything lies behind this, it might
     be that the foundation followed his victory in Galloway in 1235. Alternatively,
     the implication could be that Farquhar founded Fearn much earlier in his career;
     and as Keith Stringer has pointed out to me, by 1223 his daughter was married to
     Olaf of Man, who gave Whithorn lands and churches in Man: see Stringer's essay,
     below, chapter 6, note 142. See also above, note 135, for Farquhar's possible
     recruitment of a MacGillecongall from Galloway.
172 *Scots Peerage*, vii, 232.
173 Ibid., 233–4.

northern earldoms, but otherwise seems to have left native lords and kindreds in place despite the great rebellions. This applies not only to Ross, but also to Badenoch, the Great Glen area, the Aird, and, in a sense, Caithness in the far north. The second decade of the thirteenth century, however, saw a significant change. After the rebellion of 1211–12, against which William I had to raise two full-scale armies and also employ a force of Brabantine mercenaries, the king 'destroyed those responsible for perverting' Godfrey MacWilliam.[174] Some must have been killed, for William 'left behind him the lifeless corpses of many men';[175] and this is no doubt when the lists of 'those to whom the ... kings ... gave their peace, and those who stood with MacWilliam' were first drawn up.[176] Thus a much more draconian policy was adopted towards the local elites – which was continued, after William I's death and following fresh rebellion, by Alexander II. That perhaps helps to explain why it is so difficult to find evidence of native landowners in thirteenth-century Ross: many were no doubt removed.

Another part of the crown's new policy was the creation of military lordships in the north. In Highland Moray and the Great Glen region, important incomers such as the brother of the earl of Mar and several of the Durwards are evident in the 1220s, and after the final 1230 rebellion Walter Comyn was given Badenoch and Lochaber, which put him in charge of the central Highlands.[177] Also, as has already been seen, John Bisset became lord of the Aird and of the 'Redcastle' at Eddirdour in southern Ross; he was already there in the 1220s, and probably received his lordship in or shortly after 1212.[178] At much the same time (certainly before 1214) Hugh de Moravia, grandson of Freskin the Fleming to whom David I seems to have entrusted much of coastal Moray, was given the southern part of Caithness, namely Sutherland, as another great lordship.[179] These grants are all aspects of a new military colonisation that took place throughout northern Scotland during the second and third decades of the thirteenth century. And between Sutherland and the Aird, of course, lay Ross, where Farquhar MacTaggart was to become the earl by the mid-1220s. In the wider context, this is another example of the entrusting of a major regional lordship to a man who had proved to be a reliable military leader. Viewed in this way, therefore, what was going on in Ross in the 1210s and 1220s was part of a wider process, the final conquest of north-eastern Scotland by the kings of Alba.

---

174 Duncan, *Making of the Kingdom*, 196, 250, n.; *Chron. Melrose*, 56.
175 Ibid.
176 *APS* i, 114.
177 Barrow, 'Badenoch and Strathspey, I', 4–7.
178 See above, page 111.
179 *RRS* ii, no. 520.

That is only part of the story, however. Whereas the Bissets, de Moravias, Comyns, and most of the other lords who were put into the north were southern incomers with Anglo-Norman or Flemish origins who were imposed upon the indigenous local kindreds,[180] Farquhar MacTaggart was a native of Ross. It seems as if the territory of the earldom of Ross, in contrast to the other regions of the north, could not be entrusted to an incomer. That is reminiscent of the earldom's grant in the 1160s to Malcolm MacHeth, which probably restored him to his father's position. Furthermore, in 1212 Godfrey MacWilliam was not defeated by the royal armies sent against him, but was 'betrayed by his own followers'.[181] It is reasonable to assume that the betrayal was perpetrated, or at least supported, by local men in eastern Ross.[182] There is therefore a parallel with the events of three years later, when Donald MacWilliam and Kenneth MacHeth were killed in Ross by locals led by Farquhar MacTaggart. Perhaps, indeed, Farquhar had been involved in Godfrey's betrayal; whoever had been responsible would certainly have opposed the 1215 rebellion. Be that as it may, it is clear that in 1212–15 the MacWilliam/MacHeth cause was being rejected by at least some of the inhabitants of Ross.

Why was that? It must be remembered that the rebellions of 1211–12 and 1215 both appear to have started with landings from Ireland, and that that was probably the case, too, with the original MacWilliam rising of 1179–87. Each time, eastern Ross would have been invaded from the west. In addition, in 1196–1201 it must have experienced invasions from Orkney/Caithness, in which there was also a MacHeth connection. For the people of eastern Ross, therefore, the MacWilliam/MacHeth cause would have been a source of external incursions which, though possibly peaceful to begin with, led to intense conflicts which must have been accompanied by widespread destruction. Perhaps, therefore, by the 1210s enough was enough; although local lords apparently encouraged the rebellions, for other inhabitants of eastern Ross peace was probably much more attractive.[183] And in that case, Farquhar MacTaggart's status as the son of a (no doubt important) priest and the likely supervisor of the girth at Tain makes him an obvious leader for those who wanted an end to the rebellions in Ross.

What should be stressed in conclusion, therefore, is that when, in the

---

180 As seen with the kindred of the Aird ('del Ard'): see above, pages 112–13; cf. the Macintosh kindred in Badenoch.

181 *Chron. Bower*, iv, 466–7 (here Bower was using an early 13th-century source: ibid., iv, 631; ix, 251–5).

182 Godfrey's last known action before his betrayal was to capture one of the royal castles in eastern Ross: ibid., iv, 466–7.

183 Cf. the similar argument in Barrow, 'Macbeth and other mormaers', 113–14, 120–2.

thirteenth century, the province of Ross was finally incorporated into the kingdom, this was not simply the consequence of its conquest by the Canmore kings, by the 'Normans', or by the 'south'. Instead, after centuries when it was on or beyond the fringe, it was the actions of its own people, under Farquhar MacTaggart, that cemented this particular Highland building-block into the kingdom of Alba or Scotland. Awareness, and no doubt fear, of royal power may have helped to bring this about; but the main consideration must surely have been a desire for the peace and stability which the thirteenth-century Scottish crown offered all its loyal subjects. Certainly that is how the people of Ross could be described thereafter – at least until the Lords of the Isles became involved with the earldom during the fifteenth century.[184]

---

[184] In 1411 the then head of Earl Farquhar's kindred, Walter Ross of Balnagown, supported Donald, Lord of the Isles at the time of Harlaw: A. Grant, 'Scotland's "Celtic fringe" in the late Middle Ages: the Macdonald Lords of the Isles and the kingdom of Scotland', in R. R. Davies (ed.), *The British Isles 1100–1500: Comparisons, Contrasts and Connections* (Edinburgh 1988), 138 n.56. For 15th-century Ross see, *inter alia*, that essay and Norman Macdougall's essay in this volume, chapter 10, below.

6

Reform Monasticism and Celtic Scotland: Galloway, *c.*1140–*c.*1240

KEITH J. STRINGER

The lavish support given by the twelfth-century kings of Scots to the new continental monastic orders was part of a remarkable programme of medieval state-making that saw the gradual emergence of the Scottish realm as an increasingly unified and self-assured European-style kingdom. Of all the Gaelic-Norse potentates of the western seaboard, the rulers of Galloway were the most deeply influenced and affected by the assumptions and ambitions of the anglicised east-coast establishment. Fergus (died 1161), lord or 'king' of Galloway, embarked on modernising policies to bolster his family's prestige and regional supremacy. Yet, despite his careful power-building, dynastic feuds and inferior resources swiftly prevented the Galloways from controlling the processes of change exclusively in their own interests. They gradually came to terms with 'royal Scotland', and by the time of Fergus's grandson Roland (died 1200) and his great-grandson Alan (died 1234) – effectively the last native lord of Galloway – they had firmly embedded themselves within the Scottish magnate class.[1] In their Gaelic (or gaelicised) power base there were of course profound continuities. Confident leadership depended more on the co-operation of the kin-based society than it did on the support of the small English-speaking settler elite; and of all the regions of southern Scotland, Galloway remained the least accustomed to regular royal oversight and intervention. Nor can the vitality of provincial loyalties and interests be understated, as the rebellions of 1160 and 1174–85, and a further uprising in 1234–5 after Alan's death, amply demonstrate. In these respects and others, it has been possible to stress the superficial nature of the innovations Galloway experienced;[2] but in the last resort continuity is less

---

[1] Cf. K. J. Stringer, 'Periphery and core in thirteenth-century Scotland: Alan son of Roland, lord of Galloway and constable of Scotland', in A. Grant and K. J. Stringer (eds.), *Medieval Scotland: Crown, Lordship and Community. Essays presented to G. W. S. Barrow* (Edinburgh 1993), 82–113.

[2] See esp. R. D. Oram, 'A family business? Colonisation and settlement in twelfth- and thirteenth-century Galloway', *SHR* lxxii (1993), 111–45, which reassesses the impact of Anglo-Norman lay colonisation.

striking than the transformations it underwent. These were very similar to those charted by Robert Bartlett in his panoramic study of the dynamics of 'homogenisation' in medieval Europe as a whole;[3] and the Galloways' own links with the reformed European religious orders provided one of the most potent forces for change.

This essay is a revised version of the Society of Antiquaries of Scotland's Buchan Lecture for 1992–3.[4] At that time it seemed clear that the prominence given by historians to the kings of Scots and east-coast magnates as patrons of monastic reform had tended to obscure the important contribution from among the west-coast 'Celtic' aristocracy,[5] and it therefore appeared rewarding to choose the Galloways' role and aims as one of the leading themes. Such a choice has ceased to be entirely appropriate because their interest in establishing new religious houses is now much better known.[6] No longer can there be any doubt of Fergus's status as a major ally of the reformed orders during the earliest phase of their expansion into Scotland, or that European monasticism appealed as strongly to Fergus's successors, with the notable exception of his son Gilbert. By Alan's death, the monastic map of Galloway had largely been drawn up. The family had founded, or helped to found, the two Cistercian abbeys of Dundrennan and Glenluce; the three Premonstratensian houses of Soulseat, Tongland and Whithorn, and possibly a fourth at Holywood;[7] the Augustinian priory of St Mary's Isle; and, it seems, even the Benedictine nunnery at Lincluden. Only Sweetheart Abbey (1273) and apparently a house of Cistercian nuns – St Evoca's, near Kirkcudbright – came later; and while none of Galloway's monasteries was outstandingly wealthy, the province supported under its native lords a density of new foundations unparalleled in Scotland outside the Tay, Forth and Tweed basins. Not only that, but the Galloways helped to set the fashion: Dundrennan,

---

[3] R. Bartlett, *The Making of Europe: Conquest, Colonization and Cultural Change, 950–1350* (London 1993).

[4] 'Lordship, prestige and piety: the monastic endowments of the lords of Galloway, c.1140–1234', delivered at Kirkcudbright on 24 Oct. 1992.

[5] Though some suggestive discussions had recently appeared: e.g., B. T. Hudson, 'Gaelic princes and Gregorian reform', in B. T. Hudson and V. Ziegler (eds.), *Crossed Paths: Methodological Approaches to the Celtic Aspect of the European Middle Ages* (Lanham, Maryland, 1992), 61–82; and A. Macquarrie, 'Kings, lords and abbots: power and patronage at the medieval monastery of Iona', *TGSI* liv (1984–6), 355–75.

[6] D. Brooke, *Wild Men and Holy Places: St Ninian, Whithorn and the Medieval Realm of Galloway* (Edinburgh 1994), esp. 88–91, 104–8, 124–6; R. A. McDonald, 'Scoto-Norse kings and the reformed religious orders: patterns of monastic patronage in twelfth-century Galloway and Argyll', *Albion*, xxvii (1995), 187–219.

[7] McDonald (ibid., 198) gives no grounds for including Holywood other than its apparent status as a daughter of Soulseat; but in 1229 Alan seems to have been regarded as its patron: *CPL* i, 122.

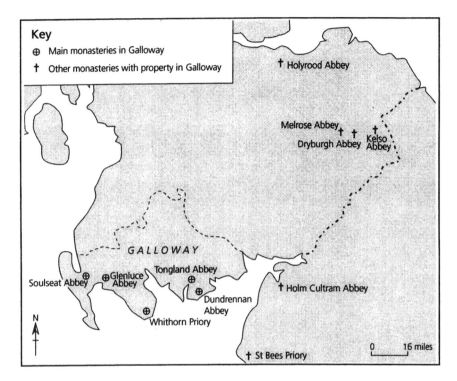

Map II. Galloway and the New Monasticism to *c*.1240

colonised from Rievaulx in 1142, was only the third Scottish Cistercian abbey after Melrose and Newbattle;[8] Soulseat (*c*.1148?), directly subject to Prémontré Abbey in Picardy, was one of the first Premonstratensian houses in Britain, and since the white canons were singularly unsuccessful in attracting Scottish royal support, that they flourished in Scotland at all was due in large measure to Fergus and his dynasty.

Here, in brief, is the clearest possible reminder that the reform of Scotland's native church was by no means exclusively sponsored by an intrusive, modernising crown, central though its interest undeniably was, especially during the reign of that 'connoisseur' of the new monasticism, King David I.[9] Since recent published studies have also commented on the

8 The arguments for redating Dundrennan to 1156 in J. G. Scott, 'The origins of Dundrennan and Soulseat Abbeys', *TDGNHAS*, 3rd ser., lxiii (1988), 35–44, do not convince. McDonald, 'Scoto-Norse kings', 193, errs in stating that the Melrose Chronicle gives 1140 as the foundation date.

9 C. N. L. Brooke, 'King David I of Scotland as a connoisseur of the religious orders', in C. E. Viola (ed.), *Mediaevalia Christiana, xie–xiiie siècles: Hommage à Raymonde Foreville* (Paris 1989), 320–34, which supplements, but in no way supersedes, Geoffrey Barrow's seminal studies.

Galloways' motivations, notably in the secular domain, it may appear that
there is little more to be said. Nevertheless, as was indicated in the Buchan
Lecture, there are good reasons for extending the agenda. It must be
stressed, for example, that the Galloways were associated with numerous
religious houses outside their province, and that this wider picture should
also be kept in view. It was in 1196 that Roland gained in right of his wife,
Helen de Morville, the lordships of Lauderdale and Cunningham, and
with them the patronage of Dryburgh Abbey (Premonstratensian) and
Kilwinning Abbey (Tironensian), not to mention that of St Leonard's
hospital at Lauder. Moreover, the family endowed, sometimes with
significant possessions in Galloway itself, the abbeys of Holyrood
(Augustinian), Kelso (Tironensian) and Melrose (Cistercian), the hospital
of Soutra, Holm Cultram Abbey (Cistercian) and St Bees Priory
(Benedictine) in Cumberland, St Peter's hospital at York, and St Andrew's
Priory at Northampton (Cluniac); gifts were also made to a crusading
military order, the Knights Hospitallers.[10] In addition, Dryburgh,
Holyrood, Holm Cultram and St Bees developed interests in Galloway by
relying on the Galloways to encourage, or at least countenance, gift-giving
by their English or Anglo-Norman dependants, including the Campanias,
Maules and Vieuxponts.[11]

More importantly, we must not lose sight of the fact that a good deal of
the initiative was owed to the religious themselves, whose aspirations
determined in fundamental ways the nature of the transformations
Galloway experienced. Concentration on reform ideology and practices
can therefore add a significant new dimension to our understanding of the
interplay between native 'Celtic' society and mainstream European life,
and this approach forms the basis of what follows. It rests on three
interlocking assumptions. First, while for monasteries located in Galloway
the serious loss of sources – including, it appears, a chronicle compiled at
Dundrennan[12] – has given rise to much pessimistic comment, the totality
of the available evidence in fact gives some cause for optimism. Most
notably, the surviving archives of Holyrood and Holm Cultram are rich
in Galloway material, and much relevant information can likewise be

---

10 K. J. Stringer, 'Acts of lordship: the records of the lords of Galloway to 1234', in
    T. Brotherstone and D. Ditchburn (eds.), *Freedom and Authority: Scotland c.1050–
    c.1650. Historical and Historiographical Essays presented to Grant G. Simpson* (forth-
    coming).
11 *Dryburgh Lib.*, nos. 64, 68, 71, 73, 75–6; *Holyrood Lib.*, nos. 49, 72; *Register and
    Records of Holm Cultram*, ed. F. Grainger and W. G. Collingwood (Cumberland
    and Westmorland Antiquarian and Archaeological Soc., Record Ser., 1929), nos.
    131, 143, 149; *Register of the Priory of St Bees*, ed. J. Wilson (Surtees Soc., 1915),
    nos. 60–1.
12 *Chron. Melrose*, p. xxxi.

gleaned from semi-historical and overtly religious tracts, especially those produced within the Cistercian milieu by Ailred of Rievaulx, his biographer and panegyrist Walter Daniel, and Jocelin of Furness. Of these commentators, Ailred was one of the foremost first-generation Cistercians and a very influential communicator of reform ideas, yet his importance for Scottish studies is still largely unrecognised. The second assumption is that ecclesiastical writings, though often disdained for their programmatic excesses and lack of 'historicity', can illuminate the monastic mind-world by providing invaluable insights into how the religious saw themselves and society itself.[13] Finally, this study takes for granted the importance of using such evidence as exists to set reform monasteries as far as possible in their wider religious, socio-economic and political contexts. Indeed, it is necessary to underline at the outset that central to the new monastic culture was the utopian concept of *caritas* or Christian love; hence, bound as they were by *caritas* to unite all Christians in an ideal Christian society, reformers were obliged to play an integral part in the world at large. For ease of presentation, an attempt will be made to separate out into different strands the main ways in which the new monasticism interacted with and influenced traditional mentalities and structures; but in the period concerned such strands were not so easily disentangled. As has been recently and cogently argued for the Cistercian order, its broad involvement in affairs resulted not so much from a corruption of the original Cistercian ideal as from the paradoxical nature of a monastic vocation that simultaneously stressed 'withdrawal' and a militaristic commitment to reforming society and building the New Jerusalem on earth.[14]

*   *   *

On the whole, the Gallovidians were seen by Cistercian and Augustinian observers as a people whose norms were far removed from those acceptable in Western Christendom. In the analysis of the Rievaulx monk Walter Daniel (c.1170), they lived in an impoverished and primitive backwater, and knew nothing of cultivated living. Nor, so far as he was concerned, did they subscribe to the moral standards of the civilised world. He was naturally scandalised by the customs of concubinage and divorce in the kin-based society; he deplored Galloway's unruliness –

---

13 See esp. T. J. Heffernan, *Sacred Biography: Saints and their Biographers in the Middle Ages* (Oxford 1988), which includes extensive commentary on Walter Daniel's *Life of Ailred*, 'one of the great works of medieval English sacred biography' (p. 77). Of modern biographies of Ailred, A. Squire, *Aelred of Rievaulx: A Study* (London 1969), remains indispensable. See also B. P. McGuire, *Brother and Lover: Aelred of Rievaulx* (New York 1994).

14 M. G. Newman, *The Boundaries of Charity: Cistercian Culture and Ecclesiastical Reform, 1098–1180* (Stanford, California, 1996).

another obvious indicator, he felt, of its people's rough and sinful nature – and his summing up was brief but graphic: 'It is a wild country where the inhabitants are like beasts, and is altogether barbarous.'[15]

These blistering attacks on native conventions and culture echoed the views of Ailred himself, who had left the Scottish court for Rievaulx Abbey in *c*.1134, became its abbot in 1147, and was a regular visitor to Galloway until his death in 1167. Although Ailred wrote disparagingly of contemporary Scottish Gaelic society in general, he singled out the shortcomings of the Gallovidians for particular condemnation. In his work *On the Saints of Hexham Church* (*c*.1155), he denounced them as a most undevout people (*impiissima gens Galwensium*) who waged war with unsurpassed barbarity.[16] The context was King David I's assaults on northern England which reached a peak in 1138, and in other writings Ailred drove the message home – nowhere more vehemently than in his quasi-historical *Battle of the Standard*, composed perhaps on the eve of Dundrennan's foundation from Rievaulx in 1142. As he perceived it, the Standard (fought near Northallerton on 22 August 1138) was a mighty struggle of the righteous against barbarians (*contra barbaros*); he identified the Gallovidians as the chief war-mongers; and in the long battle speech attributed to his patron Walter Espec (Rievaulx's founder), he told of Gallovidian war crimes, including infanticide and cannibalism, in horrifying detail.[17]

On a general level, sensationalist commentaries of this sort can be read as the common currency of men immersed in the values and assumptions of the reformed European Church, set against which the traditions and conduct of the Celtic-speaking peoples were deemed so alien and offensive that Bernard of Clairvaux could describe the Irish as 'Christians only in name, pagans in fact'.[18] More specifically, John Gillingham has argued, they reflect and express a new and radical shift in twelfth-century English culture. He has drawn on the language and ideas of contemporary writers, including the Augustinian Hexham chroniclers, to stress two interrelated points: that in the 1130s, for the first time, the crisis of Anglo-Scottish warfare helped to promote an intensified form of English self-identification and discourse; and that this heightened sense of Englishness was rooted in concepts of the effective supremacy of English culture over Scottish,

15 *Life of Ailred*, 45–6, 74.
16 *The Priory of Hexham*, ed. J. Raine (Surtees Soc., 1864–5), i, 183.
17 Ailred of Rievaulx, *Relatio de Standardo*, in *Chrons. Stephen, etc.*, iii, 182, 187–8. For 1141/2 as the possible date of composition, see D. Baker, 'Ailred of Rievaulx and Walter Espec', *Haskins Society Journal*, i (1989), 93 n.6; and for some relevant textual discussion, J. R. E. Bliese, 'Aelred of Rievaulx's rhetoric and morale at the Battle of the Standard, 1138', *Albion*, xx (1988), 553–5.
18 Bartlett, *Making of Europe*, 21–3; R. R. Davies, *Domination and Conquest: The Experience of Ireland, Scotland and Wales, 1100–1300* (Cambridge 1990), 20–3.

Welsh and Irish cultures, which were despised as inferior and 'barbaric'.[19] What also needs underlining is the key role arguably played in accentuating perceptions of difference and 'otherness' by the Gallovidians in King David's army. To their critics, familiar with the more restrained behaviour of the European knighthood, they were especially fearsome shock troops whose capacity for plunder and seemingly random killing presented a terrifying image of uncontrolled savagery.[20] Most of all, we can scarcely doubt that the men of Galloway had an unequalled reputation for waging war as a slave-hunt, a brand of atrocity which, as Gillingham has emphasised, particularly outraged English sensibilities because civilised society had recently put such frightfulness behind it.[21] It was also their decimation at the Standard that firmly endorsed the conviction that English ideals and values, and English resources and technology, were indubitably superior. The unarmoured Gallovidians insisted that they (instead of David I's knights and archers) should lead the attack on the Yorkshire army; but, as Ailred exulted, 'the frailty of Scottish spears was mocked by the mass of iron'.[22]

If the Anglo-Scottish warfare of the 1130s provided the main field day for such propaganda, later the men of Galloway acted in ways that made them appear no less repellent to reform-minded churchmen. Antipathy was shown not only by southern-based English commentators like the Yorkshire Augustinian William of Newburgh – who viewed the hostilities between Fergus's sons Uhtred and Gilbert in 1174 as a shocking exhibition of 'barbarians warring against barbarians' – but by those who wrote, as Adam of Dryburgh put it in c.1180, 'in the land of the English in the kingdom of Scots'.[23] In his account of the Anglo-Scottish war of 1215–17, the Melrose Abbey chronicler regarded the ferocity of the Gallovidians as inexcusable, condemned them as 'servants of wickedness', and interpreted as well-merited divine vengeance the drowning of some two thousand of their number in the River Eden in Cumberland.[24] In

---

19 See most recently J. Gillingham, 'Foundations of a disunited kingdom', in A. Grant and K. J. Stringer (eds.), *Uniting the Kingdom? The Making of British History* (London 1995), 48–64.

20 M. Strickland, *War and Chivalry: The Conduct and Perception of War in England and Normandy, 1066–1217* (Cambridge 1996), 291ff.

21 Specific evidence for the slave-hunt character of Celtic-style warfare in the 1130s comes almost exclusively from Hexham. Prior Richard not only interpreted slave-raiding as the hallmark of barbarism but laid the blame squarely on the Gallovidians, though he called them 'Picts': see J. MacQueen, *St Nynia* (2nd edn, Edinburgh 1990), 49–53.

22 *Chrons. Stephen, etc.*, iii, 196.

23 Ibid., i, 186–7; *Patrologia Cursus Completus, Series Latina*, ed. J.-P. Migne (Paris 1844–64), cxcviii, 723.

24 *Chron. Melrose*, 63; cf. G. W. S. Barrow, 'The army of Alexander III's Scotland', in N. H. Reid (ed.), *Scotland in the Reign of Alexander III, 1249–1286* (Edinburgh 1990), 136.

1223 this 'barbarous people' (*barbarica gens*) even made an appearance in
an otherwise soberly businesslike Melrose title deed.[25]

Nonetheless, Galloway in the 1220s was in important ways a different
world from Galloway in the 1130s. There can be no single explanation of
what spurred monastic reformers to extend their activities to the province,
but one powerful motive, we should be prepared to concede, stemmed
from their compassion and humanity. In his highly influential *Mirror of
Charity* (1142–3), Ailred eloquently urged monks to love even their
greatest enemies, for whose souls they should feel anxiety and fraternal
concern.[26] Such deeply held views, however much Ailred seemed to
contradict them in his writings on the Gallovidians, encapsulated the
belief of the reforming elite that the Church was a universal community
in which all Christians, even the ungodly, could be fully united by *caritas*.
Accordingly, it was a God-given task to bridge the perceived chasm
between the civilised, metropolitan world of English society and the
uncouth, Gaelic-speaking world of Galloway. Furthermore, as reform
churchmen needed no reminding, without effective peace-keeping there
was no hope of humankind's salvation. It followed that they had a moral
obligation to foster a new political consensus in northern Britain on behalf
of God and Christendom – and that was a role for which Rievaulx itself
was believed to be amply qualified. As Walter Daniel saw it, Rievaulx 'is a
holy place because it generates for its God sons who are peacemakers'.[27]

Reform ideology was reinforced by practical imperatives. There can be
no doubt that for monastic reform David I's attacks on northern England
had been a cataclysmic reverse fully justifying the chroniclers' apocalyptic
language. In 1138 the possessions of Furness Abbey and Hexham Priory
were ravaged; Rievaulx may have suffered as well (the Standard was fought
fourteen miles from the abbey); Calder Abbey had to be abandoned;
Newminster Abbey, still under construction, was levelled to the ground.
The Gallovidians were the chief violators, and even Ailred's friend, the
hermit Godric of Finchale, seems not to have escaped their attentions.[28]
Reformers in the north of England therefore had a real and urgent need to
achieve some sort of understanding with such formidable enemies.

Fundamental as were these considerations, however, they supplied only

---

25 *Melrose Lib.*, i, no. 195.

26 See, most accessibly, *The Mirror of Charity*, trans. G. Webb and A. Walker
(London 1962).

27 *Life of Ailred*, 37. This quotation comes from a passage on the diffusion of tensions
within the monastic community; but Walter extended the concept to society outside
the cloister. For a specific instance concerning Ailred 'the peacemaker' and
Galloway, see ibid., 46.

28 MacQueen, *St Nynia*, 50–1; *Libellus de Vita et Miraculis S. Godrici*, ed. J. Stevenson
(Surtees Soc., 1847), 114–16.

part of the inspiration for carrying the battle against sin to Galloway and sustaining a sense of mission. Another spur was provided by the age of the old missionary saints, which in English Cistercian mythology was seen as furnishing exemplary models for advancing Christian values in the Border regions. Just as Ailred in his *Life of St Ninian* (c.1160) celebrated Ninian's proselytising triumphs in Galloway and farther north, so Jocelin of Furness later promoted the cult of Kentigern, not least by stressing how he purged Galloway of 'whatever he found contrary to the Christian faith'.[29] Relatedly, Ailred had a specially pronounced grasp of the possibilities of progress and change, with whole societies, however 'barbaric', being led along new paths. In his *Eulogy of King David* (c.1153), he praised David for taming the 'total barbarity' of his subjects (among whom he numbered the Gallovidians) by introducing them to 'calm and civilised manners' and subjecting them to the rule of law:

> he brought about [peace] with such care and preserved [it] with such authority among barbarous peoples with diversities of language and customs ... that we have scarcely ever seen even among closely related peoples ... of the same race and language such harmony being observed for such a long time.[30]

For Ailred, the English or Anglo-Norman world – which he saw David I inhabiting – had a boundless capacity to expand its influence across cultural frontiers and create a new social order founded on universal norms of political organisation, personal morality, and even economic development. The only way he felt he could accurately convey this conviction was by use of hyperbole; and, naturally, in Ailred's view the quintessential dynamics of progress were spiritual revival and reform. King David, he rejoiced, 'softened [Scotland's] barbarous character by means of the Christian religion'.[31]

* * *

[29] MacQueen, *St Nynia*, 102–24; *Lives of S. Ninian and S. Kentigern*, ed. A. P. Forbes (Edinburgh 1874), 137–57, 220. Abbot Everard of Holm Cultram (d.1192) may have been another Cistercian hagiographer in northern England intent on rehabilitating the 'Celtic' saints, but the evidence is not conclusive: D. Baker, 'Legend and reality: the case of Waldef of Melrose', in D. Baker (ed.), *Church, Society and Politics* (Studies in Church History, 1975), 71. Ailred's devotion to St Cuthbert is well known; Jocelin also wrote a *Life of St Patrick*.

[30] *Pinkerton's Lives of the Scottish Saints*, ed. W. M. Metcalfe (Paisley 1889), ii, 271, 273. Here and elsewhere, I have normally adopted the recent translation of the corresponding text of Walter Bower, who, following John of Fordun, used the *Eulogy* as one of his main sources: *Chron. Bower*, iii, 143ff.

[31] *Pinkerton's Lives of Scottish Saints*, ii, 279. See also R. Ransford, 'A kind of Noah's ark: Aelred of Rievaulx and national identity', in S. Mews (ed.), *Religion and National Identity* (Studies in Church History, 1982), 137–46; and Squire, *Aelred of Rievaulx*, 84–6, for some relevant comment.

That 'renewal' and 'innovation' were the hallmarks of twelfth-century reform monasticism almost goes without saying.[32] From a Premonstratensian perspective, Adam of Dryburgh dismissed secular canons as 'black swans', and saw in the regular canonical vocation a novel sanctity symbolised by the white habits the Premonstratensians wore.[33] Ideal and reality might be far apart, as the reforming elite ruefully acknowledged;[34] and for all their professed superiority, they were quick to accept aspects of past religious tradition. In Galloway, they made use of old native ecclesiastical centres, most obviously by converting the cathedral church at Whithorn into a Premonstratensian priory, but also by subordinating to new foundations, as parish kirks or chapels, sacred sites such as Kirkcudbright and Edingham.[35] Thus did they recognise the spiritual potency and inspiration of long-established holy places. Their reverence for local saints gave another frame of reference derived from native religious culture; even Ailred's ascetic practices may have been influenced by traditional 'Celtic' spirituality.[36] But they exploited the past selectively, partly in an effort to make their arrival more palatable to Gallovidian society – and nowhere more revealingly, perhaps, than in their careful propagation of St Ninian's cult.[37] Appropriation of key features of the native religious heritage also removed potential challenges to their authority; it likewise served their purposes to legitimise change by conjuring up a lost Golden Age.[38] Above all, however, the language of reform was applied to Galloway in two main senses: to condemn its indigenous church as deformed and moribund, and to proclaim the achievements of spiritual regeneration and transformation. In his account of Dundrennan, Walter Daniel expressed these concepts, first, by depicting the native clergy of Galloway as 'ignorant and bestial and ... always inclined to carnal pleasures' and, second, by underlining that

---

[32] For a seminal analysis of these themes, see G. Constable, 'Renewal and reform in religious life: concepts and realities', in R. L. Benson and G. Constable (eds.), *Renaissance and Renewal in the Twelfth Century* (Oxford 1982), 37–67.

[33] J. Bulloch, *Adam of Dryburgh* (London 1958), 15–16, 56, 81–3; G. Constable, *The Reformation of the Twelfth Century* (Cambridge 1996), 191.

[34] For Adam's complaints about the laxity of fellow canons, see Bulloch, *Adam of Dryburgh*, 103–4; note also the criticisms added by Ailred to the *Life of St Ninian*: MacQueen, *St Nynia*, 116.

[35] For Edingham, see D. Brooke, 'The deanery of Desnes Cro and the church of Edingham', *TDGNHAS*, 3rd ser., lxii (1987), 48–65.

[36] Constable, *Reformation of the Twelfth Century*, 310.

[37] See further D. Brooke, *The Medieval Cult of St Ninian* (Whithorn 1987).

[38] Cf. Squire, *Aelred of Rievaulx*, 116, where it is stressed that Ailred's idealised view of Ninian 'as the founder of a diocese divided into parishes is inspired by the desire to discover in the past a justification for the ecclesiastical re-organization characteristic of the reign of King David'.

'Rievaulx made a plantation in this savagery, which now [that is, c.1170] ... bears much fruit.'[39] His view of the situation was partial at best. But here Walter drew on the sort of horticultural imagery typical of Cistercian writers and their confidence that new spiritual growth was possible in even the most unpromising environment.

Such a dramatic impact on a barbarian society (as the reformers saw it) naturally depended on powerful patrons and benefactors, and no one appealed for their support more eloquently than Ailred himself. In his important writings on rulership, notably the *Eulogy of King David* and the *Genealogy of the English Kings* (c.1154), a fresh emphasis was placed on encouraging rulers to accept that successful governance depended not on fear and repression, but on reforming their moral conduct, revering the Church, and showing a charitable concern for the welfare of all. Judging David I by these standards, he supplied an image of power used generally for meritorious purposes. David's sins were stressed – his reliance on brutish native warriors in the 1130s was naturally deplored – but he was shown to have regained God's favour and secured his heavenly reward through his compassion, devotion to church reform, and personal holiness. Ailred did not fail to stress the handsome political and economic benefits that would accrue to a virtuous Christian society united by *caritas* under God-fearing rulers; but at the heart of his teaching lay an appeal to strictly religious values.[40] Or, more prosaically, consider the edifying story about St Ninian and King Tudwal dwelt on by Ailred for the benefit of the lords of Galloway and their followers: Tudwal obstructed the saint's ministry and was blinded as a mark of divine displeasure; God also punished Tudwal's subjects, whose crops failed; but the king repented and miraculously regained his sight.[41]

*   *   *

What influence in practice did reform ideas have on the religious texture and culture of Gallovidian society? Virtually beyond discovery is the extent to which they affected the credo of the native community at large. But, even if we take an optimistic view, it can hardly be imagined that the teachings of the post-Gregorian Church penetrated deeply into everyday life. Certainly, ecclesiastical expectations were swiftly and painfully disappointed by the revolt begun in 1174, whose carnage left the reformers profoundly shaken; much later, the Melrose chronicler conveyed his own sense of shock when he reported that in 1258 the

---

39 *Life of Ailred*, 45.
40 For pertinent commentary, see Newman, *Boundaries of Charity*, 178, 180–2; and Squire, *Aelred of Rievaulx*, 82ff.
41 MacQueen, *St Nynia*, 109–10.

Gallovidian army fed itself on meat during Lent, even on Good Friday.[42] Yet, as should be all too evident, this is by no means the whole picture. For the moment the Galloways' monastic benefactions – and the virtue individual lords earned as protectors of the Church – can be left largely to speak for themselves. One obvious but fundamental point, however, is that their patronage of the new orders had momentous consequences for the native church in Galloway, which was denuded of many of its endowments. If, in favouring the reformers, the Galloways also relinquished control over former church property that had become secularised (as seems probable), then that would make their support of new ecclesiastical standards all the more impressive. There is no satisfactory evidence for the argument that a native clerical community at Whithorn was allowed to staff the new Premonstratensian priory established by 1177;[43] and we look in vain for survivals akin to the vigorous *céle Dé* tradition that persisted in some parts of the Scottish east midlands until the houses concerned adopted the regular life in the mid-thirteenth century. In any event, the radical shift in the Galloways' religious allegiances was graphically underscored in *c*.1173 when Uhtred, in a highly symbolic gesture, granted to Holyrood Abbey four churches in Galloway that had belonged to Iona.[44] By contrast, Uhtred's brother Gilbert (died 1185) undeniably resented the favour shown to the reformed orders, and as a result some monasteries may well have suffered serious losses. Indeed, his power-building policies, conducted with no regard for 'civilised' norms, were largely responsible for the ferocity of Gallovidian politics in the 1170s, and his career provides an especially vivid reminder of the difficulties faced by the reformers in aligning traditional Gaelic values with their own. Yet the fact remains that even Gilbert could not reverse his family's enthusiasm for European monasticism and the effective eclipse of the native church.

Otherwise, however, clear-cut answers to the question posed above are often elusive. It has to be accepted, for example, that the Galloways' support for ecclesiastical change was part of a broader attempt to enhance their position. For what now needs little further emphasis is that the aspirations of lay benefactors were composite in character – partly because the reformers themselves rarely distinguished sharply between 'spiritual' and 'material' benefits – and are best described as a desire for prestige and prosperity in both this world and the next.[45] But such a mingling of policy

---

42 *Chron. Melrose*, 115.
43 Notwithstanding the recent discussion in P. Hill, *Whithorn and St Ninian: The Excavation of a Monastic Town, 1984–91* (Stroud 1997), 23–4, 56, 60.
44 Stringer, 'Acts of lordship', no. 14.
45 Cf. J. Howe, 'The nobility's reform of the medieval Church', *American Historical*

and piety also raises the possibility that for Gaelic-Norse potentates their wish to secure practical advantages by harnessing new sources of authority and power far surpassed their religious yearnings. Arguably, however, the best way forward is to approach the question at issue through the main ways in which the reformers interpreted their own responsibilities for the laity's spiritual well-being.

Nowadays historians sometimes warn that there were few substantive distinctions between reformed monks and regular canons; yet Adam of Dryburgh apparently had no such reservations and in 1188 transferred to the stricter Carthusians because of his dissatisfaction with the canonical idea of *caritas*, which combined contemplation with Christian ministry. 'In the contemplative life', he wrote, 'we enter the tabernacle, but in the active life we go out of it.'[46] And what is striking is the purposeful manner in which Dryburgh Abbey and, yet more notably, the Augustinians of Holyrood set about their pastoral mission in Galloway. By 1174 Holyrood had been granted by Fergus and Uhtred no fewer than eleven churches in the province.[47] Spiritualities were of course important sources of revenue, and that helps to account for Holyrood's acceptance of such endowments. Nonetheless, the encouragement given by the bishops of Whithorn (Galloway west of the Urr) and Glasgow to Holyrood's amassing of local churches is manifest from their confirmation charters;[48] and there clearly was an expectation that the Augustinians would take a lead in defining Galloway's parish system and imparting new norms of Christian observance and morality, even if in practice their efforts often had only a vague, intermittent or non-existent influence on the vast majority of the population. As Janet Burton has written in a related context:

> even if they did not provide spiritual service for the community, they ... could by ... their choice of incumbent improve clerical standards [and] the enthusiastic backing given to the Augustinian canons by the higher clergy suggests that those churchmen perceived for them a very real pastoral role within the diocese as agents of reform.[49]

Review, xciii (1988), 339: 'Any single-catalyst model will have difficulty explaining all the different interests at work.'

[46] Quoted in Bulloch, *Adam of Dryburgh*, 105.

[47] Blaiket, Dunrod, Galtway (in Kirkcudbright), Kirkcudbright, Tongland, Twynholm and Urr; plus the four churches of Balmaghie, Barncrosh, Kelton and Kirkcormack, formerly held by Iona: Stringer, 'Acts of lordship', nos. 2–4, 11, 12, 14; I. B. Cowan, *The Parishes of Medieval Scotland* (Scottish Record Soc., 1967), 13, 55, 72, 93, 118–19, 198, 202, 205–6. Holyrood's later gains included Anwoth, acquired by 1206; Dryburgh held Borgue, Great Sorbie and Little Sorbie: ibid., 7, 20, 184–5.

[48] *Holyrood Lib.*, nos. 25, 49, 52–3, 67, 80, 83.

[49] J. Burton, *Monastic and Religious Orders in Britain, 1000–1300* (Cambridge 1994), 49;

Conversely, the Cistercians were excluded by their statutes from shouldering parochial responsibilities, and assumed that society's salvation was essentially the duty of the secular clergy, whom Ailred accordingly exhorted to adopt 'a better way of life'.[50] But monks and canons were evidently united in believing that they offered benefactors and their kin unique opportunities to be saved. The novelty of such views, so appealing to the gift-exchange ethos of Gaeldom, rested partly in the way that the reformers heightened lay expectations of spiritual reward by stressing the unprecedented purity of their religious life, and partly in the fact that they introduced a more authoritative and charitable doctrine of salvation, including the prospect of purging sins after death. Thus, Jocelin of Furness (adopting St Bernard's language) likened Scottish Cistercian abbeys to the rivers of Paradise and saw them as existing 'for the washing away of sins and the refreshment of souls'.[51] Ailred was more explicit when he urged that good deeds reduced the penalties of sin, and specifically linked pious donations with the counter-gift of intercession: 'We ought to realise that the men of this world give us their lands ... that they may be protected by our prayers and reconciled to God.'[52]

Such reciprocity is an important theme in the Galloways' surviving charters for the Church. Of course, the documentary record can easily mislead, as Dauvit Broun has reminded us in his recent study of the use of Latin charters in Gaelic Scotland and Ireland. Indeed, they were introduced to a previously charter-less world largely through the efforts of the reformers themselves, who as dictators or scribes would naturally stress lay piety to remind men of their Christian responsibilities. But charters could still 'reflect the donor's point of view',[53] and when we consult the Galloways' *acta*, together with other sources, it becomes increasingly apparent that the reformers' notions of penance and salvation may well have had a real impact on the family's own religious ideas. Put

cf. I. B. Cowan, 'The religious and the cure of souls', repr. in I. B. Cowan, *The Medieval Church in Scotland* (Edinburgh 1995), 62–76. Bishop John of Whithorn (1189–1209) stipulated that Holyrood was to ensure that its churches in his diocese were served by suitable priests, and he authorised the abbey to remove the less qualified after due consultation; in c.1230 Bishop Walter of Glasgow anticipated that the church of Blaiket might be served by a canon: *Holyrood Lib.*, nos. 49, 69.

50 *Life of Ailred*, 28.
51 *Vita Sancti Waldeni*, in *Acta Sanctorum*, August I (Paris 1867), 262; also (via Walter Bower) in *Chron. Bower*, iii, 364–5.
52 Quoted in Squire, *Aelred of Rievaulx*, 58. Compare Walter Daniel's passage on how almsgiving 'profited knights and monks alike': *Life of Ailred*, 28.
53 D. Broun, *The Charters of Gaelic Scotland and Ireland in the Early and Central Middle Ages* (Cambridge 1995), 25; cf. M. T. Flanagan, 'The context and uses of the Latin charter in twelfth-century Ireland', in H. Pryce (ed.), *Literacy in Medieval Celtic Societies* (Cambridge 1998), 117ff.

another way, the overall picture, however inadequate its individual parts may be, suggests that in religion (as in other matters) the Galloways gradually adopted the values of the Anglo-French aristocracy, and that in turn seems to make it 'impossible to propose a model of ... piety which involves professed religious spoon-feeding sophisticated ideas to the uncomprehending'.[54]

It was a direct reflection of the perception that favour shown to the religious was a form of good works or almsgiving that gifts by the Galloways were said to have been made 'in alms', and that on occasion the free-alms terminology was reinforced by clauses emphasising immunity from services and exactions.[55] It was usually spelled out that offerings were made directly to God, and that gift-giving was intended to assist the salvation of souls. Most of the charters lacking *pro anima* clauses record confirmations, leases and settlements of disputes. Within the culture of a vigorous gift-economy, these transactions might also be seen as involving almsgiving but, clearly, overt references to spiritual benefits were normally deemed inappropriate in such contexts.[56] An all-embracing formula might be employed, such as *pro salute anime mee et uxoris mee et pro animabus omnium antecessorum et successorum nostrorum*. Comprehensive arrangements of this nature showed a common enough desire to get your money's worth – though Roland seems to have gone to unusual lengths when he acknowledged Dryburgh's right to the church of Great Sorbie, granted to the canons by his knight Ivo de Vieuxpont. He issued his charter (c.1200) in the form appropriate to a new gift, and sought to benefit the souls of his father (Uhtred), his mother (Gunnilda of Allerdale), and all his ancestors and successors.[57] As far as can be judged, the Galloways were encouraged to think first of lessening the agonies of the dead, who were no longer masters of their own fate. For instance, when in c.1170 Uhtred and Gunnilda endowed Holyrood with the church of Torpenhow (Cumberland), the grant was made exclusively for the redemption of the souls of Gunnilda's father and Fergus and all the

---

[54] M. Bull, *Knightly Piety and the Lay Response to the First Crusade: The Limousin and Gascony, c.970–c.1130* (Oxford 1993), 156.

[55] Cf. B. Thompson, 'Free alms tenure in the twelfth century', *Anglo-Norman Studies*, xvi (1994), 221–43; and B. Thompson, 'Monasteries and their patrons at foundation and dissolution', *Transactions of the Royal Historical Soc.*, 6th ser., iv (1994), 107ff.

[56] Cf. C. B. Bouchard, *Sword, Miter, and Cloister: Nobility and the Church in Burgundy, 980–1198* (Ithaca, New York, 1987), 241, 243: '*Pro anima mea* was ... neither a well-worn cliché nor a concern behind every lay-ecclesiastic transaction. It was rather a *technical phrase*.'

[57] Stringer, 'Acts of lordship', no. 26. It cannot be ruled out that Dryburgh was anxious to recast Ivo de Vieuxpont's grant as Roland's donation because property said to have been given by the lord of Galloway was thought to be more secure than that conferred by his tenants.

grantors' forebears.[58] Significantly, the terms of reference were sometimes extended to express a sense of allegiance to and intimacy with the Scottish royal house, as in Uhtred's grant to Holyrood of the church of Blaiket for the souls of David I, Henry of Scotland and Malcolm IV.[59] As will be seen, specific examples also exist of the Galloways' seeking to build up spiritual merit through the monastic liturgy; but their routine *pro anima* grants do not refer expressly to prayers for the soul. Perhaps it was implicit that this service would normally be provided – Ailred's teaching and those waivers exempting monasteries only from *secular* services suggest as much. Nevertheless, the emphasis was usually placed on the redemptive effect of the act of giving itself.[60]

Even more revealing of the impact of religious values are those relatively unambiguous indications that in certain circumstances the Galloways were attuned to monastic ideas about personal morality. The foundation of Dundrennan Abbey in 1142 was the critical first step taken by the new monasticism in Galloway, and Fergus's wish to endow the Cistercians would assuredly not have rested on piety alone. Yet the fact remains that Dundrennan, colonised from Rievaulx within four years of the Battle of the Standard, appears to have had a very important penitential significance. The Gallovidians had been left in no doubt that they had committed great evils during their onslaughts in 1138 and had suffered divine punishment for their sins. Archbishop Thurstan of York had turned the defence of Yorkshire into a holy war,[61] while the army of Galloway had been destroyed on the battlefield within sight of the banners of Yorkshire's patron saints. Moreover, when the papal legate Alberic of Ostia came to David I's court at Carlisle on his peacemaking mission in September 1138, he brought the Gallovidians to account by insisting on the release of their captives and their pledge to spare churches and all non-combatants in the future. And shortly afterwards, at his legatine council at Westminster in December 1138, he solemnly promulgated new canons to protect churchmen and their property from violence – the unmistakable message being that those who mistreated the Church were eternally damned if they did not repent and atone.[62]

In Cistercian circles, the two men singled out for special blame were David I, who had failed to curb the atrocities, and Fergus himself, who – as

58 Ibid., no. 10.
59 Ibid., no. 12.
60 Some of the Galloways' *pro anima* charters in fact specify freedom from all burdens: ibid., nos. 3, 12, 42.
61 Compare Ailred's making Walter Espec exhort his troops to 'consecrate your hands in the blood of sinners': *Chrons. Stephen, etc.*, iii, 188.
62 Ibid., 170–1, 174; *Councils and Synods with other Documents relating to the English Church*, vol. I, ed. D. Whitelock and others (Oxford 1981), part 2, 769, 776–7.

Walter Daniel bluntly reminded his readers – 'had taken the lives of many thousands'.[63] With such a burden of sin placed on his conscience, it does not seem rash to regard Fergus's foundation of Dundrennan as a grand gesture of penance to provide him with Cistercian monks to intercede forever for his soul. A recent suggestion is that the necessary guidance was provided by Archbishop Thurstan as Galloway's 'spiritual overlord' (Whithorn diocese was subject to York).[64] But it is possible to see an important role for King David, whose vision of founding a Scoto-Northumbrian state gave him sound political reasons for healing the wounds of war.[65] Further speculation should perhaps be resisted. Yet it might be suggested that Fergus, following his humiliation in 1138, was particularly amenable to Cistercian teachings about the benefits of rulership based on moral rectitude. Nor should it be overlooked that Abbot Richard of Fountains and Abbot William of Rievaulx were closely involved in the Anglo-Scottish peace negotiations during the autumn of 1138. Since Thurstan was frail and apparently confined to York or its environs from the eve of the Standard to his death in 1140,[66] perhaps it was this Cistercian delegation that began the vital task of extending *caritas* to an enemy (the arch-enemy?) of monastic reform. It would certainly be difficult to imagine a more persuasive team. It was Abbot William who, as the secretary of St Bernard himself, led the discussions resulting in Rievaulx's foundation in 1132; and, as was argued many years ago, one of William's companions in his talks with the Scots in 1138 was none other than Ailred – whom Walter Daniel, in a passage that may have some historical basis, subsequently portrayed as Fergus's spiritual adviser.[67]

63 *Life of Ailred*, 46.
64 Oram, 'Colonisation and settlement in Galloway', 115.
65 No direct evidence exists for David I's involvement, but Oram (ibid., 114–15) and McDonald, 'Scoto-Norse kings', 194, seem unduly to minimise his role. See K. J. Stringer, 'Galloway and the abbeys of Rievaulx and Dundrennan', *TDGNHAS*, 3rd ser., lv (1980), 175; also *Chrons. Stephen, etc.*, iii, 154, 171, for some steps taken by David to calm the fears of northern English churchmen in 1138–9. In any event, David's control of Cumbria and his increasingly close links with the Yorkshire Cistercians make it inconceivable that Rievaulx colonised Dundrennan without his sanction and support: cf. K. J. Stringer, 'State-building in twelfth-century Britain: David I, king of Scots, and northern England', in J. C. Appleby and P. Dalton (eds.), *Government, Religion and Society in Northern England, 1000–1700* (Stroud 1997), 40–62.
66 *Chrons. Stephen, etc.*, iii, 169, 171–2; D. Nicholl, *Thurstan, Archbishop of York (1114–1140)* (York 1964), 223–4, 230–1, 233, 235–7.
67 *Life of Ailred*, pp. xlvi n.1, 46. Cf. McDonald, 'Scoto-Norse kings', 203–4, for the possibility that Ailred had known Fergus before his departure from the Scottish court for Rievaulx in *c*.1134; and see C. N. L. Brooke, 'St Bernard, the patrons and monastic planning', in C. Norton and D. Park (eds.), *Cistercian Art and Architecture in the British Isles* (Cambridge 1986), 13, for the suggestion that Ailred had played a part in the foundation of Melrose, colonised from Rievaulx in 1136.

The later lords of Galloway, with the important exception of Gilbert, followed a less manifestly sinful path; but when between 1201 and 1214 Alan acted with his mother (Helen de Morville) to give the land of Harehope in Peeblesshire to Melrose Abbey, he was publicly acknowledging a moral obligation to alleviate the guilt of both his uncle (William de Morville) and his father (Roland) for specific misdeeds. William had bequeathed to Melrose an estate in Cunningham; yet his intentions had not been followed up, due not least (one assumes) to Roland's refusal to accept the validity of a death-bed gift. Alan, however, provided appropriate compensation as a form of penance on their behalf, and the monks reciprocated by offering William's and Roland's souls absolution from sin. That Melrose could thereby settle this matter in its favour is some indication of the importance Alan attached to religious concepts.[68] In c.1201 he also resolved a long-standing quarrel with Kelso Abbey by giving five ploughgates of land at Oxton in Lauderdale in exchange for certain revenues in Galloway that had fallen into arrears. On their side, the monks ended the dispute by absolving Uhtred's and Roland's souls and admitting them to the 'common benefits' of their house; they similarly conferred in perpetuity the privilege of confraternity – *societas et fraternitas omnium beneficiorum spiritualium* – on Alan himself, his mother, and all their heirs, ancestors and successors.[69]

The value Alan evidently saw in these concessions reflects particularly clearly the view that monastic prayers and good works could assist the salvation of the laity as well as that of the religious themselves: 'As part of a spiritual confraternity, lay people became, vicariously, members of the convent, participating in absentia with the abbot and the monks in the liturgy. All, in turn, were part of a larger community, formed by the saints, apostles, and martyrs.'[70] But the Galloways' chief intercessory centres were naturally their own monasteries. Alan's foundation of Tongland Abbey (1218), for example, brought him greater honours than those normally associated with confraternity: on his death he was entitled to the benefits, including almsgiving and special masses, that a deceased Premonstratensian canon would receive.[71] Another of the optimal paths to Heaven was conversion. The one case concerning the Galloways was

---

68 Stringer, 'Acts of lordship', no. 38. What this charter does not reveal, however, is that the land conveyed by Alan to Melrose had been usurped by the Morvilles from Glasgow bishopric: *OPS* i, 212–13.

69 Stringer, 'Acts of lordship', no. 30.

70 B. H. Rosenwein, *To Be the Neighbor of Saint Peter: The Social Meaning of Cluny's Property, 909–1049* (Ithaca 1989), 38.

71 Cf. H. M. Colvin, *The White Canons in England* (Oxford 1951), 257–8. Fergus's obit was celebrated at Prémontré Abbey itself: I. B. Cowan and D. E. Easson, *Medieval Religious Houses: Scotland* (2nd edn, London 1976), 102–3.

Fergus's entry into the *Königskloster* of Holyrood in order to become an Augustinian canon. He converted immediately after King Malcolm IV's successful military campaigns against Galloway in 1160, and a late Holyrood source was no doubt right to stress that this was a precondition of his regaining the king's peace.[72] Yet Fergus's entry gifts were sufficiently lavish to suggest something more than an act of political submission; and, certainly, it was as an expression of genuine piety that his successors chose to interpret his conversion, for it inspired a series of substantial grants inside Galloway that intimately linked the whole family's spiritual fortunes with Holyrood.[73] Finally, the vitality of lay-religious contacts is further shown by what we know of the burials of Fergus's successors. When Roland died far from home at Northampton in 1200, he was buried in the town at St Andrew's Priory, a Cluniac house; in 1234 Alan was interred at Dundrennan. These burials and the liturgical benefits associated with them underlined the special and enduring relationship between the Galloways and the religious orders; and even St Andrew's gained Scottish endowments, albeit outside Galloway, from Helen de Morville, Alan and his brother Earl Thomas of Atholl.[74]

All in all there is little to suggest that the Galloways' support for European monasticism was mere outward show by semi-civilised 'barbarians'. Rather, they seem to have been genuinely influenced by monastic values, particularly the evolving doctrine of salvation and its evident emphasis on the concept of a purgatorial 'middle place' between Heaven and Hell, without which it would have been pointless for them to provide for both the living and the dead. Their sense of sinfulness was no doubt sharpened by the fact that 'the life of the reformed monastery ... was so diametric to the normal noble life in the world'.[75] Yet we must also recognise that the ecclesiastical elite had the inclination and ability to

---

72 *The Holyrood Ordinale*, ed. F. C. Eeles, *Book of the Old Edinburgh Club*, vii (1914), 67–8.

73 Stringer, 'Acts of lordship', nos. 2–4, 10–12, 14, 22, 31, 33–4. The souls of Fergus, Uhtred, Roland and Alan were still commemorated at Holyrood in the 15th century alongside those of its Scottish royal benefactors: *Holyrood Ordinale*, 2.

74 K. J. Stringer, 'The early lords of Lauderdale, Dryburgh Abbey and St Andrew's Priory at Northampton', in K. J. Stringer (ed.), *Essays on the Nobility of Medieval Scotland* (Edinburgh 1985), 45–6, 52, 55, 66–9; Stringer, 'Acts of lordship', nos. 42–3; *Chron. Melrose*, 83. Roland's burial-site was not wholly a matter of chance rather than choice: St Andrew's, unlike the neighbouring Augustinian priory of St James, had close connections with the Scottish royal house. For Alan's putative effigy at Dundrennan, see *Archaeological and Historical Collections relating to Ayrshire and Galloway*, x (1899), 64. W. M'Dowell, *Chronicles of Lincluden* (Edinburgh 1886), 33, reports an unsubstantiated tradition that Uhtred's mausoleum was Lincluden Priory.

75 Bouchard, *Sword, Miter, and Cloister*, 244.

bring to bear on Galloway the broader values and norms of 'civilised society'; and we turn first to economic themes, with special reference to the Cistercians.

*   *   *

In Galloway as elsewhere, one of the most obvious consequences of the arrival of the new monastic orders was a major redistribution of economic resources, and to the Cistercians the task of maximising the return from their properties was both a challenge and a duty. For all the accusations of rapacity levelled against them, it must be accepted that basic to Cistercian ideology, especially as developed and expounded by Ailred of Rievaulx, was the belief that material and spiritual well-being were inextricably intertwined. It was naturally important to Ailred that as an abbey's lands and incomes increased, so did the number of monks and 'the intensity of the monastic life and its *caritas*'. More broadly, he associated spiritual regeneration with economic transformation, and linked David I's pious governance with dynamic change in the Scottish economy whereby 'a land uncultivated and barren [became] pleasant and fruitful'.[76] Embedded in this rhetoric is the Cistercians' perception of themselves as economic pioneers in the virgin 'wildernesses' of twelfth-century Europe. While this image powerfully reflected their aspirations to follow a stricter and purer form of monastic observance, it had only a limited degree of truth, as modern studies of Cistercian economic practice have underscored. Nonetheless, even if the role of Cistercian abbeys in agricultural colonisation must not be overstated, they were major new centres of lordship, and as such contributed greatly to economic processes through more rational and efficient management.[77] Indeed, the Cistercians' development of consolidated holdings and their use of an unpaid work-force of lay brothers have long been seen as important reasons for 'the exceptional level of productivity typical of Cistercian granges in comparison with ... units worked by villein tenants'.[78] More recently, it has been argued that their economic instincts were sharpened by a desire to reshape the material world into a Garden of Eden, and that in this sense, too, their notoriously aggressive entrepreneurship was merely a logical extension of their religious culture:

---

[76] *Life of Ailred*, 38; *Pinkerton's Lives of Scottish Saints*, ii, 279.

[77] Such is the emphasis in, e.g., C. H. Berman, *Medieval Agriculture, the Southern French Countryside, and the Early Cistercians* (Philadelphia 1986); and C. B. Bouchard, *Holy Entrepreneurs: Cistercians, Knights, and Economic Change in Twelfth-Century Burgundy* (Ithaca 1991).

[78] I. Alfonso, 'Cistercians and feudalism', *Past and Present*, cxxxiii (1991), 16.

they untangled the layers of rights and obligations attached to secular property and made their land into a religious domain. Land, like love ... could be stripped of its secular ... connections [and] shaped to reflect the harmonies of divine creation.[79]

Against this backdrop, what points can be highlighted about the Cistercian contribution in Galloway? Although Dundrennan's endowment included hill ranges, and Glenluce was on the edge of the 'low moors' of Wigtown-shire, both abbeys were established in valley sites away from Galloway's mountainous interior and in what may well have been relatively settled agricultural landscapes. Closer to the Cistercian vision of a return to the 'Desert' was the base acquired at Kirkgunzeon by the Cumberland abbey of Holm Cultram, as is underlined by the boundary-marks recorded in c.1180, which included hills, trees, numerous burns and the 'great moss'.[80] Although Kirkgunzeon was not an uninhabited wasteland, its inhospitable character deeply impressed Abbot Everard of Holm – whom Jocelin of Furness admired for both his spiritual and his economic stewardship[81] – and he clearly showed his business acumen when he originally leased the place from Uhtred in c.1170 by insisting on the option of terminating the lease at his discretion.[82]

Despite Everard's initial reservations, however, Holm Cultram's economic fortunes were to be intimately linked with eastern Galloway, and the abbey's records reveal much about the growth of what became one of the province's great monastic estates. At Kirkgunzeon there were protracted disputes between Holm and other parties, and its control remained significantly incomplete since this nucleus continued to be held at rent rather than in 'pure' alms until the time of Edward Bruce (died 1318). But, overall, the emphasis in Holm's cartularies[83] is on the steady build-up of its property rights in ways that removed lands as far as possible from secular hands, on the careful clarification of boundaries to distinguish its territory from that of its neighbours, and – not least – on large-scale, direct and vigorous management. Abbot Everard felt sufficiently

[79] Newman, *Boundaries of Charity*, 69.

[80] Stringer, 'Acts of lordship', no. 15.

[81] *Vita Sancti Waldeni*, 262; also in *Chron. Bower*, iii, 364–5: Everard brought Holm 'to a high standard on the spiritual side ... and advanced it to a peak on the material side'.

[82] Stringer, 'Acts of lordship', no. 7.

[83] Calendared, not always adequately, in *Holm Cultram Reg.*; and see Stringer, 'Acts of lordship', nos. 7, 15, 23, 25, 50, for the texts of Holm's charters from Uhtred, Roland and Alan. This and the following two paragraphs are based largely on these sources, without further reference. Where necessary, however, Holm's late 13th-century cartulary in the Cumbria Record Office, Carlisle, has been consulted afresh; and for some valuable context, see R. C. Reid, 'The early ecclesiastical history of Kirkgunzean', *TDGNHAS*, 3rd ser., xiv (1926–8), 201–15.

confident by 1185 to negotiate with Roland a perpetual lease of Kirkgunzeon with an increase of rent from £6 to £10 yearly, despite the fact that Uhtred had arbitrarily withdrawn part of the estate and granted it to Walter of Berkeley as lord of Urr. By this stage the toun (*villa*) of Kirkgunzeon had been transformed into a fully-fledged grange worked by Holm's lay brethren. A demesne farm of considerable size, it embraced the whole of the modern parish (approximately 12,000 acres) and had at its centre a complex of buildings, including a chapel – to whose independent existence the bishop of Glasgow periodically objected – and, it must be supposed, barns, stables and quarters for the lay brothers.[84] Stock-farming was of necessity the chief activity. Holm was one of the leading wool-producing abbeys of the Borders, and its sheep ranches were highly organised commercial enterprises.[85] At Kirkgunzeon, however, the abbey also specialised in pig husbandry, as is shown by the steps Everard took to secure rights to drive 500 pigs from the grange into Roland's demesne woods to fatten them up in the autumn – an important concession, for it allowed Holm to stock Kirkgunzeon with more animals than could otherwise have been supported. By c.1190 Walter of Berkeley had been persuaded to restore his gains, and the grange was extended westwards towards the Urr Water; other landowners renounced their rights to adjacent territory in Colvend parish. This careful expansion of monastic lordship went hand in hand with the systematic accumulation of appendages on the Solway shore. Uhtred granted a coastal saltworks in Colvend (probably at Saltpan Rocks); Roland added a saltworks in New Abbey and another near Southerness Point, with a neighbouring fishery. The monks also made significant acquisitions alongside the Nith in the feu of Kirkconnell, where they had taken possession by c.1240 of Mabie, various other lands – including part of Kirkconnell Merse – and a fishery.

As a result, Kirkgunzeon grange was flanked by a network of outstations fulfilling a variety of key economic roles. Good supplies of salt, needed for preparing and preserving animal products, were essential to successful pastoralism; fish were no less indispensable to the Cistercians, who were forbidden to eat meat and required alternative protein-rich rations. Each saltworks needed at least four oxen for carting; but since salt-making was mainly a summer industry, the oxen were also available for ploughing. Like its salters, Holm's fishermen were also part-time farmers. The

---

84 There has apparently been no excavation or survey of the central grange site, but a rough indication of its layout can perhaps be gained from the results of recent work on the granges of Holm's sister-house, Coupar Angus Abbey: *South-East Perth: An Archaeological Landscape* (RCAHMS, 1994), 109ff.

85 Cf. E. Miller, 'Farming in northern England during the twelfth and thirteenth centuries', *Northern History*, xi (1976), 12.

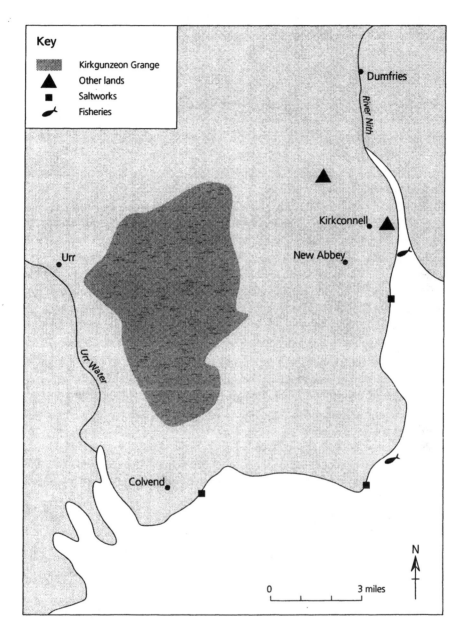

Map III. Kirkgunzeon Grange and its Appurtenances, *c*.1240

Kirkconnell fishery included pasture rights for six cows, six oxen and two horses; and the neighbouring coastlands provide one authentic example of the abbey's involvement in reclaiming new land. Holm was also careful to secure rights of way between Kirkgunzeon and its coastal outliers for men, livestock, wagons and packhorses, and permission for its boats to have free use of convenient harbours in Galloway (unfortunately unnamed) – arrangements that speak of regular comings and goings by the monks or lay brothers and much movement of stock and victuals, some for shipment across the Solway to supply English markets and the abbey itself, some for sending on to Dumfries where, at least by c.1280, Holm had commercial premises.

Here, then, between the Nith and the Urr, Holm built up a power base geared as far as possible to its sole use, and the envy and protests the abbey provoked furnish unmistakable evidence that its economic impact was profound. By 1174 conflict between Holm and Dundrennan had been resolved in a formal agreement whereby Holm was to refrain from engrossing more land, and building more houses and sheepfolds, on the western side of the Nith (that is, in Galloway), while on the eastern side, in the land of Radulf son of Dunegal (that is, in Nithsdale), neither abbey was to acquire more property without the other's consent. Dundrennan also insisted that it should be free to expand its estates in the neighbourhood of Kirkgunzeon, and in particular reserved its right to create a grange and to enclose its pastures in order to prevent incursions by Holm's stock. Dundrennan's attempts to curb Holm's expansionism evidently failed; but they graphically illustrate the economic rivalries that were bound to arise, even between abbeys of the same order, when two houses were intent on extending their influence in the same locality. Furthermore, in 1222 Bishop Walter of Glasgow belatedly complained to Pope Honorius III about the high-handed measures taken by Holm to make room for Kirkgunzeon grange, including the eviction of the toun's peasant tenants (*coloni*) – a vital step for both the introduction of direct farming and the 'transformation of secular property ... into monastic property'.[86] In sum, Holm's entrepreneurship lay not so much in widespread reclamation as in the intensification of pastoralism through a restructuring of pre-existing 'Celtic' patterns and practices. But the consequences were no less important because of that. A grange economy meant 'a change in the actual workings of the rural countryside which was as complete a transformation as any clearance of forest or drainage of swamp would have been'.[87] Nor can it be gainsaid that Holm's managerial zeal cut

---

86 Newman, *Boundaries of Charity*, 77.
87 Berman, *Medieval Agriculture*, 53.

sharply across the grain of local interests – to the extent that when the men of Galloway invaded northern England at King Alexander II's behest in 1216, they singled out Holm Cultram Abbey for specially ruthless treatment.[88]

By contrast, very little is known about how Dundrennan and Glenluce accumulated and exploited their properties. But the earliest building phases at Dundrennan, including a programme of sumptuous reconstruction beginning in the late twelfth century, can still be traced, and bear impressive witness to the abbey's wealth.[89] One source of it was pig-keeping; and as sheep-farmers both Dundrennan and Glenluce were to attract the attention of Italian merchants, perhaps because the monks also dealt as middlemen in the wool of neighbouring landowners.[90] The records of houses based outside Galloway shed some additional light. That Holyrood was at pains to secure pannage throughout the lord of Galloway's woods and forests shows that Holm Cultram and Dundrennan were not the only abbeys helping to turn parts of Galloway into areas where the pig was king.[91] Like Holm, other monasteries developed an expertise in extracting Solway salt. By 1196 Roland had given to Melrose a saltworks in Preston with land for constructing a salt-house, fuel from the adjacent wood for firing the boiling pan, and pasture for six cows, six oxen and one horse.[92] The salt industry around the Galloway coast was well established; but by *c.*1200, with Holm and Melrose – and Kelso Abbey and St Bees Priory – holding a total of eight saltworks along the sea-shore between Colvend and New Abbey, monastic lordship possibly improved on existing practices and gave Solway salt-making and the regional salt trade a significant boost.[93]

Other evidence highlights the interest of monasteries in developing more regular trading contacts through acquiring commercial facilities and privileges. Holyrood had a base in Carlisle for access to its market and fair.[94] In 1220 the English government (on Alan's petition) gave Glenluce a year's licence to buy corn and other supplies in Ireland; similar licences were issued in 1226, 1227 and again in 1252, when the abbey was allowed

---

[88] *Chron. Melrose*, 63.

[89] P. Fergusson, 'The late twelfth-century rebuilding at Dundrennan Abbey', *Antiquaries Journal*, liii (1973), 232–43.

[90] *Holm Cultram Reg.*, no. 133; A. A. M. Duncan, *Scotland: The Making of the Kingdom* (Edinburgh 1975), 430–1.

[91] Stringer, 'Acts of lordship', no. 31.

[92] Ibid., no. 17.

[93] Ibid., nos. 7, 8, 15, 17, 21, 23, 27; *St Bees Reg.*, nos. 60–1; and, more generally, G. Neilson, *Annals of the Solway until A.D. 1307* (repr. Beckermet, 1974), 44–8.

[94] H. Summerson, *Medieval Carlisle: The City and the Borders from the Late Eleventh to the Mid-Sixteenth Century* (Cumberland and Westmorland Antiquarian and Archaeological Soc., extra ser., 1993), i, 76.

to purchase a shipload of Irish corn each year for the following seven years.[95] The Cistercians also participated prominently in a broader trading network. Dundrennan enjoyed King Henry III's protection whenever it used English markets to sell wool or buy corn; from c.1170 Holm Cultram had permission to sell its wool and merchandise in any Scottish burgh.[96]

Galloway's experience of religious innovation thus had significant economic ramifications for the region and its peoples, not least those at grass-roots level. The scale of transformation naturally varied from district to district, and it would clearly be wrong to exaggerate (as the reformers did) the earlier economic isolation and backwardness of the province. The recent programme of excavations at Whithorn abundantly confirms that verdict.[97] But, equally, it would be rash to belittle the entrepreneurial innovations and successes of the new monasticism, and the general part they played in accelerating the tempo of the regional economy and integrating it more fully into the economic life of the rest of southern Scotland and of northern England.

*   *   *

Such a conclusion serves to open up fuller discussion of how far the new monasticism brought Galloway more firmly into the mainstream of affairs. Broadly speaking, reform monasteries were, for reasons quite apart from their economic contribution, focal forces in the 'deepening cultural uniformity of the Latin West'.[98] Committed to forging an ideal Christian society, they saw themselves as the epicentres of a new unifying social ethos; and their social place and function had a significance extending far beyond their much less quantifiable success in imposing on society new standards of personal morality. But what for Galloway were the more readily measurable results?

Most obviously, monastic colonisation involved a significant diversification of the traditional social structure. No doubt local recruitment became increasingly important to monasteries located in the province; but it is clear that leadership was normally provided by Anglo-Normans or by English-speaking Scots. For example, in 1165 Dundrennan's prior was Walter, formerly Walter Espec's chaplain and Rievaulx's sacristan; in c.1200 the abbey was in fact still recruiting ordinary monks directly from Yorkshire; and as late as 1244 Alan Musarde, a Rievaulx monk, became abbot of Glenluce.[99] It therefore appears that, rather than being rapidly

---

95 *CDS* i, nos. 765, 933, 974, 1891.
96 Ibid., no. 2414; *RRS* ii, no. 87.
97 Hill, *Whithorn and St Ninian*.
98 Bartlett, *Making of Europe*, 309.
99 *Life of Ailred*, 75; *Early Yorkshire Charters*, vol. V, ed. C. T. Clay (Yorkshire Archaeological Soc., Record Ser., extra ser., 1936), no. 251 (charter, c.1210, by

swamped by local attachments, the Galloway houses were in general slow to lose the trappings of colonialist institutions; and the architectural legacy at Dundrennan perhaps testifies more eloquently to this than do written sources, for the late twelfth-century building work has striking stylistic parallels with that found in Yorkshire at Byland and Roche.[100]

Nor is there a shortage of evidence for the persistence of cultural polarisation, with the reformers holding 'Celtic' society in fear and contempt, while they in turn were despised as an oppressive and palpably alien minority. Nevertheless, mutual suspicions and even outright hostility – expressed most notably in 1174 when the Gallovidians killed 'all the English and French they could seize'[101] – were to a degree modified by varying degrees of social intermeshing. Remarkably, at Whithorn Priory in 1235 nearly half of the twenty-two canons, including Prior Duncan himself, bore unmistakably Gaelic names; while later in the thirteenth century this hybrid community numbered native kindreds among its benefactors.[102] It seems probable that lay brothers – though in important respects the 'second-class citizens' of monastic society – were often local converts co-opted from the peasant community into the Cistercian (or the Premonstratensian) life. Dundrennan performed an essential social role by setting up a hospital for the sick, or perhaps an almshouse for the poor, which had at least one indigenous inmate by 1186.[103] It is also of interest that Walter Daniel presented Ailred as a saint whose miraculous powers were at the service of ordinary Gallovidians.[104]

These indications of harmonious cross-cultural encounters may not amount to much; yet such encounters occurred against a backcloth of broader personal ties of considerable social significance, for the monastic elite had a sense of identity that was at once regional, national and supranational. Many indeed were the ways in which Galloway was connected through the new monasticism with other areas. Whithorn Priory had accumulated by 1237 important possessions on the Isle of Man

Ruald constable of Richmond granting to Easby Abbey property at Thorpe under Stone, three miles west of Richmond, previously held by Walter monk of Dundrennan); *Chron. Melrose*, 91.

100 Fergusson, 'Twelfth-century rebuilding at Dundrennan', 238–43.

101 *Gesta Henrici Secundi Benedicti Abbatis*, ed. W. Stubbs (Rolls Ser., 1867), i, 67–8. The commentator was the English royal clerk Roger of Howden who, as King Henry II's envoy to Galloway in 1174, must be regarded as an authoritative source; see most recently J. Gillingham, 'The travels of Roger of Howden and his views of the Irish, Scots and Welsh', *Anglo-Norman Studies*, xx (1998), 153, 157.

102 *The Historians of the Church of York and its Archbishops*, ed. J. Raine (Rolls Ser., 1879–94), iii, 146–8; *RRS* v, no. 275.

103 Cowan and Easson, *Medieval Religious Houses*, 173.

104 *Life of Ailred*, 69.

through a series of gifts by the kings of Man.[105] Dundrennan set about
acquiring interests in Ireland, including property in Leinster possibly
bestowed on the abbey by Alan's father-in-law Hugh de Lacy, earl of
Ulster (died 1242); it also secured tenements at Egremont (Cumberland),
where it probably had an ironworks, as Glenluce – and Sweetheart Abbey –
certainly did in 1294.[106] Admittedly, such connections merely reinforced a
centuries-old tradition of cultural interchange in the Irish Sea world.[107]
But very different in nature were the new contacts serving to foster social
interaction between Galloway and anglicised Lowland Scotland. A key
point to develop here is the contribution Galloway made to the resources
of monasteries rooted in the Scottish royal heartlands: Dryburgh, Kelso,
Melrose and, most notably, Holyrood. Holyrood not only benefited from
numerous parish churches, but was entitled to take a tenth of the lord of
Galloway's cain, pleas and game between the Urr, Nith and Cluden.
These and other important gains led the abbey to establish an estate office
on St Mary's Isle which in due course became a small dependent priory, to
whose endowment Roland had added by *c*.1193 the church of Eggerness,
as well as a tenth of the provisions supplied to his residence at Kirkcudbright.[108] Holyrood, Kelso and Melrose (all were Davidian foundations)
naturally identified themselves with the culture of the Scottish court – and
here it is permissible to include Holm Cultram, founded in 1150 as an
offshoot of Melrose by David I and his son Henry when they ruled at
Carlisle. Although in 1157 Holm came under English political control, it
retained close ties with both its mother-house and the Scots crown. In
particular, Abbot Everard, who during his long abbacy (1150–92) became
a familiar figure on the Galloway scene, was a friend and former chaplain
of King David's stepson, the saintly Waltheof of Melrose (died 1159); he
attended William I's court, and was present at Melrose in 1170 for the
opening of Waltheof's tomb.[109] It can therefore be concluded that through
their ability to establish a presence in the province, all these monasteries

---

105 San Marino, California, Huntington Library, Derby Papers, MS Ellesmere 993: a
notarial copy of 12 royal, episcopal and papal documents, *c*.1220–1376, made in
1504 from the now lost cartulary of Whithorn Priory, all of which concern its
possessions on Man. On this still neglected source, see B. R. S. Megaw, 'The barony
of St Trinian's in the Isle of Man', *TDGNHAS*, 3rd ser., xxvii (1950), 175ff.
106 *CDS* ii, no. 1717; iii, nos. 967, 969, 1157; *Calendar of the Close Rolls, 1288–1296*
(London 1904), 401. Hugh de Lacy is known to have granted churches in Leinster
to St Andrews Cathedral Priory: *Liber Cartarum Prioratus Sancti Andree in Scotia*,
ed. T. Thomson (Bannatyne Club, 1841), 118–19.
107 See most recently C. Phythian-Adams, *Land of the Cumbrians: A Study in British
Provincial Origins, AD 400–1120* (Aldershot 1996); and Hill, *Whithorn and St
Ninian*.
108 Stringer, 'Acts of lordship', nos. 3, 22.
109 Baker, 'Waldef of Melrose', 68–9; *RRS* ii, no. 62.

contributed to bridging the gulf between the east-coast and west-coast worlds, as was highlighted in detail, at any rate in 1287, when Holyrood's revenue from the church of Kelton was assigned in perpetuity to the abbey's fabric fund.[110]

In addition, the social history of Galloway was naturally affected by the more efficient networks of authority and communication characteristic of the contemporary Western Church. The Cistercians were a particularly well-organised international order, and that was of crucial relevance to Dundrennan and Glenluce, for each abbey was seen as part of a close-knit family specially united by *caritas*.[111] The abbot of Rievaulx had to inspect Dundrennan annually – Ailred's visitation in 1165 lasted six or seven days[112] – and to make other official visits as required. How assiduously these duties were discharged it is impossible to say; but mother–daughter ties were strong enough for the abbot of Dundrennan to be translated to Rievaulx in 1167 and 1239.[113] Similarly, the Cistercians at Glenluce (subject to Dundrennan) were in regular contact with their counterparts outside Galloway. Not least, they had close links with Melrose, whose cellarer, William, became abbot of Glenluce in 1214. He sent a dramatic report by letter to Melrose in 1216 concerning a recent cosmic phenomenon, and afterwards visited the abbey to discuss it in person. Abbot Gilbert resigned from Glenluce in 1233 to become the novice-master at Melrose, and then returned to Galloway as bishop of Whithorn (1235–53).[114]

The outlook of such men was far from provincial; and no less revealing are the Cistercians' broader European loyalties and connections. At first Cistercian abbots in Scotland were required to join their fellows from all over Europe at the order's annual General Chapter at Cîteaux in Burgundy. From 1157 they were expected to make the journey – a round trip of eight to ten weeks – once every four years; and even the very patchy evidence available reveals several instances of attendance from Galloway at this major international assembly. Whereas the abbot of Glenluce absented himself in 1199, the abbot of Dundrennan did go to the Chapter in that year. Another who excused himself in 1217 was ordered to attend in 1218 and apparently complied; Abbot Geoffrey of Dundrennan died on his way home from Cîteaux at the Cistercian abbey of Auberive, near Dijon, in 1222; and Abbot Michael of Glenluce met a similar fate after presenting

---

110 *Holyrood Lib.*, no. 83.
111 Cf. W. E. Goodrich, 'Caritas and Cistercian uniformity: an ideological connection', *Cistercian Studies*, xx (1985), 31–43.
112 *Life of Ailred*, 74.
113 C. T. Clay, 'The early abbots of the Yorkshire Cistercian houses', *Yorkshire Archaeological Journal*, xxxviii (1952–5), 33–4, 36. Silvan, in 1167 the successor to Ailred, resigned Rievaulx in 1188 while visiting Dundrennan: *Chron. Melrose*, 46.
114 Ibid., 58, 64–6, 82–3.

himself at the General Chapter in 1243.[115] It could seriously damage an abbot's health; but membership of the Cistercian family had the general effect of broadening cultural experiences and promoting a sense of common identity among elites who were otherwise far removed from one another in their local contexts. It would be wrong, however, to imagine that such unity was unobtrusively achieved. Indeed, the unifying influence of the Cistercian system is best seen in connection with Galloway when in 1234 the General Chapter sent the abbots of Rievaulx, Roche and Sawley on a special visitation of Dundrennan and Glenluce to reform what needed reforming 'according to the constitution of the order'.[116]

Finally, the regular contacts Galloway now had with Rome provided another important sense of involvement with the rest of Latin Christendom; and a striking instance is given by an especially complex local case referred to the pope's jurisdiction, the protracted property dispute between Dundrennan and the knight Nicholas of Cardoness and his wife Cecily.[117] It was remitted to a series of judges-delegate, and thus, among others, the archdeacons of St Andrews and Dunkeld (1220), the priors of Dryburgh and Kelso (1240), and the archdeacon, chancellor and precentor of York (1241) all found themselves involved in Galloway's affairs. Towards the end of this seemingly interminable wrangle, the abbot of Dundrennan went on his own initiative to press his case at Rome; in 1241 Gregory IX intimated that he was prepared to settle the matter himself, despite the concession made to the king of Scots that his subjects should not be summoned out of the kingdom by papal letters. The dispute also produced a decretal relating to vexatious actions which became part of the general law of the Church. In these respects, as in others, the province had begun to play a small but integral part on the Western European scene.

*   *   *

A more rounded view of the impact of the new monasticism on Galloway emerges when we turn to lay authority and governance. Irrespective of their local situations, the religious knew they could not divorce themselves from the political context, for it was accepted that ecclesiastical reform and secular power-building were intimately connected. There were several aspects to this assumption, and they need only a brief rehearsal here. *Caritas* proclaimed an ethos of peace and unity, but in reality society

---

115 *Statuta Capitulorum Generalium Ordinis Cisterciensis, 1116–1786*, ed. J.-M. Canivez (Louvain 1933–41), i, 238, 249; *Chron. Melrose*, 75–6, 91.

116 *Statuta Capitulorum*, ii, 136.

117 *CPL* i, 70, 188, 196–7, 199, 228; Lord Cooper, *Select Scottish Cases of the Thirteenth Century* (Edinburgh 1944), 22–4; and, most recently, P. C. Ferguson, *Medieval Papal Representatives in Scotland: Legates, Nuncios, and Judges-Delegate, 1125–1286* (Stair Soc., 1997), 124, 141, 164–5, 168, 175, 180–1, 230–2.

was violent and tension-ridden. So reformers had no alternative but to regard lay rulers, especially royalty, as their natural allies in founding God's kingdom on earth; and they therefore saw it as their duty to support and revitalise rulership in line with Christian precepts and principles – themes manifestly to the fore in the writings of Ailred, Walter Daniel and Jocelin of Furness.[118] More practically, the influence the reformed Church exercised in society was one of the most effective means whereby a ruler's power could be projected; for their part, the reformers had a vested interest in stronger political structures, which would bring greater security to ecclesiastical landholding and greater uniformity to religious beliefs and practices.

If the broad relevance to the religious of stable and virtuous rulership needs no further emphasis, the history of Galloway graphically illustrates how this could influence 'Celtic' politics in detail. Galloway's historians have recently devoted much attention to Fergus's royal aspirations and strategies. In their view, he promoted church reform as a largely autonomous agent and simultaneously made a highly important political statement. The example most often cited is the supposed revival in *c*.1128 of the bishopric of Whithorn under the metropolitan jurisdiction of York, apparently in order to assert its freedom from King David's control and thereby enhance Galloway's claims to be regarded as an independent entity separate from 'Scotland'.[119] What deserves fuller consideration is the active role played by the religious in defining, even accentuating, Fergus's personal status and authority. Some evidently did see him as a specifically royal patron; and the most emphatic assertion of his royalty was his being accorded the title 'king of the Gallovidians' in his charter granting to the Knights Hospitallers the land of Galtway (in Balmaclellan).[120] Thus was his regal stature legitimised, and so, too, was he obliged to regard himself as a leader whose duties towards God and Christianity were greater than those of any ordinary ruler. Such royalist propaganda could not but have satisfied Fergus's desire for recognition;[121] yet it also served

---

118 For specific emphasis by these writers on the role of monks in educating and assisting rulers, see *Pinkerton's Lives of Scottish Saints*, ii, 276–7, 280 (concerning David I); *Life of Ailred*, 46 (Fergus, Gilbert and Uhtred); and *Vita Sancti Waldeni*, 262 (Malcolm IV).

119 Whithorn remained subject to York until 1355. It cannot, however, be shown conclusively that Fergus himself was responsible for reviving the see, or indeed that it needed restoring: R. D. Oram, 'In obedience and reverence: Whithorn and York, *c*.1128–*c*.1250', *Innes Rev.*, xlii (1991), 86–90, 95; Hill, *Whithorn and St Ninian*, 23.

120 Stringer, 'Acts of lordship', no. 1.

121 Cf. Hudson, 'Gaelic princes and Gregorian reform', 71: 'The reformers were choosing their words with some care and with a consideration for the agenda of their patrons.' Similarly, Flanagan, 'Context and uses of the Latin charter', 117ff.

reform interests that he should be encouraged to cease to act as a ruthless Gaelic-Norse warlord and display instead the cardinal virtues a true king was believed to possess.

While the immense advantages of kingship were not, of course, fully realised by the Galloways, it was natural that the reformed clergy should continue to look to them as the immediate guarantors of their welfare and urge them to give 'good lordship'. In *c*.1196 Roland reassured Kelso Abbey that he had taken its monks and servants residing in Galloway under his firm peace and protection; more commonly, monasteries insisted on binding the Galloways to warrandice in order to ensure compensation in the event of dispossession.[122] Yet more revealing is Uhtred's charter of *c*.1164 granting a ploughgate of land at Troqueer to St Peter's hospital at York, in which he urged all his men and friends 'for the love of God and for the souls of all your ancestors [to] help and maintain the brothers ... and their possessions, and afford them aid and counsel in all their affairs'.[123] In such ways the Galloways assumed obligations for the Church's defence in a manner characteristic of magnates in eastern Scotland, and indeed in England and France. But, as in Fergus's day, the relationship was by no means one-sided. Ecclesiastical emphasis on the lord's protective function and his responsibilities for social order projected a stronger notion of territorial lordship, in the intensification of which the religious – who were not enmeshed in the traditional kin-based society – also took a vigorous practical role. Some light is thrown by Richard, a clerk of Abbot Thomas of Dryburgh, who served as a chaplain in Alan's household; by Prior William of St Mary's Isle, who was Alan's much trusted clerk (*dilectus et familiaris clericus noster*); and by Nicholas and Geoffrey, successive abbots of Dundrennan, who witnessed Roland's and Alan's charters.[124] In other words, reform monasticism supplied not only an educated staff whose expertise transformed government practices 'according to the models of Latin literacy, documentary thinking and bureaucratic organization',[125] but a new class of major landowners who were dependent as far as possible on the Galloways themselves, and whose support provided a potent means of reworking local power balances and giving their regional superiority greater substance. Especially revealing of the interdependence of monastic and secular authority is Roland's foundation of Glenluce (1191/2) in the heart of the former power base of

---

[122] Stringer, 'Acts of lordship', no. 27. For warrandice of property in Galloway, see ibid., nos. 15, 17, 23, 50.

[123] Ibid., no. 6.

[124] *Dryburgh Lib.*, no. 229; London, Public Record Office, Chancery Miscellanea, C.47/22/9(1); Stringer, 'Acts of lordship', nos. 28, 54.

[125] Bartlett, *Making of Europe*, 285.

his uncle and sworn enemy, Gilbert son of Fergus. On Gilbert's death in 1185, Roland had embarked on the conquest of western Galloway and supervised the construction and garrisoning of castles; now he looked to his Cistercian allies to reinforce his territorial mastery.[126]

Undoubtedly, to aid the Galloways as far as circumstances permitted was of enduring relevance to the religious, and their efforts often paid handsome dividends. No more could have been asked of Alan by Dundrennan in its dispute with the Cardonesses when he coerced them into making unduly generous concessions.[127] In 1229 Holywood Abbey was similarly careful to gain Alan's support against an unnamed knight of the diocese of Glasgow who unlawfully occupied certain lands, despite his excommunication.[128] Yet the Galloways did not always deliver peace and security, and this is a very important reservation. The prolonged revolt that broke out in 1174 outraged the reformers, pointedly revealed the limitations of their influence, and left a deep imprint on their consciousness. The power struggle between Uhtred and Gilbert had precipitated a blood feud culminating in Uhtred's mutilation and the slaughter of Anglo-Norman captives; then in 1176 Gilbert allied himself with Henry II of England and insisted on driving from his lands any who recognised the sovereign lordship of the king of Scots. The savagery and turbulence of Gallovidian politics in these years – blatantly at odds with the Church's teaching and interests – can only have underlined among the religious the need for a more secure and ordered world. Furthermore, although Galloway became more peaceful from 1186, occasional confrontations reminded them of their continued vulnerability. One such concerned the land of Carsphairn on the borders of Galloway and Carrick, which the Cistercians of Vaudey Abbey (Lincolnshire) transferred to Melrose in 1223 since it was 'useless and dangerous to them, both on account of the absence of law and order, and by reason of the insidious attacks of a barbarous people'.[129]

Alternative sources of protection were actively sought within the Church itself. Individual monasteries had by 1234 obtained an impressive number of papal privileges and letters confirming their property in Galloway, protecting their rights and immunities, and granting specific favours.[130] Two letters evidently linked to the troubles of the period

---

126 Cf. Brooke, *Wild Men and Holy Places*, 124.
127 *CPL* i, 188, 196; Ferguson, *Medieval Papal Representatives*, 181, 230. It was only after Alan's death that the Cardonesses dared to reopen the case by appealing to Rome for justice.
128 *CPL* i, 122.
129 *Melrose Lib.*, i, no. 195; G. W. S. Barrow, *The Anglo-Norman Era in Scottish History* (Oxford 1980), 32.
130 For an example concerning Dundrennan, see *CPL* i, 196–7; Ferguson, *Medieval Papal Representatives*, 165.

1174–85 show that Abbot Everard drew on Pope Alexander III's authority to defend the monks of Holm Cultram and their possessions in Galloway by threat of religious sanctions.[131] The local hierarchy was also thought to have an important protective role. Bishop Jocelin of Glasgow (1174–99), himself a Cistercian (he was a former abbot of Melrose), granted to the land of Kirkgunzeon 'God's peace and protection and our own on pain of anathema, lest anyone dare harm that place or the lay brothers residing there'.[132] Bishop Christian of Whithorn (1154–86) commanded all the men of his diocese to maintain and protect the abbey of Holm and Kirkgunzeon grange 'if you wish for God's blessing and ours'; the disobedient would incur automatic excommunication and 'the punishment of everlasting fire' unless they made amends.[133] In 1210 none other than Abbot Gervase of Prémontré urged Bishop Walter of Whithorn to show 'fatherly kindness' to Whithorn Priory.[134]

But the crucial point is that monasteries also bolstered their positions in Galloway by enlisting the support of the Scottish crown. Quite apart from other considerations, the demotion of the Galloway dynasty to 'lords' would have automatically enhanced perceptions of the Scots king's role as the chief protector of Christianity in general and of ecclesiastical institutions in particular. Indeed, in reform circles an ideological basis for unitary Scottish kingship had already been shaped by the mid-twelfth century, and for its fullest expression we need look no farther than Ailred's writings. In his view, Fergus was in fact at best a sub-king or prince (*regulus*), whose authority scarcely compared to that of David I, the *rex Christianissimus*; nor could it be denied that the Scottish realm stretched across from sea to sea, or that within it the king of Scots was the chief source of justice and peace.[135] Moreover, however carefully Fergus had controlled monastic colonisation, it has to be recalled that he and his

131 *Scotia Pontificia: Papal Letters to Scotland before the Pontificate of Innocent III*, ed. R. Somerville (Oxford 1982), nos. 98–9.

132 Carlisle, Cumbria Record Office, Dean and Chapter Muniments, Cartulary of Holm Cultram, pp. 108–9; inadequately calendared in *Holm Cultram Reg.*, no. 136.

133 W. Dugdale, *Monasticon Anglicanum*, ed. J. Caley and others (London 1817–30), v, 597. Holm evidently held Christian in high regard: he was buried in the abbey, where a cult of *sanctus Christianus* took hold (*St Bees Reg.*, pp. ix–x; cf. *Holm Cultram Reg.*, 166).

134 C. L. Hugo, *Sacrae Antiquitatis Monumenta Historica, Dogmatica, Diplomatica*, vol. I (Etival 1725), no. 92. See further C. R. Cheney, 'Gervase, abbot of Prémontré: a medieval letter-writer', repr. in C. R. Cheney, *Medieval Texts and Studies* (Oxford 1973), 242–76.

135 *Life of Ailred*, 45; *Pinkerton's Lives of Scottish Saints*, ii, 271–3, 276. Cf. *Chrons. Stephen, etc.*, iii, 181, for Ailred's assumption that in 1138 the Gallovidians who invaded England were King David's subjects.

successors (except Gilbert, of course) endowed in Galloway external houses which were under the direct guardianship of the Scottish crown. Politically, that in itself made the province less distinct from the rest of the Scottish kingdom, as was already indicated in Uhtred's time when Holyrood Abbey insisted that it should hold its churches in Galloway as freely and securely as churches were held 'in the whole of Lothian'.[136] But of no less importance for monarchical influence and authority was the fact that an understandable desire to provide extra safeguards for monastic property and rights gave the Scots king specific opportunities to extend his jurisdiction by intervening in Galloway more frequently and confidently.

Even by 1164 King Malcolm IV had instructed Uhtred, Gilbert and all his responsible lieges of Galloway that he had given his firm peace to those journeying to stay at Holyrood's land of Dunrod (in Kirkcudbright). They were to have undisturbed passage; no-one was to molest them at Dunrod or occupy the land against Holyrood's wishes; and if infringements occurred, the king would impose a penalty of £10 on each offender.[137] The logic of such mandates was that eastern Galloway was already coming under the scrutiny of royal officers who could be called on by the religious to punish any breaches of the king's protection. Holyrood also secured by royal grant the right to hold a seigneurial court at Dunrod.[138] When King William I was at Selkirk in c.1196 he admonished the men of Galloway to give the lay brethren of Melrose every assistance while in pursuit of felons, 'according to my assize of Galloway'. If they were obstructed in any way, the defaulters would forfeit all their lands and goods to the crown. Again, at Jedburgh in c.1209 King William confirmed to Holyrood its Galloway churches, the implication being that he not only approved of these acquisitions but was prepared to defend Holyrood in the future if its rights were ever questioned.[139] Similarly, Holm Cultram was careful to obtain from William I and Alexander II confirmations or special grants of privileges.[140] By invoking royal authority in such ways the monasteries concerned were bringing Galloway more firmly within its ambit, and occasionally the crown can be seen to have flexed its muscles decisively. Thus when Uhtred reallocated part of Kirkgunzeon to Walter of Berkeley, Abbot Everard received a sympathetic hearing from William I, who ruled that an inquest be held, possibly in the

---

136 Stringer, 'Acts of lordship', nos. 3, 12.
137 *RRS* i, no. 230. Cf. ibid., ii, no. 103, for William I's grant of protection to St Peter's hospital, York, by 1170.
138 *Holyrood Lib.*, no. 74.
139 *RRS* ii, nos. 406, 485. For other confirmations by William I of Holyrood's property in Galloway, see ibid., nos. 39, 141, 293, 489.
140 Ibid., nos. 87–8, 256; *Holm Cultram Reg.*, no. 129.

presence of the sheriff of Dumfries. Walter relented slowly but surely; and by c.1190 Holm had equipped itself with King William's charter confirming the disputed lands to be held 'as any monks of the Cistercian order most freely, quietly, fully and honourably hold their alms in my whole land'.[141]

By contrast with this evidence, preserved by royal or royally connected abbeys, there is a dearth of contemporary information concerning the attitude towards the crown of houses inside Galloway itself. Sometimes they may have been faced with the dilemma of conflicting local and national allegiances. But, if so, such problems were eased because the Galloways increasingly recognised that their own position, as in Uhtred's and Roland's struggles against Gilbert, depended on the Scots king's political support. It is also instructive that – perhaps in the 1220s – Whithorn Priory associated itself with the expansion of crown influence in northern Scotland by planting a daughter-house at Mid Fearn in Ross on the invitation of Farquhar MacTaggart, one of Alexander II's most prominent adherents.[142] Moreover, the strength of royal authority in Galloway was at once manifested and enhanced when in 1214 Glenluce accepted William of Melrose as its abbot. From Glenluce in 1216 he reported back to Melrose how a lay brother had seen the moon assume the shape of a galley under sail, which was swiftly transmogrified into a mighty castle bearing the royal banner. It is not absurd to suppose that he believed this story, or that its political symbolism accorded with his own aspirations and informed his actions.[143] In sum, the Scots king was no longer so distant a figure; and although in Abbot William's lifetime Galloway – especially the lands west of the Cree – retained many of the characteristics typical of a far-flung frontier zone, one basic consequence of the province's experience of monastic reform was that the political boundaries of the Scottish state were extended more effectively than would otherwise have been the case.

*   *   *

141 J. G. Scott, 'An early sheriff of Dumfries?', *TDGNHAS*, 3rd ser., lvii (1982), 90–1; *RRS* ii, no. 256.

142 Cowan and Easson, *Medieval Religious Houses*, 101. In Alexander Grant's essay, above, chapter 5, note 171, it is remarked that Farquhar MacTaggart may have brought canons from Whithorn to Fearn no earlier than 1235, when he supported Alexander II as a war captain in Galloway; but it is noteworthy that by 1223 Farquhar's daughter Christiana had married Olaf of Man (*ES* ii, 458–9), whose charter for Whithorn Priory concerning lands and two churches in Man is the first of three grants or confirmations by the Manx kings recorded in Huntington Library, MS Ellesmere 993.

143 *Chron. Melrose*, 64–6. Although Abbot William used the non-specific term *navis*, he was surely referring to a galley, an instantly recognisable emblem of the status and power of Gaelic-Norse rulers on the western seaboard.

In conclusion, it can scarcely be doubted that when the reformers first came to Galloway they had a conscious sense of undertaking a special mission to a benighted region on the outer fringe of Latin Christendom. Their self-appointed task was a moral imperative demanded by the interests of peace, order and Christian unity, and the period of largely uninterrupted stability in Galloway from 1186 to 1234 is arguably some kind of testimony to their success. We must not, of course, exaggerate their impact on the traditional Gaelic ethos of Gallovidian society. Yet, to all intents and purposes, by the early thirteenth century the ecclesiastical structure of Galloway had been brought into full conformity with European norms, and as a source of political, social and economic innovation, monastic reform had left an indelible imprint of far more than localised significance. As regards the Galloways themselves, if there is little reason to doubt their basic sincerity as monastic benefactors, they often acted as expediency dictated, and their policies were always influenced by pressures other than those of ecclesiastical reform. Above all, they had to adjust to the expansionist ambitions of the Scottish monarchy, to its occasional displays of force, and to its growing might and prestige. Yet, crucial though such caveats are, it appears impossible to underestimate the extent to which the new monasticism encouraged or allowed them not only to reorganise and diversify their sources of power, but to assimilate gradually the culture of elite society in eastern Scotland, and to position themselves as men of the centre as well as of the periphery – something to which their endowment of Holyrood and other Scottish royal abbeys in itself bears striking witness. In essence, what we are seeing is a refashioning of the cultural divisions and provincial separatism that were the chief obstacles to the emergence of a cohesive Scottish polity; and although the relationship between ecclesiastical innovation in Galloway and Scottish political domination is by no means straightforward, in the event monastic reform undeniably made the work of integration a less daunting task than it might have been. The truth of this, however, has yet to be fully revealed, and in order to build up a more complete picture we also need in this concluding section to examine the circumstances of the mid-1230s when, following Alan's death without legitimate sons, King Alexander II took decisive steps to stamp his authority on the province.

Understandably, Gaelic marriage and succession customs horrified monastic commentators on Galloway, who were bound to denounce conventions such as concubinage and the assumption that bastard sons could inherit their fathers' lands. It would be rash to expand on this by suggesting that reform churchmen were largely responsible for the eventual abandonment by the Galloways of traditional practices; no doubt, as in their marriages to Anglo-Norman ladies, political aspirations often weighed more heavily than did any desire to conform to European ecclesiastical standards.[144] But reform influences cannot entirely be discounted. In particular, it can be argued that Alan's evident unwillingness to back his natural son Thomas as his heir and successor betrays the impact of the Church's teaching. And, remarkably, even the native community seemed at first to accept that Thomas's illegitimacy ruled him out, for when Alan died in 1234 its initial reaction was to petition Alexander II to take the province under his direct lordship – a declaration of loyalty that appeared finally to vindicate Ailred's conviction that under proper supervision 'barbarians' could indeed be civilised. The Gallovidians, however, were not prepared to depart further from their customs and countenance female succession. So when King Alexander snubbed them by insisting on dividing Galloway among Alan's three daughters (who were legitimate and had married English husbands), they believed they had no alternative but to rebel in support of Thomas's claims as their lord.[145]

Yet what really needs underlining is that Alexander II was able to enlist ecclesiastically approved rules of inheritance to justify not only his rejection of Gaelic law and tradition, but the dismemberment of Galloway and the simultaneous transformation of a general form of royal overlordship into direct feudal control. Moreover, although in the pacification of Galloway military pressure was obviously crucial, the resources and superstructure of the reformed Church proved to be a formidable instrument of the royal will, both in peacemaking and in helping to ensure that the peace concluded was not short-lived. In 1235 Alexander extended his authority by securing the vacant bishopric of Whithorn for his nominee Gilbert of Melrose (former abbot of Glenluce); and both Gilbert and Abbot Adam of Melrose, who 'offered to [Thomas of Galloway] the friendship they had shown to his father', were prominent in negotiating with the rebels and bringing them to terms.[146] When the Cistercian General Chapter investigated Abbot Robert of Glenluce and Abbot Jordan of Dundrennan and finally deposed them in 1236, Alexander apparently respected the order's right to settle its own affairs. But the opportunity was nevertheless swiftly seized to replace

---

144 Note that when Alan married as his third wife Hugh de Lacy's daughter, he was accused of infringing canon law on grounds of affinity, and attempts were made to have the marriage annulled by Pope Honorius III: K. J. Stringer, 'A new wife for Alan of Galloway', *TDGNHAS*, 3rd ser., xlix (1972), 52; Stringer, 'Periphery and core', 93 and n.2.

145 Ibid., 96–7, 102.

146 Oram, 'Whithorn and York', 96–8; *Chron. Melrose*, 84.

them with, respectively, Prior Michael of Melrose and Leonius, a Melrose monk. When Leonius became abbot of Rievaulx in 1239 he was succeeded at Dundrennan by Richard, another prior of Melrose.[147] In Galloway today there is disappointingly little to remind us of the scale of the Augustinian or Premonstratensian presence; yet the Cistercian legacy seems to provide one especially fitting image on which to end. Still to be found among Dundrennan's majestic ruins is a remarkable thirteenth-century effigy bearing the figures of an abbot and a kilted tribesman. A dagger is shown protruding from the abbot's breast; but the tribesman lies semi-disembowelled beneath the abbot's feet, with the abbot's pastoral staff firmly planted on the crown of his head.[148]

[147] Ibid., 85–6. It is possible that in 1234–6 Alexander used his influence at the General Chapter to discredit Robert and Jordan because they were politically ineffective or even sympathetic to the rebels; but there is no evidence that anything more than a breach of monastic discipline was at stake: cf. *Statuta Capitulorum*, ii, 136, 151.

[148] See most recently J. France, *The Cistercians in Medieval Art* (Stroud 1998), 115 (description and photograph).

7

Rebels without a Cause?
The Relations of Fergus of Galloway and
Somerled of Argyll with the Scottish Kings,
1153–1164[1]

R. ANDREW McDONALD

The laconic chronicles from which much of the history of twelfth-century Scotland must be reconstructed are full of references to struggles between the feudalised core of the kingdom and the strongly Gaelic and Gaelic-Norse periphery. These sources tell of conflicts commencing in the second decade of the twelfth century, and continuing in nearly every decade thereafter until 1230. The more serious uprisings would include those of 1130, 1153–7, 1160, 1164, 1174–85, 1187, 1211–12 – and this is not an exhaustive list. Traditionally, little more than passing attention has been devoted to them, thanks in part to a lack of evidence, but also probably because they are hard to explain, and because they provide a stumbling block for the proponents of the 'peaceful Norman Conquest of Scotland' paradigm. Originating in marginal regions which had yet to be fully assimilated into the Scottish kingdom, it is astonishing that these uprisings have been neglected when the kings of Scots spent so much time and effort in the twelfth and early thirteenth centuries suppressing them by force of arms.[2] This essay will begin to remedy this shortcoming in the historiography of medieval Scotland by exploring the conflicts of the 1150s and 1160s between Fergus of Galloway and Somerled of Argyll and the Scottish kings. Were these men merely troublesome chieftains who obstructed the path of the kings of Scots towards building a united, Europeanised kingdom of Scotland? Or was their significance deeper,

---

1 I am indebted to the following individuals for their assistance at various stages in the preparation of this essay: Ted Cowan, Dauvit Broun, Sandy Grant and Keith Stringer.

2 The story of the conquest of the marginal regions of the kingdom (esp. the North) by the Scottish kings is only beginning to be told in detail: see J. L. Roberts, *Lost Kingdoms: Celtic Scotland and the Middle Ages* (Edinburgh 1997), chs. 4, 5; and R. A. McDonald, *The Kingdom of the Isles: Scotland's Western Seaboard c.1100–c.1336* (East Linton 1997), chs. 4, 5.

pertaining to fundamental questions about the relations between kings and princes, the Europeanisation of Scotland, and the interactions between the heartland of the east and the largely autonomous, peripheral regions lying to the west and south-west? These are the questions for the present essay.

King David I, the youngest son of Malcolm Canmore and Queen Margaret, died on 24 May 1153 after a reign of nearly thirty years. His grandson succeeded him as Malcolm IV, and shortly thereafter Somerled of Argyll led an uprising along with the sons of Malcolm MacHeth.[3] The insoluble question of MacHeth's identity lies beyond the scope of this essay, but he probably had a claim to either the Scottish kingship or the earldom of Moray, which had been suppressed in 1130 following the battle of Stracathro, in which Angus, the earl (Irish sources call him king) of Moray was killed.[4] The hostilities of 1153 probably aimed at placing either MacHeth or one of his sons in the kingship of Scots, but events did not proceed favourably for the Somerled/MacHeth cause. Between 1154 and 1156 Somerled's attention was diverted to the Hebrides and Irish Sea, where he engaged in a naval battle against Godred, the king of Man, in early 1156, and this preoccupation with the Western Isles (which always seem to have been his primary sphere of activity) probably resulted in the capture of Donald MacHeth at Whithorn in 1156.[5] The capture of Donald is doubly interesting because it may link Fergus of Galloway with this conflict. It is possible that Donald was at Whithorn either because he was seeking the aid of Fergus, or because Fergus was directly involved in the rising. On the other hand, given the lack of evidence, it seems equally possible that Fergus seized Donald when he sought sanctuary at Whithorn, and Daphne Brooke has argued that the lord of Galloway, no friend to Somerled, did not lend his support to the rising, remaining 'unmoved by the claims of kin or the dictates of feud'.[6] But then, in 1157, Malcolm MacHeth was reconciled with the king of Scots, probably receiving the earldom of Ross as compensation and thereby removing the

[3] *Chron. Holyrood*, 124–5.
[4] On Malcolm MacHeth's identity, see A. A. M. Duncan, *Scotland: The Making of the Kingdom* (Edinburgh 1975), 166; *RRS* ii, 12–13; *Chron. Holyrood*, 129 n.1; and pages 108–9 of Alexander Grant's essay, above.
[5] *Chron. Man*, 67–9; *Chron. Melrose*, 75–6. For more on Somerled's involvement with the Isle of Man, see R. A. McDonald, '"Causa ruine regni Insularum": Somerled MacGillebrigde and the rise of a new dynasty in the Isles, c.1100–1164,' in S. Duffy (ed.), *A New History of the Isle of Man*, vol. III: *The Medieval Period, 1000–1405* (forthcoming).
[6] H. Maxwell, *A History of Dumfries and Galloway* (Edinburgh and London, 1896), 54; D. Brooke, *Fergus the King* (Whithorn 1991), 4, 12–13. Such a hypothesis might be supported by Somerled's activities against Fergus's grandson, Godred, the king of Man, in 1154–6.

impetus for the conflict.[7] Interestingly, however, there is no mention of a truce between Somerled and the king of Scots until 1160, when the well-known charter of King Malcolm to Berowald the Fleming was dated 'at the next Christmas after there was peace between Somerled and the king'.[8]

The year 1160 appears to have been a turbulent one for the young King Malcolm. After accompanying Henry II of England to Toulouse in the hope of winning his spurs,[9] he received a decidedly unfriendly reception from some members of the native nobility:

> When Malcolm had come to the city that is called Perth, Earl Ferteth [of Strathearn] and five other earls (being enraged against the king because he had gone to Toulouse) besieged the city, and wished to take the king prisoner; but their presumption did not at all prevail.[10]

The next paragraph then describes how 'King Malcolm went three times with a great army into Galloway; and at last subdued them'.[11]

Many aspects of this rising remain to be fully elucidated. The reliability of the sources upon which our understanding of it rests, its causes, and the involvement of Fergus are all the subject of considerable controversy. Most scholars have accepted the historicity of the event and argued that Fergus must have been involved. G. W. S. Barrow suggested that the earls believed that Malcolm's homage to Henry II threatened the kingdom, and the king had to be removed from the influence of his predominantly Anglo-Norman counsellors, while A. A. M. Duncan noted that the king's absence from the realm must also have been a contributing factor.[12] Some tension may also have been caused by feelings of antipathy toward the degree of foreign influence in Scotland at the time, reflected in Malcolm's desire to seek knighthood at the hands of the English king. Other scholars, notably Brooke, have concluded that, while the earls might have been annoyed at Malcolm for being out of the kingdom so long, it is hardly conceivable that they would have resorted to such drastic action, and even less conceivable that they would have joined forces with Fergus.[13] Brooke therefore argues that the revolt of the earls in 1160 is a non-event. She postulates instead that internal conflicts in Galloway in the late 1150s led to the unification of the warring factions against a common enemy, the

7   *Chron. Holyrood*, 129–31.
8   *RRS* i, no. 175. Fordun stated that Somerled continued to rebel after the capture of his nephew: *Chron. Fordun*, i, 255; ii, 250.
9   *Chron. Holyrood*, 132–3; *Chron. Melrose*, 76. See also W. L. Warren, *Henry II* (London 1973), 179.
10 *Chron. Melrose*, 77; trans. *ES* ii, 244.
11 Ibid., 244 n.3.
12 *RRS* i, 12; Duncan, *Making of the Kingdom*, 225–6.
13 Brooke, *Fergus the King*, 14–15.

Scots. The Galwegians then raided into Clydesdale in Malcolm's absence. The campaigns of 1160 into Galloway, in this view, should be seen as punitive expeditions entirely unrelated to the events at Perth that same year. Whatever the case may have been, their effect was certainly the same: Fergus was forced to resign his lordship and retire to a location where the king could keep an eye on him. Deprived of his status, he spent his last days in the cloisters and church of Holyrood, until he died, probably an old man, in 1161.[14]

Somerled's activities from 1160 to 1164 remain unknown, but it would appear that an uneasy peace prevailed between the ruler of Argyll and the king of Scots.[15] Then, in 1164, hostilities broke out again, when Somerled collected a fleet of 160 ships (if the figures given by the chronicles can be trusted), filled them with warriors from the Hebrides, Argyll, Kintyre, Dublin, and perhaps Galloway, and landed at Renfrew.[16] Contemporary and later sources differ on what happened next. The contemporary accounts agree that a battle was fought in which Somerled, his son, and most of his forces perished: 'And in the first cleft of battle the baleful leader fell. Wounded by a spear, slain by the sword, Somerled died ... and very many were slaughtered, both on sea and on land.'[17] By the seventeenth century, however, an alternative tradition had arisen which had Somerled assassinated through the machinations of King Malcolm's Anglo-Norman advisors.[18] Whichever account we choose to believe (and it should surely be the former), there can be little doubt that with the death of Fergus in 1161 and Somerled in 1164, two of the most prominent powerful, and mysterious figures of mid-twelfth-century Scotland had passed from the scene.

Their legacy was one of conflict with the kings of Scots, but recent scholarship has surprisingly little to say of these hostilities and particularly

14 *Chron. Holyrood*, 139. There is, however, another tradition about Fergus's retirement, which has him enter religion voluntarily thanks to the admonishment of Ailred of Rievaulx. See *Life of Ailred*, 45–6.

15 The Melrose Chronicle states that Somerled had been rebelling against the king for 12 years. This cannot be correct since it is contradicted by the evidence of the 1160 charter, and it would also place the start of the rebellion in 1152. The 12 years must be taken to be a rough estimate. See *Chron. Melrose*, 79; and A. A. M. Duncan and A. L. Brown, 'Argyll and the Isles in the earlier Middle Ages', *PSAS* xc (1956–7), 195 n.4.

16 *Chron. Melrose*, 79, records the landing at Renfrew. The diverse composition of the army is shown by *Ann. Ulster*, 1164; *Ann. Tigernach*, 1164; and the *Carmen de Morte Sumerledi*, in Simeon of Durham, *Symeonis Monachi Opera Omnia*, ed. T. Arnold (Rolls Ser., 1882–5), ii, 386.

17 Ibid., 388; trans. *ES* ii, 258.

18 *Book of Clanranald*, in *Reliquiae Celticae*, ii, 155; Hugh MacDonald, *History of the MacDonalds*, in *Highland Papers*, i, 9. On Somerled's death, see R. A. McDonald, 'The death and burial of Somerled of Argyll', *West Highland Notes and Queries*, 2nd ser., viii (Nov. 1991), 6–10.

the causes that underlie them. Explanations, when offered, range from dynastic to Celtic conservatism, but the portrayal of the uprisings as random and unconnected events leaves the impression that they were purely predatory and piratical, and that their leaders were merely troublesome chieftains, who, for no good reason, acted as thorns in the sides of the feudalising kings of Scots.[19] On the whole, then, modern views share much with medieval interpretations like that of the twelfth-century *Carmen de Morte Sumerledi*, where Somerled and his men became 'foul with treachery, the most cruel enemy'.[20]

In order fully to understand the mystery posed by these conflicts, we must turn our attention towards the peripheral regions of Galloway and Argyll, and examine the milieu from which their leaders were sprung, including the ancestry, background, and family connections of Fergus and Somerled. Such an examination will reveal that Fergus and Somerled must be placed firmly within an Irish Sea context, emphasising fundamental dichotomies between the world in which they moved and the 'new world order' being introduced by the kings of Scots in the twelfth century.

The most pressing of the questions relating to the origins and ancestry of Fergus of Galloway is, from which of the various peoples, Galwegian, Norse, Gall-Gaidhil, or Norman, did he come? What was his relation to King David I of Scotland, and to King Henry I of England? In attempting to answer these questions the lack of evidence is keenly felt. Unlike Somerled, upon whose background the genealogies shed some light, there is no direct evidence bearing upon Fergus's ancestry, and the matter is further complicated by the inventions and romantic speculations of some nineteenth-century historians.

To an earlier generation of historians, Fergus could only have been a protégé of David I, a foreign governor appointed to Galloway. This supposition rested primarily upon the marriage of Fergus to an illegitimate daughter of King Henry I of England, and his relatively late appearance on the scene sometime after 1138.[21] His marriage to the daughter of Henry I has been taken to be an indication that Fergus had spent his youth at the court of Henry I, and had there come to be associated with David. Although the marriage of Fergus to one of Henry's daughters is widely accepted,[22] it cannot be taken as evidence that Fergus spent his youth at

19 E.g., M. Lynch, *Scotland: A New History* (London 1991), 85.
20 *Carmen de Morte Sumerledi*, 386–8.
21 G. Chalmers, *Caledonia* (London 1807–24), i, 366; P. H. M'Kerlie, *The History of the Lands and Their Owners in Galloway* (Edinburgh 1870–9).
22 See, e.g., R. D. Oram, 'Fergus, Galloway and the Scots', in R. D. Oram and G. P. Stell (eds.), *Galloway: Land and Lordship* (Edinburgh 1991), 117, 119; and C. Given-Wilson and A. Curtis, *The Royal Bastards of Medieval England* (London 1984), 71.

the court of Henry. Indeed, the childhood spent at the English court 'appears to be pure fabrication, invented by nineteenth-century writers who were seeking to find suitable circumstances for Fergus to have met his future bride'.[23] Such an assessment is supported by the fact that Fergus's name nowhere appears in the charters of the Anglo-Norman kings of England, which would surely be expected if he had spent a significant part of his life at court there.[24] It is also possible to question the belief that Fergus became attached to David's court in England even though he did attest several of his charters in *c*.1136–41. Fergus first appears as a witness, along with his son Uhtred and with Radulf and Duunenald, the sons of Dunegal of Strathnith, in a charter of *c*.1136 granting Partick to the church at Glasgow.[25] It has been noted that 'the houses of Dunegal and Fergus show great interest in this area, often witnessing charters there'.[26] The presence of Fergus as a witness, then, should not be taken as indicative of his attachment to David's household, but rather of his prominence in this particular region.

The problem remains as to whether Fergus owed his status to David I. Evidence for this was adduced from the fact that he appeared solidly on the record only after the Battle of the Standard in 1138, in which Ailred of Rievaulx stated that Ulgric and Donald, leaders of the Galwegians, were slain.[27] This led to the suggestion that Fergus was appointed governor of Galloway by David in the aftermath of the conflict in order to pacify that disturbed region;[28] indeed, at one extreme, it has even been suggested that Fergus was 'clearly of the Norman race, and one of King David's own school'.[29] The deaths of Ulgric and Donald, however, need not imply Fergus's absence from the conflict. At least one chronicler could distinguish the *summo duce Loenensium*,[30] presumably from other, subordinate, leaders, and there seems little reason to suspect that the presence of Ulgric and Donald at the battle necessarily precluded that of

---

[23] Oram, 'Fergus, Galloway and the Scots', 119.

[24] See the indices of *Regesta Regum Anglo-Normannorum*, vols. II–III: *Regesta Henrici Primi, 1100–1135*, ed. C. Johnson and H. A. Cronne (Oxford 1956), and *Regesta Stephani ac Mathildi Imperatricis ac Gaufrid et Henrici Ducum Normannorum, 1135–1154*, ed. H. A. Cronne and R. H. C. Davis (Oxford 1968).

[25] *ESC*, nos. 109 (*c*. 1136), and 125 (*c*. 1139–41).

[26] A. E. Truckell, 'A proto-history of Galloway,' *TDGNHAS*, 3rd ser., lxiv (1989), 50.

[27] Ailred of Rievaulx, *Relatio de Standardo*, in *Chrons. Stephen, etc.*, iii, 196–7.

[28] W. MacKenzie, *The History of Galloway from the Earliest Period to the Present Time* (Kirkcudbright 1841), i, 167; M'Kerlie, *Lands and Their Owners*, ii, 53–4; J. F. Robertson, *The Story of Galloway* (Castle Douglas 1963; repr. Newtongrange 1985), 43.

[29] M'Kerlie, *Lands and Their Owners*, ii, 54.

[30] Henry of Huntingdon, *Historia Anglorum*, ed. T. Arnold (Rolls Ser., 1879), 264.

Fergus.[31] Like Somerled, who is thought by some to have been present,[32] his name simply did not enter the record of events. Thus, Fergus was holding a position of prominence in Galloway before 1138, but there is also another objection to his being simply a creature of David's making – one which relates to the ability of the Scottish king to interfere in the affairs of Galloway at this early period.

Upon the death of King Edgar in 1107, his brother Alexander succeeded to the kingship. David was to hold Cumbria and parts of Lothian under Alexander. The position and powers of David in the south-west from 1107 to 1124, during the reign of Alexander I, are difficult to determine through surviving documentary evidence. He held extensive lands in the south of Scotland, and the *Inquisitio* concerning the church of Glasgow, dated to *c.*1113, accorded him the description of *Cumbrensis regionis princeps*.[33] Although he received levies from the south-west in Kyle, Carrick, Cunningham, and Strathclyde, he could not have held the overlordship of Galloway as Ritchie argued.[34] A charter of Malcolm IV refers to *illa Galweia* held by his grandfather, David, suggesting that although some degree of control was exercised by David, not all of Galloway fell under his jurisdiction.[35] Moreover, the king of Scots is not known to have held any demesne land in Galloway,[36] a fact which would strongly argue against any significant royal involvement at this time.

If Fergus was not merely a protégé of David I, then the question remains of just who he was. This problem is accentuated by the lack of any reliable genealogical information concerning his ancestors. He was styled simply Fergus *de Galweia* in those charters which he attested, and the pedigrees of his descendants were carried back only to him.[37] Notwithstanding his belief that Fergus grew up with David at the court of Henry I, Sir Herbert Maxwell suggested that Fergus was 'of the line of Galloway princes or

31 Fergus's absence from the Battle of the Standard rests upon a vague story in the 'History of the foundation of the Priory of the Isle of Trail': see *Historia Fundacionis Prioratus Insule de Traile*, in *The Bannatyne Miscellany*, vol. II, ed. D. Laing (Bannatyne Club, 1836), 19–20; also in Maxwell, *History of Dumfries and Galloway*, 49–50. The story is unsupported by external evidence, and the 'History of the foundation of Trail' is described as 'fabulous' by A. C. Lawrie, *Annals of the Reigns of Malcolm and William, Kings of Scotland* (Glasgow, 1910), 67–8. It is from a 13th- or 14th-century compilation: D. and W. Stevenson, *Scottish Texts and Calendars* (Royal Historical Soc. and SHS, 1987), p. 21.
32 Duncan, *Making of the Kingdom*, 166.
33 *ESC*, no. 50.
34 Ibid., no, 125; R. L. G. Ritchie, *The Normans in Scotland* (Edinburgh 1954), 129.
35 *RRS*, i, no. 131; Oram, 'Fergus, Galloway and the Scots', 123.
36 Chalmers, *Caledonia*, i, 366.
37 *ESC*, nos. 109, 125. A charter of Dervorgilla de Balliol, *c.*1273, recorded a grant made *pro animabus Fergusii de Galwidia Uchtredi filii sui et Roulandi aui mei et Elene uxoris sue et Alani filii sui patris mei*: *RRS*, vi, no. 235.

native rulers', meaning presumably Strathclyde-Welsh blood.[38] While there might be much to commend such a view, some recent studies have argued that the last of the native British line of rulers in Strathclyde had died out by the middle of the ninth century, making it unlikely that Fergus was related to them.[39] Other historians have seen him as springing from Norse or Gall-Gaidhil stock.[40] His association with a man named Somerled (not Somerled of Argyll) in the thirteenth-century *Roman de Fergus* lends some credibility to the belief that by the early twelfth century Scandinavian elements had indeed intruded into the ruling house of Galloway.[41] Some investigators would link him to Suibne, Kenneth's son, called king of the Galwegians, who died in 1034,[42] and it has even been argued that Fergus was the son of that Somhairle, styled *rí Innse Gall*, who died in 1083.[43] Whatever the case, the most commonly held consensus among modern historians who have examined the problem is that Fergus's background was mixed Celtic-Norse, not unlike that of Somerled of Argyll.[44]

The origins and ancestry of Somerled, like those of Fergus, are all but lost. Nineteenth- and early twentieth-century historians were divided over whether his ancestry should be described as Norse, Gaelic, or mixed Celtic-Norse. Some, arguing on the evidence of his Norse name, Somerled, which means 'Summer Sailor' or 'Viking', and a distrust of the

---

38 Maxwell, *History of Dumfries and Galloway*, 47; see also Lawrie, *Annals*, 67–87 and *ESC*, 362; and *Wigtownshire Charters*, p. xvi n.1.

39 A. P. Smyth, *Warlords and Holy Men: Scotland AD 80–1000* (Edinburgh 1984), 218–19; but compare A. MacQuarrie, 'The kings of Strathclyde, *c*.900–1018', in A. Grant and K. J. Stringer (eds.), *Medieval Scotland: Crown, Lordship and Community. Essays presented to G. W. S. Barrow* (Edinburgh 1993), 1–19.

40 E.g., J. A. McGill, 'A genealogical survey of the ancient lords of Galloway', *Scottish Genealogist*, ii (2) (Apr. 1955), 3–6.

41 Guillaume le Clerc, *Fergus of Galloway: Knight of King Arthur*, ed. and trans. D. D. R. Owen (London 1991), 6. See also M. D. Legge, 'The father of Fergus of Galloway', *SHR* xliii (1964), 86; and D. P. Kirby, 'Galloway in the twelfth and thirteenth centuries', in P. McNeill and R. Nicholson (eds.), *An Historical Atlas of Scotland c.400–c.1600* (St Andrews 1975), 49. On the *Roman* itself see M. D. Legge, 'Some notes on the *Roman de Fergus*', *TDGNHAS*, 3rd ser., xxvii (1948–9), 163–72. Attempts to link the two dynasties, as in McGill, 'Genealogical survey', 5–6, have been demolished: see Oram, 'Fergus, Galloway and the Scots', 119.

42 *Wigtownshire Chrs.*, p. xi.

43 Truckell, 'Proto-history of Galloway', 50; see *Ann. Four Masters*, 1164, for the death of Somhairle *rí Innse Gall*.

44 Oram, 'Fergus, Galloway and the Scots,' 121–2; Duncan, *Making of the Kingdom*, 163–4. See also D. Brooke, 'Gall-Gaidhil and Galloway', in Oram and Stell, *Galloway: Land and Lordship*, 110, where it is argued that the place-name evidence suggests Fergus took control of the lands and residences of his predecessors without 'either shifting ground or occasioning any change in toponymy'. This strengthens the contention that he was of native Galwegian or Celtic-Norse stock, and not an outsider.

genealogical evidence, viewed his background as primarily Norse.[45] Others, following the genealogies and pointing to the Gaelic names of his father and grandfather, Gilla Brigde ('servant of St Bride') and Gilla Adomnain ('servant of St Adomnán'), stressed the predominantly Gaelic nature of his background.[46] The matter was set firmly to rest by David Sellar, who argued that Clan Donald tradition of the seventeenth century, which preserved Somerled's genealogy and was believed to be unreliable, should not be ignored: 'in later stages of Clan Donald history where facts can be cross-checked with contemporary evidence, the Clanranald historian and Hugh Macdonald are frequently wrong in matters of detail, yet in their narration of the general trend of events they are usually correct'.[47] Arguing for the authenticity of the Gaelic genealogies of the Clan Donald, Sellar traced Somerled's descent back to Godfrey, the son of Fergus, a ninth-century chieftain, 'who links Derry and Dalriada, Ireland and the Isles, and whose name has Norse associations also'.[48] Accordingly, Somerled's Celtic-Norse extraction, like that of Fergus, is now widely accepted.[49]

In their ancestry, then, both Fergus and Somerled were of mixed Celtic-Norse stock, and both had close connections with the dynasty of Man and the Isles. Marriage connections are one of the most profitable tools which can be used to illuminate the social position and the outlook of the nobility. It is therefore instructive to examine the lineal family relationships of Fergus and Somerled. One notable characteristic, common to both, is that they seem to have followed a deliberate policy of forging links outside the Scottish kingdom with little or no regard for the kings of Scots, and apparently made no attempt to ally themselves through marriage with either the line of Malcolm Canmore or newcomer Anglo-Norman families.

Fergus's marriage to a daughter of King Henry I was probably not the result of a youth spent at the court of the English king, or even less a love-match, but rather reflected the ever-present need for political alliances or mercenary troops.[50] As Brooke has perceptively noted, Henry I had arranged diplomatic marriages for several of his illegitimate daughters with ruling princes whose lands bordered on England and Normandy. Among these

---

[45] E. MacNeill, 'Chapters of Hebridean history, I: The Norse kingdom of the Hebrides', *The Scottish Review*, xxxix (1916), 254–76.

[46] C. MacDonald, *The History of Argyll* (Glasgow 1950), 73.

[47] W. D. H. Sellar, 'The origins and ancestry of Somerled', *SHR* xlv (1966), 124.

[48] Ibid., 141. See also the same author's 'Family origins in Cowal and Knapdale,' *Scottish Studies*, xv (1971), 21–37, where these arguments are further pursued.

[49] Duncan, *Making of the Kingdom*, 166; G. W. S. Barrow, *Kingship and Unity: Scotland 1000–1306* (London 1981), 108–9.

[50] Which paid off when Fergus joined with David I to support the cause of Matilda in the civil war against Stephen: see R. D. Oram, 'The Lordship of Galloway c.1000 to c.1250' (St Andrews University Ph.D. thesis, 1988), 74.

princes had been Alexander I, and 'Fergus's match to another daughter was sufficient indication of his status as a sovereign ruler.'[51] Fergus's daughter, Affrica, married King Olaf of Man, possibly shortly after Olaf's accession to the throne.[52] Their son Godred succeeded as King of Man upon the death of Olaf in 1153.[53] It was not until much later in the twelfth century that the house of Galloway would become firmly cemented through marriage alliances with families in the east of Scotland. Although Fergus's son, Uhtred, married Gunnild, the daughter of Waltheof, son of Earl Gospatrick II of Lothian, it was not until the marriage of Roland, Uhtred's son, to Helen, the daughter of Richard de Morville, that firm dynastic connections between the house of Galloway and the east became readily apparent.[54]

Somerled, like Fergus, also allied himself with west-coast dynasties, including Man. His marriage to a daughter of Olaf named Ragnhild has already been noted, although she was not the daughter of Olaf's marriage to Affrica, but rather of a concubine.[55] A sister of Somerled, whose name is unknown, married Malcolm MacHeth sometime before his capture in 1134: the *Chronicle of Holyrood* recorded that two sons of Malcolm, Somerled's nephews (*nepotes*), joined Somerled in his 1153 rebellion.[56] A daughter of this union in turn married Earl Harald Maddadsson of Orkney (1139–1206) after 1168, at a time when he, too, was locked in conflict with the king of Scots.[57]

In contracting these marriages, Fergus and Somerled were, like all medieval nobles, making a statement. But while the east-coast earls of Fife, Dunbar, and eventually Strathearn, all chose to associate themselves consciously, through marriage and other means, with the royal house and Anglo-Norman families of the east,[58] the dynasties of Galloway and Argyll demonstrate an opposite trend. They made no attempt whatsoever to forge

---

[51] Brooke, *Fergus the King*, 5.

[52] *Chron. Man* (Munch and Goss), 60, 167n. Although the Manx Chronicle, followed by its editor, Munch, stated that Olaf took the throne in 1103, it is more likely to have been 1114 or 1115. See R. Power, 'Magnus Barelegs' expeditions to the West', *SHR* lxv (1986), 115–17, and R. H. Kinvig, *A History of the Isle of Man* (2nd edn, Liverpool 1950), 54.

[53] *Chron. Man* (Munch and Goss), 60, 66.

[54] *CDS* i, no. 318.

[55] *Chron. Man* (Munch and Goss), 61. Her name is given as Ragnhild in *Orkneyinga Saga*, ch. 100. The date of the marriage is commonly given as 1140, but this rests on no contemporary authority, and it must in fact have taken place sometime between 1120 and 1150. See Duncan and Brown, 'Argyll and the Isles,' 195.

[56] *Chron. Holyrood*, 125; see also 129 n.1.

[57] *Orkneyinga Saga*, ch. 109.

[58] See, e.g., G. W. S. Barrow, 'The earls of Fife in the twelfth century,' *PSAS* lxxxvi (1952–3), 51–62; and G. W. S. Barrow, *The Anglo-Norman Era in Scottish History* (Oxford 1980), 86–8; also Roberts, *Lost Kingdoms*, ch. 3. No doubt the forthcoming volume on *Native Kindreds* edited by Steve Boardman will advance our knowledge of the Scottish earldoms considerably.

links with the Canmore dynasty nor, in the time of Fergus and Somerled, with Anglo-Norman families. The most important marriage connections were those linking these families to the Norse dynasty of Man, entirely separate from the Scottish kingdom, and with other prominent families of the north and west like the MacHeths. Indeed, while geographical factors should always be kept in mind, it is tempting to surmise that this represented a conscious policy of separation from the royal family and its attendants in the east. The marriage of Somerled's sister to Malcolm MacHeth is particularly instructive: although once thought to represent an honourable link between the royal family and that of Somerled, based upon the belief that Malcolm MacHeth was an illegitimate son of Alexander I,[59] it more probably demonstrates an association with an 'anti-feudal',[60] or perhaps anti-Canmore, faction, since Malcolm MacHeth was more likely somehow connected with the dynasty of Moray or with Ross. In short, the marriages contracted by these families are highly instructive. While in the east the focal point of such relationships was the house of Canmore, with the attraction of its Anglo-Norman style court,[61] in the west a complex network of alliances existed which extended its tentacles westward, and had as its focal point the Norse dynasty of Man. Further, these marriage alliances between the houses of Fergus, Somerled, MacHeth and Man were, in all probability, contracted without the approval of the kings of Scots, and represent alliances between families opposed, for one reason or another, to the kings of Scots.[62]

Most important of all, however, this network of lateral family connections not only reinforces the independence of these areas, but also goes far towards substantiating the continued existence of the Irish Sea Province well into the twelfth century. The concept of an Irish Sea Province implies that, during certain periods of the past, the lands bordering the Irish Sea were effectively united by 'constant and uninterrupted communication ... across the seas that separated Ireland from the mainland of Britain'.[63] Although this term is most commonly used to describe the periods from

59 Duncan and Brown, 'Argyll and the Isles,' 195. This hypothesis is no longer seriously entertained.
60 The phrase is Cowan's, although its implications have yet to be worked out for the history of medieval Scotland: see E. J. Cowan, 'The historical MacBeth,' in W. D. H. Sellar (ed.), *Moray: Province and People* (Edinburgh 1993), 131.
61 On the attraction of Anglo-Norman style courts to native kings and princes, see R. R. Davies, *Domination and Conquest: The Experience of Ireland, Scotland and Wales 1100–1300* (Cambridge 1990), 49–51.
62 R. A. McDonald, 'Matrimonial politics and core-periphery interactions in twelfth- and early thirteenth-century Scotland,' *Journal of Medieval History*, xxi (1995).
63 E. G. Bowen, 'Britain and the British Seas,' in D. Moore (ed.), *The Irish Sea Province in Archaeology and History* (Cardiff 1970), 13. See also E. G. Bowen, *Saints, Seaways and Settlements in the Celtic Lands* (Cardiff 1969), where the concept is explored at much greater length.

the mesolithic to the late eighth century, the Vikings did not destroy this unity even if they seriously altered its character.[64] As A. P. Smyth has suggested, 'by the turn of the millennium Gaelic culture was reasserting itself in south-west Scotland and something of the old unity of the Gaelic world was preserved in spite of those Norse longships'.[65] Indeed, the marriage connections of Fergus and Somerled, the formidable fleet which Somerled commanded, and the composition of his army in 1164, suggest that extensive connections were maintained down to the mid-twelfth century and beyond. This region, by virtue of its western orientation, roots in the Irish Sea world, and Scoto-Norse culture, stood apart from the east of Scotland.[66]

The last question to be addressed before turning to the causes of the conflicts between Fergus and Somerled and the kings of Scots is that of their position within twelfth-century society. Any assessment of this problem is difficult, and is further hampered by the lack of source material as well as the bias in what little evidence does exist. Were these men merely tributary lords who owed both their position and allegiance to the king of Scots, or were they something more? It has often been supposed that both Fergus and Somerled were semi-independent rulers, tributary lords, or feudal vassals, owing some sort of allegiance and tribute to the king of Scots. This interpretation is based upon the assumption that each sent troops to fight at the Battle of the Standard in 1138, and owed *cain* (tribute) from his territories to the king of Scots. In the case of Fergus, however, Richard Oram has suggested that the troops fighting on David's behalf in 1138 (as well as on earlier campaigns under Malcolm Canmore) may very well have been present as hired troops, rather than a military levy; that Fergus himself had a personal stake in the battle since he was fighting on behalf of Matilda, his wife's half-sister; and that the *cain* known to have been owed to David from Galloway was only from Desnes Ioan, something of an anomaly which does not suggest Scottish overlordship of Galloway in this period.[67] It is interesting that, to date, no scholar has made a parallel argument for Somerled. Argyll, too, may have provided mercenaries: it is well known that by the thirteenth century, the *galloclaig* (later galloglasses), fighting men from *Innse Gall*, were being utilised by Gaelic lords in Ireland.[68] And, also like Galloway, the charter evidence for

---

64 Bowen, 'Britain and the British Seas,' and P. H. Sawyer, 'The Vikings and the Irish Sea,' both in Moore, *Irish Sea Province in Archaeology and History*, 13, 86–92.

65 Smyth, *Warlords and Holy Men*, 213.

66 See McDonald, *Kingdom of the Isles, passim.*

67 Oram, 'Fergus, Galloway and the Scots,' 123–6; see 125–8 for a detailed discussion of Desnes Ioan.

68 A full discussion is in McDonald, *Kingdom of the Isles*, 154–6.

payment of *cain* from Argyll and Kintyre is not entirely unambiguous. Although David I did grant to Dunfermline Abbey 'the half part of my tenth from Argyll and Kintyre', the gift was to be given 'in that year when I myself shall have received *cain* thence'.[69] This is surely unsafe ground upon which to build any argument of the subordination of Argyll to David I. While it may be 'difficult to believe that these grants were meaningless gestures',[70] the vague phraseology of the charter ('in that year when I myself shall have received *cain* thence') can only be deliberate, and could be interpreted to indicate that David I was in fact *not* receiving any tribute.

Fortunately, better evidence of an independent and regal dignity for these men does exist. Eastern Scottish and English sources called Fergus *princeps* and once *comes*, 'earl', even though he was never so styled in the charters, while Somerled was called *regulus*.[71] But these terms prove notoriously difficult to translate, and it would be anachronistic to translate the Latin *princeps* as the modern word 'prince'; a more accurate rendering might be simply 'ruler' or 'lord',[72] while *regulus* might be rendered as 'kinglet', 'under-king' or simply 'ruler'. In general, though, the terms utilised by Scottish and English chroniclers to describe Fergus and Somerled indicate with any certainty only that they were 'rulers'. From a contemporary perspective they simply comprised part of a large group (including kings but not made up exclusively of kings), who, as *principes*, determined the fate of their subjects and the Church in their territories.[73] But it is also important to realise that Fergus and Somerled can really only be seen from the perspective of those whom they opposed: namely, the kings of Scots descended from Malcolm Canmore and Queen Margaret. Since the Scottish sources were composed at monastic centres closely connected with those rulers, very real problems of partisanship present themselves. This biased outlook of the eastern Scottish sources may be seen quite clearly in the 1164 entry in the Melrose Chronicle, which recorded how Somerled had been 'wickedly rebelling for now twelve years against Malcolm, the king of Scots, his natural lord'.[74] This invective

---

69 *ESC*, no. 209: ... *dimidiam partem decimi mei de Ergaithel et Kentir, eo scilicet anno quum* [sic] *ego ipse unde recepero can.*
70 Duncan and Brown, 'Argyll and the Isles,' 195.
71 On Fergus: *Chron. Holyrood*, 137, 139; and Richard of Hexham, *De Gestis Regis Stephani*, in *Chrons. Stephen, etc.*, iii, 177–8. On Somerled: *Chron. Melrose*, 79.
72 R. E. Latham, *Revised Medieval Latin Word-List from British and Irish Sources* (London 1965), 372; see also S. Reynolds, *Kingdoms and Communities in Western Europe 900–1300* (Oxford 1984), 259–60.
73 K. F. Werner, 'Kingdom and principality in twelfth-century France,' in T. Reuter (ed.), *The Medieval Nobility: Studies on the Ruling Classes of France and Germany from the Sixth to the Twelfth Centuries* (Amsterdam 1979), 244.
74 *Chron. Melrose*, 79.

against the presumption and insolence of Somerled could hardly be clearer: the chronicler assumed that Somerled was somehow subservient to Malcolm; the latter's 'rebellion' was therefore 'wicked'. This lens may be responsible for removing much of the regal standing that these rulers possessed, by consciously downgrading their status wherever possible in order to conform with new ideals of kingship prevalent in Scotland under David I and his successors. Such a practice is not without precedent. In seventeenth-century Ireland, tribal kings were deliberately demoted to the status of 'lord' or 'chieftain' (*tighearna* or *taoiseach*) for political reasons,[75] while in the fourteenth century terms which ascribed Irish rulers regal status ceased to be acceptable, probably as a result of Edward I's policy of promoting the central authority of the Crown and undermining local jurisdictions.[76] But the most salient point to note is that the ultimate cause of the downplaying of royal status was the arrival of the Anglo-Normans in Ireland and their 'crowding out' of native Irish dynasties.[77] These examples should be seen as closely paralleling the policy of the Canmore dynasty in Scotland in the twelfth century, providing strong evidence that, despite their immense value, the testimony of the Melrose and Holyrood chroniclers should not always be taken at face value where the status of other native dynasties is concerned.

More compelling evidence for assuming a royal status for Fergus and Somerled does indeed exist. Noting the death of Somerled in 1164, the *Annals of Tigernach*, called him *rí Innse Gall & Cind Tire*, king of the Hebrides and Kintyre.[78] The *Annals of Ulster* designated Fergus's descendants (although not Fergus himself) *rí Gall-Gaidhil*.[79] The use of these terms to describe Scottish princes has often been either ignored or explained away as representing the 'hibernicisation' of their status by Irish chroniclers.[80] Recent studies of Irish kingship, however, have suggested

---

75   F. J. Byrne, *Irish Kings and High Kings* (London 1973), 41.

76   K. Simms, *From Kings to Warlords: The Changing Political Structure of Gaelic Ireland in the Later Middle Ages* (Woodbridge 1987), 36–7. Welsh parallels could also be cited: see T. Jones Pierce, 'The age of the Princes,' in D. Myrddin Lloyd, *The Historical Basis of Welsh Nationalism* (Cardiff 1950), 50–1; and D. Jenkins, 'Kings, lords, and princes: the nomenclature of authority in thirteenth-century Wales,' *Bulletin of the Board of Celtic Studies*, xxvi (1974–6), 451–62, esp. 452–5.

77   For which see Simms, *Kings to Warlords*, 13–14; and R. Frame, *The Political Development of the British Isles 1100–1400* (Oxford 1990), 108–15.

78   *Ann. Tigernach*, 1164.

79   *Ann. Ulster* (Hennesy and MacCarthy), ii, 234–5, 240–1. See Brooke, 'Gall-Gaidhil and Galloway,' 100–3.

80   G. W. S. Barrow, 'Macbeth and other mormaers of Moray,' in L. Maclean (ed.), *The Hub of the Highlands: The Book of Inverness and District* (Edinburgh 1975), 110. Compare the comments here to the more moderate ones in Barrow, *Kingship and Unity*, 107–8.

that, far from being static, it was undergoing dramatic changes to bring it into line with continental developments in this period.[81] Within this context, then, the attribution of royal status to rulers like Fergus and Somerled cannot be disregarded entirely.

But perhaps the most compelling evidence for assuming a royal dignity for Fergus (and by implication Somerled) is found in a charter preserved in the *Monasticon Anglicanum*. Buried in a list of Hospitaller properties drawn up by the English brother John Stillingflete in the fifteenth century, there survives the record of a grant made by *Feregus Rex Galwitensium* of the land of Galtway.[82] There can be little doubt that this entry was copied from the original and represents an authentic record of the grant.[83] If so, the question remains of why Stillingflete styled Fergus *rex*. It seems impossible that the use of the title was entirely arbitrary, or that a fifteenth-century Hospitaller had any political agenda for according to Fergus royal status. The most plausible suggestion is that the title was simply copied verbatim out of the salutation of the original charter, thereby emphasising the kingly status of Fergus.

In considering the status of Fergus and Somerled it is relevant to bear in mind that, in a broader European context, the eleventh and twelfth centuries were 'not least a world of princes'.[84] Perhaps a close parallel to the position of Somerled and Fergus can be found in eleventh-century France, where the French king had only very limited power beyond his small enclaves of royal domain around Paris and Orléans.[85] The French princes were virtually independent of the king; they avoided the royal court and many carried royal powers if not actual royal titles.[86] There is, then, ample evidence to support the contention that both Fergus and Somerled were kings in the medieval sense of the word, and that the territories over which they ruled were independent kingdoms owing little obeisance to the kings of Scots.

The marriage alliances made by Fergus and Somerled and the titles accorded them are crucial to understanding their position within twelfth-century Scotland. While the eastern and southern regions of the mainland were being rapidly feudalised or Normanised, and new conventions were quickly adopted by the native mormaers or earls in these regions, the western seaboard continued to exist outside the reach of the king of Scots,

81 Simms, *Kings to Warlords*, 11.
82 R. Dodsworth and W. Dugdale, *Monasticon Anglicanum* (London 1660–73), ii, 551. See also *The Knights of St John of Jerusalem in Scotland*, ed. I. B. Cowan, P. H. R. Mackay and A. Macquarrie (SHS 1983), xxvi.
83 *RRS* i, 98.
84 Werner, 'Kingdom and principality in twelfth-century France', 243.
85 Ibid., 245.
86 Ibid., 247–8, 270–1.

and remained firmly set within the context of the Irish Sea world. There is even a sense in which some of the marriages contracted by these rulers represent the forging of links between members of an 'anti-feudal', or anti-Canmore, faction, since at one time or another all of those so connected were engaged in hostilities against the king of Scots. These districts represent, for all intents and purposes, independent kingdoms, with their own rulers in the Irish Sea tradition to whom contemporary sources, writing outside the 'core' of the feudal kingdom of Scotland, ascribed royal status. Indeed, it is doubtful whether contemporaries could have distinguished the 'constitutional' position of Somerled or Fergus from Irish kings, Welsh princes, or the kings of Man.[87] All of these factors go far towards explaining the persistence of opposition to the kings of Scots from these areas – a problem to which it is now possible to return.

There is, as we saw, no positive evidence that the ruler of Galloway was involved in the 1153–7 rising. But the campaigns of Malcolm IV against Fergus in late 1160 or early 1161 strongly suggest that, whether he was raiding into Clydesdale or was involved in the revolt of the earls, by that time Fergus had thrown in his lot with Somerled and other members of the 'anti-feudal faction' rooted in the Irish Sea world who opposed foreign influence and settlement. No doubt the cession of Cumbria by Malcolm IV to Henry II of England in 1157 would have considerably loosened Scottish control in the south-west, possibly clearing the way for Fergus's involvement in the events of 1160.[88] Only when the expansion of feudal landholdings in the south-west of Scotland is considered, however, is it possible to fully understand why Fergus moved to open conflict with the king of Scots.

In general, the process by which the south-west of Scotland, including Galloway, was feudalised and settled is less perfectly understood than that of Lothian and other regions, for which the evidence is more abundant. An examination of the distribution of estates to Anglo-Normans in the south-west indicates that the policy of the kings of Scots in this region was to encircle Galloway with a ring of fiefs, which were in the main comprised of large districts, resembling nothing so much as the Welsh marcher lordships in miniature. Indeed, Galloway must have been, as far as the Scots king was concerned, very much a frontier, and the motives for this encirclement probably included preventing disturbances and incursions into Lothian as well as keeping the important Roman road from Carlisle

---

[87] See G. W. S. Barrow, 'The pattern of feudal settlement in Cumbria,' *Journal of Medieval History*, i (1975), 128. Barrow applies this remark to Fergus, but I see no reason why the same should not be said of Somerled.

[88] On the cession of Cumbria, see A. O. Anderson, 'Anglo-Scottish relations from Constantine II to William,' *SHR* xlii (1963), 15–16.

to the western end of the Antonine wall open.[89] If the various fiefs granted
by David I and Malcolm IV are plotted on a map, they encircle Galloway.
The process began perhaps early in the reign of David I, when Annandale
was granted to Robert de Brus.[90] With its castles at Annan and Lochmaben
it was a key position.[91] The next grant was Lanark, probably under royal
control by 1150 when the church was gifted to Dryburgh Abbey.[92] Next,
Walter fitz Alan's investiture with Renfrew, Paisley, Pollok, and the
northern half of Kyle simultaneously created a buffer zone between the
kings of Argyll and Galloway, and eastern Scotland. The lordship of
Cunningham with Largs, granted to Hugh de Morville, further tightened
the snare, and the smaller holdings of Robert Avenel in Eskdale and
Ranulf de Soules in Liddesdale completed the noose.[93] Moreover, as
Barrow has observed:

> we should remark the symmetrical arrangement by which the four
> districts of Renfrew–Strathgryfe, Cunningham, North Kyle and
> South Kyle, important for the defence of the realm against attack
> from Galloway or the west, were held respectively by the Steward,
> the Constable, the Steward and the Crown.[94]

It must of course be admitted that the chronology of this process of
encirclement is only imperfectly known, and that the estates described
were granted out piecemeal over a considerable time span rather than at one
fell swoop. Nevertheless, by about 1160 the encirclement of Galloway must
be seen as essentially complete, and this pattern of feudal encroachment,
taking as its symbol the mounted knight and the motte-and-bailey castle,
combined with the relaxation of Scottish control in Cumbria, may have
prompted Fergus to throw in his lot with the discontented earls. Following
his defeat in 1160/1 the process accelerated considerably: Nithsdale was
forfeited to the kings of Scots; Dumfries was granted burghal status c.1185;
and Anglo-Norman penetration into the south-west began in earnest.[95]

Somerled, too, may have felt similar pressures, accentuated by events
taking place between 1160 and 1164. We have seen how, in 1160, Malcolm

89 *Wigtownshire Chrs.*, p. xiv.
90 *ESC*, no. 54.
91 *Wigtownshire Chrs.*, p. xiv.
92 *ESC*, no. 218.
93 On the foregoing, see: Barrow, *Kingship and Unity*, 47; Duncan, *Making of the
    Kingdom*, 135–6; *Wigtownshire Chrs.*, pp. xiv–xv; Barrow, 'Feudal settlement in
    Cumbria,' 130–2; and Barrow, *Anglo-Norman Era*, 52, map.
94 *RRS* i, 39. See also G. W. S. Barrow, *King David I and the Church of Glasgow*,
    Glasgow Cathedral Lecture Series no. 4 (Glasgow 1996).
95 See R. C. Reid, 'The feudalisation of lower Nithsdale,' *TDGNHAS*, 3rd ser., xxxiv
    (1957), 102–10; *Wigtownshire Chrs.*, p. xv.

the westward-looking Irish Sea world, the Canmore kings were aligning themselves with European cultural models, which, among other things, emphasised a hierarchy with room for only one king at its head. The conflicts originating in these regions were not, then, primarily dynastic in nature, nor were they essentially the result of a simplistic conflict between 'Celts' and 'Normans'. Rather, they were rooted in the great disparity, cultural, political, and geographical, between the west and the east of Scotland. This disparity took many forms, but it can be seen most clearly in the marriage patterns of the great families of the west and east coast: they polarised around the king of Scots in the east, and around the king of Man in the west. And it was accentuated in the twelfth century by the establishment of buffer zones or marches by the Europeanising kings of Scots on the west coast to isolate and encircle the Celtic-Norse rulers of Galloway and Argyll. Understanding the causes of the opposition to the kings of Scots from Galloway and Argyll requires reading deeper than the rebellious, treacherous vassals of the contemporary documents. It might be better described as a struggle between old and new, or perhaps more accurately as representing antangonism between the westward-looking 'marginal' kingdoms ringing the Irish Sea and the Europeanising, centralising forces of the new Scottish monarchy.

The traditional picture of the penetration of foreign, particularly Anglo-French, influence into Scotland in the twelfth century has seldom occasioned much dissent among historians. Indeed, opinion is almost universally united that there was no great discontinuity or displacement involved in the so-called 'Norman Conquest' of Scotland. Ritchie asserted that 'there was a "Norman Conquest" of Scotland', but added that 'it was not a Conquest in the military sense'.[109] Others have agreed: 'We must put firmly from our minds the belief that the earlier Celtic-speaking population was driven out.'[110] Yet it is perhaps time that this orthodoxy was modified at several junctures. Although it cannot be denied that Scotland was essentially Europeanised by its own kings, that many Anglo-Normans came as guests or were invited, and that many native Scots were quick to accept the new ideas and ways, neither can it any longer be held that the process whereby the Europeanisation of the kingdom took place was exclusively a peaceful one. The uprisings led by Fergus and Somerled, set in the context of the frequency and persistence of the other risings which threatened the kings of Scots in the twelfth century, suggest that there was a powerful opposition to the introduction of European ideas and institutions. Far from being unimportant these uprisings can serve as a

[109] Ritchie, *Normans in Scotland*, xv.
[110] Barrow, *Anglo-Norman Era*, 49. See also D. Walker, *The Normans in Britain* (Oxford 1995), 75.

barometer for measuring discontent in twelfth-century Scotland. If the
Anglo-Norman penetration of Scotland was *largely* peaceful, it should no
longer be held to have been exclusively so. When the number of times
that the Scottish kings had to defend themselves from attacks from the
northern and western margins of their kingdom are considered, it seems
clear that the sword had a much larger role to play in the Europeanisation
of Scotland than has been allowed in the past.

Finally, and perhaps most significantly, these conflicts raise important
questions about the validity of currently held opinions on the cohesiveness
of the early kingdom of Scotland. These risings, based upon marginal regions
of Scotland with strong traditions of autonomy, suggest that submission to
one king, which is held to have been well established by the twelfth century,
was weaker than has been thought, and that there was still a good deal that
was provincial and regional in Scottish politics. As one critic has suggested,
'a preoccupation with the early unity of Scotland and its subsequent strength
and (by 1286) "harmony" is perhaps misplaced'.[111] Indeed, if Argyll and
Galloway are viewed as separate kingdoms in the first half of the twelfth
century, owing little, if any, obeisance to the kings of Scots, the current
view of the early unity of Scotland cannot be sustained. Although it would
be folly to attempt to deny that, under the guidance of the descendants of
Malcolm Canmore and Queen Margaret, Scotland did emerge into the
family of European kingdoms as a relatively unified realm, the early date of
that union, as well as the strength of the ties which bound it together, should
not be overemphasised. Throughout the twelfth century, and well into the
thirteenth, regional identities, closely associated with the westward-looking
Irish Sea world, led to conflicts between these marginal regions and the
Europeanised core of the kingdom, the heartland of the Canmore
dynasty.[112] Unfortunately for the rulers of these marginal regions – rulers
like Fergus and Somerled – by the 1160s their time atop Fortune's Wheel
was past and a new element was moving into the ascendant.

---

111 D. P. Kirby, review of Duncan, *Making of the Kingdom*, in *English Historical
   Review*, xci (1976), 838. See also F. Watson, 'The enigmatic lion: Scotland, kingship
   and national identity in the Wars of Independence', in D. Broun, R. J. Finlay and
   M. Lynch (eds.), *Image and Identity: The Making and Remaking of Scotland
   Through the Ages* (Edinburgh 1998), 19.
112 It is encouraging to see regional identities receiving increased attention; see, e.g.,
   B. Webster, *Medieval Scotland: The Making of an Identity* (Basingstoke 1997).

8

Hebridean Sea Kings: The Successors of Somerled, 1164–1316[1]

W. D. H. SELLAR

Recent studies have done much to illuminate the story of the later Lordship of the Isles under its MacDonald lords, and to emphasise the role of the Lordship as a bastion of Gaelic culture and language.[2] This essay considers an earlier period in the story of the kingdom of the Isles: the century and a half after the death of Somerled at Renfrew in 1164. During this period the leading descendants of Somerled were MacDougalls and MacRuairis rather than MacDonalds, and Scandinavian influences remained strong, albeit declining. The MacDougalls have been overshadowed by the MacDonalds in Scottish historiographical tradition since their fall from power as a result of opposing Bruce in the Wars of Independence. One

[1] The genesis of this essay, delivered in the University of Guelph at the Alba Conference in 1992, was given, as 'The Early MacDougalls, Lords of Argyll: The West Highlands in the Medieval Scottish Kingdom', at the University of St Andrews's 1991–2 'Seminar in Honour of Ronald Cant: Aspects of Medieval Scotland'. It was also read to the Mull Historical Society, the Argyll Historical Society, the Edinburgh University Scottish History departmental seminar, and the Scottish Society for Northern Studies. I am deeply indebted to the many people who offered comments and suggestions on these occasions. I am also most grateful to Billy and Jean Munro for reading and commenting on a draft of the text.

It is difficult to know how best to represent personal names when writing about Man and the Isles in the Middle Ages. Should the form used be Gaelic, Latin or Scandinavian – these would, in any case, alter over a period of some hundreds of years – or should a modern English equivalent be used? There is no wholly satisfactory answer and, as yet, no agreed academic convention. I have given the names in modern English, not without some misgivings, but have also given the standard earlier Medieval Gaelic form in brackets when a name first appears: e.g., Dugald (*Dubgall*) and Olaf (*Amlaíb*). I have avoided Latin forms: thus Ewen (*Eogan*), rather than *Eugenius*, and Ranald (*Ragnall*), rather than *Reginald(us)*. I have given the English equivalents more commonly used in Scotland: thus 'Godfrey' for *Gofraid*, rather than the form 'Godred', often used of the kings of Man, or 'Guthred'.

[2] See, e.g.: *ALI*, *passim*; J. W. M. Bannerman, 'The Lordship of the Isles' in J. M. Brown (ed.), *Scottish Society in the Fifteenth Century* (London 1977), 209–40; and Bannerman's contributions to K. A. Steer and J. Bannerman, *Late Medieval Monumental Sculpture of the West Highlands* (Edinburgh 1977), esp. Appendix II, 'The Lordship of the Isles: Historical background'.

aim of this essay is to redress the balance and to place in perspective the careers of the four greatest MacDougall chiefs – Duncan, Ewen, Alexander and John – who followed each other in succession in the thirteenth and fourteenth centuries. The terminal date of 1316 has been set by the death in that year of John MacDougall of Argyll, known to generations of Scottish schoolboys as 'John of Lorn'.[3] Despite many more recent studies, the indispensable starting-point for any survey of the Lordship of Somerled and his immediate descendants remains Duncan and Brown's 'Argyll and the Isles in the Earlier Middle Ages', now over forty years old.[4]

'In 1100 the British Isles contained many and varied kings; by 1270 the rulers who had a colourable claim to royal rank had declined sharply in number, and the definition of what made a king had narrowed decisively.'[5] Robin Frame in his *Political Development of the British Isles 1100–1400* makes an eloquent and convincing plea for the study of British history in its widest sense, embracing the history of the British isles as a whole, including Ireland, as a counterpoint to the more traditional histories of England, Scotland, Ireland and Wales. As will be seen, the story of Somerled and his immediate successors is very much an exercise in British history – with an added Scandinavian dimension. It is also a story of kings. This essay follows Somerled and his descendants as far as 1266, the date of the Treaty of Perth, and the end of Norwegian sovereignty in the Isles. It considers the titles and styles which these rulers adopted, so far as is known, as also those of their relatives, the kings of Man and the northern

---

3 By way of Barbour, Blind Harry and Sir Walter Scott's *Tales of a Grandfather*.

4 A. A. M. Duncan and A. L. Brown, 'Argyll and the Isles in the earlier Middle Ages', *PSAS* xc (1956–7), 192–219. Other studies, in addition to those mentioned in note 2, include: B. Megaw, 'Norseman and native in the kingdom of the Isles', *Scottish Studies*, xx (1976), 1–44 (a revised version of this paper appears in P. Davey (ed.), *Man and Environment in the Isle of Man*, British Archaeological Reports (British ser.), liv (II), 265–314); G. W. S. Barrow, *Kingship and Unity: Scotland 1000–1306* (London 1981), esp. ch. 6, 'The winning of the West'; A. Grant, 'Scotland's "Celtic Fringe" in the later Middle Ages: the Macdonald Lords of the Isles and the kingdom of Scotland', in R. R. Davies (ed.), *The British Isles 1100–1500: Comparisons, Contrasts and Connections* (Edinburgh 1988), 118–41; E. J. Cowan, 'Norwegian sunset – Scottish dawn: Hakon IV and Alexander III', in N. H. Reid (ed.), *Scotland in the Reign of Alexander III, 1249–1286* (Edinburgh 1990), 53–73; and S. Duffy, 'The Bruce brothers in the Irish Sea world, 1306–29', in *Cambridge Medieval Celtic Studies*, xxi (1991), 55–87. C. M. Macdonald, *History of Argyll* (Glasgow 1950), remains an invaluable local history. R. A. McDonald, *The Kingdom of the Isles: Scotland's Western Seaboard c.1100–1330* (East Linton 1997), appeared while this essay was awaiting publication, as did several other specialist studies, and also A. A. M. Duncan's edition of *Barbour's Bruce* (Edinburgh 1997). Inevitably, there is a measure of overlap between this essay and McDonald's *Kingdom of the Isles* in particular, but it was thought worth while to proceed with publication.

5 R. Frame, *The Political Development of the British Isles 1100–1400* (Oxford 1990), 98.

Hebrides. Beyond 1266, it follows the careers of Alexander MacDougall of Argyll and his son John in particular. There are three genealogical tables.

* * *

Somerled (*Somairle*, Sorley) was killed at Renfrew in 1164 invading the kingdom of Scotland with an army drawn from Argyll, Kintyre, the Isles and Dublin. He is referred to by the *Melrose Chronicle* as 'regulus of Argyll' (*regulus eregeithel*), and later, after he had wrested control of Man and the Isles from his brother-in-law Godfrey (*Gofraid*), he is styled 'king of Innsegall and Kintyre'.[6] Whatever may be said about the genealogical origins of Somerled – and these appear to be as much Gaelic as Scandinavian[7] – the political origins of the kingdom of the Isles, so far as these can now be discerned, are comparable to the origins of various other polities which began to appear in Britain and Ireland around the same period as a consequence of Scandinavian invasion and settlement: in particular, the earldom of Orkney and the kingdoms of Dublin and Limerick.

There is a good case to be made for political continuity in the Isles from at least the late tenth century. Contemporary Welsh and Irish annals record the activities of Maccus and Godfrey (*Gofraid*), sons of Harald (*Aralt*) in the Hebrides and the Irish Sea province c.970–89, as do later Icelandic Sagas.[8] These were clearly powerful rulers, with large and well-organised naval resources at their disposal. They may have been related to the ruling *Uí hImhair* Scandinavian dynasty in Dublin.[9] Godfrey is described on his death in 989 as *rí Innsi Gall*, the first appearance on record of that title, the forerunner and equivalent of the later *rex* or *dominus insularum*.[10] Godfrey's son Ranald (*Ragnall*, Scand. *Rögnvaldr*) is given a similar title – *rí nan Innsi* (king of the islands) – in his obit in 1005.[11] We may compare these titles with the description of Godfrey's brother Maccus by Florence of Worcester and the *Melrose Chronicle* as *plurimarum insularum rex* on the occasion of King Edgar's famous sail on the Dee at Chester in 973, and perhaps even with that of Olaf (*Amlaíb*)

6 *Chron. Melrose*, 36; *Ann. Tigernach*.
7 W. D. H. Sellar, 'The origins and ancestry of Somerled', *SHR* xlv (1966), 124–42.
8 See, e.g.: *Ann. Ulster*; *Ann. Tigernach*; *Ann. Clonmacnoise*; *Ann. Four Masters*; *Chron. Melrose*; and *Florence of Worcester*; as in *ES* i, 478–94 and *SAEC*, 76. The forename 'Maccus' is sometimes equated with 'Magnus', but seems to lead an independent existence as a forename. It is unhappily rendered 'Mack' in *Anglo-Scottish Relations 1174–1328: Some Selected Documents*, ed. E. L. G. Stones (2nd edn, Oxford 1970), 199.
9 This is the usual suggestion, and seems not improbable. F. J. Byrne, however, suggests that they may have been sons of Harald Bluetooth, king of Denmark: T. W. Moody, F. X. Martin and F. J. Byrne (eds.), *A New History of Ireland*, vol. IX, (Oxford, 1984), 466.
10 *Ann. Ulster*, 989.
11 Ibid., 1005.

Cuarán, king of Dublin and York, in connection with the battle of Brunanburh in 937, as 'king of the Irish and of many islands'.[12] The Manx trace their present polity back to the time of these kings, for they celebrated 1000 years of their Tynwald in 1979. Although it has sometimes been suggested that the title of 'king' adopted by these and other Scandinavian rulers in the British Isles may have been taken in imitation of Irish practice,[13] it seems just as likely that it indicates a claim to descend from sacral royalty in Scandinavia. Certainly the later kings of Man and the Isles bore conspicuously royal Norwegian names, such as Olaf, Godfrey, Ranald and Harald.

Another Godfrey, son of Harald, is found in power in Man and the Isles, and also in Dublin, towards the end of the eleventh century. There can be no doubt as to the continuity of the kingdom of the Isles from his time. This is the celebrated Godfrey Crovan – the byname is Gaelic and probably means 'of the white hand' – well remembered in oral tradition and song.[14] The Manx even named the Milky Way after him: *raad mooar ree Gorry*.[15] His ancestry is not certain: it has been suggested that he may have been related to the earlier kings, Maccus and Godfrey, sons of Harald; but there is some evidence that he was a descendant of Olaf *Cuarán*, king of Dublin and York, and perhaps also of the Isles, in the mid-tenth century.[16] The Manx Chronicle relates that Godfrey had been with Harald Hardrada of Norway at Stamford Bridge in 1066, fighting Harold of England.[17] Godfrey died about 1095, in Islay, after ruling the kingdom of the Isles from the Butt of Lewis to the Calf of Man for over fifteen years.[18]

Godfrey's son Lagmann was displaced by Magnus Barefoot, king of Norway, who raided in the isles in person to establish Norwegian

---

12 *Chron. Melrose*, 15; for *Florence of Worcester*, see *SAEC*, 76, 69. Florence describes Olaf as 'king of the Irish and of many islands'.

13 Barrow, *Kingship and Unity*, 107–8; B. E. Crawford, *Scandinavian Scotland* (Leicester 1987), 192.

14 B. Ó Cuív, 'A poem in praise of Raghnall, King of Man', *Eigse*, viii (1957), 283–4, discusses the by-name Crovan, and also the by-names *Méarach* and *Méaránach* given Godfrey in Irish sources. See also: Megaw, 'Norseman and native', 16–18; and W. F. Skene, *Celtic Scotland* (2nd edn, Edinburgh, 1886–90), iii, 35–6 and Appendix II.

15 'The great track of King Orry': R. H. Kinvig, *The Isle of Man: A Social, Cultural and Political History* (3rd edn, Liverpool 1975), 61. It is at least possible that the 'King Orry' of Manx tradition is the earlier Godfrey, son of Harald.

16 G. Broderick, 'Irish and Welsh strands in the genealogy of Godred Crovan', *Journal of the Manx Museum*, viii (1980), 32–8. *Chron. Man* calls Godfrey's father 'Harald the Black of Ysland', which I take to be Iceland, rather than Isla, as is sometimes suggested: W. D. H. Sellar, 'The ancestry of the MacLeods revisited' *TGSI*, forthcoming. For the description of Olaf *Cuarán* as 'lord of many islands', see note 12 above.

17 *Chron. Man*, fo. 32v.

18 Ibid., fo. 33v. *Chron. Man* is, of course, not a contemporary witness. *Ann. Ulster* and other Irish annals give the date of Godfrey's death as 1095.

suzerainty. Duncan and Brown argue convincingly that the oft-mentioned treaty in which Scotland and Norway delimited their respective spheres of influence must have been entered into by Magnus and by Edgar, King of Scots, about 1098.[19] The Scottish mainland was recognised as part of the kingdom of Scots, but the islands to the west, with a few exceptions such as Luing and Lismore, were assigned to Norway.

After a period of confusion Godfrey Crovan's younger son Olaf succeeded to the Isles and ruled for almost forty years until his death at the hands of his nephews in 1153.[20] Around this time the bishopric of Sodor and Man was placed on a regular footing and a parochial system established. *Orkneyinga Saga* gives Olaf the Scandinavian byname of *Bitling* or *Kleining* – that is, 'the Small' or 'the little one'.[21] In later Scots Gaelic tradition he was remembered as 'the Red' (*Dearg*), in contrast to his grandson, Olaf 'the Black' (*Dubh*, Norse *Svarti*).[22] In his charters Olaf uses the style *rex insularum*, as does his son and successor Godfrey.[23] Table I (overleaf) sets out the relationships of the kings of Man and the Isles, descended from Godfrey Crovan and Olaf the Red, and notes the official style which they used.

Olaf's daughter Ragnhild, whose mother, it is argued below, was Ingibjorg of Orkney, married Somerled of Argyll.[24] As is well known, the Manx Chronicle, very much the in-house record of the kings who lived in Man, saw in this marriage the downfall of the kingdom of the Isles. Some disaffected island chiefs, unhappy with the rule of Ragnhild's brother Godfrey, approached Somerled, seeking to install Dugald (*Dubgall*), his son by Ragnhild, as king. In January 1156 Somerled defeated Godfrey at sea, forcing him to cede half his kingdom. Two years later he defeated Godfrey again, expelling him from the Isles altogether. Deprived of his kingdom, Godfrey sought help from his brother kings at the courts of

19 Duncan and Brown, 'Argyll and the Isles', 192–3. See also R. Power, 'Magnus Barelegs' expedition to the West', *SHR* lxv (1986), 107–32.
20 *Chron. Man.*, fo. 36. The history of Man and the Isles at the beginning of the 12th century is confused. I have taken the view that Olaf succeeded Domnall son of Tadg O'Brien, who took the kingship of Innse Gall by force in 1111, according to the *Annals of Inisfallen*, ed. C. O'Conor (Rerum Hibernicarum Scriptores, ii, pt 2, Buckingham 1825), and who was killed in 1115.
21 *Orkneyinga Saga*, ch. 104. These by-names have been translated in a remarkable variety of ways, including 'Morsel', 'Buttered-Bread', and 'Tit-Bit'. If they refer to Olaf's stature, they are as likely to indicate great height as stunted growth, given the Scandinavian propensity for irony.
22 For a discussion of these by-names or epithets, see Megaw, 'Norseman and native', 16–18; also Duffy, 'Bruce brothers', 62 and n.18.
23 The styles used by these kings of Man and the Isles can most readily be studied in *Monumenta de Insula Manniae*, ed. J. R. Oliver (Manx Soc., 1860–2), vol. II.
24 The modern Gaelic form of Ragnhild's name is *Raonaid*, still a popular name in the Hebrides. It is usually rendered in English as 'Rachael'.

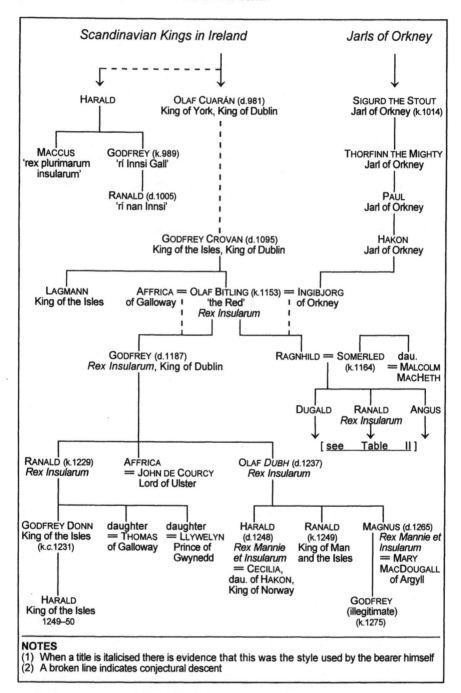

NOTES
(1) When a title is italicised there is evidence that this was the style used by the bearer himself
(2) A broken line indicates conjectural descent

Table I. The Scandinavian Connection: Kings of Man and the Isles

Scotland, England and Norway, but did not return until after Somerled's death, and then to a divided kingdom.[25]

The division of the kingdom lasted just over one hundred years, Godfrey's line ruling not only in the Isle of Man, but also in Skye and Lewis; and Somerled's line ruling in Islay and Mull, presumably also in Coll and Tiree, and perhaps in the Uists and Barra.[26] The Manx dynasty continued until the death of Magnus, son of Olaf, in 1265 (see Table I). Godfrey's sons, Ranald and Olaf, continued to use *rex insularum* as their official style; in the next generation, Olaf's sons, Harald and Magnus, preferred *rex mannie et insularum*.[27] The greatest of these kings appears to have been Ranald (*Ragnall*) (killed 1229), son of Godfrey. He is celebrated in a Gaelic praise-poem of forty-nine stanzas composed in elaborate *dan direach* metre.[28] This is one of the earliest examples of this type of metre, and a strong pointer, therefore, as Megaw has pointed out, towards a bi-lingual court around the king of Man.[29] Ranald's varied career is comparatively well recorded, and fully illustrates the theme of British history. He held his kingdom of Man and the Isles, at one time or another, of the king of Norway, of the king of England, and of the Pope. He assisted John de Courcy, who later became his brother-in-law, in his conquest of Ulster. He married one daughter to Llywelyn, Prince of Gwynedd, and another to Thomas, bastard son of Alan, Lord of Galloway.[30] He is usually identified with the Ranald *rex insularum* who assisted William, King of Scots, in subduing Harald, son of Madad, the troublesome jarl of Orkney, but it is argued below that there has been confusion here with his more obscure (at least so far as the record is concerned) cousin, Ranald, son of Somerled, who also styled himself *rex insularum*.[31]

*   *   *

Table II sets out the relationships of the descendants of Somerled who ruled in the Isles, and also the styles which they used, so far as is known. The fortunes of this branch of the house of the Isles in the forty years or so following Somerled's death are barely recorded. Somerled had at least

25 See Duncan and Brown, 'Argyll and the Isles', 197.

26 There is no direct evidence for the Uists and Barra. However, it seems a reasonable inference to place Somerled's MacRuairi descendants there before 1266 (cf. below, pages 203, 206), and to deduce, therefore, that these islands fell to Somerled's share. This is the inference made by Megaw, 'Norseman and Native', 2.

27 The English chancery used the style *rex mannie et insularum* early in the 13th century, seemingly in advance of the Manx kings themselves.

28 See Ó Cuív, 'Poem in praise of Raghnall, King of Man'.

29 Megaw, 'Norseman and native', 18.

30 For Ranald's career see, e.g., A. W. Moore, *History of the Isle of Man* (London 1900; repr. 1977).

31 For this argument, see below, pages 196–8.

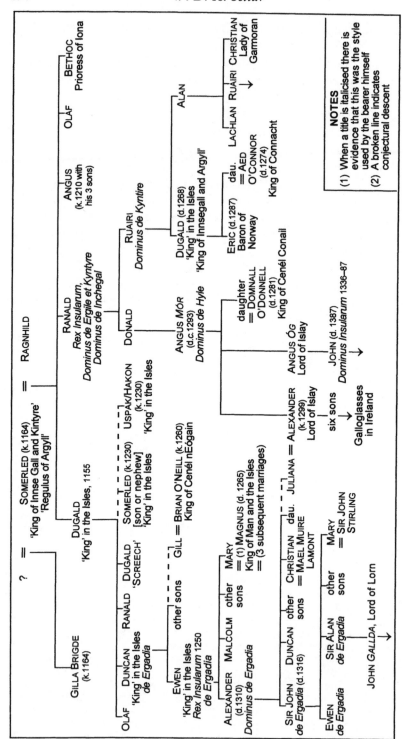

Table II. MacDougalls, MacDonalds and MacRuaris

three sons by Ragnhild – Dugald, Ranald and Angus – and probably a fourth, Olaf, as well as a son, Gilla Brigde, by a former marriage.[32] Although there is no direct evidence, a division of Somerled's territory between these sons seems likely – the obvious parallel being the Orkney earldom, rather than Gaelic or feudal society – but it is not possible to reconstruct the details.[33] There may, in any case, have been more than one partition. Of Angus nothing is known, save that he fought and defeated his brother Ranald in 1192, and was killed along with his three sons in 1210.[34] His line died out. There is only one further mention of Dugald, the eponymous ancestor of the MacDougalls, after his first appearance in the 1150s: his name appears, along with that of his sons, Olaf, Duncan and Ranald, in the *Liber Vitae* of Durham Cathedral in 1175. As has been suggested, the entry is likely to be connected with the fealty sworn by the Scots magnates to Henry II in that year.[35]

Dugald's brother Ranald is now chiefly remembered as the father of Donald (*Domnall*) and Ruairi (*Ruaidrí*), both of whom gave their name to powerful kindreds, and as the link, therefore, between the MacDonalds and Somerled. In his own time, however, although surviving sources are tantalisingly brief, Ranald would seem to have been of considerable account. In a charter to Saddell Abbey he styles himself *rex insularum, dominus de Ergile et Kyntyre*, suggesting that he claimed lordship over all the territories of Somerled.[36] Elsewhere in a charter to Paisley, in which he mentions also his wife 'Fonia' (for *Findguala?*), he styles himself *dominus de Inchegal*.[37] His rule was still remembered in the sixteenth century, when Dean Munro wrote in his *Description of the Western Isles* of 'the Laws made by Renald McSomharkle callit in his time King of the

---

32 Gilla Brigde fell with his father in 1164. 'Gellicolan', i.e. Gilla Caluim, who appears as a son in *Chron. Fordun* and some later sources, is probably a mistake for Gilla Brigde. *Chron Man* (fo. 35v) is the sole authority for the existence of Olaf.

33 Duncan and Brown, 'Argyll and the Isles', 198; Barrow, *Kingship and Unity*, 109. The later division of the Manx part of the kingdom between Ranald and Olaf, sons of Godfrey, is another parallel. The feudal distinction between succession to lands inherited and lands acquired is an unlikely explanation in this context.

34 *Chron. Man* (fos. 40v, 41r) is the only source for these events. The ascription by later historians to Angus, son of Somerled, of a son James whose daughter and heiress married the Alexander the Steward (e.g. *Scots Peerage*, v, 31) is now recognised as erroneous.

35 Duncan and Brown, 'Argyll and the Isles', 197–8; G. W. S. Barrow, *The Anglo-Norman Era in Scottish History* (Oxford 1980), 159.

36 *RMS* ii, no. 3170.

37 *Paisley Reg.*, 125. *Pace* Duncan and Brown, 'Argyll and the Isles', 198, I would not read any necessary significance into the apparent change in style from *rex* to *dominus*. The style *dominus de Inchegal* is, of course, effectively the same as *dominus insularum*, adopted in 1336 by John MacDonald of Islay.

Occident Iles'.[38] The *Book of Clanranald*, admittedly a late and sometimes garbled source, describes Ranald as 'the most distinguished of the Gall or Gaedhil for prosperity, sway of generosity, and feats of arms', and credits him with the foundation of three religious houses.[39] This last, at least, is accurate enough for, as noted below, Ranald was a notable benefactor of the Church. The date of Ranald's death is unknown. The *Book of Clanranald*, as published, gives 1207. Even if this reading is accurate – and there seems to be room for doubt – it cannot be accepted without independent corroboration. Duncan and Brown suggest that Ranald may have been killed in the conflict in 1192 with his brother Angus, but this is purely speculative, and seems unlikely in view of the fact that Ranald's son Donald appears to have issued a charter to Paisley at the same time as his father.[40] MacEwen's suggested date of *c*.1227 seems too late.[41]

Although most historians have taken the view that it was Ranald, son of Godfrey, king of the Isles and Man, who assisted William I in his campaign against Harald son of Madad, Jarl of Orkney, there are solid grounds for believing that it was rather Ranald, son of Somerled, who helped William, and who was, therefore, in the words of *Orkneyinga Saga*, 'the greatest warrior then in the western lands'. Certainly there is a conflict in the sources. Both *Orkneyinga Saga* and Roger of Howden's *Chronica* record the campaign and note that Ranald, King of the Isles, was granted Caithness in return. The saga identifies Ranald as the son of Godfrey; but Howden as the son of Somerled. The relevant passages read as follows:

> William, King of the Scots, heard that Earl Harald [the younger] had been killed, and also that Earl Harald, Maddad's son, had subdued the whole of Caithness, without asking his leave. He became enraged at this and sent men to the Sudreyar to Rognvald, Gudrod's son [Ranald son of Godfrey] the King of the Sudreyar. Gudrod's mother was Ingibjorg, daughter of Earl Hakon, Paul's son. King Rognvald was the greatest warrior then in the western lands. Three winters he had been out in

---

38 *Monro's Western Isles of Scotland and Genealogies of the Clans*, ed. R. W. Munro (Edinburgh 1961), 57.

39 *The Book of Clanranald*, in *Reliquiae Celticae*, ii, 138–309, at 157.

40 See below, page 200.

41 Duncan and Brown, 'Argyll and the Isles', 198 n.5. The dates given in the *Book of Clanranald* are not reliable. A. B. MacEwen, 'The death of Reginald, son of Somerled', *West Highland Notes and Queries*, 2nd ser., vi (Sep. 1990), 3–7, argues that the sign which follows '1200' in *Book of Clanranald* is an ampersand rather than the figure seven, and that the date indicated is, therefore, some indeterminate number of years after 1200, rather than 1200 (or 1207) specifically. I am most grateful to Professor William Gillies, who is preparing an edition of the *Book of Clanranald*, for telling me that he believes that this is, indeed, a possible reading of the text, but that an argument could also be put forward for 1201 as the year intended.

war-ships without coming under a sooty rafter. When this message came to Rognvald, he collected an army from all the kingdom of the Sudreyar and from Satiri (Kintyre). He also had a large army from Ireland. Then he went north to Caithness, took possession of the whole of the territory, and remained there for some time. Earl Harald kept in the Orkneys, and took no heed of the King's movements. Towards winter King Rognvald prepared to go home to his dominions in the Sudreyar. He left three stewards (*sýslumenn*) over Caithness ...
[*Orkneyinga Saga*][42]

Thus when Harold the younger was slain, Harold the elder came to the king of Scots ... and offered the king plenty of gold and silver to have again Caithness. And the king replied to him that he would give him that land if he dismissed his wife [and gave hostages]. But this Harold refused to do. Therefore Ronald son of Somerled and king of Man, came to William king of Scots and bought Caithness from him, saving the king's yearly revenue. [*Howden*][43]

Howden, it will be noted, although calling Ranald the son of Somerled, also describes him as king of Man, and it may be this that has persuaded historians that the Ranald in question was, in fact, the son of Godfrey, together with the existence of the fine praise-poem in praise of Ranald of Man, already mentioned, which emphasises his role as a sea-king. *Orkney-inga Saga's* statement that the mother of Godfrey was Ingibjorg, daughter of Jarl Hakon, appears to clinch the argument by giving Ranald, son of Godfrey, a colourable claim to Caithness.

However, *Orkneyinga Saga* to the contrary, it appears Ingibjorg was not the mother of Godfrey of Man. The *Chronicle of Man* names Godfrey's mother as Affrica, daughter of Fergus, Lord of Galloway.[44] Its evidence, as the semi-official account of the Manx dynasty, is clearly to be preferred on this. The appearance of the name Affrica later in the Manx dynasty tends to confirm the Chronicle's account. A further pointer is the appellation *a hi Fhergais* (descendant of Fergus) accorded Ranald of Man in the praise-poem in his honour: as the editor, Brian Ó Cuív, comments, this is likely to refer to Fergus of Galloway rather than to a remote ninth-century ancestor of Somerled of the same name.[45] The Manx Chronicle, in fact,

---

42   This memorable and oft-quoted translation is by J. A. Hjaltilin and G. Goudie, in Joseph Anderson's edition of *Orkneyinga Saga* (Edinburgh 1873), ch. 114.
43   Roger of Howden, in *SAEC*, 317.
44   *Cron. Man.*, fo. 35v.
45   Ó Cuív, 'Poem in praise of Raghnall, King of Man', 301. For Somerled's alleged 9th-century ancestor, Godfrey son of Fergus, see Sellar, 'Origins and ancestry of Somerled', 124–42.

devotes some attention to the marital status of Godfrey's father Olaf. It mentions Olaf's marriage to Affrica, and then continues: *habuit & concubinas plures de quibus filios tres ... et filias multas generavit. Quarum una nupsit Sumerledo regulo herergaidel* (he also had many concubines by whom he had three sons ... and many daughters, one of whom married Somerled of Argyll).[46] The Chronicle therefore insists that Ragnhild, the wife of Somerled and mother of his son Ranald, was only a half-sister of King Godfrey, and the daughter of a concubine. Marriage customs in contemporary Gaelic and Scandinavian society were lax by canonical standards, and the Chronicle may have fastened on a technicality in its desire to discredit the rival dynasty. However that may be, it is likely that the mother of Ragnhild, through whom Somerled's descendants acquired their claim to the Isles, was a woman of high status.

Orkneyinga Saga, then, is mistaken in making Ingibjorg of Orkney the mother of King Godfrey and grandmother, therefore, of Ranald of Man. This leaves Ranald of Man with no known hereditary claim to Orkney or Caithness. *Orkneyinga Saga*, however, may be correct in noting a marriage between Ingibjorg and Olaf of Man. Suppose Ingibjorg to have been the mother not of Godfrey but of his sister Ragnhild, all falls into place: Ranald, son of Somerled, as the grandson of Ingibjorg of Orkney, would inherit a claim to the Orkney earldom. This would square with Howden's statement that it was Ranald, son of Somerled, who assisted William. On balance this seems to be the solution that best fits the known facts. If the matter seems confusing to us, it can hardly have appeared less so to contemporaries.

Ranald, son of Somerled, is the only descendant of Somerled known to have used the style *rex insularum*, although Ewen of Argyll is said to have adopted the same style in Man in 1250 – much to the irritation of the Manx![47] This charter style and, it would seem, Ranald's seal, derives from the Manx kings who used it (or the later *rex mannie et insularum*) regularly from at least the first half of the twelfth century, as already noted.[48] The title is the equivalent of the Gaelic *rí Innse Gall*, first recorded of Godfrey, son of Harald in 989, and the precursor of the later *dominus insularum*. Given this tenth-century origin, it seems likely that the title was first adopted in a Scandinavian context, although Gaelic parallels are, of course, not difficult to find. By the twelfth century the use of the title would seem to indicate the conferring, or at least the approval, of 'kingship' by the king of Norway. Had a charter of Somerled survived, granted after 1156, it is reasonable to assume that he would have used the style *rex insularum*.

[46] *Cron. Man.*, fo. 35v.
[47] See below, page 205.
[48] See R. A. McDonald, 'Images of Hebridean lordship in the late twelfth and early thirteenth centuries: the seal of Raonall MacSorley', *SHR* lxxiv (1995), 129–43.

How far, or at what point in time, succession to the kingship was influenced by tanistry in the Gaelic manner is not easy to determine. Nor is it easy to know exactly how the titles *rí Innse Gall* and *rí Airir Goídel* (king of Argyll) related to each other. There is some evidence that Irish annalists used these styles rather loosely, making it difficult to know what weight to put upon the evidence.[49] As regards the latter title, all the record evidence suggests, as will be seen, that the MacDougall descendants of Somerled were located in Argyll proper from *c.*1225 onwards and consistently used *de Ergadia* as their style.

Which of these two sons of Somerled who founded lasting kindreds, Dugald or Ranald, was the elder? The question has been debated vigorously over the centuries. MacDonald apologists have been prominent among those who have argued for Ranald's seniority. Some have even suggested that the later MacDougalls descend not from Dugald son of Somerled at all, but from another Dugald, a son, rather than a brother, of Ranald.[50] Such evidence as there is, however, all points towards Dugald being the elder brother; while the case for the descent of the later MacDougalls from Dugald son of Somerled is, in my view, incontrovertible.[51] Briefly, the early sources which mention both brothers place Dugald before Ranald.[52] Second, as already noted, Dugald appears on record earlier than Ranald. Third, it was Dugald rather than Ranald who was offered the kingdom of the Isles in the place of Godfrey, King of Man and the Isles. Fourth, and most significantly, although there is some evidence that the appellation *MacSomairle* (son of Somerled) was applied at first to all male line descendants of Somerled, it is the MacDougalls, rather than their cousins the MacDonalds and the MacRuairis, who are styled *Clann Somairle* in later medieval Gaelic pedigrees.[53] This suggests that it was the MacDougalls who were thought of as representing in some sense the main stem of Somerled's descendants. To lay much store by primogeniture at this period is, however, anachronistic.

*   *   *

49 I am not wholly convinced by Bannerman's argument ('Lordship of the Isles', 202) that *rí Airir Goídel* was a title subsidiary to *rí Innse Gall* and normally held with it. For the title *rí Airir Goídel*, see below, pages 201, 207, and 217 note 155.

50 E.g., A. and A. MacDonald, *The Clan Donald* (Inverness 1896–1904), i, 64–7; *Scots Peerage*, v, 32. Macdonald, *Argyll*, 89–90, argues that Dugald was the elder brother.

51 Duncan and Brown regard the argument that Dugald was a younger son, or that the later MacDougalls did not descend from him as being 'contrary to all the evidence' ('Argyll and the Isles', 197 n.8), a judgement with which I heartily concur.

52 *Chron. Man.*, fo. 35v; *Orkneyinga Saga*, ch. 104.

53 E.g., 'MS 1467' gives the main MacDougall line under *Clann Somhairle*, as does the *Book of Lecan*. For a discussion of these and other early MacDougall pedigrees, see W. D. H. Sellar, 'MacDougall pedigrees in MS 1467', *Notes and Queries of the Society of West Highland and Island Historical Research*, 1st ser., xxix (Aug. 1986), 3–16.

In the generation of Somerled's grandchildren, little is known of the sons of Ranald. The *Annals of Ulster* record the defeat of unnamed sons of Ranald in 1209 at the hands of the men of Skye.[54] The same annals note a great naval assault on Derry and Inishowen in 1212, launched by Thomas of Galloway, earl of Atholl, and sons of Ranald, again unnamed, in alliance with the Cenél Conaill.[55] Over seventy galleys are said to have been involved. Thomas of Galloway repeated the operation in 1214 with Ruairi son of Ranald, and plundered the treasures of Derry.[56] Donald son of Ranald may have participated in the events of 1209 and 1212, but he appears on record by name once only, granting land to Paisley Abbey.[57] As Duncan and Brown observe, similarities between Donald's charter to Paisley and that of his father Ranald strongly suggest that the two grants must have been made at or about the same time.[58] A daughter of Donald would appear to have married Domnall Óg O'Donnell, king of Cenél Conaill (1258–81), for the Ulster Annals record the deposition in 1290 of Aed O'Donnell, king of Cenél Conaill, by his half-brother Toirrdelbach (killed 1303), acting with his mother's kin, the Clan Donald, and many other galloglasses.[59]

Donald (*Domnall*), son of Ranald, is, of course, the eponym and ancestor of the MacDonalds; and the 1290 annal marks the first appearance on record of the Clan Donald by name. This is the first time the name 'Donald' occurs among the descendants of Somerled. Hugh Macdonald's late and garbled 'History of the MacDonalds' claims that 'Reginald [Ranald] was married to MacRandel's daughter, or, as some say, to a sister of Thomas Randel, Earl of Murray ...' This is, of course, impossible, as the Randolphs did not become earls of Moray until later; but might not the tradition refer to an earlier earl of Moray, William son of Duncan II and father of the claimant Donald mac William (killed 1187)?[60] If so, could the MacDonald eponym have been named after Donald mac William? A slender argument, but worth airing. Ruairi (*Ruaidri*), son of Ranald, styles

54 *Ann. Ulster*, 1209.
55 *ES* ii, 393.
56 Ibid., 395. Thomas of Galloway had a speculative grant of some Cenél nEógain lands in Ulster from King John, and built the castle of Coleraine about 1213. For Thomas of Galloway, see, e.g., K. J. Stringer, 'Periphery and core in thirteenth-century Scotland: Alan son of Roland, Lord of Galloway and Constable of Scotland', in A. Grant and K. J. Stringer (eds.), *Medieval Scotland: Crown, Lordship and Community* (Edinburgh 1993), 82–113.
57 *Paisley Reg.*, 126. Despite what is stated in MacDonald and MacDonald, *Clan Donald*, i, 486 (repeated in *Scots Peerage*, v, 33, and *ALI*, 280), Donald is not styled *dominus de Inchegal* in this charter, but merely *Douenaldus filius Reginaldi filii Sumerledi*. I am grateful to Professor Barrow for alerting me to this discrepancy.
58 Duncan and Brown, 'Argyll and the Isles', 198 n.8.
59 *Ann. Ulster*, 1290. This is one of the earliest mentions of galloglasses by name.
60 *Highland Papers*, i, 13; for the MacWilliams and Moray, see *RRS* ii, 12–13.

himself *dominus de Kyntire* in a charter of lands in Kintyre.[61] He is, I would suggest, the descendant of Somerled, styled simply *Mac Somurli*, who met his death at the battle of Ballyshannon in the west of Ireland in 1247, assisting Mael Sechlainn O'Donnell, king of Cenél Conaill, who was also killed, against a strong Anglo-Irish force.[62] The *Annals of Connacht* style this *MacSomairle* 'king of Argyll' (*rí Airir Gaídil*). However, later entries in the same annals suggest that this may be rather a loose description: thus they style Dugald, son of Ruairi, 'king of Argyll' in his obit in 1268.[63] Some have suggested that the *MacSomairle* killed at Ballyshannon may have been Ruairi's cousin Duncan of Argyll, son of Dugald. The arguments in favour of Ruairi seem stronger. The death of *MacSomairle* in 1247 is likely to be connected with the appearance in Bergen the following year of Ewen, son of Duncan, and Dugald, son of Ruairi, each seeking kingship in the Isles (see below). However, as Duncan of Argyll is already on record in 1175, the probability must be against his playing an active overseas role in 1247.[64]

As noted, three sons of Dugald son of Somerled – Olaf, Duncan and Ranald – are entered with their father in the *Liber Vitae* of Durham Cathedral in 1175. Nothing further is known of Olaf or Ranald. Indeed, Dugald's family disappears from the record for fifty years. Duncan (*Donnchad*) is found again in 1225 or thereabouts, witnessing a charter of Maoldomnaich, Earl of Lennox, as Duncan *de Ergadia*.[65] This seems to be the first appearance of the familiar style *de Ergadia* (of Argyll). We can only speculate as to what happened in the intervening years. Alexander II is known to have mounted an expedition against Argyll in 1221 or 1222, or both, resulting in some reallocation of territory. Duncan and Brown suggest that land in Kintyre may have changed hands, as does Cowan, who conjectures that Donald son of Ranald may have replaced his brother Ruairi there; but the focus must surely have been on Argyll proper, at that time distinct from Kintyre.[66] Whoever was displaced from Argyll in 1222, it does not appear to have been Duncan. Perhaps Dugald's family were beneficiaries of the royal expedition, and Donald and Ruairi, sons of Ranald who had styled himself *dominus de Ergile*, the losers.

61 *RMS* ii, no. 3136.

62 *Ann. Ulster, Ann. Connacht*, and others, for 1247.

63 See below, page 207.

64 Duffy, 'Bruce brothers', 68, suggests that it was Donald son of Ranald who was killed in 1247, but this is quite speculative. There are no grounds, incidentally, for holding that Ruairi son of Ranald is the same as the Ruairi of the 1263 campaign who was granted Bute by King Hakon, as was once supposed.

65 *Paisley Reg.*, 216–17.

66 See Duncan and Brown, 'Argyll and the Isles', 199–200; Cowan, 'Hakon IV and Alexander III', 114; J. G. Dunbar and A. A. M. Duncan, 'Tarbert Castle', *SHR* l (1971), 2; and Macdonald, *Argyll*, 100–2.

A few years later, in 1228, Norwegian sources record a punitive expedition launched against kings of Somerled's race, who are said to have been unfaithful to King Hakon. Duncan is specifically mentioned, and described as 'king' in the Sudreys, as is his brother Dugald 'Screech'. A second Somerled is also mentioned, either a brother or cousin of Duncan. The Scandinavian byname 'screech', like the Gaelic bynames of the thirteenth-century Manx kings, is a further reminder of the hybrid nature of Hebridean society at this time. The leader of the Norwegian expedition, whom King Hakon intended to set up as 'king' in the Isles, was Uspak, named as 'son of Ogmund', but said to have been a brother of Duncan and Dugald. Perhaps Ogmund was his foster father. The attempt ended with the death of Uspak in 1230.[67] It has sometimes been conjectured that the Scandinavian name 'Uspak' may stand here for Gaelic *Gillespic*; although clearly not impossible, such an equivalence of names would be unique, and there is no supporting evidence.[68] Duncan last appears on record in 1244 – assuming that he was not the *MacSomairle* slain at Ballyshannon – by then an old man, as one of the magnates of Scotland who wrote with Alexander II to the Pope.[69] Again he is designed 'of Argyll'. According to Sir Iain Moncreiffe, Duncan had a daughter Gill (*Egidia*) who married Brian O'Neill (killed 1260), king of Cenél nEógain.[70]

One has the impression, admittedly on slender evidence, that Duncan was more involved in the affairs of the Scottish kingdom than his cousins, tempering somewhat his career as Hebridean sea-king. He is the founder of the Valliscaulian priory of Ardchattan on Loch Etive, and probably also the builder of the great castle of Dunstaffnage, part of the thirteenth-century walls of which still stand.[71] Both Barrow and Cowan draw attention to the castle-building activities of the descendants of Somerled, Barrow describing their castles as 'indisputably the most remarkable collection of thirteenth-century lords' strongholds to be found in any single region of Britain'.[72] Duncan of Argyll, or if not he then his son

---

67 The story of this expedition is well covered by Duncan and Brown, 'Argyll and the Isles', 200–1.

68 Thus Barrow, *Kingship and Unity*, 110, and A. A. M. Duncan, *Scotland: The Making of the Kingdom* (Edinburgh 1975), 547. The forename Uspak (or Ospak) gives the surname MacCuspic.

69 *SAEC*, 356; Duncan and Brown, 'Argyll and the Isles', 202.

70 I. Moncreiffe, *The Highland Clans* (2nd edn, London 1982), 133. I have not found Sir Iain's authority for this statement.

71 For these see RCAHMS, *Inventory of the Ancient Monuments of Argyll*, vol. II: *Lorn* (Edinburgh 1975).

72 Barrow, *Kingship and Unity*, 112–13; compare Cowan, 'Hakon IV and Alexander III', 125.

Ewen, was also responsible for building the castle of Aros in Mull, one of the largest hallhouses in Scotland.[73]

Duncan's foundation of Ardchattan can be seen as part of a tradition of religious patronage in his family. Either Somerled himself, or more probably his son Ranald, founded the Cistercian abbey of Saddell.[74] Either Dugald, son of Somerled, already noted as appearing in Durham's *Liber Vitae*, or perhaps Ranald, is likely to have been instrumental in the foundation of the see of Argyll in the 1180s.[75] Later it seems to have operated to an extent as a MacDougall family see.[76] Ranald appears to have founded both the Benedictine monastery and the Augustinian nunnery on Iona, his sister Bethoc being the first prioress.[77] Bethoc was also credited by later generations with the foundation of *Teampull na Trionaid* (the Church of the Trinity) in North Uist.[78] Ranald and his son Donald both made grants to Paisley Abbey.[79] Ranald and his son Ruairi both made grants to Saddell Abbey in Kintyre.[80] As in the case of the castles, this adds up to an impressive tally by any contemporary standards.

The career of Duncan's son Ewen (*Eogan*) is well known. Of all the island rulers he was the most affected by the competing expansionist ambitions of Scotland and Norway. Although his name appears in the sources in a bewildering number of guises, there can be no doubt that he bore the Gaelic forename *Eogan*. Some of the confusion is due to the similarity in sound between *Eogan* (Ewen) and *Eoin* (John; later *Iain*) in Gaelic. In Norwegian sources he is *Jon Duncansson*, in Matthew Paris's Chronicle *Oenus de Ergadia*, in the Manx Chronicle *Johannes Dugaldi*, and in charter Latin *Eugenius de Argadia*.[81] Among his own people, however, he was probably *Eogan MacSomairle* or even *Eogan MacDubgaill*.

During his father's lifetime – in 1240, as Duncan and Brown have demonstrated – Ewen granted lands in Lismore to the see of Argyll.[82] In

---

73 For Aros, see RCAHMS, *Argyll Inventory*, vol. III: *Mull, Tiree, Coll and Northern Argyll* (Edinburgh 1980).
74 For Saddell Abbey, see RCAHMS, *Argyll Inventory*, vol. I: *Kintyre*.
75 Duncan and Brown, 'Argyll and the Isles', 209; D. E. R. Watt, *Fasti Ecclesiae Scoticanae medii aevi ad annum 1638* (2nd edn, Scottish Record Soc., 1969), 26.
76 Sellar, 'MacDougall pedigrees', 13.
77 RCAHMS, *Argyll Inventory*, vol. IV: *Iona*.
78 *Book of Clanranald*, 156–7.
79 See above, pages 195–6, 200.
80 *RMS* ii, no. 3170 (and see above, pages 195, 203).
81 The sources for Ewen's career are well covered in Duncan and Brown, 'Argyll and the Isles', 207–16. *Pace* Kenneth Jackson ('Argyll and the Isles', 209 n.2), 'Oenus' in Matthew Paris's account stands for 'Ewen' and not 'Angus'; cf. 'Audoenus' for Ewen's grandson and namesake (see below, page 213). *APS* i, 115 gives *Eugenius de Argadia*.
82 Duncan and Brown, 'Argyll and the Isles', 211 and Appendix IV.

1248 he sailed to Bergen, as did his second cousin Dugald son of Ruairi (*Duggal Rudrisson*), both seeking the title of 'king' in the Hebrides from Hakon of Norway. Ewen was recognised as king in 1248, while Dugald 'took kingship' in 1249.[83] Late in 1248 Harald son of Olaf of the Manx dynasty, who had also been recognised as 'king' by Hakon, was drowned in Sumburgh Roost off Shetland. Ewen was sent by Hakon to take control of Man and the Isles for the time being. Alexander II moved swiftly against him. The story of this expedition and of Alexander's subsequent death on the island of Kerrera, so vividly told by Matthew Paris and *Hakons Saga*, has often been recounted. Alexander demanded that Ewen give up his allegiance to Hakon and surrender the castle of Cairn na burgh, that remarkable fortress in the Treshnish Isles, together with three further unnamed castles. Ewen refused. There has been much speculation as to the identity of the unnamed castles. One must surely have been Dun Chonnuill, the equally remarkable fortress in the Garvellachs. Another, I would suggest, must have been Aros in Mull. The fourth may have been Ewen's mainland stronghold of Dunstaffnage, or alternatively another island castle, such as Duart or the elusive 'Iselborg'.[84] Undeterred by dreams in which the saints of Scotland and of Norway alike sought to restrain him, Alexander pressed on, but caught fever and died: 'while wishing to disinherit an innocent man he unexpectedly breathed out with that ambition the breath of life'.[85] Later island tradition claimed that Alexander died on the farm of Ardchork in Kerrera where he had been brought ashore to a holy well.[86]

Duncan and Brown suggest that King Alexander's expedition may have been intended 'not only to attack the lordship of Ewen ... but to restore the see of Argyll', which had lain vacant for most of the preceding twenty years.[87] However, it is difficult to see how moving the see from Lismore to Kilbride, only five miles from Dunstaffnage, which they suggest may have been in prospect, would have resulted in the bishopric being any less under the control of the lords of Argyll. Judging from the names of later

---

83 *ES* ii, 548ff., following the *Icelandic Annals* and *Hakon's Saga*.
84 Duncan and Brown, 'Argyll and the Isles', 208, suggest Dunconnel, Iselborg and Dunstaffnage. For these castles generally, see the RCAHMS *Argyll Inventory*. Both Aros and Duart are dated by the Commission to the 13th century. If they were already in existence or under construction in 1249, it seems very likely that one or both would have been among the three further castles which Ewen was to surrender.
85 Duncan and Brown, 'Argyll and the Isles', 208–9; Cowan, 'Hakon IV and Alexander III', 115–17.
86 The well is said to have been at 'Dalrigh' on Ardchork farm (information from the late Mrs Catherine Pape who was brought up on Ardchork in the early years of this century).
87 Duncan and Brown, 'Argyll and the Isles', 209–10.

bishops the MacDougalls kept a firm grip on the see well into the fourteenth century.[88]

After 1249 Ewen, deprived for a time of his mainland territory of Argyll, continued his career as Hebridean sea-king. He appears in the Isle of Man in 1250 together with Magnus son of Olaf, later to be king. According to the Manx Chronicle, Ewen gave offence by issuing commands and adopting the style *rex insularum*. As a result, he and his men were forcibly expelled from Man.[89] In 1253 he and Dugald son of Ruairi are found once again in Bergen with King Hakon whence all three sailed in an expedition against Denmark.[90] In 1255, however, through the intercession of yet another king, Henry III of England, Ewen was restored to his lands in Argyll.[91]

Eight years later King Hakon arrived in person in the Isles to confront the Scots – the first Norwegian king to do so since Magnus Barefoot. There is little need to elaborate here on the 1263 campaign, as it has been well covered in recent accounts.[92] The distinguished company on Hakon's own ship included Eric, son of Dugald son of Ruairi (*Eirik Duggalsson* son of *Duggal Rudrisson*).[93] Again Ewen was put to the test: which king would he serve – Alexander or Hakon? This time Ewen opted for Scotland and surrendered his person and his island possessions to King Hakon who treated him honourably. Later in 1263, defeated by the Scots at Largs and battered by the weather, Hakon made his way as far back as Orkney, where he died. Three years later sovereignty over the Isles was ceded by Norway to Scotland by the Treaty of Perth.[94] By the terms of the treaty Ewen was restored to his island possessions. His title 'king' does not recur, however, in any surviving source. Nevertheless, Ewen's career must be accounted a success: twice within twenty years he had been confronted by two powerful kings, to both of whom he owed allegiance, his lands being central to the conflict between them, yet he managed to retain both his honour and his possessions. He last appears in 1268 as witness to a charter of Malise, Earl of Strathearn.[95] The occasion may have been the marriage of his daughter Mary, widow of King Magnus of Man, to Malise.[96]

88 Sellar, 'MacDougall pedigrees', 13.
89 *Chron. Man* is our only source for this episode (fos. 48–9).
90 *ES* ii, 577.
91 Duncan and Brown, 'Argyll and the Isles', 211–12.
92 E.g., Barrow, *Kingship and Unity*, ch. 6; Cowan, 'Hakon IV and Alexander III'.
93 *Hakon's Saga*: see *ES* ii, 213.
94 For a discussion of the Treaty of Perth, see R. I. Lustig, 'The Treaty of Perth: a re-examination', *SHR* lviii (1979), 35–57.
95 *Inchaffray Charters* (SHS, 1908), 87 (*domino Ewgenio de argadia*).
96 For Mary of Argyll's successive marriages to Magnus, king of Man (d.1265), Malise, Earl of Strathearn (d.1271), Sir Hugh Abernethy (d.1291 × 2) and Warin FitzWarin (d.1299), see *Inchaffray Charters*, p. lxiv, and G. E. C[ockayne], *The*

If Ewen appears ambivalent in his attachment to Norway, the same cannot be said of his cousin and fellow ruler Dugald son of Ruairi (*Duggal Rudrisson*), whose power base may have lain in Garmoran and the Uists. As already noted, Dugald was in Bergen with Ewen in 1248 and 1249, and again in 1253. In 1258 he led a great fleet from the Hebrides to Ireland. The *Annals of Connacht* style him 'MacSomurli' and note that he sailed round the west of Ireland to Connemara 'and robbed a merchant ship of all her goods: wine, copper, cloth and iron'.[97] As in the days of Dugald's Viking ancestors, trading and raiding were clearly closely connected. The English sheriff of Connacht, Jordan de Exeter, gave chase with a fleet, but was defeated and killed by Dugald. 'The fleet of the Galls [that is, the English] retired after losing the best of their lords,' runs the annal, 'and MacSomurli went back to his land, joyful and laden with spoil.'[98] Was Dugald avenging the death of his father ten years before – if the identification proposed above is correct? The following year Dugald was in Ireland again, at Derry, accompanied by his brother Alan [*Ailín*], this time with peaceful purpose. The occasion was the marriage of Dugald's daughter to Aed O'Connor, king of Connacht, her tocher, or dowry, being 160 warriors.[99] This tocher is reminiscent of the celebrated *tochradh nighean a'Chathanach* (tocher of the daughter of O'Cathan) said to have accompanied Aíne O'Cathan on her marriage to Angus Óg MacDonald of Islay a generation or so later.[100]

It comes as no surprise, then, to learn that in the 1263 campaign Dugald was a full-blooded supporter of King Hakon. Norwegian sources generally refer to him as 'king' Dugald. His son, Eric, as has been noted, sailed in Hakon's own galley. Dugald and his brother Alan, together with their cousin Angus of Islay, Murchad MacSween and Magnus, King of Man, did not participate in the battle of Largs, being engaged at the crucial moment on a raiding expedition into the Lennox, by way of Loch Long and Arrochar, from where they transported their galleys across the *tarbert* to Loch Lomond.[101]

Complete Peerage, vol. XII(1) (London 1953), 382–3. Mary is known to have had children by Sir Hugh Abernethy. She died in London in 1302, surrounded by her MacDougall kin (*CDS* v, no. 290).

97 Although *Ann. Connacht* do not mention Dugald specifically, the inference made by most commentators that he was the 'MacSomairle' involved seems highly likely, given the entries for the following year.

98 M. Dolley, *Anglo-Norman Ireland* (Dublin 1972), 151, regards this incident as an attack by 'Hebridean pirates'!

99 *Ann. Connacht*; *Annals of Loch Cé*, ed. W. M. Hennessy (Rolls Ser., 1871). These warriors (*oclaech*) appear to be galloglasses (see note 59 above).

100 For the *tochradh nighean a'Chathanaich*, see, e.g., J. Bannerman, *The Beatons: A Medical Kindred in the Gaelic Tradition* (Edinburgh 1986), 10–11.

101 *ES* ii, 625–6; and see Cowan, 'Hakon IV and Alexander III', 121. This, p. 119 and genealogical table, and Duncan and Brown, 'Argyll and the Isles', 213 and genealogical

Even after the failure and death of King Hakon, Dugald continued to defy the Scots from his ships.[102] He died in 1268, perhaps in Norway, his obit recorded in Irish and Icelandic annals, but not in any Scottish source.[103] *The Annals of Connacht* style him 'king of Argyll' (*rí Oirir Gaídel*), and those of Loch Cé 'king of Innse Gall and Argyll'. His son Eric opted to stay in Norway, where he died in 1287, a leading Norwegian baron.[104]

Less is known of the activities of Dugald's cousin Angus *Mór*, lord of Islay, the first MacDonald. Later tradition recorded that he had been fostered by Dubside, ancestor of the MacDuffies or MacPhees.[105] Angus followed Hakon in 1263 with some reluctance, and cast his lot with Scotland thereafter, surrendering his infant son as a hostage to Alexander III in 1264.[106] Although the record evidence is sparse, Angus, like Ranald of Man before him, is the subject of a memorable Gaelic praise-poem.[107] Unlike many examples of the genre, which tend to be predictable, formalistic and dull, this poem is vibrant and humorous. It seems to have been composed to celebrate Angus's succession to his father Donald:

> Purchase thy father's poem, Angus, thou hast the king's house.
>
> To thee he left his dwelling place, thine is each breastplate, thine each treasure and his tapering swords ... his brown ivory chessman.

Ships and control of the sea are a constant theme:

> Thou hast come round Ireland; rare is the strand whence thou hast not taken cattle; graceful ships are sailed by thee; thou art like an otter, O scion of Tara.
>
> To Lough Foyle, to Erris, thy path is straight from the Hebrides ... [*a hInnsibh Gall*]
>
> The host of Islay has been with thee beside Aran. Corcumroe thy fleet has reached ... thou art a salmon that searches every strand.

---

table, are mistaken in making Murchad (*Margadr*) a brother of Angus of Islay: he is properly Murchad MacSween. See W. D. H. Sellar, 'Family origins in Cowal and Knapdale', *Scottish Studies*, xv (1971), 21–37.

102 *ES* ii, 649.

103 Ibid., ii, 660; *Ann. Connacht*, 1268 (compare the entry for 1247, at note 62 above).

104 In *Chronica Regum Manniae et Insularum*, ed. P. A. Munch (Christiania 1860), 134, Munch notices Eric's death in 1287. See also K. Helle, *Konge og Gode Menn I norsk riksstyving, ca. 1150–1319* (Oslo 1972), 582; I am indebted to Dr Barbara Crawford for this reference.

105 'A Fragment of an Irish MS History of the Macdonalds of Antrim', *TGSI* xxxvii (1934–6), 277.

106 *ER* i, 5.

107 'An Address to Aonghus of Islay', in O. Bergin, *Irish Bardic Poetry*, ed. D. Greene and F. Kelly (Dublin 1970), 169–74, 291–4. The full poem has 31 stanzas. I have followed Bergin's translation. See also *Scottish Gaelic Studies* iv (1934–5), 57–69.

The poet makes considerable play of the fact that he himself is a landsman, unhappy at sea:

> I should be an ill hand at the oar against the perilous sea, O blue-eyed prince: on a calm river I tremble when I take charge of a boat's rudder.

> How to settle myself I know not, when going over the waves: I know not whether it is better to sit; I fear to lie down in the ship.

> In my native district men ask about the form of a ship, O lord of the Gall:[108] little of the sea is visible from the highest steep mountain in it.

Angus's ancestry is referred to, stretching back through Somerled and Godfrey to Colla Uais.[109] But his Scandinavian associations are not neglected. One stanza begins, intriguingly,

> Around thee are Thorkell, Ivar and Olaf ... heroes of Dublin of bright hazels.[110]

Nothing could be more evocative of the world of the thirteenth-century sea-kings than this marvellous poem. Praise-poems must have been written for Ewen of Argyll and Dugald mac Ruairi also, but none are known to have survived.

*   *   *

The career of Ewen's son Alexander of Argyll takes us into a different milieu entirely, as a glance at Table III makes clear. The first references to Alexander occur in 1275. In the summer of that year Alexander III wrote to Edward of England noting that a ship and some men of Alexander of Argyll had been detained at Bristol and asking for their release.[111] Edward was happy to comply. Alexander's trading activities are mentioned again in 1292, when Edward I granted him a licence to trade in Ireland, narrating that Alexander regularly sent men and his merchants to Ireland – *frequenter mittit homines et mercatores suos ad partes Hiberniae* – to buy and sell goods and commodities.[112] Alexander, his men and his merchants were to have safe conducts in Ireland. Edward also granted a licence at the same time to Alexander's remote cousins Angus *Mór* of Islay and his son Alexander.

---

108 'Gall' here refers to the 'foreigners' of the Isles, of mixed Gaelic and Scandinavian stock.
109 See Sellar, 'Origins and ancestry of Somerled'. I did not know of this poem when I wrote that article.
110 Are these ancestors, retainers or, as Duffy plausibly suggests ('Bruce brothers', 68), kings of Dublin? In any case the Scandinavian associations are clear.
111 *CDS* ii, no. 55.
112 Stevenson, *Documents*, no. 276.

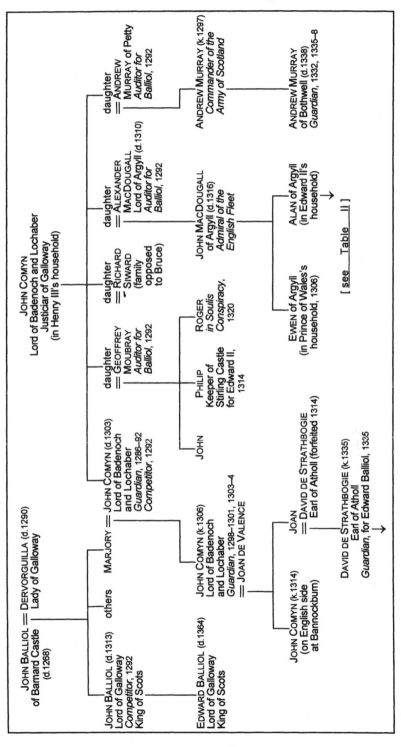

Table III. MacDougalls, Comyns of Badenoch and Balliols

The second reference to Alexander of Argyll in 1275 relates to the expedition launched by Alexander III against the Isle of Man. The last king of the Manx dynasty, Magnus son of Olaf (who had married a sister of Alexander of Argyll) died in 1265, shortly after doing homage to Alexander III.[113] By the Treaty of Perth in 1266 Man was formally ceded to Scotland. In 1275, however, Godfrey, an illegitimate son of Magnus, rose in rebellion seeking to establish himself as king. The revolt was crushed by the Scots, and Godfrey killed. The Scottish leaders included 'Alan fitz Rother', that is, Alan son of Ruairi and brother of Dugald, last noticed ravaging in the Lennox in 1263 in the Norwegian interest, and Alexander 'fitz John of Argyll'.[114] This last is a significant entry, as it is the only contemporary source which specifically names Alexander's father as Ewen (allowing for the persistent confusion between *Eoghan* and *Eoin*), thereby confirming later genealogical tradition and putting the relationship between Alexander and Ewen beyond reasonable doubt.[115]

The next reference to Alexander occurs in 1284, when he attended a Scottish council or colloquium held at Scone, together with his cousins Angus of Islay and Alan mac Ruairi.[116] About the same time, it has been deduced, Alexander received a royal commission over Argyll, Kintyre and perhaps also the Isles, similar to the Campbell lieutenancy of later centuries. Alexander's activities over the next twenty years can conveniently be considered under two heads: his participation in matters central to the governance of Scotland, and his drive for supremacy in the West Highlands and Islands, in which he bid fair for a time to recreate the hegemony of his ancestor Somerled.

Looking first to Alexander's role as a leading member of the community of the realm of Scotland, his marriage gave him an entrée into the highest circles of the Anglo-Scottish baronage. Although the name of his wife is unknown, it seems clear that she was a member of the most powerful magnatial family in Scotland, the Comyns, and probably a daughter of John Comyn (I), lord of Badenoch, as Wyntoun says.[117] Table III,

---

113 Duncan and Brown, 'Argyll and the Isles', 214; *ES* ii, 653.

114 *SAEC*, 382. The entry comes from an English source with close links to Man: the *Annals of Furness*.

115 As it probably would have been anyway, but for the unhappy suggestion made in 1836 by W. F. Skene in his *Highlanders of Scotland* (2nd edn, ed. A. Macbain, Stirling 1902), 242–6 and 411, that Ewen died leaving no heirs but daughters. Although Skene later recanted (*Celtic Scotland*, iii, 293–4, 330, 470) the damage was done (and see Sellar, 'MacDougall pedigrees', 4–5).

116 *APS* i, 424.

117 *Chron. Wyntoun* (Laing), iii, 312. Alexander's grandson, Alan of Argyll, used a seal bearing a lymphad within a bordure wavy, charged with garbs (the armorial emblems of the Comyns) with a dragon at the sinister side of the shield (*CDS* iii, no. 647). For the Comyn family generally, see now A. Young, *Robert the Bruce's Rivals: The Comyns, 1212–1314* (East Linton 1997).

'MacDougall, Comyn of Badenoch and Balliol', discloses a network of relationships radically different from those in Tables I and II. It illustrates Alexander's place within the Balliol/Comyn affinity, central to the governance of Scotland. Alexander's role in the community of the realm must be viewed against this background.

In March 1290 Alexander was one of the magnates who wrote to Edward I anent the marriage of the Maid of Norway.[118] Later that year he approved the Treaty of Birgham agreed with Edward.[119] In the Great Cause Alexander was one of Balliol's auditors, as too were Geoffrey Moubray and Andrew Murray of Petty, married like Alexander to daughters of John Comyn (I).[120] John Comyn (II), lord of Badenoch, was nominally a competitor in his own right as a descendant of Donald Ban (deposed 1097), but had indicated that he did not wish to press his claim to the prejudice of Balliol.[121] Alexander witnessed Balliol's fealty to Edward I in November 1292 shortly after Edward had given judgement in favour of Balliol.[122] In 1296, like most prominent Scots, Alexander did homage to Edward.[123] Later that year he fell out with Edward, who instructed the earl of Menteith to take possession of Alexander's lands and those of his son John. Alexander was imprisoned in Berwick Castle until May 1297.[124] Relations with Edward continued strained until 1301 when Edward instructed his admiral of the Cinque Ports to take Alexander into his peace, together with his sons John and Duncan, and his son-in-law and kinsman Lachlan, son of Alan mac Ruairi (*Loughlan le fiz Aleyn*).[125] By 1305 Edward had abandoned the idea of a subordinate Scottish kingdom and was seeking to forge one kingdom in the British Isles. He appointed his nephew John of Brittany as his lieutenant in Scotland with a council of twenty to advise him. Alexander of Argyll was nominated to that council, as were his wife's nephews John Comyn (III) of Badenoch and John Moubray; so too was the earl of Carrick, Robert Bruce, the future king.[126]

Despite his involvement at the heart of Scottish affairs Alexander was also active in the Highlands and Islands. Indeed his activities in both spheres of operation were to a considerable degree complementary: there

118 *APS* i, 441.
119 Stevenson, *Documents* i, no. 92.
120 *Edward I and the Throne of Scotland, 1290–1296*, ed. E. L. G. Stones and G. G. Simpson (Oxford 1978), ii, 84; and see note 117 above, and Table III.
121 *Edward I and the Throne of Scotland*, i, 15; ii, 138.
122 Ibid., ii, 254.
123 *CDS* ii, no. 791; as did his brother Malcolm de Ergadia: ibid., no. 823, p. 200.
124 Ibid., ii, p. 225; *Rot. Scot.*, i, 40b.
125 *CDS* ii, no. 1204; Stevenson, *Documents*, ii, no. 610. This essay does not consider the careers of Lachlan (Roland) and his brother Ranald.
126 *Documents and Records illustrating the History of Scotland*, ed. F. Palgrave (London 1837), i, 292–3, and pp. cli–clii.

is much truth in the observation in the much later *Book of Clanranald* that in the war of the Balliols and the Bruces the race of Dugald son of Somerled took the side of the Balliols and the race of Ranald son of Somerled that of the Bruces.[127] In 1292 Alexander was engaged in legal dispute with his kinsman Alexander MacDonald, younger of Islay, over land in Lismore, the case being notoriously appealed by MacDonald and his wife Juliana from John Balliol to Edward I in 1295.[128] In 1293 Alexander of Argyll was appointed sheriff of the newly created sheriffdom of Lorn. This included the lands of Angus MacDonald of Islay, Colin *Mór* Campbell and of Alexander himself, the mainland area covered extending from Ardnamurchan in the north to Knapdale in the south.[129] In or about 1296 the MacDougalls, traditionally led by Alexander's son John, killed Colin *Mór* Campbell in a skirmish near Loch Avich in Brae Lorn.[130] It may not be irrelevant that Colin had been a Bruce auditor in the Great Cause.[131] Later, in 1304–5, Alexander is found paying the rents of the Campbell heartland of Lochawe and Ardscotnish (Kilmartin) to Edward I.[132]

In 1297, Alexander, with his son Duncan and brother-in-law, Comyn of Badenoch, burned and devastated the lands of Alexander MacDonald of Islay.[133] Two years later he killed MacDonald. The *Annals of Ulster* record that 'Alexander Mac Domnaill, the person who was best for hospitality and excellence that was in Ireland and in Scotland, was killed together with a countless number of his own people that were slaughtered around him, by Alexander Mac Dubghaill.'[134] Remarkably, this annal long passed unnoticed by Scottish historians, who continued to credit Alexander MacDonald of Islay after 1299 with many activities, for which there is, unsurprisingly, no record evidence.[135] The identity of Alexander MacDonald has been

---

127 *Book of Clanranald*, 156–7. Compare G. W. S. Barrow, *Robert Bruce and the Community of the Realm of Scotland* (3rd edn, Edinburgh 1988), 163: 'As long as John Balliol had been king, the Macdougalls were patriots and the Macdonalds pro-English.'

128 *Foedera, Conventiones, Litterae, et Cuiuscunque Generis Acta Publica*, ed. T. Rymer (Record Commission, 1816–69), i, 761; *Rot. Scot.*, i, 21b; and see Barrow, *Bruce*, 57–8. Alexander's wife Juliana is sometimes said to be the sister or daughter of Alexander of Argyll. While this may be so, beyond the fact that she claimed a hereditary right to part of Lismore, there seems to be no hard evidence.

129 *APS* i, 447.

130 See: 'Ane Accompt of the Genealogie of the Campbells', in *Highland Papers*, ii, 85; P. H. Gillies, *Nether Lorn* (London 1903), 144–6; and Macdonald, *Argyll*, 120. The date is often given as 1294, but Colin was still alive in 1296: W. D. H. Sellar, 'The earliest Campbells – Norman, Briton or Gael?', *Scottish Studies*, xvii (1973), 111.

131 *Edward I and the Throne of Scotland*, ii, 82.

132 *CDS* ii, no. 1646, p. 439. For the early Campbells generally, see Sellar, 'Earliest Campbells'.

133 Stevenson, *Documents*, ii, no. 445.

134 *Ann Ulster*, 1299; also *Ann. Connacht*.

135 E.g., Macdonald, *Argyll*, 126–7, 134.

disputed, but there can be little doubt that this was the lord of Islay, son of Angus *Mór*, and leader of his kindred.[136] The 1299 annal is also of interest as being the only contemporary reference to Alexander of Argyll as 'MacDougall', and the first appearance on record, therefore, of that surname.[137]

By 1306, Alexander of Argyll, now an elderly man, was at the apex of his career. He had achieved supremacy in the West, unsurpassed since the time of Somerled. Within the space of a few years he had defeated and killed the chief of the Campbells and the chief of the MacDonalds, the latter, it would seem, in a major engagement. In some ways Alexander's achievement foreshadows that of the MacDonald lords of the Isles. But perhaps it is more truly comparable to that of the Campbells, later to adopt Alexander's designation 'of Argyll'. Alexander had become a leading member of the community of the realm. He had integrated with the centre in a way which the MacDonalds were never to do.

The year 1306 marks the turning-point in Alexander's fortunes. In that year his grandson Ewen, heavily disguised on the record as 'Audoenus Dargail', is found in the household of the Prince of Wales, soon to be Edward II.[138] Ewen was following a family tradition, for his great-grandfather, John Comyn (I) of Badenoch, had been in Henry III's personal service in the 1260s.[139] However, 1306 was also the year in which Robert Bruce killed John Comyn III, Alexander's nephew by marriage, in hot blood at Dumfries, and was shortly afterwards proclaimed king of Scots.[140]

That same year King Robert's reign nearly came to a premature end at the hands of Alexander's son John, cousin of the slaughtered Comyn, who defeated and nearly captured the king at Dalrigh, by Tyndrum. Barbour recounts this skirmish and adds that King Robert's escape was so miraculous that John of Argyll compared it to Goll mac Morna's escape from Finn mac Cumhail.[141] Do we hear in this anecdote the authentic voice of John

---

136 *Pace* S. Duffy, 'The 'Continuation' of Nicholas Trevet: a new source for the Bruce invasion', *Proceedings of the Royal Irish Academy*, xci (1991), 311–12. And see W. D. H. Sellar, 'MacDonald and MacRuari pedigrees in MS 1467', *Notes and Queries of the Society of West Highland and Island Historical Research*, 1st ser., xxviii (Mar. 1986), 7–8.

137 Unless one counts *Johannes Dugaldi* in *Chron. Man* (see above, page 203).

138 *CDS* iv, appendix, p. 489; also *CDS* v, nos. 471 (g), 472 (q).

139 Young, *Comyns*, 81, 138. It is not clear whether it was John Comyn himself or his brother Richard who was captured with Henry III at the battle of Lewes in 1264 (see *CDS* i, no. 2678).

140 Comyn's killing – to use the word 'murder' for a killing in hot blood is an anachronism – was doubly offensive to Edward I, as he was married to Edward's cousin Joan de Valence.

141 *Barbour's Bruce*, ed. M. P. McDiarmid and J. A. C. Stevenson (Scottish Text Soc., 1980–5), ii, 48 (III, ll. 61–75). I have altered 'y' to 'th', 'z' to 'y', and (twice) 'w' to 'u'.

of Argyll, or is the story a mere literary conceit? It would seem the former, because Barbour goes on to criticise John for making the comparison: far better, says Barbour, and more in keeping with fashion, to have compared Bruce to some hero of French romance:

> Quhen that the lord off Lorne saw
> His men stand off him [Bruce] ane sik aw
> That thai durst nocht folow the chase
> Rycht angry in his hart he was,
> And for wondyr that he suld swa
> Stot thaim him ane but ma
> He said, 'Me think, Marthokys sone,*
> Rycht as Golmakmorn was wone
> To haiff fra Fyn[gall] his mengne,
> Rycht swa all his fra us has he.'
> He set ensample thus mydlike
> The-quhethir he mycht mar manerlik
> Lyknyt hym to Gaudifer de Larys
> Quhen that the mychty duk Betys
> Assailyeit in Gadyrris the forrayours ...

[*Marjory's son, i.e. Robert Bruce]

This is the occasion on which a dying MacDougall is traditionally said to have wrested the 'Brooch of Lorn' from Bruce.

After 1306 all was disaster, and MacDougall power shattered for ever. In 1307 Edward I died. His successor appointed John of Argyll sheriff of Argyll and Innse Gall (Argyll and the Isles).[142] In 1308 Bruce launched a major offensive against the MacDougalls and defeated John of Argyll on the slopes of Ben Cruachan.[143] After this reverse, Alexander, seeing his lands ravaged, surrendered his castle of Dunstaffnage to King Robert and came temporarily into his peace. His son John, however, fled in his ships, according to Barbour:

> Schyr Alexandir off Arghile that saw
> The king dystroy up clene & law
> His land sent treyteris to the king
> And come his man bot mar duelling
> And he resawyt him till his pes,
> Bot Ihone off Lorne his sone yeit wes

---

[142] *CDS* iii, no. 18.

[143] The date and details of this campaign have been much discussed. Here, I follow Barrow, *Bruce.*

> Rebell as he wes wont to be,
> And fled with schippis on the se.
> Bot thai that left apon the land
> War to the king all obeysand.
> And he thar hostage all has tane
> And towart Perth agayne is gane.[144]

Alexander, together with the *barones de tocius Ergadie et Ynchgallye*, attended Bruce's St Andrews Parliament in March 1309.[145] Some time later, however, he slipped off to England, for he is found, together with his son John, attending Edward II's council at Westminster in June 1310.[146] He seems to have died late in that year, perhaps in Ireland, for in January 1311 Edward II sent a letter to the treasurer and chamberlain of the exchequer in Dublin directing the payment to Alexander and John of £100 each for their men in Ireland. A note adds that Alexander had since died.[147]

What a strange and varied career had this chief of the MacDougalls! As a child he may have watched his father Ewen set sail to claim kingship in Bergen in 1248. The following year he would have heard of Alexander II's expedition against Argyll and death in MacDougall territory on Kerrera. As a young man he would have seen King Hakon's fleet sail down the Isles and known of his father's decision to surrender all his island possessions. The son and brother-in-law of a king himself, in maturity he knew and served two kings of Scots, Alexander III and John Balliol, and two kings of England, Edward I and Edward II. He established himself as the greatest power in Argyll and the Isles since the time of Somerled; but, unlike Somerled, he was also a leading member of the community of the realm of Scotland. Even when that realm seemed destined to disappear as a sovereign kingdom he retained his influence at the heart of affairs. But in the end his career was inextricably linked with that of the king he opposed, Robert Bruce; and he died in old age and exile, shorn of all his possessions, a pensioner of the English king.

* * *

John (*Eoin*) of Argyll's career overlaps that of his father, but he is a considerable figure in his own right. From Barbour onwards he has had a place in the rogues' gallery of Scottish history as John 'of Lorn', implacable opponent of Robert Bruce. Yet even the most biased pro-Bruce accounts

---

144 *Barbour's Bruce*, ii, 243 (X, ll. 123–34). Barrow suggests that John MacDougall escaped down Loch Awe, rather than Loch Etive.
145 *APS* i, 459.
146 *CDS* iii. no. 95.
147 Ibid., iii, no. 191.

accord John a grudging respect. Although he is often referred to, following Barbour's lead, as John 'of Lorn', there seems to be no contemporary evidence for this style: he is invariably styled 'of Argyll', like his father, grandfather and great-grandfather before him.[148] It is possible also that the byname *bacach* (the lame), first found attached to him in a seventeenth-century genealogy, may result from confusion with the byname attached to a MacDougall cousin and namesake, *Eoin Bogach* (the soft).[149]

As already noted, John was probably the grandson of, and may well have been named for, John Comyn (I) of Badenoch. If Wyntoun's evidence is to be trusted, his cousins included not only John Comyn, killed in 1306, but also Andrew Murray, Commander of the Army of Scotland at Stirling Bridge and Philip Moubray, keeper of Stirling Castle for Edward II in 1314 (see Table III). He first appears (as *Johannes de Ergadia*) in 1291 when he swore fealty to Edward I.[150] Again, as noted, tradition credits John with the slaying of Colin *Mór* Campbell about 1296. In 1306 he defeated Bruce at Dalrigh, but was defeated in his turn at Ben Cruachan ('the battle of the pass of Brander') in 1308. John was much trusted by Edward I. In a letter written in 1304 Edward expresses his full confidence in him.[151] In 1306, John's son Ewen was in the household of Edward, Prince of Wales, following a family tradition of royal service. A second son, Alan, also served in Edward's household after he became king.[152] In 1307 John was appointed sheriff of Argyll and Innse Gall. In 1310 he attended Edward's council at Westminster. Troubled, it would seem, by ill health, John survived his father by less than six years. On at least three occasions, in 1311, 1314 and 1315, he was appointed – as *Monsire Jehan Dargail* – admiral and captain of an English fleet.[153] In 1315

---

148 I too referred to him as 'John of Lorn' in my 'MacDougall Pedigrees in MS 1467'. It is conceivable that during his father's lifetime, John may have been addressed as 'of Lorn'; but it seems more likely that he was anachronistically given the style of his grandson and namesake, Barbour's contemporary, John *Gallda*, lord of Lorn. Alternatively, the Gaelic epithet *Latharnach* (literally, 'of Lorn') may have been attached to John in the Gaelic vernacular.

149 Sellar, 'MacDougall pedigrees', 12.

150 *Edward and the Throne of Scotland*, ii, 125, 368.

151 Stevenson, *Documents*, ii, no. 637. For the charter of lands in Lismore (*RMS* ii, no. 3136) usually said to have been granted by John in 1304, see note 158 below.

152 For Ewen, see above, page 213. He is mentioned again in 1311, and also by Wyntoun: *CDS* v, no. 562 (d); *Chron. Wyntoun* (Laing), ii, 312, 'Ewyn off Lorne'. For Alan, see *CDS* iii, nos. 647, 684. An 'Ivo de Ergadia' (for 'Ivar'?) also appears around this time: *CDS*, ii, no. 302; v, nos. 562 (a–c), 575 (d).

153 John appears in the list of English admirals in *Handbook of British Chronology*, ed. E. B. Fryde and others (3rd edn, London 1986), 136, as 'John Argyll, kt.' (for *Monsire Jehan Dargail*). His appointment in 1315 (*Rot. Scot.* i, 139a) does not appear in the *Handbook*.

he won back for the English the Isle of Man, lost earlier to the Scots.[154] Later that year he was in Ireland assisting the English in opposing the brothers Robert and Edward Bruce. His MacDonald and MacRuairi cousins, by contrast, supported King Robert.[155]

In 1316 John of Argyll was granted a pension of 200 marks per annum by the English crown. He died in September 1316, 'being impotent in body, and his lands in Scotland totally destroyed', at Ospring in Kent, on pilgrimage to Canterbury.[156] The appropriate reference now shifts from the world of the sagas and Gaelic praise-poetry to that of Chaucer's 'verray parfit gentil knight'. John died in debt: his executor Dungal MacDowall, head of another displaced Scottish family, was still coping with claims of John's creditors almost ten years later.[157]

John's son Ewen (*Eogan*) may have returned briefly to Argyll in the train of Edward Balliol.[158] A younger son, Alan, became a member of Edward II's household, as already noted. It was Alan's son John (*Eoin*), appropriately remembered as *Gallda* (the Foreigner), who finally made peace with the house of Bruce and re-established his family in Argyll, albeit with much diminished territory. John *Gallda* seems to have left an illegitimate son, Alan, ancestor of the later MacDougalls of Dunollie, by

154 *CDS* iii, no. 420; and see Duncan's comment in *RRS* v, 378–9.
155 According to *Ann. Ulster* and other Irish annals, a MacDonald *rí Airir Goidel* and a MacRuairi *rí Innse Gall* were killed in 1318. For the story of the Bruce involvement in Ireland see, *inter alia*: R. Frame, 'The Bruces in Ireland, 1315–1317', *Irish Historical Studies*, xxiii (1982–3), 61–7; A. A. M. Duncan, 'The Scots' invasion of Ireland, 1315', in Davies, *British Isles*, 100–17; Duffy, 'Bruce brothers'; Duffy, '"Continuation" of Nicholas Trevet', 303–15; and, now, Duncan, *Barbour's Bruce*, and C. McNamee, *The Wars of the Bruces: Scotland: England and Ireland, 1306–1328* (East Linton 1997), 166–205.
156 *Archaeologia*, Society of Antiquaries of London, xxvi (1836) 341. I am most grateful to Donald Galbraith, formerly of the Scottish Record Office, for first alerting me to the existence of this record, so long in print. Barbour's account (*Barbour's Bruce*, iii, 111 [XV, ll. 309–14]) of the capture of John of Argyll by Bruce and his subsequent imprisonment and death in Loch Leven Castle is quite mistaken and remains a puzzle. A garbled version of this story may lie behind later, equally unhistorical, accounts of the fate of Alexander MacDonald, son of Angus *Mór* (see above, page 212). The quotation comes from *CDS* iii, no. 912.
157 Ibid. The MacDowalls, staunch Balliol supporters from Galloway, were a different kin from the MacDougalls of Argyll, despite their identical surname (for *Dowall* and *Dougall* represent the same forename).
158 I have argued that this Ewen (*Eogan*), son of John (*Eoin*) of Argyll, is the Ewen, lord of Lorn, who granted a ten-pound land in Lismore to Andrew, Bishop of Argyll, at Achadun on 10 September 1334 (*OPS*, ii (2), 828); and that this grant should be compared with that recorded in *RMS* ii, no. 3136 as having been made by *Eugenius*, lord of Lorn, Benderloch and Lismore to Andrew, Bishop of Argyll, of various pennylands in Lismore, at Achadun on 10 Sep. 1304 (Sellar, 'MacDougall pedigrees', 6 and n.15). The latter is usually ascribed to John of Argyll, but it seems more likely that it has been misdated by 30 years.

Oban.[159] His main lands, however, descended to the Stewarts of Lorn, by daughters of his marriage with Janet Isaac, granddaughter of Robert Bruce, and thus the lordship of Lorn finally left the possession of the MacDougalls. Its subsequent history is traced by Steve Boardman in the following chapter.

[159] As argued in Sellar, 'MacDougall pedigrees', contrary to the account usually given of the descent of the later MacDougalls of Dunolly. A 'Thomas Ergaill' appears in 1348–9 as a valet or esquire of Edward Balliol: R. C. Reid, 'Edward de Balliol', *Trans. Dumfries and Galloway Natural History and Antiquarian Soc.*, 3rd ser., xxxv (1956–7), 50.

9

The Tale of Leper John and the Campbell Acquisition of Lorn

STEVE BOARDMAN

In 1865, in Port Appin on the eastern shore of Loch Linnhe, two old men met to share tales of days bypast. One was John Dewar from Rosneath, a man employed by the eighth duke of Argyll and his agent J. F. Campbell as a collector of traditional histories from the inhabitants of the Highlands and Islands.[1] The other was Gillespie MacCombie, an eighty-three-year old widower and a native of Appin who had lived much of his long life as a farmer on the land of the laird of Airds.[2] MacCombie's stories were duly recorded in Dewar's massive collection of traditional lore as 'A tale of Gillespie MacCombie in Port Appin, and of those from whom he is descended, according to his own telling of it'.[3] Overall, it was a strange yarn that MacCombie unfolded for his guest. It began with the death of an unnamed lord of Lorn at the hands of the MacDougalls of Dunollie who thereafter 'brought caterans with them and went to dwell in Castle Stalker, and they sought sustenance ... by plundering the country'.[4] Relief was at hand, however, in the shape of Dougall Stewart, an illegitimate son of the slain lord of Lorn, who 'was staying at Balquhidder among his mother's relations' and who determined to recover the lands between 'Loch Creran and Loch Linnhe up to Glenduror (the *Ceathramh Fearna*, as MacCombie described it)'. Recruiting men from Dumbarton, Loch Lomondside and, most especially, MacLarens from Perthshire with the promise that 'they and their descendants should have farms so long as Dugald Stewart or his offspring should have lordship', Dougall 'took possession of the Ceathramh Fearna, and ... gave farms to the MacLaurins'.[5]

Within fifteen years of MacCombie and Dewar's meeting a more elaborate and detailed version of the tale of Dougall Stewart found its way

1 J. Dewar, *The Dewar Manuscripts*, ed. J. Mackechnie (Glasgow 1964) i, 11, 30–1.
2 Ibid., 258–9.
3 Ibid., 255.
4 Ibid.
5 Ibid.

into print in a family history of the Stewarts of Appin.[6] The Appin history combined the local oral traditions evidenced by MacCombie's tale with the 'authority' of manuscript accounts of the Stewarts of Appin and the MacLarens of Ardvech. The editors of the history also had recourse to the printed documentary sources then available for late medieval Scotland. The result was a rousing, but still apparently fabulous, account which explained the origins of Stewart lordship in Appin in the fifteenth century. Agreeing with MacCombie, the Appin history asserted that the progenitor of the Stewarts of Appin was Dougall, an illegitimate son of John Stewart, lord of Lorn. The tale narrated how, late in life, John Stewart (also known to tradition as John _Mourach_ or Leper John) decided to marry Dougall's mother, a daughter of the MacLaren lord of Ardvech (near Lochearnhead), and retrospectively legitimise their son so that he might succeed to the lordship of Lorn. On the morning of the wedding, as John's bride-to-be and his son approached Dunstaffnage Castle with a MacLaren escort, banners flying and pipes playing, the lord of Lorn received a fatal wound from an assassin, Allan MacDougall. John was made of stern stuff, however, and if there is any substance to his byname he may have been long prepared for his own death and long inured to physical suffering. In a melodramatic conclusion to the tale the old lord, his life ebbing away, ground through the marriage ceremony in order to secure the lordship for his son. After John's death, the Appin history resentfully records the sweeping aside of Dougall's rights by the naked political and military power of his adversaries, notably Colin Campbell, earl of Argyll and his uncle Colin Campbell of Glenorchy, who were married to Dougall's legitimate sisters.[7]

At first sight the Stewart tale seems an obvious invention, the wish-fulfilment of a family whose illegitimate ancestor was rightly debarred from succeeding to his father's lands and title. Manuscript histories associated with Clan Campbell, such as the _Black Book of Taymouth_, provide a far more prosaic and bland account of the circumstances behind Earl Colin's acquisition of Lorn. The earl's right, we are told, rested squarely on his marriage to Isabel Stewart, one of the three daughters and co-heiresses of John Stewart, the last Stewart lord of Lorn, who was

---

6 J. and D. Stewart, _The Stewarts of Appin_ (Edinburgh 1880). The tale was obviously considerably older, for its outlines can be discerned in a manuscript associated with Clan Campbell dating from 1756: _Argyll Records_, 9–10.

7 Stewart and Stewart, _Stewarts of Appin_, 73–96. The account also includes four stanzas of a Gaelic poem apparently commemorating the march of Dougall and his mother from Loch Earn to Dunstaffnage. It may be significant that John's by-name is found only in Campbell sources: _Argyll Records_, 9.

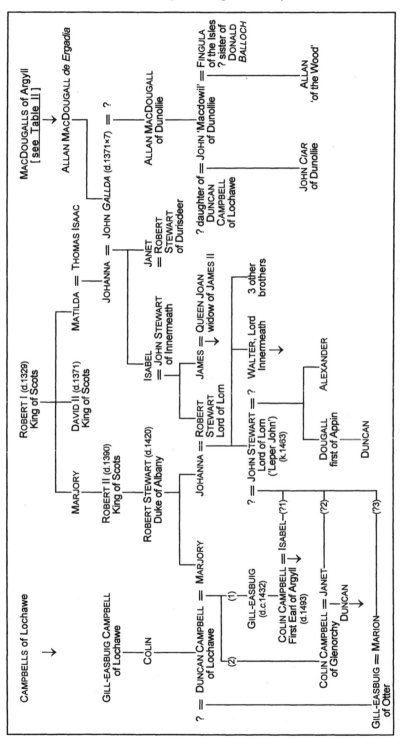

Table IV. The Lorn Inheritance: MacDougalls, Stewarts and Campbells

assassinated in his own castle of Dunstaffnage in December 1463 by Allan MacDougall.[8]

We can be sure, however, that there was no automatic Campbell succession to Lorn in 1463/4. After John Stewart's death the lordship of Lorn passed, under the terms of an entail drawn up in 1452, to John's brother Walter. It was not until 17 April 1470, six years after John Stewart's demise, that Colin Campbell, first earl of Argyll, received a royal grant of the lordship of Lorn following on Walter Stewart's resignation.[9] Moreover, behind the mundane conveyancing which apparently brought Lorn into Campbell possession in 1469/70 lay a far more compelling story centred on the ambitions of the indefatigable 'leper John' and his disinherited son. There are, in short, substantial grounds for believing that the traditions of the Stewarts of Appin, although heavily dramatised, contain a number of observations which accurately reflect the aims and ambitions of the chief protagonists in the complex and prolonged struggle which ended with the absorption of the lordship of Lorn into the Campbell empire.

Campbells, Stewarts and the reign of James II

It would be easy in hindsight to explain Earl Colin's acquisition of Lorn as typical of the way in which Clan Campbell expanded their power and authority in the west: a succession crisis in a neighbouring lordship providing an opportunity for the ruthless application of political, legal and military pressure. In truth, however, the tensions and conflicts of the 1460s were unexpected because they emerged from a background of close political co-operation between the Campbells of Lochawe and the Stewarts of Lorn in the years prior to John Stewart's death. In fact, the association between the two families was probably well established by the time of John Stewart's birth around 1400.[10] John was the eldest son of Robert Stewart and Johanna, a daughter of Robert, first Duke of Albany. Robert Stewart's marriage to Johanna had secured his place in the extensive Albany affinity, a group which included another of Duke

---

8   *Taymouth Book*, 10–11. John Stewart is misnamed William, Lord of Lorn. *Argyll Records*, 9–10, also emphasise the rights of John's daughters as heirs to the lordship of Lorn, but also indicate that there was resistance from 'the Stewarts of Inner-meth, who pretend to be Lords of Lorn by tailzie'.

9   *RMS* ii, no. 989.

10 A dispensation for Robert and Johanna's marriage was granted on 27 Sep. 1397; he was described as Robert, son of John Stewart of Innermeath: *Calendar of Papal Letters to Scotland of Benedict XIII of Avignon, 1394–1419*, ed. F. McGurk (SHS 1976), 75. The marriage was certainly concluded before 20 October 1407, when Robert witnessed one of Duke Robert's charters as *filius suus*: *RMS* i, no. 926.

Robert's sons-in-law, Duncan Campbell, lord of Lochawe.[11] The friendship between the Stewarts of Lorn and the Campbells of Lochawe extended to the political sphere, where the two families steered parallel paths through the upheavals of the early fifteenth century. In particular, Duncan Campbell and Robert Stewart escaped relatively unscathed from James I's devastating assault on their Albany kinsmen in 1425, although neither went on to enjoy the trust and patronage of the king.[12] In Campbell's case, it was probably extreme good fortune that he had been chosen as one of the hostages to be sent to England in 1424 in order to guarantee payment of James I's ransom. When, in May 1425, Murdoch, Duke of Albany, his sons and his father-in-law Duncan, Earl of Lennox, faced the executioner's axe in Stirling, Duncan Campbell, the duke's brother-in-law, was still in custody in England.[13]

The mutual suspicion and alienation which seems to have characterised the relationship of the Campbells with the royal court during the remainder of James I's reign was transformed in the wake of the king's assassination on 20 February 1437 in the Blackfriars of Perth.[14] In the aftermath of the murder, the Campbells of Lochawe and the Stewarts of Lorn swiftly established themselves as prominent supporters of the king's widow, Joan Beaufort, and her infant son James II. After the king's death Queen Joan fled to Edinburgh, from where she and her adherents attempted to take action against the men involved in the plot to kill her husband.[15] One of the first men active on the queen's behalf was the eldest surviving son of Duncan Campbell of Lochawe, Colin Campbell of Glenorchy. On 27 March 1437 Colin was in Edinburgh, where he received the right to use a portable altar from the papal nuncio Bishop Anthony Altani of Urbino.[16] Colin's appearance in Edinburgh indicates that he attended the coronation of James II at Holyrood on 25 March 1437, and it seems likely that he was knighted as part of the celebrations surrounding that event.[17] Thereafter, Colin Campbell was involved in the rooting out of the earl of Atholl and his fellow conspirators in February/ March 1437; he was certainly later given a grant of lands in Strath Tay for his capture of Thomas Chambers, one of the men directly involved in the assassination.[18] Duncan Campbell also seems to have given his active support to the queen, and was present

---

11 S. Boardman, *The Early Stewart Kings: Robert II and Robert III, 1371–1406* (East Linton 1996), 181–2.
12 M. Brown, *James I* (East Linton 1994), 66–7.
13 *CDS*, iv, nos. 941–2, 952–3, 960, 964, 973, 981, 983.
14 Brown, *James I*, 186–8.
15 C. McGladdery, *James II* (Edinburgh 1990), 10.
16 NAS, Breadalbane Collection, GD112/3/2.
17 Colin was a knight by 27 Mar. 1437: *Argyll Trans.*, at date.
18 *RMS* iii, no. 316.

in Stirling early in May 1437 at a general council called by Queen Joan which sanctioned the execution of Sir Robert Graham 'with many of his coveen' (perhaps including Thomas Chambers).[19] Given Duncan Campbell's links to the queen's party in and after 1437, the lord of Lochawe's supplication for the elevation of the kirk of Kilmun to collegiate status in 1442 for 'the weal of the souls of the late James king of Scots and of Johanna his consort, and also of James, the present king', may reflect sentiments which extended beyond conventional rhetoric.[20]

Loyalty to the queen and the young king also held out the prospect of more material reward. In the months after James's murder, Duncan Campbell embarked on a campaign to reclaim lands and offices denied him by the dead king and made a number of significant territorial and political advances as the beleaguered queen cast around for political and military support. While Duncan was attending the Stirling general council he had a notarial copy made of the 1382 charter by which Robert II (1371–90) had created Gill-easbuig Campbell (Duncan's grandfather) the king's lieutenant in Argyll.[21] The witnesses to the instrument included Duncan's brother-in-law, Robert Stewart, lord of Lorn, and two figures who were to play a dominant role in the politics of James II's minority, James Douglas, earl of Avondale and Alexander Livingstone of -endar. Duncan's claim to the lieutenancy was conceded by 4 August 1442, when the lord of Lochawe issued a charter in which he was styled 'locumtenens deputatus domini nostri regis infra partes Ergadie'.[22] The re-establishment of the Campbell lieutenancy in Argyll formed only one part of Duncan's plans for the expansion of his lordship after 1437. In or shortly after 1437 Duncan took possession of the strategic 'royal' fortress of Dunoon which dominated the northern reaches of the Firth of Clyde, as well as the king's portion of Glendaruel in the lordship of Cowal, estates which lay almost under the shadow of the Campbell fortress of Eilean Dearg in Loch Riddon.[23] The Campbells also made significant gains in Strathearn, where

19 Argyll Trans., 10 May 1437.
20 *CSSR* iv, no. 791.
21 Argyll Trans., 10 May 1437. The notarial instrument was probably intended to assist Duncan in pleading his case for a restoration of the lieutenancy before the royal council. It seems likely that James I had rescinded the lieutenancy because of Duncan's political links with the Albany Stewarts.
22 *RMS* ii, no. 346.
23 In Jul. 1445 Duncan Campbell was noted as having received all the rentals from the crown lands of Dunoon and Glendaruel in Cowal for the previous two years: *ER* v, 202. As this was the first account of the reign for the crown's lands in the Firth of Clyde, the Campbell occupation of the castle of Dunoon can probably be traced back to an earlier date than 1443. On 12 Mar. 1440, Duncan Campbell issued a charter from the castle of Dunoon in favour of Dunoon parish kirk: NAS, Register House Charters, RH6/304.

the execution and forfeiture of Walter, Earl of Atholl and Strathearn in 1437 allowed patronage to be directed towards the men active in the queen's service. By 1445 Colin Campbell of Glenorchy was occupying the lands of Glen Lednock, while his father received a £20 pension from other lands in the earldom of Strathearn.[24] It seems probable that the Campbell expansion into Strathearn was assisted by David Murray of Tullibardine, reputedly the brother-in-law of Robert Stewart and another man associated with Queen Joan. Murray appears to have replaced Malcolm Drummond of Concraig as Steward of Strathearn in the aftermath of Earl Walter's execution.[25]

In 1439 the political links between Queen Joan and this tight-knit band of Perthshire/Argyllshire lords were strengthened by her marriage to James Stewart, the brother of Robert, Lord of Lorn. The match seems to have taken place around July 1439 and it provoked an immediate response from other members of the royal establishment, worried about the increasing influence of the lord of Lorn and his allies in the dispensation of royal patronage.[26] On 3 August 1439 Sir Alexander Livingstone of Callendar, the constable of Stirling Castle, imprisoned the queen, her new husband and one of his brothers in the royal fortress before negotiating their release through a deal ratified by a general council held in the burgh of Stirling on 4 September 1439.[27] The terms of the so-called 'Appointment' of September 1439 saw Livingstone retain custody of the young King James and thus a central role in the political life of the kingdom. Queen Joan's 'men and retenew' were required to swear not to take action against the Livingstones for their seizure of the queen. The reconciliation no doubt explains the presence of Robert, Lord of Lorn and Sir David Murray in Stirling on 5 September.[28]

The new Livingstone-dominated regime which emerged from the political jockeying of 1439 seems to have been disinclined to take direct action against the Queen's allies, but the next major political crisis of the reign, in 1444–5, saw a sustained assault on the interests of Joan, the Stewarts of Lorn and the Campbells. In October/November 1444 Alexander Livingstone and his principal ally William, eighth Earl of Douglas, arranged a revocation of all grants made in the name of James II since the start of his minority.[29] The revocation cleared the way for a

24 *ER* v, 173, 205.
25 NAS, Drummond Writs, GD160/1/9 and 10; S. Boardman, 'Politics and the Feud in Late Medieval Scotland' (St Andrews University Ph.D. thesis, 1989), 161–2.
26 McGladdery, *James II*, 17.
27 Ibid., 18, 160; *APS* ii, 54.
28 *RMS* ii, no. 205.
29 McGladdery, *James II*, 32.

concerted Livingstone/Douglas attack on their political opponents through the withdrawal of grants of royal lands and offices obtained during or after 1437. The queen mother and her political ally James Kennedy, bishop of St Andrews (who, as bishop of Dunkeld, had sought papal confirmation for the queen's marriage to James Stewart in 1439) responded with a letter to the burgh of Aberdeen (and presumably many others) demanding that no payments should be made from the burgh 'to tha persownis that now has the Kyng in gouernance'.[30] Kennedy and the queen, however, did not have the political and military clout to compete with Livingstone and Douglas. Early in 1445 the lands of the bishopric of St Andrews were subjected to a great raid by the earl of Crawford, James Livingstone 'that tyme kepar to the king and captain of Stirling' and others, while at around the same time Queen Joan seems to have been forced to seek refuge with Sir Adam Hepburn of Hailes in Dunbar Castle.[31] The triumph of Livingstone and Douglas was confirmed by a parliament which opened in Perth in June 1445 and was then adjourned on 28 June to Edinburgh. On 14 June the Perth session of the parliament confirmed that any lands which had been held by James I on the day of his death should remain in possession of the young James II 'undemandit and unpleyit of ony man befor ony Juge within the Realme on to the tym of his lauchful age'.[32] Although the statute can be regarded as part of a general attempt to place the administration of royal lands and revenues on a more regular basis it also confirmed the ability of the current guardians of the young king to take action against those possessing royal lands on the basis of grants made after James I's death.

The exchequer audit held in Edinburgh from 5 July 1445 was supervised by Alexander Livingstone of Callendar and his son James, keeper of Stirling and guardian of the young king, and presented a clear opportunity for Livingstone and Douglas to punish the adherents of Queen Joan. Any last hope Duncan Campbell may have harboured of being able to defend his position in Cowal disappeared on 15 July when Queen Joan died under siege in Dunbar Castle; there was now no legitimate alternative to the Livingstone/Douglas axis.[33] On the day after the queen's death the exchequer auditors dealt with the accounts for the 'royal' lands of Dunoon and Glendaruel for the previous two years.[34] It was noted that

---

30 Ibid., 34; *Extracts from the Council Register of the Burgh of Aberdeen, 1398–1570*, ed. J. Stuart (Spalding Club, 1894), i, 399.

31 According to the so-called 'Auchinleck Chronicle', conveniently reprinted in McGladdery, *James II*, Appendix 2, 162.

32 *APS* ii, 33.

33 McGladdery, *James II*, 162.

34 *ER* v, 201–2. Cowal had never featured as an area of fiscal account in James I's reign, nor in the years 1437–43.

Duncan Campbell had uplifted all the rents of Dunoon and Glendaruel during this period. The response of the Livingstone regime was to dismiss Campbell and appoint Robert of Callendar, a Livingstone retainer who was already serving as custodian of Dumbarton Castle, as keeper of Dunoon. Callendar was also to receive the ferms of the king's lands of Glendaruel to supplement his fee as custodian of Dumbarton.[35] Similarly, the Campbell gains in Strathearn were annulled in July 1445 with the cessation of payment of Sir Duncan's pension and the re-classification of Glen Lednock as an estate illegally occupied by Sir Colin of Glenorchy.[36]

By the summer of 1445, then, the ambitions of the Campbells and the Stewarts of Lorn lay in tatters. One man in a particularly vulnerable position was Sir James Stewart, the husband of the dead queen. James, the so-called Black Knight of Lorn, had failed to answer a summons to the parliament of June 1445 and, in consequence, his goods and lands were to be forfeited to the crown unless he submitted to the law within a year.[37] By 22 November 1445 Sir James was clearly contemplating leaving Scotland, although he and his young sons by Joan Beaufort probably did not depart the kingdom until shortly after 20 November 1447, on which date he obtained a four-year safe-conduct to pass through England to France and elsewhere.[38] The Stewarts of Lorn suffered another blow with the death of James's brother, Robert, Lord Lorn, sometime before 15 March 1449, by which date Robert's son, John, had succeeded to the lordship.

One of the earliest acts of the new lord of Lorn was to contract a marriage between his daughter, Janet, and Colin Campbell of Glenorchy. On 15 March 1449, at Sir Colin's 'castle of Glen Orchy', John gave over to Colin and Janet a considerable estate in Braelorn to be held by the couple and their male heirs.[39] Despite the later ramifications of the marriage John's choice of son-in-law was hardly surprising, for Colin was both a kinsman

[35] *ER* v, 246. For Robert of Callendar's career in the service of the Livingstones see A. R. Borthwick, 'The King, Council and Councillors in Scotland, c.1430–1460' (Edinburgh University Ph.D. thesis, 1989), i, 71–2.

[36] *ER* v, 205, 246–9. Glen Lednock had not appeared on the charge side of the 1444 account for Strathearn, perhaps indicating that it was, at that stage, part of Sir Colin's 'bailiary' within the earldom: *ER* v, 173. In 1445–6 the lands of Glen Lednock still only produced £5 of the expected £30.

[37] J. Pinkerton, *The History of Scotland from the accession of the House of Stuart to that of Mary, with Appendixes of Original Papers* (London 1797), i, 477, Appendix XIV; R. Nicholson, *Scotland: The Later Middle Ages* (Edinburgh 1974), 342–3.

[38] *CDS* iv, no. 1181. A year long safe-conduct was issued on 22 Nov. 1445: ibid., no. 1203.

[39] NAS, Breadalbane Coll., GD112/1/7. One small obstacle in the way of the union was that Sir Colin was already married to Dame Janet Borthwick, Lady Dalkeith. However, on 7 May 1449 Colin obtained an annulment of the marriage to Janet on the grounds that he had enjoyed a prior relationship with a woman who was related to her in the fourth degree of consanguinity: *Argyll Trans.*, 7 May 1449.

and (in the circumstances of the 1440s) a trusted political ally. The strengthening of the political and social ties between Lorn and the Campbells of Lochawe through the marriage of Janet and Colin became evident in the families' co-ordinated response to the major political crises of James II's reign and, in particular, the king's confrontation with the Douglas earls during the 1450s. The first indication of the end of the king's minority and James's growing political independence came in the autumn of 1449. On 20 September 1449 James Livingstone, onetime guardian of the king, and a number of his kinsmen and adherents, including Robert Callendar, custodian of Dumbarton and Dunoon, were arrested on the orders of James II.[40] While Duncan Campbell immediately reoccupied the royal estates of Glendaruel which had been held by Robert Callendar, there was no indication of any wider political gains by the Campbells or their Stewart kinsmen in the wake of the rapid collapse of the Livingstone faction.[41]

It was not long, however, before James II's political aggression offered more substantial opportunities to Duncan Campbell and the Stewarts of Lorn. A simmering dispute between William, eighth Earl of Douglas and James erupted in spectacular fashion on 22 February 1452 when Earl William was killed by the king and a number of his retainers during a meeting between the two men in Stirling Castle.[42] In the months after Earl William's death, James II cast around for the political and military support which would enable him to ride out the crisis provoked by the death of the head of the most powerful magnate family in the Scottish kingdom. In June 1452 James held a parliament in Edinburgh in order to give official sanction to his slaying of William, eighth Earl of Douglas, and to organise support in his continuing struggle with the earl's relatives.[43] The parliament also saw the showering of royal patronage on those prepared to support the crown, including Duncan Campbell and John Stewart, lord of Lorn, both of whom attended the gathering in Edinburgh.[44] One of the most significant royal concessions saw the king give his approval to a radical

---

40 McGladdery, *James II*, 172.
41 *ER* v, 414. There was less joy for Duncan elsewhere in Cowal, as the fortress of Dunoon was claimed in the immediate aftermath of Callendar's disgrace by Walter Graham. At the same time, Walter's nephew, Patrick, Lord Graham, replaced Callendar as keeper of Dumbarton: *ER* v, 411, 414, 418. The Grahams' domination of the Clyde fortresses was short-lived, for in July 1450 Dunoon was handed over to William Turnbull, bishop of Glasgow, one of James II's loyalest councillors, and, after Turnbull's death, it was given over to the bishop of Argyll: *ER* v, 456; McGladdery, *James II*, 49.
42 Ibid., 66–7.
43 Ibid., 78–9.
44 Ibid., 78–9; Both men witnessed Bishop Kennedy's 'Golden Charter' of 14 Jun. 1452: *RMS* ii, no. 1444; *APS* ii, 73.

reworking of the inheritance to the lordship of Lorn. In 1452, John Stewart was probably in his early fifties and, given his byname, he may have been suffering from the onset of a chronic and debilitating disease. It would be understandable, therefore, if John's thoughts were increasingly directed towards the need to provide for his succession and to secure the future of his lordship. John was 'blessed' with a number of illegitimate sons, but his only canonically legitimate children were his three daughters, one of whom was already betrothed to Colin Campbell of Glenorchy.[45] John's marital status in 1452 is uncertain, although he left an unidentified widow when he died in 1463.[46] It seems likely that this woman was the mother of John's daughters and of an age in 1452 to make the appearance of any further legitimate children unlikely.[47] The political situation in 1452, however, allowed John to make alternative arrangements for the preservation of Lorn as a Stewart lordship. The Auchinleck chronicler, running through the various gifts made by the king in the course of the parliament of June 1452, noted that 'the lord of Lorne John Stewart talzeit all his landis to the male and surname in the said parliament'.[48] James II's charters in favour of John Stewart were issued on 20 June 1452, and confirmed to John the lordship of Lorn, along with the baronies of Innermeath and Redcastle, with a detailed entail in favour of John's brothers Walter, Alan, David, and Robert and their heirs male in succession, whom failing, the male lines descending from John's uncle Archibald Stewart, Sir James Stewart and John's cousin Thomas Stewart.[49]

There is little indication that Duncan Campbell and Colin of Glenorchy objected to an entail which effectively annulled any claim Sir Colin might have to inherit part of the lordship of Lorn through his wife Janet. Significantly, the Campbells were also the beneficiaries of considerable royal largesse during the parliament of June 1452. The Auchinleck chronicler noted that both Duncan and Colin received legally dubious grants of 'sundry landis' from the king during the parliament.[50] On 19

---

45   Aside from Dougall, John also had an illegitimate son named Alexander: NAS, John MacGregor Collection, GD50/1/54.

46   Argyll Trans., 29 Apr. 1466.

47   Traditional sources suggest that John Stewart's wife and the mother of his legitimate children was a daughter of a Lord of the Isles: Stewart and Stewart, *Stewarts of Appin*, 62.

48   McGladdery, *James II*, 166.

49   *RMS* ii, no. 573. On the same day the king confirmed the annexation of estates scattered through Strathearn, Kinross, Fife and Forteviot to the barony of Innermeath (Innerdunning, Baldinnies, Coldrain, Maw, 'Coltrane', Kildinny): ibid., no. 574.

50   McGladdery, *James II*, 166. The grants involved the heritable alienation of crown lands. The Auchinleck Chronicler emphasised that the gifts had been made on the advice of the 'king's secret counsall' rather than approved by parliament, and suggested that in the opinion of many the grants could not be maintained in the long term.

June 1452, Duncan, Lord Campbell received heritable title to the third of Glendaruel held by the crown which was granted to him as a free barony called 'Kanloch-Rowel' (Kinlochruel), ostensibly for his service to James II's father at the siege of Roxburgh Castle in 1436–7.[51] Duncan must have returned to Cowal directly from the June parliament in which James II had made arrangements for the gathering of a royal host at Pentlandmuir on 8 July to carry war against the Douglas earls. On 6 July, in a charter issued from Kilmun, Duncan passed on the lands of Kinlochruel to one of his grandsons, Colin Neilson Campbell of Ormidale in return for Colin's service to the king and Duncan.[52] Colin Neilson's prospective service to the king was undoubtedly related to the imminent royal campaign in the south, which saw James's army marching through the country around Peebles, Selkirk and Dumfries.[53]

Sir Colin Campbell of Glenorchy was another beneficiary of the king's generosity in the June parliament, receiving a pension of forty merks from the crown lands around Loch Tay.[54] The king may have had particular reason to reward Campbell of Glenorchy's loyalty in 1452 as a man with recent connections to the murdered earl of Douglas. In November 1450 Sir Colin had obtained an English safe-conduct to accompany Earl William on his celebrated visit to Rome during the papal jubilee, thus earning his Gaelic byname *Colin dubh na Roimh* (Black Colin of Rome).[55]

By the end of 1452, then, the future of the lordship of Lorn seemed secure. Title to Lorn was destined to pass, in the first instance, to John's brother Walter and his male heirs. Even if Walter's line failed, then the entail of 1452 meant that the wider Stewart of Lorn kindred were unlikely to be displaced from the lordship. Colin Campbell of Glenorchy seems to have been prepared to live with the implications of the entail and there was certainly no attempt to annul his marriage to Janet Stewart. Indeed, in 1454, two years after the entailing of Lorn, Colin and his wife sought and received a papal dispensation allowing their marriage despite the fact that

---

[51] *RMS* ii, no. 571. The charter may well have been couched in these terms to justify the alienation of royal lands by presenting them as a reward for services already rendered to the crown and perhaps to suggest that the Campbells had an established record of supporting the monarchy in times of political crisis. In reality, of course, the grants were intended to secure Campbell support in the king's immediate political struggle with the Black Douglases: *ER* vi, 48–9, 427–8, 536, 632.

[52] *RMS* iv, no. 791.

[53] McGladdery, *James II*, 166.

[54] *ER* v, 542, 657.

[55] *CDS* iv, no. 1229, 9 Nov. 1450, where Colin appears as Sir Nicholas Campbell; Nicholas was often used in documents of English provenance for the name Colin. Campbell tradition claimed that Colin visited Rome three times, and at least two expeditions, including the 1450 jubilee trip, can be verified: *Taymouth Book*, 13–14.

they were within the forbidden degrees of consanguinity.[56] The couple received the papal letters from George Lauder, bishop of Argyll at Inishail in Lochawe, in the presence of John Stewart and Colin Campbell, the new Lord Campbell, who had succeeded to that title and the lordship of Lochawe on the death of his grandfather Duncan in 1453. The fact that Colin of Lochawe, who was created first earl of Argyll in 1457/8, eventually married Janet's sister Isabel, confirms that John Stewart and his family did not view their Campbell neighbours as a danger to the operation of the 1452 entail.[57] Indeed, the Campbell marriages apparently helped to secure the Stewart succession by providing the problematic 'heiresses' with husbands who were kinsmen and allies of the lord of Lorn. Within a decade, however, John Stewart, the architect of the successful settlement of 1452, would bring the Stewart hold on Lorn to the brink of destruction. There would be many prepared to assist him in this enterprise.

Storms at Sea

The first indication of the problems which would engulf the lordship of Lorn in the 1460s occurred shortly after the death of James II at the siege of Roxburgh on 3 August 1460.[58] In the immediate aftermath of King James's demise a fierce dynastic struggle broke out within the MacDougall kindred in Lorn. It drew in a number of outside powers, including Colin Campbell, earl of Argyll, in support of the rival candidates for control of the MacDougall lordship. The stakes were high, for the MacDougall lords of Dunollie occupied a unique and powerful position within the lordship of Lorn.

The Dunollie family was descended from John *Gallda*, the last MacDougall lord of Lorn,[59] who had died sometime in the period 1371 × 7 leaving two legitimate daughters Isabel and Janet.[60] John, however, also left an 'illegitimate' son Allan, who would undoubtedly have been regarded as the leader of the kindred after his father's death.[61] Unfortunately for

---

56 NAS, Breadalbane Coll., GD112/1/7. It was noted that James II had supplicated on behalf of the couple.

57 The exact date of Colin and Isabel's marriage is unknown. The couple were certainly married by December 1462: NAS, Reg. Ho. Charters, RH6/372. The fact that Colin was arranging a marriage for his *second* daughter, Katherine, on 6 Feb. 1465 suggests that his liaison with Isabel Stewart must have commenced in the 1450s: Argyll Trans., 6 Feb. 1465.

58 McGladdery, *James II*, 169.

59 See Table II in David Sellar's essay, above, p. 194.

60 John was still apparently alive on 12 Oct. 1371: *Highland Papers*, ii, 147, 148 n.1. According to Fordun's chronicle, after John's death his widow married Malcolm Fleming of Biggar: *Chron. Fordun*, i, 369 n.17. In 1377 a Johanna of Lorn received a papal dispensation to marry Malcolm Fleming: Theiner, *Vetera Monumenta*, 362.

61 W. D. H. Sellar, 'MacDougall pedigrees in MS 1467', *Notes and Queries of the Society of West Highland and Island Historical Research*, 1st ser., xxix (Aug. 1986), 7-8.

Allan, the king at the time of John *Gallda*'s demise, Robert II, may have felt compelled to intervene in the Lorn inheritance in 1377 for dynastic rather than simply territorial reasons. Robert II had come to the throne in 1371 as the half-nephew and heir of David II (1329–71), but the relationship between the two men had been poor for most of David's reign and on a number of occasions King David had attempted to amend the succession in order to by-pass Robert.[62] John *Gallda*'s wife, the mother of Isabel and Janet, was Johanna Isaac, the niece of David II.[63] Thus, as far as David II was concerned, the heirs of John *Gallda*'s marriage to Johanna may have represented a possible alternative line of succession to Robert and his family, and it is significant that King David displayed considerable favour towards the lord of Lorn and his 'royal' bride in the period after 1357.[64] Having earned the suspicion of the future King Robert, the waning of John *Gallda*'s fortunes after 1371 was perhaps inevitable.[65] In the years after his accession Robert pursued a number of policies designed to secure the position of his new royal dynasty. Most notably, on 4 April 1373, a parliament meeting at Scone approved the creation of a male entail, naming Robert's five sons and their male heirs in order of seniority, to regulate the descent of the kingship after Robert II's death.[66] The demise of John *Gallda* in c.1376–7 allowed the cautious king to neutralise the residual claims to the throne vested in the lord of Lorn's widow and her two daughters by marrying the women off to his own adherents. Johanna Isaac was betrothed to Malcolm Fleming of Biggar, while Isabel and Janet were married to two brothers from a cadet branch of the Stewarts, John Stewart of Innermeath (the grandfather of leper John) and Robert Stewart of Durisdeer.[67]

John *Gallda*'s son, Allan, who might otherwise have been able to ignore the claims of his half-sisters to the lands and lordship of Lorn, thus found himself facing powerful and well-connected adversaries. The terms on which Allan, as the chief of the established ruling lineage in Lorn, eventually

---

62 Boardman, *Early Stewart Kings*, 8–9, 19–22; A. A. M. Duncan, 'Honi soit qui mal y pense: David II and Edward III, 1346–52', *SHR* lxvii (1988), 113–41; A. A. M. Duncan, 'A question about the succession, 1364', *Miscellany of the Scottish History Society*, xii (1994), 1–57.

63 *Chron. Bower*, vi, 377; vii, 275.

64 *ER* ii, 352; *RMS* i, no. 237; *RRS* vi, no. 165. John of Lorn's marriage to Johanna took place before Aug. 1362: *ER* ii, 106. It seems likely that the association between David and John developed in England after David's capture at Neville's Cross. John's by-name *Gallda* (the foreigner) probably derived from the fact that he had been brought up in England after his grandfather and father (Allan) had been forced into exile by Robert I and his supporters early in the 14th century.

65 Boardman, *Early Stewart Kings*, 76.

66 *APS* i, 549.

67 *Chron. Fordun*, i, 369 n.17.

accepted his new Stewart overlords in the second half of the fourteenth century may well be preserved in a charter granted by Leper John to Allan's son and grandson in January 1451.[68] By the terms of the 'gift' Stewart gave over to 'John Allani de lorn, nominato makdowil' and his first-born son John *Ciar* (left-handed) a great tract of land inside the lordship of Lorn. The charter probably did no more than confirm the MacDougalls in possession of lands which they held as the descendants of John *Gallda*. More striking were the offices confirmed to the MacDougalls. These included the bailiary of all the lord of Lorn's lands in the lordship with the care and fosterage of the lord's heir. While John Stewart and his heirs were to receive one third of the revenue from the lands granted to the MacDougall lords, John Allanson and John *Ciar* were to collect one third of the income from all the lands of Lorn. In return, the MacDougalls were to support Stewart 'by land and sea' against all mortal men, the king excepted.[69]

Effectively, the MacDougalls had retained possession of most of their estates and, through the hereditary bailieship, a claim to exercise a wider political and social leadership inside Lorn under the Stewart lords. The privileged position of the MacDougalls of Dunollie was further attested and guaranteed by their hereditary right to foster the heirs to the Stewart lordship.[70]

The immediate aim of John Stewart's formal grant of 1451, however, was to head off an attempt to displace John *Ciar* as the heir to his father's lands, offices and title. John *Ciar* was under threat from his younger half-brother Allan 'of the Wood', the son of John Allanson and Fingula of the Isles. In 1447 John Allanson had supplicated the pope to allow his marriage to Fingula, despite the canonical impediments, and to legitimise their children retrospectively.[71] Fingula was probably the sister of Donald *Balloch* (freckled), the head of Clan Donald south and the most powerful aristocrat in the southern Hebrides. The Auchinleck Chronicle certainly later identified Allan 'of the Wood' as Donald's nephew.[72] John *Ciar* thus had every reason to be apprehensive about his position in the years after 1447 as he faced the challenge of a recently legitimised young half-brother

68 Argyll Trans., 4 Jan. 1451.
69 This phrase is similar to the stipulation found in contemporary Campbell charters that the recipient should render 'special retinue' service to their Campbell lords.
70 See K. Nicholls, *Gaelic and Gaelicised Ireland in the Middle Ages* (Dublin 1972), 79, for a brief treatment of the political/social significance of fosterage.
71 *CSSR* v, no. 101; *CPL* x, 336. The supplication was made simply in the name of John of Lorn. It seems unlikely that this referred to John *Ciar*, since as John son of John of Lorn he had supplicated the pope to legitimise his relationship with Margaret daughter of Murdoch MacLean in 1441: *CSSR* iv, no. 807. It also seems unlikely that the John of Lorn supplicating the pope in 1447 could have been John Stewart, because the latter would have been styled lord *of* Lorn.
72 McGladdery, *James II*, 170.

whose ambitions were supported by the formidable Donald *Balloch* and, apparently, by John's own father.

In these circumstances it is hardly surprising that John *Ciar* sought outside assistance to maintain his hold on the MacDougall inheritance. A natural source of support would have been John's maternal kinsmen. The identity of John's mother is uncertain, but there is a possibility that she was a daughter of Duncan Campbell of Lochawe.[73] John Stewart's charter of 1451 clearly indicated that John *Ciar* also enjoyed the backing of the lord of Lorn, but perhaps the most significant aspect of the grant was that it was issued at Ardtornish in Morvern on the shores of the sound of Mull. Ardtornish was a stronghold of John MacDonald, earl of Ross and Lord of the Isles. Earl John was a close kinsman of Donald *Balloch*, but he may also have been related to the lord of Lorn, who is reputed to have married the daughter of an unnamed Lord of the Isles.[74] Stewart was certainly an occasional witness to the earl of Ross's charters and had appeared as a member of his council in Dingwall Castle on 28 May 1450.[75] Moreover, John *Ciar* may have had other allies in the Isles, notably his brother-in-law John MacLean of Lochbuie, prepared to plead his case before the earl of Ross.[76] In any case the 1451 charter, which gave over the MacDougall lands and offices to John Allanson *and* John *Ciar* (pointedly described as John Allanson's first-born son), was clearly issued with Ross's approval. The grant may well represent the results of an arbitration presided over by Earl John at Ardtornish, as Ross and his council sought to avoid a confrontation over the MacDougall inheritance which had the potential to pitch Donald *Balloch* and his allies against the Stewart lord of Lorn and the Campbells of Lochawe.

Secured in his inheritance and apparently backed by Ross, John Stewart of Lorn, and the Campbells of Lochawe, John *Ciar* could face the future with renewed confidence. Indeed, John may well have been able to exclude his rival from land and influence inside Lorn after 1451; certainly Allan's byname 'of the Wood' seems to indicate a considerable period spent as the leader of an 'outlaw' band.

73 The Auchinleck Chronicler described Colin Campbell, 1st earl of Argyll, as John *Ciar*'s cousin: ibid. One later Campbell genealogy gives Duncan a daughter called Mary 'of Lorn', perhaps the wife of John Allanson of Lorn and the mother of John *Ciar*. I am indebted to David Sellar for this reference and suggestion. For an alternative and plausible explanation of the relationship between Earl Colin and John *Ciar*, see K. A. Steer and J. W. M. Bannerman, *Late Medieval Monumental Sculpture in the West Highlands and Islands* (Edinburgh 1977), 136; *Black Book of Taymouth*, 11–13; and *Scottish Verse from the Book of the Dean of Lismore*, ed. W. J. Watson (Scottish Gaelic Texts Soc., 1937), 175.

74 Stewart and Stewart, *Stewarts of Appin*, 62.

75 *ALI*, nos. 51, 54.

76 *CSSR* iv, no. 807; for John MacLean as an occasional witness to the charters of Ross and his father Alexander, see *ALI*, nos. 21, 42, 51, 73, 76, 96.

The death of James II in 1460, however, saw Allan mount a spectacular comeback. The Auchinleck chronicler noted that shortly after the king's decease 'John Keir of Lorne ... was tane be his brother Allane of Lorne of the wod, sister son to downe balloch' and imprisoned on the Isle of Kerrera in Oban Bay. John *Ciar*'s position was desperate for, according to the Auchinleck chronicler, Allan intended 'to distroye him [so] that he [Allan] mycht have succedit to the heretage'. John was saved by the dramatic intervention of his cousin Colin Campbell, earl of Argyll, who steered his galley-host to Lorn and unleashed a devastating sea-borne assault on Allan and his men on Kerrera. Taken by surprise, Allan's force, unable to escape in its galleys which were set afire as Earl Colin's men fought their way ashore, was almost utterly destroyed. Allan himself escaped 'richt narowly with his lyf', but John *Ciar* was liberated and restored to his lordship.[77]

Allan's desperate flight from Kerrera across the bows of the Campbell galleys as they drove into Oban Bay, and the ruthless destruction of his military following, might suggest that his renewed ambitions had suffered a swift and fatal blow. Despite the carnage on Kerrera, however, Allan of the Wood was not yet a spent force; the nephew of Donald *Balloch* would make one more dramatic contribution to the story of the lordship of Lorn.

The attempted coup against John *Ciar* in the winter of 1460/1 and Earl Colin's belligerent response were simply the opening shots in a contest for regional dominance between Argyll and Donald *Balloch*. Away to the south of Lorn the two men clashed again in a struggle for control of the seaways of the Firth of Clyde and, in particular, the isle of Arran. Arran had long been vulnerable to the political and military power of the various branches of Clan Donald south based in Kintyre and Knapdale. From the 1430s to the 1450s 'royal' estates in the north of the island had been occupied by one Ranald MacAlexander who consistently refused to render ferms to the king, while other 'crown' estates were frequently recorded as being 'waste' due to the depredations of the *maledictos invasores* of Kintyre and Knapdale.[78] Occasional attempts by the crown or its agents to impose effective lordship in Arran met with little success. On

77 McGladdery, *James II*, 170.
78 For Ranald MacAlexander's lands, see *ER* v, 86, 165, 211–12, 251, 289, 333–4, 359, 365, 575–6; vi, 44, 327–8; and for references to the activities of 'invaders' from Knapdale and Kintyre, ibid., v, 167, 213, 253. The identity of Ranald MacAlexander is uncertain; he may have been a close kinsman of Donald *Balloch* or a member of the Clan Alexander, a branch of Clan Donald apparently descended from Alexander, son of Angus *Mór*: *ALI*, Appendix D, 279–81, no. 5; K. Nicholls, 'Notes on the genealogy of Clann Eoin Mhoir', *West Highland Notes and Queries*, 2nd ser., viii (Nov. 1991), 11–12. I should like to thank David Sellar for referring me to this article.

14 April 1452, for example, James II granted a ten-year lease of the right to uplift the ferms of the king's lands in Bute, Arran and Cowal along with the great customs of Ayr, Irvine and Dumbarton to William Turnbull, bishop of Glasgow.[79] In the following month the king gifted Kinlochransay (Lochranza) and the other 'royal' estates which had been long occupied by Ranald MacAlexander to Alexander, Lord Montgomery and his heirs.[80] It seems likely that Lord Montgomery was to act as the bishop's secular arm in an attempt to facilitate the collection of royal rents in Arran by breaking Ranald MacAlexander's hold on the island. Montgomery was notably unsuccessful, however, in his attempt to dislodge MacAlexander. By the summer of 1453 Bishop Turnbull had given up the attempt to extract revenues from Arran and had assigned over his right to all crown rents from the island to Ranald, who from then on until his death in 1457/8 simply uplifted for his own use all the rents and duties due to the king from the island.[81] It is tempting to view the attempt by James II, Bishop Turnbull and Lord Montgomery to recover control of Arran in 1452 as the provocation for the great raid on the Firth of Clyde undertaken by Donald *Balloch* 'with the powere of the Isles with him' at around this time, although the description of the expedition provided by the Auchinleck Chronicler seems to suggest a date in 1454.[82] Donald's campaign graphically illustrated the military resources at his disposal and the ability of his galley forces to hit targets across the Firth of Clyde. After devastating Inverkip on the Renfrewshire coast, Donald 'with his ost of the Isles' harried Arran and the two Cumbraes, and took a levy from the inhabitants of Bute. That Arran was the prime target for Donald's campaign, however, is indicated by the fact that the king's castle of Brodick was beseiged, taken

---

79 *RMS* ii, no. 542. The grant was made to repay Turnbull for 800 merks he had diverted from the sum raised by the diocese for the papal jubilee to support the king in his struggle with the Douglas earls.

80 Ibid., no. 563.

81 *ER* vi, 44, 229, 327–9, 419.

82 McGladdery, *James II*, 167–8. The raid has been assigned to every year from 1452 to 1455 on the basis of the Auchinleck Chronicle's description of a meeting between James Douglas, brother of the deceased William, 8th Earl of Douglas, and John, Earl of Ross in Knapdale on 12 May (year unidentified) as a prelude to Donald's attack on Inverkip (10 Jul.). The episode between these two entries, the king's siege of Blackness Castle, is specifically said to have occurred in the same month and year as the Knapdale meeting and can be shown to date to the summer of 1454: M. Brown, *The Black Douglases: War and Lordship in Late Medieval Scotland, 1300–1455* (East Linton 1998). It is interesting to note that the description of Donald's raid is less securely linked to the Blackness episode and is followed by an entry relating to events of August 1452. Moreover, a general raid on Arran in the summer of 1454 makes little sense if Ranald MacAlexander was an ally of Donald *Balloch*. If it took place in 1454 the raid may have been designed specifically to strike against areas still held by crown agents, such as Brodick Castle.

and then 'kest ... down to the erd'.[83] The destruction of Brodick suggests a deliberate attempt to disrupt the crown's ability to intervene in Arran in the long term, and implies that Donald's interest in the island extended beyond occasional raiding.

The death of Donald's ally Ranald MacAlexander in 1457-8 allowed the crown and others to reassert their interests in the island, and by the summer of that year Lord Montgomery made good the king's grant of 1452 by occupying the estates at the head of Lochranza which had lain at the heart of Ranald's influence in the island.[84] The demise of James II, however, flung the tentative revival of crown influence in the Firth of Clyde into reverse. In the wake of the king's death Donald *Balloch* and his supporters once again reoccupied the vulnerable crown estates on Arran, and the exchequer auditors of July 1462 gloomily declared Arran to be utterly 'waste' in terms of the rentals delivered to the crown.[85] The importance of Arran to Clan Donald south was illustrated by the specific provisions made for the island in the famous (and much misunderstood) treaty concluded in February 1462 between the English king Edward IV on the one hand and John, Lord of the Isles, Donald *Balloch*, and John of the Isles, Donald's son and heir, on the other.[86] The treaty stipulated that if Edward IV concluded a truce with the government of the young James III after Whitsunday 1462 (by which stage the three islesmen were due to have become liegemen of the English king) then Edward was to ensure that Ross, Donald *Balloch* and his son John were to be included in the peace. In particular the lordships, lands and possessions of the three men within Scotland, 'and also the island of Arran', were to be safeguarded in any pacification between Edward IV and James III.

While Ross and Donald *Balloch* dabbled in negotiations with the English king, the years after James II's death saw the earl of Argyll consolidate his position as the political and military mainstay of James III's minority government in the west. During 1460 the earl recovered possession of the vital castle of Dunoon and became the royal bailie for the wider lordship of Cowal, grants which may well have been inspired by the renewed threat of Donald *Balloch* in the Firth of Clyde.[87] The defence of the northern reaches of the Firth of Clyde was now in the hands of a magnate capable of responding in kind to the maritime raids of Clan Donald south. By 1462 Earl Colin and the royal administration were preparing to go on

---

[83] McGladdery, *James II*, 168.

[84] *ER* vi, 531.

[85] Ibid., vii, 109.

[86] *ALI*, no. 75; *Foedera, Conventiones, Litterae, et Cuiuscunque Generis Acta Publica*, ed. T. Rymer (London 1704-35), xi, 484-7; *Rot. Scot.*, ii, 405-7.

[87] HMC, *Fourth Report*, Appendix, 480.

the offensive. The anxiety displayed by Donald *Balloch* during his negotiations with the English crown over the position of Arran proved to be well founded. During or shortly after the exchequer session of July 1462 the thankless task of uplifting the crown rents from Arran was assigned to, or was assumed by, Earl Colin.[88] Earl Colin's family had an ancient but apparently moribund claim to Lochranza Castle and other estates on the island through a mid-fourteenth-century grant by John Menteith, lord of Knapdale and Arran in favour of Gill-easbuig Campbell, Earl Colin's great-great-grandfather.[89] Having already intervened success-fully to frustrate Donald *Balloch*'s ambitions in Lorn, Earl Colin was now being given an open invitation to take on Clan Donald south in the Firth of Clyde. While war gathered in the south in 1462, however, events were also moving swiftly in the lordship of Lorn. John Stewart was about to make a last desperate and ill-advised gamble with the future of his inheritance. The fates would not be kind to Leper John.

A Lord Forlorn?

Earl Colin's successful defence of the rights of John *Ciar* in the MacDougall lordship may have temporarily stabilised the lordship of Lorn, but in 1462 a new succession crisis was taking shape, this time affecting the Stewarts of Lorn. On 11 December 1462, at Inistrynich on Loch Awe, Earl Colin and Walter Stewart, the brother and 'apperande ayr' of John Stewart, lord of Lorn, entered into an agreement by which the earl pledged to defend Walter and his heirs against any attempt by John to cancel or amend the terms of the 1452 entail.[90] If John did attempt to change the succession arrangements then Argyll, who was highly influential at the court of the young James III, was to allow 'na thing [to] ga throu in preve nor in apertht [openly]'. The price of Argyll's support for Walter Stewart's position as the heir to Lorn was high. Walter agreed that in return for the earl's 'supple, mantenans, defens and resisting of al and sundry' he would assign over to Colin one hundred merks-worth of land within Lorn. In particular, Earl Colin and his heirs were to have all the lands between Loch Awe and Loch Etive, with the remainder 'al togeder in maist comptent plasis to the said lorde erll' either around 'Erdmaddy' (Ardmaddy) or in Benderloch.[91]

---

88 *ER* vii, 385–6; 405–6.
89 As recently as 13 May 1433, however, Duncan Campbell of Lochawe had had a notarial instrument drawn up recording the terms of the grant: Argyll Trans., 13 May 1433.
90 NAS, Reg. Ho. Charters, RH6/372.
91 Ibid. In addition to the Lorn lands, Stewart agreed to give Argyll a charter for 20 merks-worth of land in the Perthshire barony of Innermeath. Walter was to give the earl 'lachfull charter' of the 120 merks-worth of land as soon as he was given sasine of the lordship of Lorn, 'be in heyland and lowlande'. Argyll and his wife,

The indenture at Inistrynich confirms the essential elements of the traditional Stewart of Appin tale. By December 1462, John Stewart was clearly attempting to revise the descent of the entailed lands of Lorn, Innermeath and Redcastle. Walter Stewart, the chief beneficiary of the threatened 1452 entail, was sufficiently convinced of the seriousness of John's intentions to promise huge concessions from the Lorn and Innermeath estates to Earl Colin, John's son-in-law, an influential figure at the royal court and a powerful local magnate, in the hope that the earl could maintain Walter's position as John's heir. The alliance between John's brother and the husband of one of John's legitimate daughters indicates that the lord of Lorn's proposed revision of the 1452 entail threatened the interests of both men, and there is little reason to doubt the view that John *Mourach* was, in his twilight years, attempting to secure the lordship for his 'illegitimate' son.[92]

John Stewart's plans made little headway before his assassination on 20 December 1463 in Dunstaffnage Castle by one Allan MacCoule or MacDougall.[93] It seems more than likely that this Allan was the tenacious Allan of the Wood, at last revenged on one of the men who had consistently supported his brother in the struggle for control of the MacDougall lordship.[94] Despite Earl Colin's obvious interest in stopping John's plans for the descent of the lordship of Lorn there is little to suggest that the

Isabel Stewart, also agreed to give up all right and claim they had to the entailed lands associated with the lordship of Lorn. The earl further promised to assist Walter in defending the third of the unentailed lands to which Isabel Stewart had claim as John, Lord Lorn's heiress of line.

92 Although the Inistrynich indenture does not specifically name the potential beneficiaries of John Stewart's revision, Earl Colin was charged with preventing the inheritance passing to 'ony man that pertenes to' Lord Lorn.

93 *Chronicle of Fortingall*, in *Taymouth Book*, 113; *APS* xii, Supplements, 31.

94 Traditional histories insist that Allan of the Wood and the assassin of the lord of Lorn were different men. This notion, however, is clearly derived from the work of the 16th-century chronicler Hector Boece. Boece's work was informed by a desire to exhibit the effectiveness of Scottish royal government in previous ages. As part of this programme, Boece was prone to rewrite episodes involving outrageous acts of disorder to suggest that the perpetrators of violence were the subject of swift retribution. See R. Mason, 'Chivalry and citizenship: aspects of national identity in Renaissance Scotland', in R. Mason and N. Macdougall (eds.), *People and Power in Scotland* (Edinburgh 1992), 61. Boece's claim that Allan of the Wood was captured by the earl of Argyll in 1460 and died in captivity shortly after is flatly refuted by the contemporary Auchinleck Chronicle, which stresses that Allan was one of the few men to escape from the slaughter on Kerrera; cf. Hector Boethius, *Scotorum Historiae* (2nd edn, Paris 1574), 383. For another example, see Boece's description of the probably fictitious imprisonment of Alexander Stewart, earl of Buchan, after his burning of Elgin cathedral in 1390: *The Chronicles of Scotland compiled by Hector Boece, translated into Scots by John Bellenden, 1531* (Scottish Text Soc., 1938–41), ii, 353; I am grateful to Charles Borden, M.Sc. student in the Department of Scottish History, University of Edinburgh, for this observation.

earl had connived in the assassination; indeed, Allan MacDougall's capture of Dunstaffnage in the aftermath of John's death struck a major blow against Campbell ambitions in the region. Stewart's death, then, appears to have resulted simply from his involvement in the disputed MacDougall succession, but it had a major effect on the wider struggle for regional dominance in the west. A parliament held in the early months of 1464 (and probably called in response to news of Lorn's death) expressed the outrage of the estates over the death of the king's kinsman, and called for James III to make a personal expedition to the west to punish Allan and recapture Dunstaffnage when the weather would allow royal forces to campaign in the region.[95] Significantly, royal letters were also sent to John, Earl of Ross, commanding him not to offer any support to Allan in his occupation of the castle. Earl John and, more particularly, his kinsman Donald *Balloch* could be expected to provide substantial assistance to the new MacDougall lord in Dunstaffnage in his renewed bid to assume a dominant role within Lorn. In fact, however, Lorn's death seems to have been a significant turning-point in the stormy relationship between Ross and the minority government of James III. The men who dominated the young king's administration had every reason to find a way to curb or conciliate Earl John. Since James II's death the forces of the lordship had been on the offensive against a wide range of targets over an area which stretched from Orkney to Arran.[96] Perhaps most seriously, from the viewpoint of those who moulded crown policy, the earl and his adherents had occupied a number of royal lordships and estates around Inverness and had taken customs revenue from the royal burgh, although Ross may well have claimed to be acting lawfully as sheriff of Inverness.[97] Ross had been summoned to the first parliament of the reign in February 1461, presumably to answer for the actions of his men and kinsmen, but little effective action seems to have been taken against him.[98] Attempts to reach an accommodation with Ross continued sporadically over the next two years, including a delegation headed by Argyll, and Lords Montgomery and Kennedy, which negotiated with the earl sometime in the period July 1462 to August 1463.[99]

Although the demands for the king's direct intervention in Lorn after John Stewart's death went unheeded, in the autumn of 1464 James III was

95 *APS* xii, Supplements, 31.
96 E.g., *Records of the Earldom of Orkney*, ed. J. S. Clouston (SHS 1914), nos. 22–3.
97 *ER* vii, 20, 128–9, 296–7.
98 McGladdery, *James II*, 170.
99 *ER* vii, 204. The fact that two of the crown's representatives, Argyll and Montgomery, were actively pursuing claims in Arran suggests that the activities of Donald *Balloch* were likely to feature prominently in the negotiations.

moved north to confront the earl of Ross.[100] The earldom of Ross and Earl John's interests around Inverness were vulnerable to the application of pressure by the men acting in the name of the young king. By threatening Ross, James III's advisors probably hoped that the earl would be forced to curtail the activities of Clan Donald in other areas. The presence of the earl of Argyll as Master of the King's Household (an office he obtained before 11 April 1464) meant that the price for settlement probably included Earl John's agreement not to threaten Earl Colin's interests in Arran and Lorn. That the arrangements of 1464 saw a personal bargain between Argyll and Ross as well as a settlement between John and the king's Council is suggested by the fact that Earl Colin acted, alongside Gilbert, Lord Kennedy, as Ross's representative in the parliament of October 1464.[101]

Donald *Balloch* may have been less than happy with John's apparent willingness to abandon the claims of Donald and his adherents in Lorn and Arran in order to protect his own position in Ross. Tensions within Clan Donald over the settlement of 1464 may have contributed to the attacks made on Donald *Balloch* and his family in their Irish lordships during the following year. In the spring of 1465 the *Annals of Ulster* record the death of Donald *Balloch*'s son Angus, 'slain ... by John, son of Alexander. And Domnall, son of the bishop MacDomnaill, it was that mortally struck him with one stroke of a sword'.[102] Later in the same year the Ulster annalist noted the death of another of Donald *Balloch*'s kinsmen, his nephew 'John, son of Alexander, son of John MacDomnaill Mor', at the hands of the O'Neills of Clandeboye.[103]

The withdrawal of Ross's active support and the problems in and around his lordship of the Glens of Antrim seem to have hamstrung Donald's efforts to defend his agents in Arran and Lorn. By 1466 Argyll

---

[100] *ER* vii, 296–7.

[101] *APS* ii, 84.

[102] *Ann. Ulster*, iii, 212–13. Interpretation of the incident depends on the identification of the men involved in the attack on Angus. Kenneth Nicholls has suggested that the 'bishop MacDomnaill' was Angus, Bishop of the Isles, a son of Donald, Lord of the Isles; if this were the case, the assassin would have been a cousin of John, Lord of the Isles: Nicholls, 'Genealogy of Clann Eoin Mhoir', 11–12; *ALI*, 300–1; but cf. S. Kingston, 'The Political Development of Ulster and the Lordship of the Isles, 1394–1499' (Oxford University D.Phil. thesis, 1998).

[103] *Ann. Ulster*, iii, 214–15. Kingston, 'Ulster and the Lordship of the Isles', 84–5, suggests plausibly that the origin of this dispute lay in Donald's negotiations with the English crown in 1462–3, and his subsequent policy of support for the inhabitants of the Anglo-Irish burgh of Carrickfergus, traditional enemies of the O'Neills of Clandeboye. The garrison at Carrickfergus had been under the command of the exiled James, Earl of Douglas, since 1463. Douglas had played a leading role in the negotiations which had culminated in the treaty of Ardtornish: Brown, *Black Douglases*, 319.

seems to have cleared Donald's men from Arran. The island was certainly considered an attractive prospect by Robert, Lord Boyd, after he seized control of the young King James on 9 July 1466.[104] Before 22 February 1467, Boyd arranged the transfer of the royal lands in Arran from Argyll to his own son, Thomas, who was also given the title earl of Arran.[105]

Of the position in Lorn in the immediate aftermath of John Stewart's death we can say little. Unsurprisingly, the family history narrated in *The Stewarts of Appin* lays a heavy emphasis on the heroic role of John's son, Dougall Stewart, in the events after his father's death. While young Dougall valiantly attempted to avenge his father, Walter Stewart and Colin Campbell, respectively the murdered lord's brother and son-in-law, were claimed to have displayed a cynical indifference to Lord Lorn's fate.[106] Left without allies, Dougall's first attempt to confront Allan MacDougall was said to have ended in defeat at the battle of Leac-a-dotha on the slopes of Bendoran in Lochawe because, bizarrely, the Campbell earl had encouraged his adherents, the MacFarlanes of Loch Lomond, to intervene on MacDougall's behalf. There may be more substance in the history's assertion that Dougall and his supporters were effectively forced to abandon lower Lorn and Benderloch and flee north of Loch Etive into Appin after John's assassination (an event described in the history as the 'Inveich mor', or 'great flitting'). Eventually, we are informed, Allan MacDougall was killed at the battle of Stalc on the hillside overlooking the island fortress of Castle Stalker, as he attempted to drive Dougall Stewart from his last stronghold in Appin.[107]

The history thus provided a satisfying explanation of the origins of the Appin Stewarts and laid out the family's independent claim to their Appin lands. The tale preserved the fact that Dougall had been regarded in the early 1460s, at least within his father's following, as a potential heir to the entire lordship of Lorn. Dougall and his descendants were thus portrayed as the legitimate heirs of John Stewart, unjustly excluded from a wider inheritance, but secured in Appin by right of descent and through the independent military prowess and valour of Dougall. These themes were undoubtedly important for the Stewarts of Appin after 1463, as they sought to define and defend their lands and status in Appin against the potential claims of the men who obtained title to the lordship of Lorn.

The assumption of Campbell villainy obviously colours the Stewart narrative, but does reflect a very real aspect of the response to John

---

104 N. A. T. Macdougall, *James III* (Edinburgh 1982), 70–5.
105 Ibid., 75; *CDS* iv, no. 1368; *RMS* ii, no. 914.
106 Stewart and Stewart, *Stewarts of Appin*, 80–5.
107 Ibid., 83–5.

Stewart's death, namely the profound disagreements which broke out between Lord Lorn's many potential 'heirs' during 1464.[108]

Early in 1464 Walter Stewart received sasine of the lordship of Lorn and the barony of Innermeath under the terms of the 1452 entail, and by 15 May 1464, five months after his brother's death, Walter was using the style Lord Lorn.[109] Walter's hold on his new inheritance, however, can hardly have been secure. The chief fortress of Lorn, Dunstaffnage, was probably still occupied by his brother's assassin, Allan MacDougall. Moreover, Walter may not have enjoyed the unequivocal support of his brother's retainers and adherents in Lorn given John Stewart's belated attempts to promote Dougall Stewart as his heir. Finally, the shadow of Walter's desperate agreement in the winter of 1462 with Colin, Earl of Argyll must have assumed a darker and more menacing aspect as his ambitions came close to fulfilment. It is impossible to know whether Argyll did, in fact, help to prevent John Stewart's proposed reworking of the 1452 entail, but regardless of the effort expended, Earl Colin would undoubtedly have been keen to enforce the terms of his bargain with Walter. The new lord of Lorn must have known that his onetime ally would soon be pressing claims to the entire territory between Lochawe and Loch Etive.

Once secured in the title to Lorn, Walter appears to have been understandably reluctant to fulfil his obligation to hand over 120 merks-worth of his new lordship to Argyll. Earl Colin's response was to deploy and prosecute the claims of his wife and her sisters, even to estates which had been specifically included in the entail of 1452. As early as May and August 1464 Walter and Argyll were to be found in litigation before the king's court over various elements of the Lorn inheritance. That the succession to John's lands and possessions had become a matter of open dispute was confirmed on 1 July 1464, when Earl Colin and Colin Campbell of Glenorchy granted a bond of maintenance to Thomas Rogerson of Drumdrewin, by which they were bound to defend Rogerson against all men, but especially 'aganys ony of thaim that pretendis thaim ayeris to the ... Lord of Lornis gudis and of all the lave of the forsaid lordis

---

108 The censorious description of the earl of Argyll's self-seeking behaviour after Lord Lorn's death was openly influenced by the work of 19th-century historians available to the editors of the Appin history. Earl Colin's attitudes and ambitions were 'explained' with the help of an extensive quote from Skene's *Highlanders* (first published in 1837), which proclaimed that the political success of the medieval Clan Campbell was built on a 'policy characterised by cunning and perfidy, though deep and far sighted, and which obtained its usual success in the acquisition of great temporal grandeur and power': W. F. Skene, *The Highlanders of Scotland* (2nd edn, ed. A. Macbain, Stirling 1902), 359.

109 Blair Atholl, Blair Castle, Atholl Muniments, Box 7, Parcel IV, no. 4.

barnyis'.[110] Prolonged legal action before the royal courts was hardly in the interests of Walter Stewart. Walter's adversary was Master of the King's Household, a royal justiciar, and a man with real influence in government at the highest level – as Walter himself had recognised when he approached Argyll in 1462 to uphold the entailing of Lorn. Walter was hardly friendless; his brothers and cousins formed an impressive political network with their own claims on James III's favour. In particular, Walter's cousins, John Stewart, earl of Atholl and the earl's younger brothers James and Andrew were the king's half-brothers. Overall, however, Lorn lacked the political strength to match his opponent.

As the 1460s wore on, Argyll's legal campaign began to take its toll. Despite Walter's objections, Earl Colin's wife and her sisters received sasine in the bulk of their father's unentailed lands. These losses may have been anticipated, but the disruption of Walter's hold on estates which had been included in the 1452 entail was much more damaging. In 1465 Earl Colin's wife, Countess Isabel, Marion Stewart, and Duncan Campbell of Glenorchy (the son of Colin of Glenorchy and the third Stewart heiress, Janet) obtained possession of the lands of Kildinny, Innerdunning and Baldinnies.[111] These lands had been annexed to the entailed barony of Innermeath in June 1452 and should, therefore, have passed to Walter after his brother's death.

Earl Colin's relentless legal assault eventually provoked a violent backlash from the lord of Lorn. In April 1465 Isabel Stewart, Duncan Campbell and Marion Stewart each received sasine in one third of the lands of Dollar and Gloom in the barony of Dunkeld as heirs to John, Lord Lorn.[112]

---

110 Atholl Muniments, Box 7, Parcel IV, no. 4, and Box 2, Parcel XVI, no. 3. Rogerson's concern with John, Lord Lorn's 'heirs' was that he had just paid over a sum of money to Earl Colin (acting on behalf of his wife), Duncan Campbell (son of Colin Campbell of Glenorchy and Janet Stewart), and Marion Stewart as 'aieris of umquhile John Stewart, Lord of Lorne' for the partial redemption of lands in Strathyre which he had set in wadset to Lord Lorn on 10 Jan. 1463: *Calendar of the Laing Charters 854–1837*, ed. J. Anderson (Edinburgh 1899), no. 151. Argyll's and Glenorchy's maintenance was clearly related to this financial transaction, with the two men pledging themselves to assist Rogerson against any others, claiming to be Lord Lorn's heirs, who sought to recover the redemption money due from Rogerson for the Strathyre lands.

111 On 16 Aug. 1465 the Lords of Council gave judgement in an action between Earl Colin, his wife Countess Isabel, Marion Stewart and Duncan Campbell of Glenorchy (the son of Colin of Glenorchy and the third Stewart heiress, Janet) on the one hand, and the lord of Lorn on the other. The judgement recorded that a recognition had been made of the lands of Kildinny, Innerdunning and Baldinnies because of the disputes between the parties. Walter, Lord Lorn failed to appear, and the lands were given over to Earl Colin as procurator for his wife. Before the end of the year Walter's opponents had obtained sasine of the lands: Argyll Trans., 20 Aug. 1465.

112 HMC, *4th Rep.*, 483 (nos. 187–9).

Walter's response was vigorous if rather misjudged. A papal writ of April 1466 recorded that shortly after Earl Colin's wife had received possession of the tower of Gloom near Dollar it had been attacked, burnt and destroyed by Walter, Lord Lorn and his men.[113] The effect of the attack was counter-productive, in that it gave Argyll further grounds for litigation. The settlement of Earl Colin's new claims against Walter occurred on 29 April 1466 in Perth in the presence of Andrew, Lord Avandale, the Chancellor, Walter's kinsman, John, Earl of Atholl, and David Guthrie, the royal treasurer. On that date the lord of Lorn granted various lands in Perthshire to Argyll, while Earl Colin gave Walter a charter of reversion for the same lands which could be redeemed once Walter had paid the earl the sum of £433. These arrangements were almost certainly intended to compensate Argyll for Walter's attack on Dollar and the tower of Gloom.[114]

By the end of 1466 the lord of Lorn had been reduced to a parlous position. All of John Stewart's unentailed lands, as well as the estates in Fife, Aberdeenshire, Strathearn and Perthshire which had been annexed to the barony of Innermeath in 1452, had been lost to the Campbells of Argyll and Glenorchy and Marion Stewart. Walter was, moreover, heavily in debt to Earl Colin and the guarantee for the payment of this sum was the remaining part of the barony of Innermeath. Of all the lowland lordships and estates enjoyed by John Stewart only the barony of Redcastle in Angus was securely held by his 'heir'. In the west, in Lorn itself, Walter had probably fared little better. Given Walter's failure to fulfil the terms of the 1462 agreement with Earl Colin and the ensuing conflict between the two men it was hardly surprising that the military and political might of Clan Campbell was not deployed in support of the Stewarts within Lorn. Without Argyll's backing, Walter and his allies clearly struggled to impose any form of lordship in the region. In truth, Walter seems to have abandoned the fight in the west, and effective leadership of the Stewart cause in Lorn fell to John's son, Dougall, who carved out a lordship in the lands north of Loch Creran far removed from the centres of MacDougall and Campbell power. There may be some substance in the traditional view that Dougall was assisted not only by his mother's kin, the MacLarens, but by adventurers from Dumbarton and Loch Lomondside recruited with the promise that 'they and their descendants should have farms so long as Dugald Stewart or his offspring should have lordship'.[115]

---

113 NAS, Breadalbane Coll., GD112, Box 66, Bundle 1, Item 1.
114 *RMS* ii, no. 876; NAS, John MacGregor Coll., GD50/1/38. The papal writ obtained by Argyll in April 1466 allowed the bishop of Lismore to threaten Walter and his men with excommunication if they failed to submit themselves to legal judgement.
115 Dewar, *Dewar Manuscripts*, i, 255.

By 1469, the ageing Walter Stewart was prepared to make significant concessions in order to retrieve some tangible profit from the increasingly hollow titles he had inherited in 1463/4. In November 1469, during a parliament in Edinburgh, the weary lord of Lorn concluded his long dispute with the earl of Argyll. By the terms of an indenture between the two men drawn up on 30 November Walter agreed to resign the lordship of Lorn in favour of the earl. In return, Argyll would resign the lands of Coldrain and Maw in Fife, Kildinny, Baldinnies, Innerdunning, Balgowan and 'Ladboth' in Perthshire, Cockairney in Kinross, and Latheris and Rothiebrisbane in Aberdeenshire to Walter.[116] In essence, Walter was giving up his unenforceable rights of lordship in Lorn, in order to secure possession of the lowland estates which had been held by his brother. In addition, Walter was to receive the office of coroner of Perth, while Earl Colin was to use his influence with the king to ensure that Walter remained a lord of Parliament, to be styled Lord Innermeath.

The exchange of lands and titles proceeded smoothly over the following five months.[117] By 13 April 1470 Walter was to be found enjoying his new title of Lord Innermeath.[118] On the following day Walter formally resigned the lordship of Lorn into the hands of James III, and on 17 April the king granted the lordship to Earl Colin and his heirs. After almost a century the Stewart lordship of Lorn had come to an end. In May 1471 Argyll's grip on his new lordship was tightened still further when Earl Colin was given the office of justiciar within the bounds of Lorn by James III.[119]

The Stewart presence in Lorn, however, persisted in the shape of the immovable Dougall of Appin. Dougall and his brothers may have been party to the settlement between Walter and Earl Colin, although there were no specific guarantees for the position of the Appin Stewarts in the agreements of 1469/70.[120] The extension of Campbell overlordship into Lorn was a period of potential danger for kindreds with no formal title to the lands they occupied. Legal rights to the estates of Lorn, Benderloch

---

116 Argyll Trans., 30 Nov. 1469; HMC, *4th Rep.*, 474 (no. 9). The parliament opened on 20 Nov.: *APS* ii, 93.
117 For the various stages in the transfer of property rights in mind-numbing detail, see Boardman, 'Politics and the Feud', 37–8.
118 HMC, *4th Rep.*, 474 (no. 11).
119 Ibid., 474 (no. 12), 485.
120 A Dougall Stewart, almost certainly John Stewart's son, acted as procurator for Walter, Lord Lorn, in receiving sasine of the lordship of Lorn on 21 Mar. 1470, in preparation for Walter's resignation of the lordship to Argyll: Argyll Trans., 21 Mar. 1470. Dougall's brother Alexander had become bound in manrent to Walter Stewart some time before 26 Apr. 1482, on which date Walter was discharged from providing Alexander with 'feall and household' on the basis that the latter had entered the service of James, Earl of Buchan without Walter's licence: NAS, John MacGregor Coll., GD50/1/54.

and Appin now lay in the hands of a powerful lord who had to provide patronage to an extensive network of ambitious kinsmen and allies eager for land and office. One such was Duncan Campbell of Glenorchy, who on 17 December 1470, as the heir of Janet Stewart, received a grant of one third of the lands of Lorn from Earl Colin.[121] Overall, however, Earl Colin and Duncan Campbell of Glenorchy were unwilling or unable to initiate a large-scale displacement of Lorn kindreds in favour of their own kinsmen in the years after 1471. In particular, Argyll and Glenorchy reached an accommodation with the MacDougalls of Dunollie and the Stewarts of Appin, which saw promises of good and faithful service exchanged for heritable title to land.[122] In a repeat of the process by which Stewart lordship had encroached on Lorn in the fourteenth century, the Stewarts of Appin now joined the MacDougalls of Dunollie (in each case the direct male heirs of former lords of Lorn) as a subordinate kindred which retained a reduced and more localised influence under a new overlord.

After 1470, Dougall's son and successor, Duncan, was occasionally found in Earl Colin's retinue, but the relationship between the Appin Stewarts and their new 'masters' often appears to have been tense. At the very northern limit of Campbell territorial lordship the Stewarts of Appin seem to have retained a capacity for independent political action which was a consistent source of worry to the Campbell lords of Lorn. The traditional history of the family reflected and supported the notion that Dougall Stewart and his descendants were not wholly Argyll's men; their local lordship had been won with blood and iron and not through the gift and favour of Earl Colin and his successors. Originally promoted as part of the validation and definition of aristocratic rights in Appin, the story of Leper John and his son seems to have taken on a wider significance in defining local identity for those who lived under Stewart rule in the lands north of Loch Creran. The tale told by Gillespie MacCombie in 1865 of the passing of the Stewart lords of Lorn and the foundation of the Stewart lordship of Appin was written in the local population and landscape. The men of Appin were the descendants of the adventurers from Balquhidder, Dumbarton and Loch Lomond who had followed Dougall Stewart to the *Ceathramh Fearna* and won it from the MacDougalls. The action in MacCombie's tale was centred around nearby Castle Stalker rather than Dunstaffnage, and cairns on the shore above Eilean Stalker still marked the spot where Allan MacDougall had made his last stand.

---

121 NAS, Breadalbane Coll., GD112/2/109, nos. 1, 4, 5.
122 *Argyll Records*, 10.

10

Achilles' Heel?
The Earldom of Ross, the Lordship of the Isles, and the Stewart Kings, 1449–1507

NORMAN MACDOUGALL

Early in May 1449 Alexander MacDonald, earl of Ross and Lord of the Isles, in Hugh Macdonald's famous phrase 'a man born to much trouble all his lifetime', died at Dingwall and was buried in the Chanonry of Ross (Rosemarkie).[1] His son and heir John, the eldest of a sizeable progeny, succeeded at the tender age of fifteen, without any apparent difficulty, to Alexander's vast inheritance – the Northern and Southern Hebrides, the lordships and lands of Lochaber, Garmoran, Kincardine in the Mearns, Kingedward in Buchan, and Greenan in Ayrshire, Knapdale and the peninsula of Kintyre in the south-west.[2] Of this huge empire, some of the lands – Kincardine, Kingedward, and Greenan – remained in ward until John's majority, probably in late 1455, by which time he had also been formally recognised as keeper of Urquhart Castle on Loch Ness. John was sheriff of Inverness by 1458, had the sheriffship of Nairn in his gift by the 1460s, and – above all – succeeded at once to his father's earldom of Ross, being present at a meeting of the council of the earldom at Dingwall as early as May 1450.[3] If John's father Alexander had been, in Sandy Grant's words, 'easily the greatest magnate in the entire Highlands', John himself, as a youth of fifteen in 1449, seemed to have even greater potential; for in that summer he married Elizabeth Livingstone, daughter of James Livingstone of Callendar, the royal chamberlain, keeper of Stirling Castle, and – most important of all – custodian of the person of the young king, James II.[4]

---

1 *Highland Papers*, i, 47.
2 *ALI*, introduction and no. 51. In much of what follows, my indebtedness to the editors of this splendid volume, the scholar's 'bible' for the history of the Lordship, will be readily apparent.
3 Ibid., 80–2.
4 A. Grant, *Independence and Nationhood: Scotland 1306–1469* (London 1984), 218; R. Nicholson, *Scotland: The Later Middle Ages* (Edinburgh 1974), 350; National Library of Scotland, MS. Acc. 4233 (the 'Auchinleck Chronicle'), fos. 122r–v; C. McGladdery, *James II* (Edinburgh 1990), 50, 53, 172.

Yet John MacDonald would lose it all – the earldom of Ross, the Lord-ship, his influence both with the king and with his kin and allies in the north and west – within his own lifetime, and would end his days as a pathetic pensioner of the Crown. If the Sleat *seanchaidh*, Hugh Macdonald, is to be believed, in the late 1470s John MacDonald's position was challenged by his son Angus, who drove him from his manor house on Islay and forced him to shelter for the night under an upturned boat, from which John emerged in the morning to lay a curse upon his son.[5] The curse would be fulfilled, and would indeed fall upon other members of the MacDonald kin apart from Angus himself, though not, perhaps, in the manner anticipated by John MacDonald. In any event, such a spectacular decline and fall requires explanation, and what follows is an attempt to provide some answers.[6]

* * *

First, there is the question of young John MacDonald's inheritance in 1449. In theory, his lands and offices made him potentially the most powerful magnate north of the Forth; but as Grant has convincingly shown, John also inherited more than two generations of Crown–MacDonald hostility, based largely on the policy of expansion eastwards into Ross and the Moray coastal plain of the fourth Lord's two predecessors.[7] Thus although Alexander, John's father, ended his life as earl of Ross and royal justiciar north of the Forth, his relationship with the Crown had been stormy for most of his life; and reluctant royal recognition of Alexander as earl of Ross had come possibly a year before, but only openly after, James I's assassination in February 1437, when Stewart government was plunged into a period of weakness and civil war in the south, and there was no option but to accept the gains made by the third Lord in the north.[8] It may well be asked how safe these gains would remain once an adult Stewart king, in the person of James II, began to rule for himself. Certainly the omens were not good. Between 1428 and 1431, James I, that consummate master of the pre-emptive strike, had sought to

[5] *Highland Papers*, i, 47–8.
[6] There has been an abundance of scholarly work on the Lordship in recent years. Apart from the superb volume of the *Acts of the Lords of the Isles*, the following are of major importance: Grant, *Independence and Nationhood*, ch. 8; A. Grant, 'Scotland's "Celtic fringe" in the late Middle Ages: the Macdonald Lords of the Isles and the kingdom of Scotland', in R. R. Davies (ed.), *The British Isles 1100–1500: Comparisons, Contrasts and Connections* (Edinburgh 1988), 118–41; J. W. M. Bannerman, 'The Lordship of the Isles', in J. M. Brown (ed.), *Scottish Society in the Fifteenth Century* (London 1977), 209–40; D. H. Caldwell and G. Ewart, 'Finlaggan and the Lordship of the Isles: an archaeological approach', *SHR* lxxii (1993), 146–66; Nicholson, *Later Middle Ages*, chs. 6–18 *passim*.
[7] Grant, *Independence and Nationhood*, 215–18.
[8] M. Brown, *James I* (Edinburgh 1994), 160.

acquire direct control of Ross by a policy of arrests and executions, and ultimately by invasions of Kintyre, Knapdale, Lochaber and Sutherland, undertaken either by himself or his lieutenants, of whom by far the most influential, until his death in 1435, was Alexander Stewart, earl of Mar. Although King James had some initial success, his Highland policy, as Michael Brown has recently shown, was misconceived; and royal strong-arm tactics simply provoked a powerful reaction in the west and north in support of the MacDonalds. This was a dangerous time for James I. Until October 1430 he had no male heir; and when he released Alexander MacDonald from imprisonment in Tantallon Castle, the third Lord not only responded by burning Inverness but by allying with his kinsmen, Alastair *Carrach* of Lochaber and Donald *Balloch*, the young and aggressive son of John *Mór* of Dunivaig and the Glens of Antrim, in an abortive plot to bring home James the Fat, the last survivor of the Albany Stewarts whom James I had annihilated in 1425, in order that he might be made king. The plot failed because of James the Fat's timely (for James I) death in the spring of 1429. But subsequent efforts by royal lieutenants to dismantle MacDonald power on the mainland by seizing control of Lochaber and the Great Glen ended in ignominious defeat at the hands of a Lordship army at Inverlochy in September 1431, swiftly followed by criticism of King James's policy in parliament the following month, and in effect the abandonment of direct royal intervention in the north and west. Mar, as the king's lieutenant, was left to provide a barrier to further Lordship expansion; but his death in 1435 was rapidly followed by Alexander MacDonald styling himself earl of Ross, and being officially recognised as such by the government after 1437.[9]

Nonetheless, it was a tenuous inheritance, dependent for its continuance on royal acquiescence of a *fait accompli*. The frightening alternative – for the MacDonalds – was the possibility of the re-emergence of a strong Crown with the power to further James I's Highland policies effectively – that is, to take over Ross, to acquire control of Lochaber, and to secure Kintyre and Knapdale, the latter lands part of the principality created by Robert III for his son Prince James (James I) in 1404, and therefore an obvious royal target. Certainly the violent events of 1428–31 had shown that the Crown could be threatened from abroad with Lordship assistance, that royal armies could be defeated by Lordship forces – as had happened at Inverlochy and at Drum nan coup in Strathnaver in September 1431 – and that the relatively good Crown–Lordship relations which had obtained in the late fourteenth century, prior to the death of the first Lord in 1387, were unlikely to return.

9 Ibid., 74–5, 93–118, 135–40, 145–8, 157–60.

In the summer of 1449, therefore, the young fourth Lord and his advisers were probably looking both for an insurance policy to preserve the Lordship gains of the 1430s and 1440s, and also to take advantage of a Crown which was still in minority. This would explain the marriage of John MacDonald to Elizabeth Livingstone, the Chamberlain's daughter, an alliance which – in spite of the subsequent poetic condemnation of the Livingstones for climbing high above their station in Holland's *Buke of the Howlat*[10] – appeared to make very good sense at the time. It brought the young fourth Lord into close contact with the family which ran the court, controlled some of the principal royal castles, and had charge of the adolescent James II; the marriage might help to ease Crown–Lordship tensions; and, in the short term, if the contemporary Auchinleck chronicler is to be believed, it seems that James II encouraged the marriage, granting John MacDonald the custody of Urquhart Castle on Loch Ness for three years, and promising him good lordship.[11]

In effect, the king's good lordship lasted only a few weeks. Thereafter James II's actions signalled the reopening of crown aggression, a second and major factor in the weakening of the MacDonald Lordship. Apparently without warning, on Monday 23 September 1449, the king ordered the arrest of Chamberlain James Livingstone, the young fourth Lord's father-in-law, together with his brother Alexander, and Robert Livingstone, the Comptroller, and incarcerated them in Blackness Castle.[12] Further arrests followed, and in the parliament of January 1450 the Livingstones were forfeited with their allies the Dundases, and Alexander and Robert Livingstone were executed. The principal charge brought against the entire family, the treasonable incarceration of James I's widow, Queen Joan Beaufort, more than a decade before, is less than convincing, for both the main perpetrators of that act – Alexander Livingstone senior and his son James – survived the assault on their kin. Alexander appears to have been expelled from the kingdom, while James, according to the Auchinleck chronicler, 'eschapit subtelly fra the king and his counsall out of the abbay of halyrudhouss'. His daughter Elizabeth had preceded him; perhaps forewarned of the king's coup, she had fled from Dumbarton to her husband in Kintyre.[13] Furious retaliation followed for what the young fourth Lord can only have regarded as royal treachery. Grant has convinc-ingly demonstrated that John MacDonald's revolt occurred in March of

10 M. Stewart. 'Holland's "Howlat" and the fall of the Livingstons', *Innes Review*, xxvi (1975), 67–79.
11 'Auchinleck Chronicle', fo. 118v.
12 Ibid., fo. 122r.
13 *APS* ii, 61; McGladdery, *James II*, 50–4; 'Auchinleck Chronicle', fo. 122r.

1451 rather than 1452 as had previously been widely assumed.[14] Indeed, one might wonder why he waited so long, a full eighteen months after the fall of his Livingstone kinsmen. Possibly he delayed launching a rebellion until his father-in-law James Livingstone, who was clearly in royal custody for some time, was safely out of royal hands. But it seems much more likely that John MacDonald and his advisers wished to secure areas vital to the Lordship's mainland territories. So there was no immediate attack on Stewart lands in the Clyde, but rather a seizure of royal castles in the Great Glen and Badenoch, Inverness, Urquhart on Loch Ness, and Ruthven. According to the Auchinleck chronicler, MacDonald gave the keepership of Urquhart to his father-in-law James Livingstone, and 'kest dovne' Ruthven Castle.[15]

King James II, by his sudden strike against the Livingstones, had indicated that he saw his role as continuing his father's aggressive kingship. However, there was little that he could do personally to respond to the Lord of the Isles' revolt. But in April 1451, a month after the revolt, the king took an action which was to have far-reaching consequences: he granted the lordship of Badenoch with Ruthven Castle – or what was left of it – to Alexander Gordon, first earl of Huntly, the head of a family with expansionist ambitions in the north-east which by the beginning of the next century would have reached their full flowering.[16] In April 1451, however, Alexander Gordon was an earl of only six years standing; and his creation as such in 1445, at the outset of the Douglas–Livingstone ascendancy at court and during the minority of James II, was hardly likely to endear him to the adult king. One writer has described Huntly as the Crown's chief supporter in the north,[17] and this is true in the sense that he was prepared to attack rebels in pursuit of crown rewards. But the grant of Badenoch to Huntly by the king was probably little more than a retrospective royal nod of approval towards the earl in a local contest with the Lordship which was already under way, and in which the earl himself had become involved to further his family's territorial ambitions. Twenty years earlier, Huntly's father had been on the losing side against Lordship forces at the battle of Inverlochy; and a generation later, his son George, second Earl of Huntly, would be the principal royal enforcer following the forfeiture of the earldom of Ross.[18] The Stewart kings seem

---

14 A. Grant, 'The revolt of the Lord of the Isles and the death of the earl of Douglas, 1451–1452', *SHR* lx (1981), 169–74.

15 'Auchinleck Chronicle', fo. 118v.

16 *RMS* ii, no. 442.

17 Grant, 'Revolt of the Lord of the Isles', 171 n.6.

18 *Highland Papers*, i, 40–1; *Miscellany of the Spalding Club*, vol. IV, ed. J. Stuart (Spalding Club, 1849), 133.

to have been more reluctant observers of the Huntly–Ross struggle than active participants in it. Certainly for James II there was no alternative but to approve the extension of Gordon power in Badenoch as a barrier to further Lordship expansion; but the king remained suspicious of Huntly aggrandisement. The following year, when Huntly defeated the rebel earl of Crawford at Brechin in what appears to have been another piece of Gordon private enterprise, there were no royal rewards forthcoming; and after 1455, James II seems to have been pursuing a deliberate policy of checking Huntly expansion in the earldom of Moray, frustrating both the earl and his son and at some point provoking their devastation of lands in Mar.[19]

In 1451, then, the power struggle in the Great Glen, Badenoch, and the Moray coastal plain was of vital interest to the young MacDonald earl of Ross and his Gordon opponent, Alexander, Earl of Huntly. To the king, however, this contest was little more than a sideshow, as he had become involved in the south in what was to prove the greatest conflict of the reign, with the Black Douglases – William, eighth Earl of Douglas and his brothers the earls of Moray and Ormond. This is not the place to consider that conflict in detail, but some mention must be made of that part of it in which the Lord of the Isles played a role, albeit a passive one, namely the famous (or notorious) Douglas–Ross–Crawford bond. A great deal of ink has been spilled in efforts to analyse this contract which brought together three unnatural allies – William, eighth Earl of Douglas, John MacDonald, earl of Ross and Lord of the Isles, and David Lindsay, fourth earl of Crawford – but as the bond itself no longer exists, its contents can only be a matter for speculation.[20] What it *may* have been, as Christine McGladdery suggests, was a bond of friendship bringing to an end territorial or other disputes, for example between the earl of Ross and the Douglas earls in the north-east.[21] Such an argument might well alarm James II, who, like most successful rulers, counted on being able to exploit local enmities to his advantage. However, we cannot be sure of this. We cannot even be sure when the bond was made. Opinions vary from 1445 (when of course two of the parties, the earls of Ross and Crawford, were different individuals) to 1451–2. Perhaps there is something to be said for a late date; for Douglas was present at court on 13 January 1452, yet needed a safe-conduct to visit his sovereign at Stirling a month later, two facts which

---

19 'Auchinleck Chronicle', fos. 123r–v; McGladdery, *James II*, 104–5; *ER* vi, 269.
20 See, e.g., Nicholson, *Later Middle Ages*, 358–9; Grant, 'Revolt of the Lord of the Isles', 172–4; G. Donaldson, *Scottish Kings* (Edinburgh 1967), 90–1; *ALI*, no. 45. The contemporary source for the bond is 'Auchinleck Chronicle', fo. 114v, with – probably – an oblique reference to it in the parliament of June 1452: *APS* ii, 73.
21 McGladdery, *James II*, 63–4.

would fit the making, or renewal, of the bond sometime between 13 January and Douglas's arrival at Stirling on 21 February 1452.[22]

There are only two certainties – first, that Douglas had made a bond with a rebel, John MacDonald, earl of Ross; and secondly that James II was so incensed with his failure to make Earl William 'break' the bond that this issue, rather than all the southern territorial disputes, provided the immediate cause of Douglas's killing, stabbed by the king himself and finished off by seven others present in an exuberant and gory demonstration of their loyalty to the Crown.[23]

In one sense, the death of the earl of Douglas at the king's hands may be seen to have worked to the advantage of John MacDonald. If James II had had problems before, these increased enormously after the Stirling killing; and for more than three years the king, preoccupied with intermittent civil wars and constant walking of a very dangerous political tightrope, could do little more than accept the status quo created by the fourth Lord's rebellion in the north. On the other hand, Douglas's murder, a dramatic display of the withdrawal of good lordship if ever there was one, probably prompted the rebellion which followed on the part of the Lindsay earl of Crawford; and according to Auchinleck, James, the new ninth earl of Douglas and brother of the murdered earl, had a meeting in Knapdale with the Lord of the Isles in May 1454, presumably in an attempt to win his support for the Douglas cause against the king. Auchinleck is both cryptic and obscure in his account of this meeting; having recorded the lavish gifts given to the fourth Lord by Douglas – wine, clothes, silver, silk and English cloth – he remarks: 'And quhat was thar amangis thaim wes counsall to conwines (i.e. convince); And thai demyt Ill all.'[24] This last may perhaps be read as an indication that the talks failed. Certainly John MacDonald gave no known direct military assistance to the Douglases for the remainder of the reign. His reward, if that is the correct word, was crown acceptance of his possession of some of the lands in the Great Glen which he had seized by rebellion in 1451. In spite of the Act of Annexation of 4 August 1455, by which the castle and lordship of Urquhart were specified as properties inalienably annexed to the royal patrimony, within a year a compromise solution had been reached whereby John MacDonald was formally granted the farms of Urquhart and Glenmoriston, worth

---

22 *RMS* ii, no. 523; 'Auchinleck Chronicle', fo. 114v.
23 Ibid., fos. 114v–115r.
24 Ibid., fo. 117r. Auchinleck dates the Knapdale meeting to 12 May 1452; but see M. Brown, *The Black Douglases: War and Lordship in Late Medieval Scotland, 1300–1455* (East Linton 1998), 303–4 and n. 33, in which a convincing argument is made for 1454. Michael Brown also argues that the 4th Lord's ultimate adherence to the king may have been influenced by the restoration to royal favour of his father-in-law James Livingstone: ibid., 311.

£100 annually, for life;[25] and he was to enjoy control of both these important strategic lordships for almost twenty years. By 1458 MacDonald is also described as sheriff of Inverness.[26] Thus in terms of his stewardship of the earldom of Ross which he had inherited from his father, the fourth Lord may at this stage be accounted a success, taking advantage of royal government weakness to press his territorial claims. Indeed, Ross seems to have been John MacDonald's main concern during the 1450s; surviving charter evidence from this decade places him at Dingwall and Inverness on many occasions, but seldom within the Lordship, and only once at its centre, Loch Finlaggan on Islay.[27]

* * *

There was a price to be paid for all this, of course. It may be that in the fourth Lord's concentration on Ross – and, for that matter, his father's – the MacDonald hegemony was becoming too large to be run effectively by one leader, and indeed that the MacDonald kin and the major families within the original Lordship were looking to others to pursue a more aggressive policy in the west. It is surely significant that, although the fourth Lord appears to have made no response to Douglas appeals for aid after the killing of the eighth earl by James II, MacDonald's kinsman Donald *Balloch* of Dunivaig and the Glens, whose galleys had helped to secure victory for the Lordship at Inverlochy in 1431, launched a major assault on crown lands in the Firth of Clyde in July 1454, attacking Inverkip on the Renfrewshire mainland, harrying and burning on the Cumbraes, Bute and Arran, where Brodick Castle was taken and razed to the ground. According to Auchinleck, Donald *Balloch* had a force of 5–6,000 in a fleet of 100 galleys; and accompanying him was John Douglas, an illegitimate son of Archibald, fourth earl of Douglas.[28] This great raid is surely the Lordship's real answer to James II's acts of aggression and killing against the Douglases; and it also suggests that Donald *Balloch*, in 1454 a mature man in his forties, had assumed effective leadership of the forces of the Lordship, presumably with the concurrence of his young eighteen-year-old kinsman, the fourth Lord.

An even more striking example of the hawkish influence within the Lordship of Donald *Balloch* is to be found ten years later, in the rather fancifully named 'Treaty of Westminster–Ardtornish' of February 1462. James II had died at the siege of Roxburgh in August 1460, and royal

25 *APS* ii, 42; *ER* vi, 68, 217.
26 *ALI*, no. 69.
27 Ibid., nos. 53–69.
28 'Auchinleck Chronicle', fos. 117r–v. For the dating of Donald *Balloch*'s raid, see Steve Boardman's essay, chapter 9 above, note 82; and Brown, *Black Douglases*, 303–4 and n. 33.

government during the minority of his successor James III was not only
initially weak but also divided in its attitude towards the Yorkist victor in
the English civil war, King Edward IV.[29] Royal government weakness
invited Lordship aggression, and on 19 October 1461 John MacDonald
sent two ambassadors from his castle of Ardtornish on the Morvern coast
with full power to negotiate a treaty on his behalf with Edward IV.[30] The
first of those ambassadors, Ranald of the Isles, was Donald *Balloch*'s
brother; and the treaty which followed in February 1462 is remarkable in the
prominence which it accords to Donald and his family. John MacDonald,
as earl of Ross and Lord of the Isles, is named first; but then follows not
only Donald *Balloch*, but also his son and heir John of Islay. All three
agreed to become liegemen of Edward IV of England, and to take the
English king's part in wars in Scotland or Ireland in return for an annual
pension; but the most interesting part of the indenture is the proposed
territorial division of Scotland should the country be conquered and
brought under the overlordship of Edward IV. In that event, all of
Scotland north of the Forth would be divided equally among John, Earl of
Ross, Donald *Balloch*, and the exiled James, Earl of Douglas, the last-
named the mainstay of the Scottish 'fifth column' in England. Should
Douglas play an active part in the conquest of Scotland for Edward IV, he
should be restored to all his former possessions *south* of the Forth.[31]

This treaty is of great interest not because there was any real chance of
its contents being implemented – an accommodation between the minority
government of James III and that of Edward IV soon put paid to that –
but because it reveals English perceptions of the relative importance of
potential allies among the Scots. Donald *Balloch* was presumably highly
rated by the Yorkists because he had already twice led expeditions against
royal forces in Scotland with some success, and also on account of his
direct links with Antrim in Northern Ireland. So Donald's brother
negotiated the English treaty, and Donald himself and his son and heir
John were to be two of its principal beneficiaries. And if the earl of
Douglas were to be restored in the south of Scotland, then the country
north of the Forth would have been divided between the two MacDonald
kinsmen, John, Earl of Ross, and Donald *Balloch*.

How that division would have been made if the treaty had been followed
up is indicated by John MacDonald's activities in the early 1460s. For at
the outset of the reign of James III, the fourth Lord is to be found mainly,
if not exclusively, in the north-east. He was apparently at Rosemarkie

[29] For a discussion of Anglo-Scottish relations in the early 1460s, see N. Macdougall,
James III: A Political Study (Edinburgh 1982), 57–61.
[30] *ALI*, no. 74.
[31] Ibid., no. 75.

when summoned to attend the parliament of February 1461, a summons which may have been prompted by claims that he had appropriated to himself crown revenues in Moray amounting to over £200 Scots.[32] Subsequently he was summoned to answer charges of treason – the seizure of royal ferms and victuals at Inverness – in a parliament which was to have been held in Aberdeen in June 1462; there is documentary evidence that such a parliament was planned, but it did not take place because the king did not travel north at that time.[33] In the spring of 1463 Ross laid waste crown lands in the vicinity of Inverness, and in August 1464 he was confronted by Bishop Kennedy and the entire royal Council at Inverness on the young James III's first northern progress. On this occasion Ross admitted to the seizure of £74.12s.3d. from Inverness burgh customs.[34] All this evidence suggests strongly that John MacDonald's main interest lay in consolidating and extending his power in Ross and the Moray coastal plain, acting aggressively in the expectation – incorrect as events proved – that a Stewart minority government would be too weak to resist. Probably, therefore, the fourth Lord's contemporary alliance with Edward IV was made with the same aim of securing and extending his father's difficult north-eastern legacy.

By contrast, in the 1460s and 1470s John MacDonald appears to have played little part in the politics of the Lordship proper, and it seems probable that Donald *Balloch* and his son John were the real makers of policy in the west, and would have expected to succeed to the Lordship if the English treaty of 1462 had borne fruit. Even as things stood, the fourth Lord seems to have spent much time negotiating with the royal government in response to charges which should have been brought against others. Thus it may be that the MacDonald Lordship of the Isles was already, as early as the 1460s and perhaps much earlier, a house divided, with the MacDonalds of Dunivaig and the Glens of Antrim, in the persons of the hawkish Donald *Balloch* and his family, challenging what Dean Monro calls the 'royal blude of Clandonald' in the person of John MacDonald, fourth Lord.[35] In this sense, the latter's preoccupation with the earldom of Ross proved an Achilles' Heel, for it was in Ross that the MacDonalds were most vulnerable; and the loss of that earldom in 1475–6 would make the fourth Lord's position in the Isles untenable.

---

[32] *ER* vii, pp. xxxix–xl, 20. The revenues in question were appropriated from the former Douglas earldoms of Moray and Ormond, which had come into crown hands by forfeiture as recently as 1455.

[33] 'Auchinleck Chronicle', fo. 120v; *ER* vii, 143.

[34] Ibid., vii, 296–7.

[35] *Monro's Western Isles of Scotland and Genealogies of the Clans*, ed. R. W. Munro (Edinburgh 1961), 57.

An obligation of 8 October 1475 reveals the extent of Donald *Balloch*'s power. His kinsman the earl of Ross and Lord of the Isles had shortly before granted to John Davidson the lands of Greenan on the Ayrshire coast; but it was Donald *Balloch*, described in the obligation as the fourth Lord's *'primus et principalis conciliarius'*, who was required to defend Davidson in his Ayrshire lands.[36] And when Donald died, sometime between August 1476 and June 1481, it was not only to the Lord of the Isles, but also to Donald's son and successor John – who had been associated with his father in the treaty of Westminster–Ardtornish of 1462 – that Edward IV looked for assistance against James III in the Anglo-Scottish war of 1480–2.[37] Presumably the English king was unaware of John MacDonald's political impotence; for the fourth Lord had demonstrably failed in the Isles by this stage; his inheritance had proved too much for him, and the struggle, both in Ross and in the Lordship, had already passed to stronger and more ruthless men.

Indeed, there can be little doubt that John MacDonald's personality played a major role in the collapse of the Lordship. He was of course unfortunate to succeed at the age of only fifteen, and doubly unfortunate that his marriage to Elizabeth Livingstone in 1449 rapidly lost its political *raison d'être* with the fall of the Livingstones a few weeks later. Also, there can be little doubt that during his minority, the crucial early years of the 1450s, decisions affecting the future of Ross and the Lordship of the Isles were being made for him by others. Yet when all this has been said in mitigation, it is hard to forget the Sleat *seanchaidh* Hugh Macdonald's damning verdict on the fourth Lord as 'a meek, modest man and a scholar, more fit to be a churchman than to command so many irregular tribes of people'.[38] John's weakness, according to the same source, was to attempt to retain the allegiance of the important families of the Isles through a policy of bestowing gifts of lands and possessions, thereby greatly diminishing his own rents and impoverishing his family. The *seanchaidh* specifically mentions MacDonald generosity to the MacLeans, who received the lordship of Morvern; and the record evidence bears this out, with extensive grants not only in Morvern but also in Lochaber, Mull and Jura to MacLean of Lochbuie.[39] Such grants undoubtedly gave the major Lord-ship families – the MacLeans of Duart and Lochbuie, the MacLeods of Lewis,

---

36 *ALI*, no. 107. It has been suggested to me by David Sellar that Donald *Balloch*'s title in this obligation of *primus et principalis conciliarius* of the earl of Ross might mean that Donald had been chosen as a tanist within the Lordship.

37 *CDS* iv, no. 1469. The name of John, 4th Lord, omitted by Bain, should be included in Edward IV's commission: see *ALI*, p. lxxviii.

38 *Highland Papers*, i, 47.

39 Ibid.; *ALI*, nos. 72, A42–A45.

Dunvegan and Harris – good reason to support the MacDonald Lordship against external (and internal) threats, but only so long as the head of Clan Donald remained firmly in control. When, as in the case of the fourth Lord, he was simultaneously and successfully challenged by his king *and* his own kin, the Lordship families' problem of allegiance became acute.

There was also a further, perhaps major, problem, created by John MacDonald's wife, Elizabeth Livingstone. Although MacDonald–Livingstone relations may have been cordial as late as 1461 – according to Auchinleck, both the fourth Lord and his Livingstone father-in-law were present at James III's first parliament in February of that year[40] – by January of 1464 Elizabeth was to be found complaining to the pope that her husband had ejected her both from cohabitation with him and from his lands, in spite of the fact that the marriage had been properly consummated and that she had borne him offspring. Children of this marriage cannot however be identified, and the marital break-up may have been caused by the fourth Lord's fears for the succession to the Lordship; thus by 1464 he was cohabiting with what his wife's petition calls 'a certain adultress'. By contrast, Elizabeth's real fears may have been the prospect of losing lands in Ross acquired through her marriage; and a decade later the situation had deteriorated still further. Another petition, presumably sent to the pope after John MacDonald's forfeiture of Ross (as he is referred to only as Lord of the Isles), omitted to claim the birth of children by the marriage, but tried a different tack, namely that when Elizabeth had been pregnant, her husband had imprisoned her and attempted to poison her. She had therefore fled from the Isles to the court of the queen of Scots (at Stirling), where in March 1478 she was still living. It is difficult to date these dramatic events, but it seems most likely that Elizabeth's flight preceded her petition by quite some time, perhaps a few years, and certainly occurred before the MacDonald forfeiture of Ross in December 1475; for as early as the following February, Elizabeth received from the Crown extensive lands in Ross, Moray, Aberdeenshire, and Ayrshire for her maintenance. These grants, it was claimed, were made for service to the late James II, James III himself and his queen, Margaret of Denmark, and because Elizabeth had given no assistance to John MacDonald in his treasons.[41] All this suggests that the MacDonald–Livingstone marital estrangement was long-standing; it may even have gone back to the 1450s, within a few years of the wedding, when the Livingstones, newly rehabilitated at court after their spectacular fall in 1449, must have found their family connection with a rebellious Highlander difficult to live with. And

---

[40] 'Auchinleck Chronicle', fo. 120r.
[41] *Highland Papers*, iv, 206–9; *RMS* ii, no. 1227.

by the 1460s, when Elizabeth Livingstone was becoming, for whatever reason, less and less of an asset to her husband, she may well have been developing into more and more of an asset to the royal government. It is difficult to believe, for example, that John MacDonald's 1462 Westminster–Ardtornish treaty with Edward IV remained a secret from James III until after the Anglo-Scottish treaty of 1474; certainly it must have been 'leaked', at the latest, when Elizabeth Livingstone fled for succour to the enigmatic but politically shrewd Margaret of Denmark.

Thereafter John MacDonald became little more than a observer at the dismemberment of his own empire. In October 1475 he was summoned to answer charges of treason which included the making of treasonable leagues with Edward IV and with the forfeited James, Earl of Douglas – a clear reference to 1462 – the usurpation of royal authority by making his bastard son Angus his lieutenant, and the besieging of Rothesay Castle and laying waste of the island of Bute.[42] This last charge may in fact relate to Donald *Balloch*'s great raid on the Clyde in 1452, for which John MacDonald as Lord of the Isles was now called to answer; but it is strange that the indictment does not specify Ross's own undoubted rebellion of March 1451, which had resulted in the seizure of Inverness and Urquhart, and the assault on Ruthven in Badenoch.

In any event, John MacDonald failed to appear in parliament at Edinburgh on 1 December 1475, and sentence of forfeiture was duly passed by Chancellor Avandale.[43] In the same week, commissions of lieutenancy were granted to four magnates – John Stewart, Lord Darnley, styled (briefly) earl of Lennox, Colin Campbell, first earl of Argyll, John Stewart, earl of Atholl, and George Gordon, second earl of Huntly – to execute the forfeiture.[44] There followed vigorous action on the part of at least two of them – Atholl and Huntly. Atholl would be rewarded – belatedly – with a royal grant of the forest of Cluny and park of Laighwood in Perthshire in March 1481, expressly for his trouble and expense in suppressing the rebellion of John of the Isles.[45] But Huntly's intervention appears to have been even more decisive; sometime before 28 March 1476 he had recovered Dingwall Castle, at the heart of the earldom of Ross, and had invaded Lochaber with great success. James III, writing to the earl, promised to reward him, at the same time exhorting Huntly to be 'of gude perseverance and continuance in the invasion of our said rebellis'.[46]

---

42 *APS* ii, 109–10.
43 Ibid., 111.
44 Inveraray, Inveraray Castle, Argyll Muniments; *RMS* ii, nos. 1210–12; Macdougall, *James III*, 121–2.
45 Blair Atholl, Blair Castle, Atholl Charters, Box 13, Parcel vii.
46 *Spalding Miscellany*, iv, 133.

Huntly needed no second bidding. His Commission of Lieutenancy simply gave him royal authority to pursue a feud with John MacDonald which had been under way at least since the spring of 1474.[47] Indeed, the Huntly–Ross feud may be said to have its origins in James II's grant of Badenoch to Alexander, first Earl of Huntly, in April 1451.[48] The second earl is likely to have been one of the main instigators in urging the forfeiture of Ross; and clearly he was off his mark earlier than anyone else, launching attacks on Lochaber and Ross in the space of a few months. He clearly hoped to be rewarded by the king with the keepership of Dingwall Castle; although denying Huntly this office, the devious king encouraged further assaults on Ross's territories in the Great Glen by granting to Huntly a fee of 100 merks from the ferms of Urquhart and Glenmoriston. These lands, together with the keepership of Urquhart Castle – which had been in John MacDonald's hands for a quarter of a century – had been granted to Huntly by July 1476; and by 1478 the earl had also been reappointed as bailie of the crown lands of Petty, Brachly, and Strathnairn in Moray, lands whose revenues the earl of Ross had appropriated in the early 1460s.[49] These moves by Huntly and the king effectively elevated the Huntly–Ross feud to the level of national politics, and helped to promote a war in Ross and its adjoining territories which would explode intermittently over the next thirty years. But the winners, without a doubt, were George Gordon, second earl of Huntly, who at his death in 1501 was James IV's Chancellor, and was buried in Cambuskenneth Abbey near James III and Margaret of Denmark; and his son and successor Alexander, third earl, who both inherited and built upon a huge Gordon sphere of influence in northern Scotland.

The losers were the MacDonalds, in the first instance John MacDonald himself. On 10 July 1476, before a very full assembly of parliament, he appeared and submitted to the royal will. He was stripped of the title of earl of Ross, the earldom being annexed to the domains of the Crown; James III was to have the liberty to grant Ross to his second son James, and in fact he did so in 1481. In addition, however, John MacDonald was deprived of the sheriffships of Inverness and Nairn, together with their castles; and the Crown also struck at the MacDonald heartland by forfeiting the lordships of Knapdale and Kintyre.[50] Five days later, John received a new crown charter of Islay and his other Hebridean lands, together with the mainland territories of Morvern, Garmoran, Lochaber, Duror and Glencoe, Kingedward and Greenan. These were entailed upon his legitimate male heirs, whom failing his illegitimate sons Angus and

[47] *TA* i, 48.
[48] *RMS* ii, no. 442.
[49] *Spalding Miscellany*, iv, 134.
[50] *APS* ii, 113.

John, to be held for the customary services performed by other barons and for obedience to the laws and customs of the kingdom.[51]

*   *   *

In many respects, these agreements of July 1476 amounted to the real forfeiture of the Lordship of the Isles. For John MacDonald had lost far more than Ross; the surrender to the Crown of Knapdale and Kintyre (although some of the Lordship lands therein were subsequently regranted to John) greatly weakened the Lordship; and John's rather tame acceptance of his demotion to a lordship of parliament undermined his authority – or what was left of it – in the Isles and created enormous problems for his son and heir. The scene was set for a long struggle in the Isles and Ross, as the main branches of Clan Donald sought to dominate both areas, while the Lordship families, MacLeans, MacLeods, and MacNeills, who had prospered under a period of extensive MacDonald grants, tried to ally themselves with the likely winner. There followed, as the author of *The Book of Clanranald* aptly puts it, 'a great struggle among the Gael for power'.[52]

John MacDonald's designated heir, Angus (Angus Óg) soon emerged as a resolute and capable warlord who refused to accept the imposed settlement of 1476; and from the late 'seventies his aim seems to have been nothing less than the recovery by force of arms of both Ross and those areas of the Lordship which had been surrendered by his father.[53] Initially Angus may have tried to secure his father's support for resistance to crown annexation of Knapdale; for in April 1478 parliament accused the fourth Lord of 'stuffing' Castle Sween in Knapdale with men, victuals, and arms of war. John MacDonald may have been summoned to answer for acts which in fact had been committed by his warlike son; probably fearful of losing his Lordship altogether, he again came to Edinburgh to submit to the king, and duly received a confirmation of his 1476 charter.[54] He also received the support of one of the greatest magnates in the kingdom – Colin Campbell, first earl of Argyll, Master of the Royal Household and future Chancellor, an individual who managed to reconcile the functions of Highland clan chief and principal 'man of business' at the Stewart court, and to profit enormously from both. It is dangerous to assume Campbell–MacDonald enmity in the late fifteenth century because we are so familiar with its most dramatic manifestation, the Massacre of Glencoe, at the end of the seventeenth; in fact, once John MacDonald had accepted that his only future lay in behaving as a loyal vassal of the Crown, Argyll – and his son and heir Archibald, second Earl –

51   *RMS* ii, no. 1246.
52   *Reliquiae Celticae*, ii, 163.
53   *Highland Papers*, i, 48–9.
54   *APS* ii, 115; *RMS* ii, no. 1410.

though of course continuing to pursue Campbell expansionist aims, might well act as a prop for the shaky Lordship; and it is significant that the second earl of Argyll took no part in the eventual forfeiture of 1493.

In any event, Angus of the Isles is soon to be found taking on his father – Hugh Macdonald's story of the fourth Lord's cursing of his son relates to this period – the earl of Argyll, the earl of Atholl, and the forces of the Lordship families, apparently with remarkable success. He was aided in his efforts by the virtual collapse of effective Stewart government; for James III, although he managed to gather in some rents from Ross for the first time in 1479, was in the same year confronted by parliamentary complaints about 'the gret trubill that now is in ross, caithness and suthirland'; within a year he was at war with his former ally Edward IV of England; in 1482–3 he faced a major domestic crisis in which the lead was taken by members of his own family, and which he only just survived; and in the early months of 1488 he was confronted with a massive rebellion to which he eventually succumbed at the battle of Sauchieburn.[55] Periods of royal Stewart weakness traditionally provided a springboard for Lordship gains; and in the short term Angus of the Isles achieved some spectacular successes. On some date during the Anglo-Scottish war of 1480–2 – 1481 is probably the most likely – he rounded Ardnamurchan point with a large fleet and won a convincing sea-battle, generally described as the battle of Bloody Bay, near Tobermory, against the galleys of the MacLeods of Lewis and Harris, MacLean of Duart and MacNeill of Barra, all of whom had come to the Sound of Mull at the request of Argyll, Atholl, and Angus's father, the fourth Lord. Angus's decision to fight rather than negotiate was vindicated by his victory; and he may well have been supported by Donald *Balloch*'s son, John of Dunivaig, whom Edward IV of England was seeking to enlist in 1481.[56]

Probably in the same year Angus won another victory, this time over a royal army led by John Stewart, earl of Atholl, at Lagabraad, somewhere in Ross; if Hugh Macdonald is to be believed, 517 of Atholl's force were killed, which suggests a very sizeable battle; and the follow-up seems to have been the occupation of Easter Ross by Angus, possibly reoccupying Dingwall Castle for the two years 1481–3.[57] Thus, at least temporarily, Angus had recovered many of his father's lost territories. But the task proved too much for him, and with the ending of the English war and domestic Stewart crisis in the spring of 1483, Angus appears to have retreated to the west, burning Inverness as he withdrew. The two most prominent royalist northern earls, Atholl and Huntly (who had played a

[55] *APS* ii, 122; Macdougall, *James III*, chs. 8 and 11 (for the crises of 1482 and 1488).
[56] *Highland Papers*, i, 49–50; *CDS* iv, no. 1469.
[57] *Highland Papers*, i, 49.

major part in the crisis of 1482–3, initially by seizing James III and latterly by backing him against his brother, the duke of Albany) had returned to their estates by the autumn of 1483; wisely, Angus MacDonald appears to have stayed out of Huntly's way, for we find him back in the Isles in November 1485, apparently reconciled to his father and conveying land in Mull with the consent of the Council of the Lordship.[58] However, the great magnate rebellion of 1488, in which Angus's father-in-law Argyll was prominently involved against James III, again provided the Master of the Isles with an opportunity to attempt to recover Ross. Either in this year or the following one, when a second huge rebellion distracted the country for about nine months, Angus seized Inverness. Here, according to the Sleat *seanchaidh*, his father's curse caught up with him. Angus's Irish harper Art O'Carby had composed an obscure prophetic poem about the danger to the rider of the dapple horse if there was poison in his long knife, which he called Gallfit. Suiting the action to the words, the harper rose in the night and cut Angus's throat while he was asleep.[59]

No subsequent military leader within the Lordship would present a similar threat, or indeed win victories against royal armies; but many tried. Alexander MacDonald of Lochalsh, Angus's cousin, launched a devastating raid on Inverness in 1491; but later the same year he was heavily defeated by the MacKenzies at Park near Strathpeffer.[60] He continued, however, to grant charters within the Lordship in 1492 – from Colonsay, Oronsay, and Iona, two of them with the consent of the Council of the Isles, and one only in association with his uncle, John MacDonald, the fourth Lord.[61] Clearly, therefore, whatever the attitude of those in charge of the minority government of James IV, Alexander of Lochalsh – *not* the fourth Lord – was accepted by the Council of the Isles as effective Lord of the Isles, with the power to grant lands and offices within the Lordship. Indeed, John, fourth Lord, made no known independent grants in the Isles between 1486 and his last charter, made at Aros on Mull on 6 December 1492, giving the patronage of the church of Kilberry in Knapdale to Robert Colquhoun, bishop of Argyll.[62] So the charter evidence of 1492 shows the last Lord of the Isles dithering between collaboration with his hawkish nephew, Alexander of Lochalsh, and granting church patronage to the royalist bishop of Argyll. Divisions amongst the Lordship families, together with the disintegrating authority of John MacDonald, probably convinced those in charge of James IV's

---

58 *ALI*, no. 119.
59 *Highland Papers*, i, 51–2. Angus was still alive on 8 August 1488: *ALI*, no. 121.
60 *Highland Papers*, i, 55.
61 *ALI*, nos. 122–4.
62 Ibid., no. 125.

government that the time had come to launch a full-scale assault in the West; and Jean Munro argues convincingly that those loyal to the Crown within the Lordship expected firm intervention by the king.[63]

The result, the forfeiture of the Lordship in the parliament of May–June 1493, is a well-known event. Yet it is also rather a mysterious one, partly because there is no surviving record of it in the parliamentary records, but also because, although the forfeiture is frequently described as the act of a dynamic young ruler determined to make his mark in the Isles, in fact James IV is unlikely to have been its instigator, for he did not take personal charge of royal government for another two years.[64] And perhaps most strange of all, the earl of Argyll (Archibald, second earl) not only took no part in the forfeiture but suffered a total political eclipse between 1493 and 1495.[65]

The key to this mystery is provided by the great political maverick of the reign, Archibald Douglas, fifth earl of Angus. This ambitious but unsubtle individual had contrived to join the winning side in the rebellion against James III in 1488, and yet was denied major office under the early governments of his successor; indeed, he lost much of his influence as a powerful border magnate, and by 1491 had become so jaundiced with the regime that he entered into treasonable negotiations with Henry VII of England and had to endure a siege of his castle of Tantallon by James IV in October of that year.[66] However, his political comeback was spectacular; at the turn of the year 1492–3 the Chancellor, Colin Campbell, first earl of Argyll, died, and Angus, thanks partly to his growing friendship with the young king and partly to the fact that Angus's niece, Marion Boyd, was James IV's first mistress, managed to secure the Chancellorship for himself. It seems likely that he planned to use this powerful secular office to develop his influence in Ayrshire and the west, where he had had roots since his Boyd marriage a quarter of a century before. This also meant taking part in the major feud against Hugh, Lord Montgomery, the new earl of Argyll's brother-in-law, and in removing Campbell influence from royal government.[67] It was a risky and only temporarily successful plan; and one of its first fruits was the forfeiture of the Lordship in the summer of 1493. The young king may, of course, have actively sought this, together with other frustrated members of the government and Lordship families who longed to settle the issue of their allegiance; but that Angus was the principal instigator of the forfeiture is strongly suggested by the

63 J. Munro, 'The Lordship of the Isles', in L. Maclean (ed.), *The Middle Ages in the Highlands* (Inverness 1981), 33.

64 N. Macdougall, *James IV* (Edinburgh 1989), 112–15.

65 Ibid., 101.

66 *TA* i, 181, 182.

67 Macdougall, *James IV*, 97–9.

very first royal grant of Lordship lands, that of the lands of Greenan in Ayrshire, which went to Angus's second son William, displacing the Davidson family who had held Greenan for a generation and who were to protest against the arbitrary change for the next twenty years.[68]

However, there can be no doubt that, after years of uncertainty in the west, the forfeiture of 1493 produced a dramatic response and changed the lives of those directly affected by it. John MacDonald, the former fourth Lord, had come almost to the end of the road; he gave up the unequal struggle of trying to reconcile the Crown and the forces of the Lordship, and by 1494 had been brought into the royal household with a generous annual pension of £133.6s.8d.[69] This last may have been a security measure, to prevent John being used by those who wished to restore the Lordship. But there were other methods of doing this than making use of the enfeebled John MacDonald; for he had a grandson, Donald *Dubh*, the son of Angus of the Isles and a daughter of the first earl of Argyll, a child of about three years of age in 1493. Sometime after the forfeiture, John Stewart, earl of Atholl, removed Donald *Dubh* from the keeping of his mother and transferred him to Argyll's powerful stronghold of Inchconnell, on an island in Loch Awe.[70] The possession of the person of the direct heir to the forfeited Lordship gave Argyll a powerful bargaining counter in his – temporarily – strained relations with the royal government.

It remained for that government to make the forfeiture effective if it could. As the start of what a later parliament would rather grandly describe as 'the daunting of the Isles', James IV, attended by his mentor, Chancellor Angus, and the royal Council, sailed north, reaching Dunstaffnage Castle on the Firth of Lorn by 18 August 1493.[71] We have no record of what happened there, and while it is tempting to envisage a grand set-piece, with the galleys of John of Dunivaig, Alexander of Lochalsh, and MacIan of Ardnamurchan, emerging from the mists of the Firth or the Sound of Mull, bearing the leaders of the Lordship to submit to their masterful sovereign, the facts suggest that little was achieved. It is possible that John of Dunivaig and Alexander of Lochalsh were knighted on this occasion; but if so, both can hardly have failed to remark the absence from the king's party of Archibald Campbell, earl of Argyll – and that in the heart of his lordship of Lorn. The conclusions which both men might have drawn from Argyll's absence could have been that their submission was a waste of time, that the crown magnate with whom they had to deal most in the west was excluded, and that James IV's government was weak and divided.

68 *RMS* ii, no. 2172; *ALI*, nos. A40, A68.
69 *ER* x, 534; *TA* i, 233–4.
70 *Highland Papers*, i, 50.
71 *RMS* ii, no. 2171.

Certainly both men remained conspicuously undaunted, for both were in rebellion the following year. They received short shrift, not through direct crown action, but because of the ambitions of John MacIan of Ardnamurchan, who although the representative of a junior branch of the MacDonald kin seems to have aspired to dominate a revived Lordship; as a first step he could kill its leaders and secure substantial rewards from a grateful government.[72] His success was total. Some time in 1494, MacIan killed Alexander of Lochalsh – who may have led an abortive raid on Ross in that year – on the Isle of Oronsay. The place of Alexander's death suggests treachery, for Oronsay had been used as a meeting place for the Council of the Isles as recently as August 1492, on which occasion both Alexander of Lochalsh and MacIan had been present. It was possibly during a similar meeting in 1494 that Alexander was assassinated at MacIan's instigation.[73] As for Sir John of Dunivaig, Donald *Balloch*'s son, his defiance of James IV was impressive but short-lived. The area of potential conflict was the Kintyre peninsula; the king summoned part of the host to meet him at Tarbert, and made repairs to the castle there, and to Dunaverty at the southern end of the peninsula. However, according to the Sleat *seanchaidh*, John of Dunivaig stormed Dunaverty and killed King James's keeper, displaying the corpse outside the castle wall in view of the departing royal fleet.[74] By September of 1494 Sir John had been summoned for treason;[75] and for a second time it was MacIan of Ardnamurchan who did the government's work for it. Before the end of the year he surprised and captured Sir John and three of his sons – John *Cattanach*, Ragnall the Red, and Domnall the Freckled – at the very centre of the Lordship, Loch Finlaggan on Islay. All four were brought to Edinburgh, to languish in prison until 1499, when James IV, still seeking a final solution to the Lordship problem which he had been bequeathed, hanged them on the same gallows.[76] The immediate beneficiary of their removal and ultimate

---

[72] John MacIan of Ardnamurchan's ambition to dominate the Lordship may originate in the predominance of his branch of the family in the early 14th century. Around 1341 his ancestor Angus, founder of the MacIans of Ardnamurchan, had received a royal charter of the island of Islay, all of Kintyre, Gigha, Jura, Colonsay, the lands of Morvern, and some lands in Mull (*RMS* i, app. Ii, no. 114; *ALI*, no. A1). The grant does not appear to have taken effect; but if it had, it would have placed the MacIans of Ardnamurchan at the very heart of the Lordship of the Isles. See also *Highland Papers*, i, 45.

[73] Ibid., i, 56, 60; *ALI*, no. 123.

[74] *TA* i, 217, 237, 244, 253–4; D. Gregory, *A History of the Western Highlands and Isles of Scotland, 1493–1625* (Edinburgh 1836), 89.

[75] *TA* i, 238–9.

[76] Gregory, *Western Highlands*, 89–90, gives 1494 as the date of the capture *and* execution of Sir John and his sons; but a more reliable source is the contemporary Ulster annalist, who places the executions in 1499: *Ann. Ulster*, 1499. The location

demise was MacIan of Ardnamurchan, who received extensive lands on Islay and the office of crown bailie on the island; and by March of 1507 MacIan's power in the Isles was so formidable that Hugh O'Donnell of Tyrone, styling himself Prince of Ulster, wrote to James IV asking him to provide him with 4,000 fighting men, to be led by John MacIan of Ardnamurchan, 'the chief of his clan', who would choose such 'leaders of Clandonnell' as he wished to accompany him.[77] More immediately, MacIan's new status as royal hatchet-man in the Isles was confirmed by the king's visit, in May 1495, to MacIan's castle of Mingary on the Ardnamurchan peninsula.[78] This was significant because James had taken effective control of royal government only two months before, and because the visit to Mingary would prove to be the king's last excursion to the former Lordship; henceforth, to borrow a twentieth-century Glaswegian phrase, James IV's trips would only be 'doon the watter', within the confines of the Firth of Clyde.

For the truth was that the young king had inherited rather than created a policy in the Isles; that his interest in the west was confined to the matters of establishing some kind of authority in a sensitive area, of drawing rents from the forfeited Lordship, and perhaps above all of providing adequate protection for the Stewart lands in the Firth of Clyde. In this last area we find personal royal intervention on a scale unmatched elsewhere.

Consider for a moment the eastern side of the peninsula of Kintyre. As Dunaverty Castle at its tip had proved only too vulnerable in 1494, in 1495 James began the construction of a new royal fortress at Kilkerran, within the present-day Campbeltown Loch. In 1498 he paid three visits to it, and spent no less than two months of the summer in it, receiving submissions and promises of loyalty from some Lordship families.[79] Further north on the same coast, in 1508 he had the Cistercian abbey of Saddell suppressed and its endowments annexed to the bishopric of Argyll and erected into the free barony of Saddell. The recipient of royal favour in this case was the young, loyalist David Hamilton, bishop of Argyll, who was also empowered to build castles for the barony's defence; some time before February 1512 he had completed an impressive tower house.[80] A few miles further north, at Carradale, the spectacularly sited Aird's Castle, a former Lordship fortress, was granted to the royal familiar Adam Rede of Barskimming in September 1498, on condition that Rede installed

of their capture – Finlaggan on Islay – suggests treachery on the part of MacIan, with the arrests taking place during a meeting of the Council of the Isles.

77 *ALI*, nos. A57, A58; *RMS* ii, no. 2895; *The Letters of James the Fourth, 1505–1513*, ed. R. L. Mackie (Edinburgh 1953), 70–1.

78 *RMS* ii, no. 2253.

79 *TA* i, 382, 389–90; *RMS* ii, nos. 2424–40.

80 *RMS* ii, no. 3170; *RSS* i, no. 2369.

six archers well supplied with bows and arrows and remained in the castle during the king's wars with the Islesmen.[81] Further north still, on the same side of the Kintyre peninsula though technically within the bounds of Knapdale, Skipness Castle went first to another royal familiar, Sir Duncan Forrester, and subsequently to Archibald, second earl of Argyll;[82] and the royal castle of Tarbert, strategically the most important of all, was extensively rebuilt on James IV's orders from 1494 onwards, and a new tower house added to the fortifications.[83] Tarbert was also James's last port of call in the Highland west, in 1500; and on the available evidence, one is tempted to speak of the royal 'daunting' of Eastern Kintyre and southern Knapdale rather than the 'daunting' of the Isles. For James IV, already attracted by the prospect of playing an important European role, had turned his eyes from the Clyde to the Forth; and his main enthusiasm, the creation of a royal navy, would find its outlets at Leith and Newhaven rather than Dumbarton.

* * *

Thus it was largely left to others to make effective the forfeiture of the Lordship in 1493. What James IV clearly wanted was a quick solution to the problems which he had inherited; but in fact he had exacerbated them by first regranting lands to loyal Lordship families in 1495, and then issuing his Act of Revocation in March 1498 requiring immediate confirmation of recently granted Lordship charters – and at a price.[84] In any case, those chiefs who had been appeased by the king – MacLean of Duart, Alan, captain of Clan Cameron, and MacNeill of Barra – must have been thoroughly alarmed by an act of the Lords of Council of 3 October 1496, ordering that any royal summons issued against any person dwelling in the Lordship before 16 April 1497 was to be executed by the chief of his clan; any failure on the chief's part to do so would lead to proceedings being taken against him as though he were the defendant in the case.[85] Arguably this act made the position of chiefs who were as yet uncommitted difficult if not impossible with their clansmen, undermining their authority in an effort to drive them along the road towards acceptance of crown control of the Lordship. The main instigator of this insensitive act was Archibald, second Earl of Argyll, whom the king had brought back into the royal fold as Master of the Household in March 1495.[86] Two years

---

81 *RMS* ii, no. 2454.
82 RCAHMS, *Inventory of the Ancient Monuments of Argyll*, vol. I: *Kintyre* (Edinburgh 1971), 178.
83 *RSS* i, no. 413; *TA* i, 215; *ER* xi, 162.
84 *TA* i, 383.
85 *Acts of the Lords of Council in Civil Cases, 1496–1501*, ed. G. Neilson and H. Paton (Edinburgh 1918), 41.
86 *RMS* ii, no. 2240.

later, King James sacked Angus as Chancellor and replaced him with Huntly.[87] The great Highland magnates had come into their own at last.

Or so it seemed. On 22 April 1500 Argyll was appointed royal lieutenant within the old Lordship – excepting Kintyre and Islay – for a period of three years, with the power to make statutes in the king's name, to seize and execute rebels, to lay siege to their castles and homes, and where necessary to grant remissions.[88] Given the bewildering changes in royal policy since 1493, it must have seemed to many within the Lordship that what Argyll had been given was a royal commission which simply legalised further Campbell aggrandisement. Furthermore, the issue was complicated in August 1501, when a second commission of lieutenancy was issued, this time to Alexander Gordon, who had just succeeded his father as third earl of Huntly. Huntly's commission, unlike that of Argyll, was not subject to a time limit; and he was authorised to receive 'bandis and oblissingis' – in effect submissions – of magnates north of the Mounth, if necessary by force; he was also to collect royal rents in Lochaber and use force against anyone who resisted payment.[89] Huntly's remit – anywhere north of the Mounth – was geographically vast and imprecise, including large areas of the former Lordship of the Isles and the earldom of Ross; and the Gordon earl, hungry for power in the north and west, had already gained the trust of James IV through his involvement with the king's Act of Revocation of 1498, and its circulation to the Island chiefs.[90] Huntly also had useful connections in the north-west and the Isles; his father, the second earl, had probably received assistance from Hugh MacDonald of Sleat, John the fourth Lord's half-brother, in taking Dingwall Castle as long before as 1475; and Hugh himself had married MacIan of Ardnamurchan's daughter Finvola by 1469.[91] So there already existed dangerous rivalries amongst the MacDonald kin which the Gordon earls, father and son, were in a position to exploit.

Argyll had no such advantage. He was caught as the man in the middle, given temporary vice-regal powers which he was expected to use against recalcitrant Lordship families, by some of whom he was already regarded with deep suspicion. One of their leaders, Torquil MacLeod of Lewis, was Argyll's son-in-law, having married the earl's daughter Catherine as recently as 1498. Torquil's disaffection may have been caused primarily – and with some justification – by his fear of Huntly, whose 1501 lieutenancy was likely to be pursued much more vigorously than that given to

---

[87] Ibid., nos. 2374, 2382.
[88] *RSS* ii, nos. 413, 513, 520.
[89] Ibid., nos. 722–3.
[90] *TA* i, 383.
[91] *ALI*, p. lxx, and no. 96.

Torquil's kinsman Argyll the previous year. To resist, Torquil MacLeod needed a cause; and he found it in a projected restoration of the MacDonald Lordship of the Isles. Probably some time in the autumn of 1501 – that is shortly after Huntly's royal commission – the MacDonalds of Glencoe released from captivity in Argyll's castle of Inchconnell on Loch Awe, Donald *Dubh*, grandson of John MacDonald, fourth Lord, an eleven-year-old youth who could be presented as the rightful heir to the forfeited Lordship.[92] As Argyll had taken charge of Donald *Dubh* as an infant in 1493, it may be that the earl also connived at his grandson's release in 1501 as a means of checking the growing power of his rival Huntly. Certainly by October of 1501, the king knew that Donald *Dubh* had been transferred to the custody of Torquil MacLeod of Lewis, and that royal plans for the former Lordship were in danger of total collapse.[93]

The Crown's response to these ominous changes was threefold: first, Torquil MacLeod was declared guilty of rebellion by the Lords of Council, who on 13 August 1502 decreed that Torquil had failed to show any title to his lands in Lewis, Skye, and Wester Ross, and ordained that his estates now belonged to the king (Argyll was – perhaps significantly – not present to condemn his new son-in-law).[94] Secondly, still more power was given to Alexander, third Earl of Huntly; on 21 March 1502, only six days after Torquil MacLeod had been cited as a rebel by the Lords of Council, Huntly was given a royal commission, together with Fraser of Lovat and Munro of Fowlis, authorising him to let the royal lands in Lochaber and Mamore for a period of five years to reliable men who would expel all 'trespassouris and brokin men'; and in addition Huntly and his two allies were empowered to let Torquil's lands of Assynt and Coigach in Wester Ross to 'gud trew men, being afald (i.e. afield, in the field) in our souerane lordis opinion', an indication that the Gordon earl was already in the field and had much support from those seeking to acquire Torquil's estates.[95] Huntly needed no second bidding to raise a royal army in Lochaber to attack all those who resisted paying the king's rents; and there is some evidence that he undertook a wholesale removal of sitting tenants from Lochaber in 1501–2.[96]

Thirdly, the king played his last Lordship card. In September and October of 1502 preparations were made for John MacDonald, the forfeited fourth Lord of the Isles, and as we have seen a court pensioner for the previous

92 Ibid., 313–14.
93 *RMS* ii, no. 2162; *Acts of the Lords of Council, 1501–1503*, ed. J. A. Clyde (Stair Soc., 1943), 174–5.
94 Ibid., 187.
95 *RSS* i, no. 792.
96 Ibid., nos. 723, 792.

eight years, to travel to the Isles and to Lochaber, presumably to earn his annual pension as part of a crown propaganda exercise in areas where King James might expect open rebellion as a response to his lieutenants' severity.[97] Producing John of the Isles, Donald *Dubh*'s grandfather, in the Highlands might well help to nip unrest in the bud. But John MacDonald probably never made the journey; for in January 1503 he fell ill and died at Dundee.[98] He was in his late sixties, but had arguably been a broken reed in the Isles for more than a quarter of a century; and his role in crown service was purely symbolic. But symbolism, when allied to deep-seated political grievances, can exercise a powerful influence; and following John MacDonald's death, the disaffected families in the Isles, Lochaber and Ross could claim with more conviction that they sought a restoration of the Lordship with Donald *Dubh* as the rightful heir of his recently deceased grandfather. Hence the royal government's repeated claim that Donald was the illegitimate son of an illegitimate son; but such statements appear to have had little effect in the Isles.

Donald *Dubh* was the necessary figurehead; the intrusion of Huntly into the Highland west was the grievance; and at Christmas 1503 Torquil MacLeod and Lachlan MacLean of Duart swept into the Gordon earl's Lordship of Badenoch, looting and burning.[99] Even more ominous, the royal lands on Bute had been assailed by Islesmen throughout the previous year, and so much damage was done that royal tenants on Bute were excused payment of rents for three years;[100] and the king was moved to summon parliament, the first to be held for eight years, on 18 December 1503. A week later the Christmas raid on Badenoch made the need to convene the estates even more urgent; and parliament met at Edinburgh on 11 March 1504.[101]

The Donald *Dubh* rising was the closest James IV, an able king, came to a major internal crisis during his adult rule. He dealt with it forcefully, even ruthlessly. At the very beginning of the parliament, he issued an act of revocation – the fifth of the reign – revoking not only all donations and gifts, but also statutes of parliament and general council 'and all vthir thingis done be him in tymis bigane othir hurtand his saule, his crovne or halikirk' – an enormous brief, open to any interpretation which King James wished to place on it. Above all, all revocations made in this way were to be 'put furtht of the bukis and writingis' – or, in modern parlance, shredded.[102] In

97 *TA* ii, 301, 344.
98 Ibid., 354, 357.
99 *APS* ii, 263.
100 *ER* xii, 247–8.
101 *TA* ii, 410; *APS* ii, 239.
102 *APS* ii, 240.

effect, the king was freeing himself of the Angus government's unhappy decisions regarding the Isles in 1493 – or indeed some of his own later schemes – by ordering their removal from the original records and making a new beginning in 1504.

We may pass over quickly the estates' efforts to create new sheriffdoms in Ross and Caithness, and the division of the Isles into north and south for judicial purposes. 'For lak and falt of Justice Airis', moaned the estates, 'the pepill ar almaist gane wild.' Yet these administrative plans were shelved in 1509; and the real problem confronting parliament in 1504 was of course to identify the rebels and crush the rebellion. As neither king nor estates seemed at all certain of the exact stance taken by some of the Lordship families even in 1504, we may be forgiven for failing to identify the rebels with any clarity now. There is no doubt, however, that MacLean of Duart was initially feared by the government because he was believed to have taken possession of Donald *Dubh*, and that his castle of Cairn na burgh in the remote Treshnish Isles, west of Mull, was besieged by a royal fleet largely for that reason. It is also likely that Archibald, second Earl of Argyll, had fallen under suspicion for a short time before and during the 1504 parliament, possibly for collusion with those who released Donald *Dubh*, possibly for allowing Torquil MacLeod and MacLean of Duart to pass through Argyll lands on their way to the Badenoch raid of 1503, certainly for failing to make his lieutenancy of 1500 a success in royal terms.[103] In the long run, the king discovered that there was no alternative to Argyll in the west; but even more striking was the further power given to Huntly in the north. Together with the earl of Crawford, the Earl Marischal, and Lord Lovat, Huntly was entrusted with the overall command of the royal forces sent to subdue 'the northt ylis'; as a first step, he was to lay siege to the castles of Strome and Eilean Donan in Wester Ross, the taking and garrisoning of which were regarded as 'rycht necessar for the danting of the Ilis'; James IV undertook to assist Huntly with a ship and artillery; and parliament recommended that the king entrust the Gordon earl with the building of a castle at Inverlochy on Loch Linnhe.[104]

The Donald *Dubh* revolt dragged on for two years, necessitating the summoning of a second parliament in 1506 and a revision of the government's list of forfeitures. But perhaps we should not exaggerate the threat which it posed to James IV's authority; for the temporary adherence to Donald *Dubh* by major Lordship families may have been inspired more by their desire to check MacIan of Ardnamurchan's growing power than by any affection for the legitimate heir to the MacDonald hegemony. In

---

[103] For a full discussion of Argyll's position, see Macdougall, *James IV*, 183–5.
[104] *APS* ii, 240, 248.

June 1506, the earl of Argyll, restored to favour at court, intervened to obtain a promise from MacIan that both MacLeans – of Duart and Lochbuie – would remain unharmed in their persons and goods for a year, and that in the meantime any disputes between MacIan and MacLean of Lochbuie would be submitted to the king and Council for arbitration.[105]

The extent of royal power delegated to James's lieutenant Huntly in the north is clearly demonstrated by what followed. John Ogilvy, sheriff-depute of Inverness, was given the unenviable task of summoning Torquil MacLeod of Lewis, who had retired to his castle of Stornoway with Donald *Dubh*, to appear to answer charges of treason in Edinburgh. Ogilvy, an understandably cautious man, chose to serve the summons at eleven o'clock on the morning of Christmas Eve 1505, but no nearer Stornoway than the market cross of the burgh of Inverness, more than a hundred miles and a good sea journey distant.[106] Torquil and Donald *Dubh*, no doubt enjoying Christmas in Stornoway Castle, may perhaps be forgiven for not having heard, far less responded to, the summons; and in any earlier reign they would probably have been able to sit on Lewis and defy the government with impunity. But in 1506 there was no hiding place even in the most remote territories of the Lordship. In late August or early September, Huntly, assisted by MacKay of Strathnaver and possibly also by the reconciled MacLeans, provided by the king with a hired ship, the 'Raven', and the royal gunner Robert Herwort, landed an expeditionary force on Lewis and even penetrated as far as Uig, on the west coast of the island. Most important of all, the Gordon earl secured the surrender of Stornoway Castle; by early September 1506, Donald *Dubh* was captured and remained a prisoner, either in Stirling or Edinburgh Castle, for almost the whole of the remainder of his life, while Torquil MacLeod fled and died, a forfeited rebel, five years later.[107] James IV visited both Badenoch and Inverness in the autumn of 1506, ostensibly en route for Tain in Easter Ross on pilgrimage, but probably also with a strategic purpose, to lend personal support to the recent gains made by his ruthless Gordon lieutenant; and in the summer of 1507, the king made his spectacularly swift ride to Tain, with only a few attendants, perhaps to demonstrate in a showy way that royal Stewarts were perfectly safe in Ross, the Achilles' Heel of the MacDonalds and their adherents.[108]

In the southern Isles, the king had finally been forced to use Argyll to restrain the activities of his over-zealous supporter MacIan of Ardnamurchan; but no such restraints were put on Alexander Gordon, third earl of

105 R. L. Mackie, *King James IV of Scotland* (Edinburgh 1958), 195–6.
106 *APS* ii, 263–4.
107 *TA* iii, 200, 209, 338, 340, 342–3; *ALI*, 313–14; *RSS* i, no. 1690; *RMS* ii, no. 3202.
108 Macdougall, *James IV*, 293–4.

Huntly, because King James had no wish – and arguably lacked the power – to control him. James needed Huntly to control the Northern Isles, Ross and the Great Glen, and royal grants poured in from 1506 onwards – commissions to set royal lands in Glengarry, Invergarry, and Knoydart, the hereditary sheriffship of Inverness, and the power to appoint deputies to the sheriff courts of Caithness, Ross, and Lochaber. By the early months of 1509, Huntly and his associates controlled almost the whole of Scotland north of the Great Glen, the lordships of Lochaber and Badenoch, and the huge tracts of Aberdeenshire territory which formed the heartland of the earldom. Between 1506 and 1508 Huntly was even employed as royal enforcer as far south as Perthshire, eventually being given the power to attack and arrest all those at the king's horn in Fortingall, Rannoch, and Lochaber.[109]

Times would change, of course. In a few years, James IV would die at Flodden with many of his magnates, including Argyll, who had temporarily sinned in 1493 and perhaps in 1501–4, and who atoned for these lapses by getting himself killed. Huntly, the ruthless loyalist and pragmatist, had the good sense to escape. And there would be further risings in the Isles, in 1513–15, 1516–19, 1529–31, 1539, and a final spectacular but abortive attempt to restore the Lordship in 1545. But the consistent objective of successive Stewart monarchs and their lieutenants throughout the fifteenth century – to reduce the threat which they perceived to emanate from the Lordship as early as Inverlochy in 1431, perhaps even from Harlaw twenty years earlier – had been achieved to the extent that James IV was concerned but not overly troubled by the major rising of 1504. He was not, after all, at the sieges of Cairn na burgh or Stornoway in person; he did not have to be.

In the last analysis, however, it is difficult to avoid the conclusion that the Lordship collapsed not because of royal Stewart hostility, but because the MacDonald empire became too large for any single individual to control; and the accession of John MacDonald in 1449, a minor who grew up into a weak man, inevitably produced a major split amongst the MacDonald kin and confusion and unrest amongst the principal Lordship families. Paralleling this weakness was the unremitting hostility of three successive earls of Huntly, catalogued most clearly perhaps in the struggles over Badenoch and Ross from the 1450s onwards; and in the end this proved fatal.

---

[109] *RSS* i, nos. 1283, 1344, 1532, 1543, 1579, 1668, 1773, 1820, 1825; *RMS* ii, no. 3286.

Index

The following abbreviations have been used: ab. = abbot; abp. = archbishop; bp. = bishop; d. = died; dau. = daughter; e. = earl; k. = king; pr. = prior; s. = son

Places in Great Britain are located by pre-1973 county, as far as seems necessary, except in the Western Isles, where the island has been noted instead.

Index